GOOD GOVERNMENT

GOOD GOVERNMENT

Democracy beyond Elections

PIERRE ROSANVALLON

Translated by Malcolm DeBevoise

Harvard University Press

Cambridge, Massachusetts
London, England
2018

Copyright © 2018 by the President and Fellows of Harvard College
Originally published in French as *Le Bon gouvernement*, by Pierre Rosanvallon.
Copyright © Les Éditions du Seuil, 2015
All rights reserved
Printed in the United States of America

First printing

Library of Congress Cataloging-in-Publication Data
Names: Rosanvallon, Pierre, 1948– author. | DeBevoise, Malcolm, translator.
Title: Good government : democracy beyond elections / Pierre Rosanvallon;
translated by Malcolm DeBevoise.
Other titles: Bon gouvernement. English
Description: Cambridge, Massachusetts : Harvard University Press, 2018. |
"Originally published in French as Le Bon gouvernement, by Pierre Rosanvallon.
Copyright "Les Éditions du Seuil, 2015." | Includes bibliographical
references and index.
Identifiers: LCCN 2017036976 | ISBN 9780674979437 (hardcover : alk. paper)
Subjects: LCSH: Democracy. | Political science.
Classification: LCC JC423 .R169313 2018 | DDC 321.8—dc23
LC record available at https://lccn.loc.gov/2017036976

CONTENTS

Introduction: From One Democracy to Another   1

I. *Executive Power*

  1. Consecration of the Law and Demotion of the Executive   23

  2. The Cult of Impersonality and Its Metamorphoses   32

  3. The Age of Rehabilitation   45

  4. Two Temptations   59

II. *The Presidentialization of Democracies*

  5. The Pioneering Experiments: 1848 and Weimar   75

  6. From Gaullist Exception to Standard Model   91

  7. Unavoidable and Unsatisfactory   104

  8. Limiting Illiberalism   114

III. *A Democracy of Appropriation*

  9. The Governed and Their Governors   127

  10. Legibility   146

  11. Responsibility   172

  12. Responsiveness   190

IV. *A Democracy of Trust*

    13. The Good Ruler in Historical Perspective   209

    14. Truthfulness   224

    15. Integrity   243

    Conclusion: The Second Democratic Revolution   261

    Notes   271

    Index   329

GOOD GOVERNMENT

INTRODUCTION

From One Democracy to Another

O UR REGIMES ARE DEMOCRATIC, but we are not governed democratically. This apparent paradox is at the root of the disenchantment and dismay that are so widely felt today. Our regimes are democratic
in the sense that power comes from the ballot box at the end of an open
competition, and that we live in a legally constituted state that recog-
nizes and protects individual liberties. To be sure, democracy has by no
means been fully achieved. People often feel abandoned by their elected
representatives; once the campaign is over, they discover that they are
scarcely more sovereign than they were before. But this reality must not
be allowed to mask another common phenomenon: bad government.
Though it is still poorly understood, no one doubts its power to erode
the foundations of our societies.

Political life is organized around institutions that, taken together, define a type of regime. But it is also bound up with governmental action,
which is to say with the day-to-day management of affairs of state, the
authority to decide and command. It is where power—which in constitutional terms means executive power—is exercised. Politics affect
people directly, every day of their lives. By the same token, the center
of political gravity in democratic societies has imperceptibly shifted: until
recently it was located in the relationship between representatives and
those who are represented; now it is the relationship between governors

and those who are governed that matters. This shift does not amount to a complete break with the past, however. The question of representation continues to occupy a prominent place in public discussion; indeed, one is forever being told that there is a "crisis of representation" today. I will come back to this point. For the moment it is important to emphasize that the feeling that there is something wrong with democracy, that it is not working as it should, now clearly derives from some deeper discontent. The chief failing of democracy in the minds of many is that their voice is not heard. They see their leaders making decisions without consultation, failing to take responsibility for their actions, lying with impunity, living in a bubble—in short, a government shut off from the world, a system whose workings are opaque.

Politics never used to be thought of in this way. Democracy has traditionally been understood as a kind of regime, very seldom as a specific mode of government. The fact that, historically, the words "regime" and "government" were used more or less synonymously is proof of this.[1] Considering the earliest modern form of democratic regime, the *parliamentary-representative* model, in which the legislature dominated the other branches, the question may well appear to be of only minor significance. But now that the executive has the upper hand, we have entered into a *presidential-governing* era. Whereas dissatisfaction once sprang from a sense of being poorly represented, lately it has grown out of a sense of being poorly governed. In what follows I examine the history of this shift, and the reasons for the mistrust of executive power that preceded it. I then go on to lay the foundations of a democratic theory of government.

The Presidentialization of Democracies

Let us start out, then, from the fact that for some thirty years now the growth of presidentialism has marked a major change in the nature and form of democracy. The change is obvious in one way, because the simplest and most natural way of conceiving of presidentialism is in terms of the election by popular vote of the head of the executive branch. Everywhere today events remind us of the central place it occupies in the political life of people in all parts of the world. At the same time the implications of this change have yet to be fully appreciated. One reason

by the persistence of constitutional monarchies. This is still the case today in the United Kingdom, Belgium, the Netherlands, Luxembourg, Denmark, Sweden, and Norway, creating the impression of something rather like a museum of the institutions of liberal democracy as they existed in the nineteenth century. Under these monarchies the question of electing a chief executive, the prime minister, by universal suffrage never arises. Indeed, it could not arise, for it would undermine in its very principle the accepted preeminence of the crown. It was always in his or her capacity as leader of the party or coalition that had prevailed in the general election, and therefore won a parliamentary majority, that the prime minister was appointed to this office. Next there is the case of the countries that survived Nazism and Fascism, Germany and Italy. They are both provided with a president of the Republic, but this person is elected by the parliament and has a merely representative function; although the prime minister is named by the president, again it is only in acknowledgment of the majority formed by the election of parliamentary representatives. Germany had experimented after 1919 with the popular election of the president of the Reich, which ended with Hitler's rise to power, and in Italy Mussolini had established a dictatorship in 1925. The memory of this tragic period between the wars led both nations after 1945 to adopt their current constitutions. The countries of southern Europe that belatedly emerged from dictatorship in the 1970s— Spain, Greece, and Portugal—took a cautious view of the return to democracy. In Spain this was done through the reestablishment of a monarchy, in Greece through the adoption of a traditional parliamentary regime in which the president is elected by the parliament without acting as head of the executive. Portugal was the exception, instituting the election of a president by universal suffrage. And yet this arrangement concealed a novel conception of the presidency, shaped by the importance attached to the old liberal idea of a moderating power. At the same time, though the Portuguese view was undoubtedly influenced by political theory (in no other twentieth-century country could one have so thoroughly updated the writings of Benjamin Constant), it was nonetheless political practice that gave the chief executive a peculiar position from 1976 onward: relatively unassertive in ordinary times, while intervening more actively in moments of crisis, his power to affect government policy depended on being able to bring to bear both his moral and his electoral legitimacy as a function of circumstances. The countries of eastern Eu-

rope, for their part, unlike the new ones issuing from the dismember-
ment of the Soviet Union, subsequently made much the same kind of
choice by equipping themselves for the most part with prime-ministerial
regimes[3] after the breakup of the Communist bloc in 1989.

With the exception of France—evidently a major exception,[4] since
it may be considered to have set in motion the modern history of presidentialism with the adoption by referendum, in 1962, of the election of
the president by direct universal suffrage—European countries seem in
their various ways to have stood apart from the movement toward presidentialism that swept the rest of the world. The French example sup-
plied a universalizable model for a form of constitutional government
that, in its American version, devised long before, had not been successfully reproduced in the twentieth century.[5] Embraced by a majority of
voters, while long remaining suspect in the eyes of the political class,
the presidentialization of democracy in France had its formal basis in
a constitution that was felt by some to be potentially dangerous for
reviving memories of the country's Caesarist past. Those who criticized
the Gaullist regime on this ground, though they failed to grasp why it
was welcomed by a great many people as a step forward, nonetheless
grudgingly admitted the lack of any viable alternative. The phrase "unavoidable but unsatisfactory" was often heard, suggesting that presidentialism was regarded as a sort of national disease for which a cure
would have to be found, and not as a promising attempt to construct a
new form of democratic government.

The Predominance of the Executive

Putting aside these differences in historical development, presidentialism
can be seen to be the consequence of a more profound phenomenon:
the growing influence of the executive branch. Today, when one speaks
of *government*, what is really meant is executive power. Directly and continually active, inseparable from the decisions it makes every single
day, constantly expressing and asserting its will, it is this power that citizens expect to positively manage the conditions under which they live
and work. Accordingly, they require both that the executive give proof
of an effectual will—evidence that it can actually accomplish what it
sets out to do—and that it be held accountable for its actions.[6] This is

the source of the tendency of executive power to polarization and personalization. While presidentialism in the formal or procedural sense—the practice of electing the head of the executive by popular vote—has not everywhere been adopted, the twin effects of polarization and personalization associated with the modern preeminence of the executive are themselves universal.[7] It is therefore very much a global transformation of democratic life that has taken place, whatever local differences there may be in constitutional expression.

A persuasive account of this transformation will have to consider what may be called *governing organs,* as distinct from the presidency itself, even if it is this institution that unites the various agencies of government and guides their operation in the great majority of countries today. These organs are an indispensable part of the new presidential-governing form of democracy. The term "executive power," though it is still almost invariably used today, does not give any real idea of the initiative and the influence such agencies now enjoy, in large part because of the passively mechanical connotation that has clung to it for so long. The legislative branch itself, as we shall see shortly, has become effectively subordinate to the business of governing. It is therefore necessary to regard all these organs as forming an integrated whole. We are today so accustomed to taking for granted the supremacy of governing in relation to representation that the dramatic shift of power from the legislature to the executive that has taken place over the last two centuries seems scarcely to be of any interest. Looking at the matter with the eye of a historian, however, one cannot help but see that it amounts to a complete reversal of perspective by comparison with the founding vision of modern democracy, particularly in the form given it by the American and the French Revolutions. If we fail to work out what this shift in perspective implies, we will be unable to understand the real reasons for the current mood of disenchantment—and therefore incapable of deciding what must be done if democracy is once more to flourish.

The Parliamentary-Representative Model

The parliamentary-representative model of democracy, as it was originally conceived by the authors of the American and French constitutions, rests on two principles: the rule of law and the idea of the people as its own legislator.[8] Law was understood as the vehicle of impersonal rule, an essentially nondominating kind of authority. Because impersonality was considered to be the highest political virtue, indissociably liberal and democratic, a government could be good only so long as it embodied this quality. The break with absolutism, which is to say the structurally arbitrary power of a single person, was motivated by exactly this assumption. One need not look any further to see how conspicuously the modern presidential-governing model, founded on personalization, differs from the eighteenth-century conception.

With the advent of the people-as-legislator, in accordance with the second principle, they were henceforth recognized as the generative source of all powers of government. In America the people were called the "fountain of power," in France "sovereign." Law could then be seen as "the expression of the general will," in the famous phrase of Article 6 of the Declaration of the Rights of Man and the Citizen of 1789, which stipulated furthermore that "all citizens have the right to take part, in person or through their representatives, in its formation." The central power was therefore understood to reside in the legislature, whereas the executive was considered secondary, not only in view of the theoretical primacy of the people but also because the practical opportunities for governmental action were limited by comparison with our own time. How the legislative branch should be organized therefore became the major question in debates about democratic institutions during the eighteenth and nineteenth centuries. At the heart of this question was the nature of representation itself.

Public attention was concentrated on three main issues. First, the *democratization of election,* which was recommended as a way of reducing partisan influence on popular opinion. In France, both in 1848 and under the Second Empire, workers' groups vigorously opposed the domination of electoral committees by lawyers and journalists. A generation later, at the turn of the twentieth century in America, the same impulse led to an ultimately victorious campaign by progressives to create a system of primaries aimed at curbing the power of party bosses over political life. Battles were also fought, though much less often crowned with success, to limit the concurrent holding of public offices and the duration of terms of office. There was much talk in the nineteenth century, too, of instituting a system of imperative mandates.[9] Although incompatible with the classical doctrine of parliamentarism, which was based on the principle of the independence of the representative in relation to his constituents,[10] the idea gained indirect support with the drafting of programs and platforms that, even if they lacked the force of law, nonetheless implied a recognition that elected officials were in some sense constrained by the will of voters.

The second issue involved a search for ways of *improving the representative character* of elected bodies, chiefly with regard to the representation of various social groups. This was to be the driving force behind the formation of class-based parties. The call for "special representation of the proletarians" had been heard in Europe as early as the 1830s. In the decades immediately following, a campaign on behalf of proportional representation mobilized support for strengthening the "expressive function" of Parliament, as it was called in Great Britain, where the movement had first been given a theoretical foundation and where it was to become the object of intense political rivalry.

There was a great debate, finally, about the introduction of referendum procedures in both Europe and the United States in the last decades of the nineteenth century, especially in connection with the idea of *direct legislation by the people,* championed by American progressives, German and French socialists, and the heirs of Bonapartism. Even some conservative figures, notably in Great Britain, expressed their approval, reasoning that under certain circumstances granting the people a veto power might usefully serve as a safety valve.

The origins of these various proposals for making parliamentary-representative democracy more robust may be traced back to the time of the French Revolution. Bitter complaints about "representative aristocracy" first began to be heard in the autumn of 1789. Two centuries later, it is striking to observe that fits of impatience and disappointed expectations of democratic progress very often continue to crystallize around the same three issues. Some things have changed, of course. Demands for greater minority representation and for gender equality, for example, have supplanted the cause of class representation. In other respects, however, the degree of continuity is remarkable. The only real innovation has been the idea of a *lottery.* Nonetheless, because at bottom it amounts to substituting for voting a procedure thought likelier to make political institutions more representative, a lottery does not depart in any fundamental way from the parliamentary-representative paradigm.[11] Similarly, the notion of *participatory democracy* is inspired in large part by a desire to remedy the defects of representative democracy, by going beyond the status quo. In all these cases, it is the nature and the quality of the relationship of representatives to constituents, as well as the possibility of direct citizen involvement, that are seen as cornerstones of the democratic ideal.

The Relationship between Governed and Governing

In an age when the power of the executive branch is predominant, the success of a democracy depends on society's ability to exert some measure of control over the executive. The crucial issue, in other words, is the relationship between those who govern and those who are governed. The aim cannot be an unattainable ideal of complete self-government (as against some more feasible arrangement, such as the people-as-legislator), inasmuch as the very notion of government presupposes a basic distinction between governed and governing.[12] The aim must be to preserve the strictly functional character of this relationship, by setting forth the conditions of legitimate governmental action, that is, the conditions under which government will be government of, for, and by the people, and not an instrument of domination, an expression of oligarchic power cut off from society. The problem is that the only way of doing this that so far has been devised is direct popular election of the head of the executive. But this amounts merely to establishing a *democracy of authorization,* a democracy that grants permission to govern—nothing more, nothing less. One has only to look around and see how many of world's elected presidents behave undemocratically to realize that this cannot be regarded as a satisfactory solution.

While election may be considered an adequate means, under certain circumstances, of determining the relationship between representatives and constituents,[13] the same cannot be said of the relationship between governors and governed. This is an essential point. Historically, the popular designation of a representative has consisted in principle in expressing an identity and in transmitting a mandate—precisely the two things that one wants an election to accomplish. Election, it was held, establishes a representative's intrinsic status *and* his functional role, together with the sense of permanence that the notion of holding a public office implies. The election of a governor, by contrast, serves only to legitimize his institutional position, without conferring any distinctive status or quality on him. The democratic value of electing a governor is in this sense inferior to that of electing a representative.[14]

Hence the urgent necessity of extending a democracy of authorization by means of a *permanent democracy*[15] that grows out of a responsibility exercised by citizens themselves for the purpose of reaching agreement about the qualities that are to be insisted upon in those who govern and about the rules that ought to order their relations with the governed. It is the very absence of such a democracy that permits a freely elected chief executive to preside over an illiberal (and indeed in certain cases a dictatorial) regime. In the nineteenth century, the French tradition of Caesarism inaugurated by Napoléon Bonaparte furnished the outstanding example. The murderous and self-destructive perversions of democracy that gave rise to totalitarian regimes in the twentieth century were, at bottom, pathologies of representation. Here what one saw were governments claiming to be able to break through the impasses inherent in a representative system, and to overcome its inevitable incompleteness, by perfectly embodying society. Their absolutism was justified on just this ground, as a consequence of the need to make the governed identical with the governor. Although it is quite true that pathologies of representation are with us still, the new pathologies of the twenty-first century are of a different kind. Now they arise from the identification of democratic governance with the simple procedure of authorization. If presidentialism is diseased today, it is owing to a sort of atrophy.[16]

My chief purpose in this book is to describe the mechanisms of vigilance and oversight on which a permanent democracy must rely. These mechanisms are what in an uncertain and very general way community activists and people in many areas of civil society are trying to create today, whether they call for greater *transparency*, or for the construction of a *networked democracy*, or for the practice of *open government*, to mention just a few of the most common slogans. My aim is to organize these aspirations and ideas by identifying the qualities that those who seek to govern must display as well as the principles that sustain a healthy relationship between governors and governed in a democracy. Taken together, these things form the basis of *good government*.

Among the principles that ought to regulate the behavior of those who govern toward those who are governed, three are paramount: *legibility, responsibility, responsiveness*. They mark out the contours of what elsewhere I have called a *democracy of appropriation*,[17] in which citizens are able more directly to exercise democratic functions and duties that have long been monopolized by parliamentary prerogatives. Giving practical effect to these principles will also make it clear that power is not a thing, but a relation, and that it is therefore the nature of this relation that separates an unhealthy situation from one in which a properly functional distinction between governors and governed makes the civic appropriation of power possible.

With regard to the personal qualities that a good governor must have, I am not interested in drawing up a list of traits from which a composite portrait of an ideal ruler could be assembled, a sort of IdentiKit superposition of all relevant talents and virtues. I am interested instead in considering in a pragmatic way which ones are necessary for creating the bond of mutual confidence between governors and governed that a *democracy of trust* requires. Trust is one of a number of "invisible institutions" whose vitality has assumed a decisive importance in the present age of personalized democracy. I shall examine two such institutions: *truthfulness* and *integrity*.

Democratic progress in an era of presidential government depends on constructing both a democracy of trust and a democracy of appropriation. The principles of good government they embody must be applied not only to the various agencies of the executive branch, but also to all persons and institutions having a regulatory function, including nonelected officers of independent authorities, magistrates appointed to the courts and other bodies of the judiciary, and indeed anyone who holds an office of public administration. These are persons and institutions that in one manner or another exercise authority over others and, in this capacity, direct the organs of government.

Decline and Redefinition of Parties

Political parties have historically played a major role in the functioning of parliamentary-representative democracy. With the advent of universal suffrage (male, to begin with), they helped to shape the expression of public opinion once it had been channeled in a preferred direction. They were an instrument for organizing and rallying the "many," as the masses used to be called in the nineteenth century, particularly by regulating electoral competition through the selection of candidates. Alongside this function, they structured parliamentary life through the formation of disciplined factions whose bargaining, either directly or in the form of alliances, allowed majorities to emerge. In both these respects they marked a break with the old interlocking circles of notables that dominated political and parliamentary life in an earlier age of property-based suffrage and two-round voting.

At the same time, and in a progressive sense, parties were mass organizations. Beyond their electoral and parliamentary functions, they promoted social representation by giving voice to classes and ideologies, which is to say to particular interests and competing visions of a better society. And yet, though they were an integral part of the parliamentary-representative system of the period, their bureaucratic and hierarchical character very quickly provoked sharp criticism. In France, beginning in 1848 with the first elections based on universal direct suffrage, the electoral committees that drew up lists of candidates came under withering attack from one of the leading political theorists of the day. "The first time that you exercise your public right," Lamennais warned prospective working-class voters, "you are ordered to assemble, a list is put in your hand that you have never discussed or even read, and you are instructed in no uncertain terms: drop that in the ballot box. You are made into a voting machine."[18] The same case was made still more vigorously, and in harsher terms as well, by many authors at the turn of the twentieth century, most notably in two groundbreaking works of political sociology: Moisei Ostrogorski's *La démocratie et les partis politiques* (1902), devoted to the United States and Great Britain, and Robert Michels's *Zür Soziologie des Parteiwesens in der modernen Demokratie* (1911), treating the Social Democratic Party in Germany. Both authors described the ways in which aristocratic tendencies were automatically recreated within parties. Ostrogorski stressed the conversion of parties into mechanical devices ("machines") that in the hands of professionals could be made to operate in an almost autonomous fashion, whereas Michels analyzed the success of party leaders in establishing themselves as a new type of oligarchy. It is scarcely surprising, then, that parties should have aroused highly ambivalent feelings. But in spite of institutional inertia, and notwithstanding a determination to impose their will on party members—variable in its extent, to be sure, depending on levels of education and training, but nowhere more extreme than in the case of the discipline enforced by Communist parties—it cannot be denied that parties gave a voice, a face, and access to a public forum to people who had previously been kept out of political life.

The traditional representative function of parties began to erode in the early part of the twentieth century, and by the end had all but disappeared. There are two reasons for this. The first, and the most obvious, has to do with the fact that society itself had become more opaque, to the point of illegibility in some respects, and therefore less easily represented than the old class society with its well-defined gradations and boundaries. We have entered into a new age that I call the individualism of singularity,[19] marked not only by a growing complexity and heterogeneity of social relations, but also by the fact that the course of people's lives is now determined as much by their personal background as by their social standing. Representing society in this sense requires an awareness of new social conditions in an age when capitalism itself, now shaped by the economics of permanent innovation, has gone beyond the highly organized industrial society described by Galbraith fifty years ago, while at the same time taking into account all the situations, all the trials, fears, and expectations, that influence individual destinies. The social invisibility from which so many people suffer in democracies today is the result of failing to do either of these things. The old parties had a representative capacity that might be called identitarian, owing to the very fact of their mass character. They no longer have this capacity. The nature of society has changed. Accurately mapping a new and far more complicated social landscape—honestly representing it, in other words—means that politics must henceforth have a "narrative" dimension that parties are not presently capable of imagining. For the moment, because parties have distanced themselves from the world of everyday experience, their rhetoric, filled with grand abstractions having no point of contact with people's daily lives, echoes into a void.

The sociological roots of this new age of malrepresentation, as it may well be called, are now better understood than they once were.[20] But another factor, less noticed and more important for the purposes of the present work, has also powerfully contributed to the decline of parties, namely, their retreat from the responsibilities of good government. They no longer see themselves as intermediaries between society and political institutions. Here two reasons stand out among many. The first is that parliaments themselves have ceased to be lawmaking bodies in any true sense. Once the motive force of legislation, now they are content to cede to the executive the prerogative for proposing and drafting new laws. But the main reason is that the principal function of parliamentary majorities today is to support the government in power and the principal function of opposition parties is to criticize the government until they can to take its place. Parties have therefore become auxiliary forces in wars of executive action, whether they lead the charge in support of the government's policies or prepare the way for its defeat in the next elections by demonstrating their harmful character.[21] In either case they are more concerned with the interests of governments than the interests of citizens. Parliamentary deputies, despite the fact that they have been elected by their respective constituencies, represent these districts only as an afterthought, because their primary duty is to carry out the political tasks assigned to them by their party.[22] They constitute the dominated, or at least the relatively passive, part of the governing oligarchy. It is this shift in orientation toward the executive that explains why elected officials are increasingly cut off from society, having become professionalized to the point that they are now purely political creatures.[23] Their "reality" is the world of insiders, a product of the collision of policy agendas, party congresses, and bureaucratic infighting that determines the balance of power from which governments emerge.

In the meantime party activity has been reduced mainly to managing the election calendar, whose most important date, superseding all others in the nation's political life, is the presidential election. The number of regular party members[24] is now in sharp decline almost everywhere on account of this withdrawal into an auxiliary governing function, with the result that parties make an effort to recruit support only with a narrow view to controlling primary outcomes (where a primary system exists). Here their ability to get out the vote remains a decisive asset. In this and all other respects, one cannot help but conclude that parties' democratic function is confined solely to assisting the smooth operation of an authorizing democracy of the sort I described earlier.

Now that the representative dimension of democracy has effectively been abandoned by the parties, life must now be given to it through other channels. New forms of narrative representation, new ways of representing social problems, as it were, must be developed in cooperation with civic associations in all walks of social and cultural life in order to combat the debilitating sense of malrepresentation that gnaws away at democracies and weakens their will to resist the sirens of populism. In my last book,[25] which served as a manifesto for the "Raconter la vie" project launched in 2014,[26] I proposed instruments of analysis and action for bringing about just such a "post-party" revitalization of representation.

Toward New Democratic Organizations

Parties having now become subsidiary structures of executive organs, they are no longer in a position to play an effective role in giving the governing–governed relation a properly democratic form. This is plain to see when they participate in a coalition government. But it is no less true when they find themselves in opposition, for in criticizing the government their interest is much more in regaining power than in improving the situation of the citizens for whom they are deputized to speak, however often they may call for the increased use of referendums.[27] Their attention is focused instead, and especially, on the relationship of the government to the parliament, while taking the side of the latter.[28]

It is in this context that political entities quite different from the old party organizations have emerged. There are new-style parties that compete in elections while taking care not to compromise their participatory character, such as Podemos in Spain, the most successful example of its kind (no doubt in part because its leader is highly charismatic); protest movements of a novel kind as well, such as the Indignant movement, which appeared in various countries in the early 2010s, and Occupy Wall Street, which described itself in 2011 as a "leaderless resistance movement" claiming to speak for the 99 percent of a population that is no longer willing to tolerate the greed and the corruption of the 1 percent; also spectacular mass demonstrations in capitals across the world that have rocked the foundations of hated regimes. In combination they have had the effect of revitalizing the notion of representation, and with it the notion of a democratic forum. Alongside these spontaneous outbursts of activism, which have been widely covered in the media and commented upon at great length by political analysts, more deliberate and possibly more enduring citizen initiatives have taken shape, known in Anglo-American countries as good government organizations. The aim of these initiatives is not to take power, but to monitor and restrain it. Less well known than the others, they now work on five continents to hold governments accountable, to force them to tell the truth, to listen to citizens, to behave in a responsible fashion, to lift the veil of secrecy behind which they often dissemble. Doing these things, I believe, will give still greater scope for citizen involvement. The present work is meant to clarify the role of organizations of this type, and to examine the initiatives they have so far sponsored and the expectations their work has aroused. It is meant also, and not less importantly, to situate these organizations in an enlarged theory of democracy that can provide a more adequate explanation of contemporary governmental behavior. By showing how a presidential-governing regime can be made more truly democratic, it will be easier, or so one may hope, to resist the appeal of ideas that would have exactly the opposite effect.

A Different Democratic Universalism

A permanent democracy is not something that only countries in the West can imagine being theirs one day. The same prospect prompts citizens to take action even in countries where they are still prevented from going to the polls. This is what is happening now in China, to take only the most prominent example. Ordinary people have rallied there against corruption, governmental indifference, the lack of transparency in policy making, the irresponsibility of political leaders. What they are demanding, in a word, is accountability.[29] In countries under authoritarian rule, people are insisting that governments meet at least certain minimal democratic standards. Here one finds further evidence that the establishment of a system exhibiting the rudimentary features of a permanent democracy may precede the establishment of an electoral democracy. Historically, this is what occurred in the oldest democracies, particularly in Europe. But it need not happen again today. Many new democracies, alas, have gone no further than a mere democracy of authorization,[30] and some have installed illiberal, populist regimes (in the case of Belarus and Kazakhstan, ones with frankly totalitarian overtones). A democracy of authorization is a fragile thing: under presidential rule, its institutions are open to manipulation and may even be perverted by the corrosive dynamics of personalization and polarization. A permanent democracy, by contrast, owing to its decentralized and multiform character, is much less likely to be corrupted. This is why it represents the positive face of democratic universalism today.

The Four Democracies

This book concludes a cycle of works, the first of which appeared almost ten years ago, on the transformations of contemporary democracy, considered in its four dimensions: civic activity, political regime, form of society, and form of government. The institution of citizenship emerged in stages, beginning with the achievement of universal suffrage, of which I made a preliminary study more than two decades ago.[31] In this first stage, suffrage defined not only a political right, which is to say the power of being an active citizen, but also a social status that allows each person to be recognized as an autonomous individual participating on a basis of equality with fellow citizens. Before long, however, growing impatience with the idea that voting is the sole means by which the people can affirm its sovereignty caused suffrage to be expanded and supplemented. Alongside the original electoral-representative sphere there gradually came into being a whole set of new democratic habits and reflexes, relating to oversight, preventive action, and judgment, through which society was able to exercise powers of correction and coercion. In addition to the citizen's primary responsibility as a voter, there was now a broader conception of the people as monitor, as gainsayer, and as judge—but with this crucial difference, that whereas voting is a mechanism for instilling confidence, oversight and its companion forms of supervision entail a duty of distrust. I examined the history and the theory of this new way of thinking about citizenship, which played a major role in political developments in France and elsewhere during the 1980s, in the first book of the quartet, *La contre-démocratie* [2006].[32]

Democracy as regime is defined by institutions and procedures designed to shape the general will. The institutions are of two types. On the one hand, there are institutions of representation. Once more I had first examined their history and structural tensions in an earlier book, published in 1998.[33] On the other hand, there are institutions of sovereignty, whose problematic evolution I retraced in my next book, published two years later.[34] Then, in the second volume of the present tetrology, *La légitimité démocratique* [2008],[35] I showed how a new understanding of the general will has sought to go beyond the limitations of strictly majoritarian expression. On this view, a government can be considered to be fully democratic only if it is submitted to procedures of formal review and control that are at once in conflict with and complementary to the will of the majority. It is expected to satisfy a threefold requirement of neutrality with regard to partisan positions and special interests (legitimacy of impartiality), tolerance in the face of rival conceptions of the common good (legitimacy of reflexivity), and recognition of particularities (legitimacy of proximity). Independent public authorities and constitutional councils now occupy an increasingly large place in democracies for just this reason. In the meantime I have analyzed the contemporary crisis of representation, and considered what must be done to overcome it, in an essay on what I call the parliament of invisible people.[36]

Democracy as a form of society constitutes the third dimension. Here again I had taken up the topic more than twenty years ago, with the aim of showing that the modern revolution in politics was first and foremost a revolution of equality, where equality was now understood as a relation, a way of constituting a society of fellows; from the beginning it was seen as a democratic quality, a figure of communality, and not only as a mode of wealth distribution.[37] But it was not until I came to write the third volume of the four, *La société des égaux* [2011],[38] that I was able to consider this question more fully, and to demonstrate that the breakdown of this idea of equality was an essential cause of the explosion in inequality that today threatens to undermine democracy as a form of society, and in so doing to bring about a more general abandonment of democratic ideals.

With this, the fourth and final volume, I turn finally to *democracy as a form of government,* reviewing the stages by which it acquired its current preeminence with the advent of the presidentialist system. No one should suppose that, having now completed the task I had set for myself, I have exhausted all the questions that led me to undertake so vast a project in the first place. Far from it. There are many more books yet to be written if we are to understand the history of democracy and how it has changed. But I may at least hope to have provided other scholars with a set of tools they will find useful in carrying on with the work that remains to be done. History is now breathing down our necks. Perhaps never before has it been a more urgent necessity that we try to make sense of it. Rushing headlong into the future, the present is in danger of losing its balance. Beneath lies the abyss.

PART I

EXECUTIVE POWER

Consecration of the Law and Demotion of the Executive

The Idea of the Rule of Law

The democratic ideal derives from a conception of society as a purely human creation. This was taken to imply that the sovereignty of the people had to be extended by making the people its own legislator. In the eighteenth century, the democratic ideal came to be conjoined with a veritable sacralization of the law. The powers of government, it was believed, must possess a generality that is both procedural and substantial, in accordance with a wholly novel approach to the management of human affairs. There was a practical and rationalizing purpose in this, namely, simplifying and stabilizing the administration of justice by imposing a uniform order on the existing jumble of legally sanctioned customs. But the political reformers of the period had something much more ambitious in mind. Their aim was to revolutionize public action, not only by ridding it of its arbitrary aspects, but also, and more fundamentally, by desubjectivizing it, as it were, by substituting an objective form of authority for the will of a single person.

Cesare Beccaria, the great philosopher of law of the Enlightenment, brilliantly expounded the new conception of the role of law in a work that was to have a lasting influence, *Dei delitti e delle pene* [On Crimes and Punishments, 1764].[1] Its point of departure was classically liberal.

Beccaria sought first of all to remedy the incoherence of a system of justice that inflicted very different punishments for the same crime. Like many philosophers, he was haunted by the specter of judicial error and appalled by the arbitrariness of sentencing. Arguing that the source of these harmful inconsistencies lay in the discretionary power allowed to judges, he endeavored to make the law fairer by standardizing the treatment of facts and evidence. True justice, whose very impersonality, he held, was sufficient to prevent arbitrariness, therefore consisted in the literal interpretation and strict application of the language of the laws. His guiding idea, shared by all the reformers of the age, was that a law, by virtue of the generality of its expression, comprehends and encompasses every particular case, whose facts therefore cannot help but exactly coincide with it. Near the end of the eighteenth century, Jeremy Bentham, the father of utilitarianism, went a step further in calling for a *science of legislation* as the basis of a revolution that would be at once democratic, moral, and methodological.[2] In *A Fragment on Government* [1789] he had drawn up a prospectus for "a Complete Body of Laws," or *pannomion*, which, along with the panopticon scheme undertaken later in connection with prison reform, was to occupy him for the rest of his life.[3] From Beccaria to Bentham, then, the consecration of law was part of a larger project aimed at bringing forth an objective power, generality, on which a new political order could be founded. One consequence of this was that the rule of law came to eclipse good government in Enlightenment thinking about the conditions of a just and effectual polity. The prevailing opinion was that only a few laws were needed to govern society, provided they were good. As Louis de Jaucourt put it in his article on law in the *Encyclopédie* of Diderot and d'Alembert, "a multiplicity of laws proves, all else being equal, the bad constitution of a government."[4] Good laws, general and few in number, therefore deserved to be permanent. What is more, in uniting the properties of generality, simplicity, and immutability, they presented a way of ordering human affairs through a convergence of liberalism and democracy.

Veneration of man-made laws, together with the cult of the market, thought to be governed by a natural law, the law of the invisible hand, caused the scope of politics as a *sphere of decision* to be diminished. These two views of the nature of law, one belonging to positive philosophy, as it was called, the other to natural philosophy, came together to marginalize both the idea of executive power and the idea of an immediately active political will, distrusted on the ground that it was bound to work in favor of particular interests. Now that the social sciences, dominated by the thinkers of the Scottish Enlightenment, had devoted themselves to imagining a world in which the will, assumed to be inherently arbitrary, no longer played any role, the idea of government found itself correspondingly depreciated. The most influential exponents of this determination to break with the old order of things turned out to be the revolutionaries of 1789. Their radicalism was to make the French Revolution the foremost laboratory for the consecration of law, in both its theoretical and its practical aspects, and so a natural starting point for our inquiry into the reasons for the supremacy of the legislative branch and the demotion of the executive that accompanied it.

It is no accident that a French grammarian should have suggested at the very outset of the Revolution that his country was now destined to form a "lawdom."[5] Three years later, in the spring of 1792, a "festival of law"—one of the first revolutionary festivals, after that of the Federation—was organized with great pomp in the streets of Paris. Waves of banners passed by bearing the inscriptions "The law," "Respect the law," "Die to defend it," and the crowds spontaneously and fervently exclaimed "Long live the law!" in response. Reverence for the law was a constant feature of appeals both to reason and to the emotions.[6] Of the seventeen articles that make up the Declaration of the Rights of Man and the Citizen, seven refer to the law and its functions. Small wonder, then, that Michelet should have characterized the first phase of the Revolution as the "advent of the Law." But things were not so simple. On closer inspection it will be clear that the apparently unequivocal invocation of the law concealed three distinct ways of looking at it.

The first, which may be described as liberal, contrasted the virtues of a state based on law with the errancies and transgressions of arbitrary power. This was hardly a new idea. It was the classical English view, and no less familiar to the men of 1789 from their reading of Montesquieu, who had stigmatized despotism as a regime in which "a single person, without law and without rule, directs everything by his own will and caprice."[7] Despotism was likened to a power of particularity (the prince's arbitrary "good will"), whereas liberty was guaranteed by the generality of lawful rule in all its aspects: it was general in its origin (having been created by a parliament), in its form (owing to the impersonal character of legal norms), and in its mode of administration (as embodied by the state). The prestige of the law proceeded from this threefold equivalence. Law was at once a *principle of order* that made it possible to "transform an infinite number of men . . . into a single body," and a *principle of justice,* because in its generality it knows no one in particular, which permits it to be an "intelligence without passion."[8]

The revolutionary celebration of law accorded in the second place with the concern for juridical rationalization that had emerged in the eighteenth century, and gave rise to a vast enterprise of codification. The very term "Code" suggested the extent of the reformist ambition to substitute uniform and rational legislation for the motley mass of customs and conventions that until then had governed legal judgment. For the members of the National Constituent Assembly, codification amounted to a kind of therapeutics, as much intellectual as political in its purpose, that went far beyond the earlier, purely technical, exercise of composing a digest of laws that would serve merely to ratify existing practices.

Thirdly, and not less importantly, law had a democratic dimension. As the "expression of the general will," it ought therefore to be the business of the people in its capacity as legislator. Article 6 of the Declaration, as we saw earlier, insisted on just this point: "All citizens have the right to take part, in person or through their representatives, in its formation."

A Political Utopia

This threefold conception of law had a totalizing aspect that was bound up with a utopian vision of government as a power capable of grasping the whole of society and driving it forward on every front. The reign of generality that political philosophy sought to bring about was not solely procedural in nature. In the minds of the French revolutionaries, law not only enforced an effective and legitimate set of civil and criminal norms; it had political force as well. In banishing any and all interest in particularity, law was meant to lay the foundations for a just and well-ordered society. The urge to simplify and codify sprang from a conviction that if the world could be comprehended in its entirety, having first been reduced to a manageably compact body of propositions, it could then be perfectly governed. No one has more vividly described the affinity between the psychology of lawmakers and a certain political ideal than Jean Carbonnier, one of the great French jurists of the twentieth century: "To legislate is a more exquisite pleasure than to command. [The law] is more than the crude order that the master hurls at the slave, the officer at the soldier; more than an immediate imperative without a future. No, it is the *law,* a faceless order that aspires to be universal and eternal, after the example of the divine, and equal to it, an order launched into space and into time, where an anonymous crowd meets invisible generations."[9] It was exactly this quality that the men of 1789 cherished about the power of generality. The sovereignty of the law did something more than merely affirm the powers of a legally constituted state; it gave legislators the authority they needed to absorb all political functions, above all those of the judiciary and the executive.

The Downgrading of the Judiciary

The radical conception of law that triumphed with the Revolution implied in the first instance a downgrading of the judiciary. In this regard one has only to look at the great debate over judicial reform that occupied the attention of the Constituent Assembly for several months in 1790. I cannot treat it here in its entirety. But it is nonetheless worth recalling, even very briefly, by way of example, the reasons that were advanced then for establishing a Court [*Tribunal*] of Cassation.[10] While they justified the institution of a procedure for overturning the rulings of lower courts as "an evil, but a necessary evil,"[11] the deputies were in no doubt as to the danger that an autonomous power of judicial review carried with it. Notwithstanding that such a court might serve the technical purpose, as one of them put it, of "maintain[ing] the unity of legislation,"[12] they dreaded the possibility that a court that was intended to act as the guardian and protector of the laws might insidiously become their master. They therefore resolved to create the court as a chamber of the Assembly itself, uniquely seated *in the legislature,* so that the wording of a disputed law could be directly clarified in each case, without giving rise to a body of jurisprudence in the usual sense.[13] "This word 'jurisprudence' . . . must be erased from our language,"

Robespierre revealingly remarked, on this point expressing the general feeling. "In a state that has a constitution, that makes laws," he went on to say, "the jurisprudence of the courts is nothing other than the law [itself]."[14] As a practical matter, the activity of the Court of Cassation was limited during this period to the annulment of enactments deemed to be "plainly in breach" of an existing statute or to derive from an "incorrect application of the law."[15]

The Discrediting of the Executive

The executive likewise found itself marginalized and held in disrepute, since it operated in the main only by particular acts. "Executive power cannot belong to the general public in its capacity as legislator or sovereign," Rousseau had argued earlier, "because this power consists wholly of particular acts that fall outside the province of the law, and consequently that of the sovereign, whose acts can only be laws."[16] While he recognized the role of the executive, he thought of it as merely subordinate and derivative. The question was all the more important in view of the structural dissymmetry that obtained between the legislature and the executive under the ancien régime, the former being intermittent and the latter permanent. The reign of law, identified with the sovereignty of the people, therefore required that executive power be channeled and very strongly constrained; in the best case it could be kept to a strict minimum.[17] Abbé Sieyès, one of the chief authors of the first French constitution of 1791, drew the same conclusion and urged that the legislature be established on a permanent basis as well, the better to act as a check on the executive.[18]

All the revolutionaries shared this sentiment. Their intellectual restraint was all the more striking as the executive power of the ancien régime was by then generally despised. Because the king remained still untouchable in 1789, resentment and dissatisfaction were concentrated instead on his ministers. Recriminations against their "crimes" filled the lists of grievances [cahiers de doléances] of the period, and from the first days of the Revolution a stream of books and pamphlets drew up an indictment of ministerial misconduct. "Since the origin of the monarchy," one read in a commentary on events prior to publication of the first issue of the weekly newspaper Révolutions de Paris in July 1789, "we have groaned alternately under [the yoke of] feudal despotism and ministerial despotism."[19] The widespread willingness to protest the second kind of tyranny was a way of criticizing the executive while absolving the monarchy itself by means of a "pious fiction" (the phrase is due to Mirabeau).[20] If some at first took the precaution of saying that ministerial power "degraded" executive power, it was executive power—suspected of being a natural enemy of the nation, capable of every crime against it—that very rapidly found itself the object of public wrath. The constitutional debates of 1791 gave ample evidence of this suspicion.[21]

In August of that year, when the deputies firmly rejected the idea of granting the king and his ministers a right of initiative in legislative matters, one of them said straight out what was on the minds of many: "The executive will always be the enemy of the legislature and will do it all the harm it can. This is an established [form of] combat in political systems."[22] Significantly, it was the very term "power" that they sought to eliminate in connection with the executive, recharacterizing it more modestly as a "function" or "authority." Sieyès, ever in the vanguard of semantic innovation, proposed a variety of alternatives: "executorial commission," "initiatory and regulatory thought," "headmaster of the public institution," "intermediary commission of powers."[23] Execution itself, the carrying out of policy, was shrunk to accommodate the narrowest and most mechanical construction that could be placed upon it, so that it could in no way threaten the power of the law as the expression of the general will. Condorcet dreamed even of exploiting the possibilities offered by the new science of automata in order to produce a *roi-machine*, a mechanical king.[24] "A people that wishes to be free and peaceable," he wrote, "must have laws, institutions that reduce the action of the government to the least quantity possible." He went even so far as to speak of a necessary "nullity of government" resulting "from a profoundly considered system of laws."[25]

The discrediting of executive power was a consequence not only of the veneration of generality. It was also nourished by the widespread idea that government is in principle a simple matter, and that a small number of laws suffices to regulate social activity. The liberal utopia of government on the cheap held very great appeal for the members of the Constituent Assembly. Most of them sincerely believed that the abnormal growth of executive power was purely an effect of absolutism. While opposing the doctrine of separation of powers on the ground that there was only a single power, residing in the legislative body, they were so impressed by what they took to be the immediate and direct application of the law in the political sphere that they could not imagine its application in the judicial sphere being any less straightforward.[26] In the same spirit, as a symbolic gesture, it was proposed that all ministers be renamed *ministère des Lois de* ____ (where the blank was to be filled in with the title of each one's portfolio) in order to emphasize their subordinate character.[27] Some suggested that the king, supreme holder of executive authority, be considered no more than the "first public functionary"—an epithet that was to be formally approved. After the adoption of the Constitution of 1791, measures to limit the power of ministers—for example, by reducing their salary—became commonplace.

Later, when the powers of the Committee of Public Safety, a creature of the National Convention, were codified in December 1793, it was remarked, as though it were something quite obvious, that "the ministry is only an executive council charged with carrying out policy in its details, [a body] monitored with great vigilance, whose leaders come each day, at appointed hours, to receive the orders and decrees of the Committee."[28] Robespierre himself described the ministers as "mere instruments" of the Committee,[29] this in connection with a decree specifying that "the National Convention is the unique source of impetus for the government."[30] The actual exercise of power was understood to be lodged in the committees of the Convention. It is significant that all the acts of this same Convention were subsequently presented as "laws," even when it was a matter of purely circumstantial decisions or of simple administrative actions having specific purposes.[31] In 1793 and 1794, personal decisions made by members of the Convention sent on official business, to the departments of the country or among the armies, were themselves described as laws. The movement to deny executive power was to culminate on 1 April 1794 (12 Germinal, Year II) in the abolition of the Executive Council (with the approval of its six ministers), now replaced by twelve committees answering directly to the Committee of Public Safety.[32] Executive power was to regain a certain practical influence after Thermidor, it is true, and the Constitution of Year III was to sanction it. But this cannot be said to have represented a true break with what had gone before. The same thing is true with regard to the introduction of bicameralism and the concomitant recognition of the positive role that some form of separation of powers might play. These changes in attitude were the result of prudence and pragmatism. Even so, the principle of legislative centrality had not been abandoned, it had only been modified. The idea that it was necessary "to liberate the legislative body from its oppression by the executive" had lost none of its force.[33]

2

The Cult of Impersonality and Its Metamorphoses

I F THE LAW CAN express the general will, it is because it is impersonal. Generality and impersonality are its two characteristic and complementary traits, both substantively and in respect of the form of the power it enjoys. It is on account of this second quality, impersonality, that it was cherished by the thinkers of the Enlightenment, then by the American and French revolutionaries, and long before them, of course, by the ancient Greeks.[1] For if law can rule without oppressing its subjects, it is because it is objective, impartial, detached from all interested aims and purposes. Law is the just master par excellence, a power that obliges human beings without dominating them, that constrains without doing violence or humiliating those who obey it.

Government without a Head of Government

The discrepancy between this benign view of the impersonality of law and the conception of executive power as residing in the person of the king alone was not immediately apparent to the French in the late eighteenth century. Retaining the monarchy was not perceived to contradict revolutionary values and institutions. Because the king occupied an office inherited from the past, his position did not have to be created and justified as it would have had to be if it were a question of establishing a monarchy in the first place. A positive opinion of English institutions continued to exert a certain influence in the early stages of the Revolution as well. And in any case, a monarch was not really a person, for his individuality had been absorbed by the royal function of embodying a collective identity. What is more, the indissociably juridical and psychological principle of sovereign immunity ("the king can do no wrong") was no less firmly fixed in people's minds than before.[2] The fact that he exercised executive power was considered to be secondary.

All these notions were overturned in the days following the flight to Varennes. It is by no means a coincidence that the term *acéphocratie* should have been coined at this very moment, elevating the image of a government without a head into a constitutional category. The author of an essay bearing this title went to great lengths to explain that "once one man holds the police power as his own, he will be surrounded by slaves."[3] The word was to be forgotten, but not the idea. Now that Brissot and Condorcet had begun openly to describe themselves as republicans, the first to do so, few if any of the revolutionaries thought of the new form to be assumed by the executive after the fall of the monarchy on 10 August 1792 as somehow carrying on the old institution. The debates of the period over removing the figure of the king from the official state seal and replacing it with an image of the republic are proof of this. With the adoption of a first version of Marianne, shown holding a pike surmounted by a Phrygian cap familiar from ancient Roman iconography,[4] the revolutionary enterprise of depersonalizing power found a potent visual symbol. The choice of a female allegory of liberty only further emphasized this purpose, since no one could imagine a woman actually presiding over the country's destiny.

If constitutional experts were divided over many of the points at issue in 1792, all were agreed in dismissing the notion of a solitary exercise of executive power. Once the people were thought of as forming a body, having now replaced the king as sovereign in everyone's mind, it was inconceivable that the king should have any kind of successor as head of government. The very term "president" was understood then only in a technical sense. When the National Convention assembled for the first time in September 1792, a proposal that the president of the Convention take the title of "President of France," and that he be seen to embody the dignity and grandeur of revolutionary institutions and the sovereignty of the people by taking up residence in the Tuileries Palace, met with immediate and violent disapproval.[5] One member of the Convention pointedly summed up the general mood: "It is not only royalty that must be excluded from our Constitution, *it is every kind of individual power that would tend to restrain the rights of the people and injure the principles of equality.*"[6] Seven years later, when the institution of a "President of the Republic" was suggested (the first time this phrase had been used), the idea was dismissed at once.[7] Bonaparte himself greeted it with ridicule—a few weeks before being appointed first consul with full executive powers!

An Unelected Collegial Power

On 15 August 1792 a Provisional Executive Council of six ministers was put in place, with a de facto presidency, which rotated among the ministers on a weekly basis, imparting a functionally collegial character to the institution.[8] Condorcet, on presenting a draft constitution to the Convention in February 1793, emphasized the importance of establishing the principle of collegiality in order to prevent a lapse into authoritarian rule. While taking care not to offend the dominant sensibility—by insisting that it was not a matter of installing a "real power," only an organ "responsible for ensuring that the national will is carried out"—he plainly specified the conditions under which such a principle would be protected against corruption: constant renewal, through the replacement annually of half of the Council's members (numbering eight in all, seven ministers plus a secretary), so that it could never form an autonomous body; strict subordination to legislative authority, with the legislative body being reserved the right of passing judgment on the members of the Council, and even of relieving them of their duties in case of "incapacity or grave negligence"; a rotating presidency, now contemplated on a biweekly basis.[9]

The Constitution finally approved in June of that year was to adopt these principles in the main, strengthening the collegial aspect through an enlarged Executive Council of twenty-four members chosen directly by the legislative body (even if they had been selected from a list drawn up in the departments) and subject to no principle of rank or hierarchy.

The aim at first was a pure government of representative assembly, the executive being explicitly confined to the subordinate position of an "arm of the Assembly." As Barère put it, "There is only one power: the national power that resides in the legislative body."[10] If the Committee of Public Safety subsequently was to exercise genuinely directive—indeed dictatorial—power, it was nonetheless in its essence merely an outgrowth of the legislative-representative branch. After the fall of Robespierre, the idea remained paramount that the executive ought to be an adjunct of the legislature and nothing more. The constitutional plan presented in Year III stated the matter frankly: "The Convention must not at this moment abandon the reins of government to foreign hands, it could not relinquish them without danger."[11] And yet if the theoretical model of a government located *in* the legislative-representative body was unchanged, the Thermidorians were determined to put an end to the excesses of the Committee of Public Safety, calling for a "steady government."[12] The problem was that a government capable of responding promptly to political and social challenges, of maintaining order and stamping out popular insurrections, was also liable to pose a threat to liberties. The solution was a form of executive dualism. This is what the Constitution of Year III was designed to put into effect, on the one hand by forming a Directory of five members that would express the "government's thinking," and on the other by making ministers subject to its orders, serving at its pleasure and charged with overseeing "details of administration." Whereas the Directory was a deliberative body, it was made clear that "the ministers in no way form a council." All this echoed the recommendations of Saint-Just, who in the spring of 1793 had warned against the grave risks of instituting a "royalty of ministers" and suggested dividing executive power into two organs: a council for purposes of deliberation and a group of ministers deputized to carry out its decisions.[13] An early form of the modern executive therefore came to be introduced in France at some remove from the idea of "ministerial power," still mistrusted as a way of surreptitiously bringing back the ancien régime. What was wanted instead was a collegial institution capable of being constantly revitalized, in this case through the appointment of one new member each year—an extreme form of depersonalization meant to dispel widespread fears that a royal figure might soon reappear (one recalls the influence of rumors that Robespierre wished to make himself king).[14]

In the meantime the idea of an executive directly elected by the citizens had not occurred to anyone, not even to the most radical men of 1789 or of 1793. Neither Babeuf nor Robespierre, not even Hébert or any of his fanatical followers imagined that such a thing might be possible, or at least desirable. Only Condorcet had raised the issue, in a pamphlet published in July 1791 under the title "On the Institution of an Elective Council," but his argument in favor of a council elected by the citizens that would take the place of the king, composed of persons "chosen by the same electors as the members of legislatures," went unnoticed.[15] His position was all the more original considering that he still considered the executive to enjoy the same legitimacy as the legislature. What Condorcet had in mind, anticipating the later republican ideal, was an executive power that would owe its authority to the fact that it had been democratically sanctioned by popular vote. He continued to defend this idea a year and a half later, as part of his constitutional scheme of February 1793, emphasizing that "the members of the Council will not be elected by the legislative body, since they are the officers of the people, and not of their representatives."[16] But his proposal on this point, no less contrary to the prevailing opinion than before, was not even discussed.

Bonaparte: Return of a Proper Name, New Regime of the Will

From 1789 to 1794, owing to the breathless pace of events and the constant need to deal with crises, revolutionary thinking about governmental powers had preserved its mostly theoretical character. Only afterward, during the period of the Directory, the five years that followed the adoption of the Constitution of Year III (1795), was it to be put to the test in a practical way. It soon came to be realized that the new regime was incapable of managing the nation's affairs with the institutions that had been put in place earlier. Threatened on both its right and its left, the Directory was torn between a desire to lower the political temperature, to avoid returning to a time that had been dominated by the "magic of words," as Sieyès put it,[17] and a resolve to use the force of the state, beginning in Year IV, in order to stem the tide of royalist feeling that had resurfaced with popular election. These years, in which parliamentary impotence was compounded by intellectual confusion, inexorably brought about the regime's downfall. An era was soon to come to an end, though not before one last attempt was made to solve a specifically French constitutional and political problem.

With the Constitution of Year VIII, composed with an immediate view to finding a way out from the crisis, a new regime was installed that marked a decisive break with the political culture of the previous decade. In order to "put an end to the revolution"—the great watchword of the day—the main concern was to concentrate power in the hands of an executive. This meant, among other things, revoking the principle of impersonality. If the principle seemed still to be honored by the formal establishment of a triumvirate, as a practical matter the first consul had been granted permission to dominate the scene all by himself. For some, these measures did nothing more than respond to the circumstances of the moment. "People were tired of assemblies," as Bonaparte himself said, looking back on the period.[18] In reality, however, yet another model for the exercise of popular sovereignty of the people was about to be tried out.

Madame de Staël, in a few lines that were long to remain famous, recounted the shock of Bonaparte's ascendency on his return from Egypt. "It was the first time, since the Revolution, that one heard a proper name on everyone's lips," she wrote. "Until then one said: the Constituent Assembly has done such and such, the People, the Convention; now one spoke only of this man who was destined to take the place of all others, and render the human race anonymous, by monopolizing celebrity for himself alone, and preventing anyone else from ever being able to acquire it."[19] There is no finer brief description of the period, which dealt a fatal blow to the ideal of impersonality. To be sure, the general owed his promotion to a certain acquiescence, a disillusioned willingness to revive a monarchical order after the acknowledged failure of the previous ten years of constitutional experimentation. Cries of "Vive le roi!" were heard with increasing frequency in 1799.[20] But at the same time something else was going on. There was no question whatever of resurrecting the hereditary principle or reverting to a hierarchical view of society. Even once he had become Napoleon, Bonaparte was to remain in a certain sense loyal to the egalitarian ideal that ultimately defined the revolutionary break with the past (and ensured his popularity). Above all it was executive power that was magnified, in the person of Bonaparte himself. Nostalgia played no part in its new preeminence; there was no longing for a restored monarchy. To the contrary, the power he embodied was seen as a necessary completion of political modernity, where the idea of completion depended on reinterpreting the old notion of embodiment. Bonaparte was by no means the abstract figure theorized by Hobbes in *Leviathan* [1651], nor a reminder of the remote power of a Sun King. Instead he was the "outstanding example of the gift of personification"[21] in a democratic age; a man capable of "absorbing into himself a whole generation," to recall Edgar Quinet's phrase.[22] He was the first to be described as a *man-people*.[23] Quinet himself addressed to him the plea: "You bear our name, rule in our place."[24]

What Bonaparte did was redefine the ideal of democratic will. The Revolution, though it celebrated the cult of impersonality, had not done away with the notion of will. Like the thinkers of the Enlightenment, the revolutionaries followed Bacon in taking as their end "the Enlarging of the bounds of Humane Empire, [with a view] to the Effecting of all Things possible."[25] But what they hoped to see was the triumph of a depersonalized will, the general will as expressed by law—an ideal that itself was reinforced by the notion of *progress*, a forward movement, independent of the decisions of particular individuals, that was the result of bringing forth, through education, a new man, entirely devoted to the common good. With Bonaparte it was the military application of the will that was admired, a power of solitary decision whose effect was amplified by its immediacy, freed from the inertia of collective deliberation. Bonaparte consulted often, but he decided alone. It was this very talent for deciding that captivated so many, both during his lifetime and after. If the image of the man-as-people celebrated by popular singers during the first half of the nineteenth century counted for a great deal in the creation of the Napoleonic legend,[26] it was still more the manifestation of a directly active will, harnessed to extraordinary reserves of energy, that fascinated contemporaries and made him one of the great heroes of the romantic age[27]—all this at a moment when many had grown tired of the dreary monotony of the new bourgeois world.

The New Age of Impersonality

The truth about the cost of Bonaparte's wars, and the disasters to which they led, brought the Napoleonic interlude to an end. With the onset of a century of relative peace, faith in the virtues of impersonality was restored and the figure of Napoleon, in the minds of the nation's elites, came to stand for the exact opposite of what a good ruler ought to be. Even if the lower classes, and especially those in the countryside, succeeded in keeping the legend alive—as the ease with which the emperor's nephew, Louis-Napoleon Bonaparte, acquired power in his turn was to testify—the democratic heresy of personal power united liberals, republicans, socialists, and communists of all persuasions in unforgiving disapproval. Madame de Staël spoke for them all in holding up to public obloquy "a man elected by the people, who desired to put his gigantic *ego* in the place of the human race."[28] But their joint condemnation was not enough to bring back the utopian and abstract radicalism of the old revolutionary doctrine of impersonality. On the left, impersonality was henceforth to have a human face, whether in the form of revolutionary mobs or electoral majorities. Whatever the mode of expression, the underlying feeling remained the same one immortalized by Michelet: "The masses do everything and the great names do little, . . . the supposed gods, giants, titans manage to give a false idea of their size only by raising themselves up on the shoulders of the good giant, the People."[29] Quoting Anacharsis Cloots, he looked forward to the day when France would be "cured of individuals."[30]

For liberals and republicans, impersonality had a different face. It was associated with a type of regime, parliamentarianism, and also a type of social power, whether rule by *notables* or by a political class. One might go so far as to speak of *class impersonality,* for it was in this fashion that revolutionary ideals were to assume a stable constitutional form in France, stripped of their exalted language and grand abstractions. Indeed, the revolutionary trinity of impersonality, legislative supremacy (with a corresponding marginalization of the executive), and reverence for the law constituted a creed that was common to all the various regimes of nineteenth-century France, notwithstanding the different ways in which they tried to square these ideals with the reality of popular sovereignty. The Third Republic is the outstanding case, for having erected the system of assembly government into a constitutional dogma.

The new republican cult of impersonality came to be lastingly established with the crisis of 16 May 1877. Marshal MacMahon was then president of the Republic, having succeeded Adolphe Thiers in 1873. On 8 March 1876, the outgoing National Assembly, elected five years earlier, had transmitted its powers to two new chambers, the Senate, presided

over by an Orleanist, and the Chamber of Deputies, headed by a moderate republican, Jules Grévy. Relations with MacMahon, an ultracon-
servative, quickly proved to be very tense. There were disagreements
not only on the religious question and how the administrative functions
of the state should be organized, but also on symbolic issues, such
as amnesty for the Communards. More fundamentally, however, it was
the very nature of the regime itself that was in question. MacMahon
and his party still clung to the hope of putting in place an authoritarian
regime, doing away with the Republic and parliamentarianism. The
crisis of 16 May settled the matter. Taking advantage of the fact that
Jules Simon, his prime minister, now commanded only a minority in
the Chamber of Deputies, MacMahon forced Simon to resign, justifying his interference in the affairs of the lower house with the words,
"While I am not responsible to the Parliament, as you are, I do have a
responsibility to France." On 17 May 1877, at Léon Gambetta's urging,
the Chamber approved a motion affirming that "the preponderance of
parliamentary power, exercised by ministerial responsibility, [is] the
first condition of the government of the nation by the nation, which the
constitutional laws were meant to establish." The test of strength had
begun. MacMahon moved at once to adjourn both chambers, as the
Constitution permitted him to do, thus opening the way to their formal
dissolution.[31] The victory of the republican camp in the October elections
that year finally broke the impasse, with the result that a new regime
was brought into being, the office of the president having been deprived
of perhaps its most jealously protected prerogative. The doubts and uncertainties arising from the prospect of a return to an authoritarian conservative order had been removed with the unambiguous adoption of a
parliamentary system, triumphant at last.

That the new system, marked by an obsession with ridding France
of what Gambetta called "excessively important persons," did in fact
amount to a change of regime may be seen from the list of prime ministers in the years that followed. No fewer than fifty presidents of the
Council of Ministers succeeded one another from 1876 to 1914, under
eight presidents of the Republic. The leading figures of the republican
world played only a relatively minor role in the workings of government
during this period. Gambetta, Léon Bourgeois, and Émile Combes each
served only once as president of the Council, Jules Ferry twice. By contrast, the more obscure Charles Dupuy and Jules Dufaure held the of-

fice five times each, and Alexandre Ribot four times; almost no one today who is not an expert on the period will have heard of Ernest de Cissey, Gaëton de Grimaudet de Rochebouët, Pierre Tirard, Jean Sarrien, or Ernest Monis, all of whom nonetheless headed governments under the Third Republic. It was in the Chamber of Deputies and the Senate that the important decisions were taken and the major directions of policy decided upon, there that the activity and influence of the great names manifested themselves—as though there had been a deliberate preference for the highest responsibilities of government to be exercised by weak figures, a quasi-systematic enterprise of depersonalization, inaugurating what Daniel Halévy was later to call the "dark times."[32]

The debates over the introduction of a party-list system of balloting provide further evidence of how seriously the ideal of depersonalized politics was taken. With this method of voting, the choice of candidates was determined in principle by the positions they defended and the ideas they argued for. Considered to be "intrinsically republican" (having first been proposed in 1848), it was nonetheless used only for four years, from 1885 to 1889, owing to the fear of the *notables* who comprised the great Parisian bourgeoisie, remnants of the old aristocracy, that their influence would be eclipsed by the growing leverage of professional party officials. Depersonalization was only the flip side of a diffuse and hidden power, exerted in the first instance by the *notables* and later by the parties—which is to say the power of a faceless oligarchy. Already by the late 1880s, the Boulanger affair had shown how far removed from the lives of ordinary citizens this power really was, and how profound the disenchantment to which it gave rise.

French Exception or Democratic Modernity?

France presents an exemplary instance of the ambiguities of nineteenth-century political life, not only for its celebration of the twin cults of law and democratic impersonality but also in its ability to convert, not once but twice, to the contrary religion of Caesarism and the man-as-people. Later we will see how the oscillation between these two poles generated a distinctive constitutional system. First, however, we need to ask whether the revolutionary rejection of executive power constituted an exception in the history of democratic regimes or whether it merely reflected, albeit in exaggerated fashion, a tendency common to all countries whose constitutional history belongs to the liberal-democratic tradition. In trying to answer this question, a brief detour across the English Channel will be unavoidable. For if Great Britain was the birthplace of parliamentarianism, it was also the source of the liberal conception of an executive coexisting with a legislature in a relation of checks and balances. There, more than anywhere else in Europe, executive power early on enjoyed a real measure of autonomy. The price of such autonomy—and the originality of the British system consists in just this—was having to devise a mechanism for consolidating and sustaining executive power through the exercise of political responsibility by the cabinet, which in turn was associated with an openness to the idea that the independence of the executive might assume various forms.

The constant strengthening of this branch, from the beginning of the eighteenth century onward, therefore concealed no absolutist intent or imperial ambition; to the contrary, it was accompanied by greater powers of legislative oversight, corresponding to an enlargement of the rights and prerogatives of Parliament.[33] In striking contrast to the French conception of unitary and rational government, relations between the executive and the legislature under the British model amounted to a positive-sum game, as opposed to the zero-sum game that prevailed across the Channel.[34] They were part of an evolving relationship with the monarchy, in a game with three actors—the cabinet, the houses of Parliament, and the crown, the first two entering into alliances with each other in order *jointly* to offset and lessen royal primacy. More than anything else, the inclination to regard law as a modifiable set of rules, and not as a fixed basic principle of society, was decisive in creating the shifting balance of power characteristic of common-law systems.

Paradoxically, then, the position of a British prime minister in the nineteenth century was much stronger than that of an American president or a president of the Council in France. It is true that in the United States the head of state was practically irremovable, but his authority was limited; the French prime minister, for his part, was a toy in the hands of successive parliamentary coalitions. A cooperative system of the British type, which gradually came into existence without having been preconceived, was more constraining but, on balance, more favorable to the growth of executive power.[35] *To begin with,* however, Parliament had the upper hand. In his magisterial study of the British Constitution as it actually functioned, published at the midpoint of the Victorian Age, in 1867, Walter Bagehot was to say of the Cabinet: "By that new word we mean a committee of the legislative body selected to be the executive body."[36] "The legislature has many committees," he hastens to add, "but this is its greatest."[37] The control exercised by Parliament assumed the form of a *fusion*—the word frequently recurs in Bagehot's writings on the subject—of the executive and the legislature. "The Cabinet," he emphasizes, "is a combining committee . . . , a *buckle* which fastens the legislative part of the State to the executive part of the State. In its origin it belongs to the one, in its functions it belongs to the other."[38] The peculiarity of the English executive, in other words, is that it acted on its own authority while at the same time remaining under a form of legislative oversight that was as vigilant as it was permanent. Power was therefore understood on the other side of the Channel from France to consist in a *dynamic relation* between initiative and supervision. In this sense it was opposed to the conception of assembly government, which the French model had more or less closely approximated for many years.

Power was also more personalized across the Channel, where figures such as Benjamin Disraeli and William Ewart Gladstone dominated the political scene under circumstances wholly absent from nineteenth-century republican France. This was due in part to the British two-party system. In France, by contrast, conditions for forming majorities made complex and invariably precarious negotiations between various circles of *notables* inevitable. Paradoxically, again, the existence of the monarchy favored the rise of figures such as Disraeli and Gladstone, by structurally relativizing their position. The inferior status of even the most brilliant and popular prime ministers in Great Britain was never in doubt; and yet it was the very distinction between two kinds of power that allowed the visible splendors of sovereignty and the effective authority of the Cabinet to peacefully coexist. No prime minister could dream of becoming king, nor could anyone else hope to improve his political standing in this fashion. In addition to permitting greater flexibility than a republic, a constitutional monarchy swept away fantasies of one day restoring a deposed regime. But on the fundamental question of what good government ought to be, the differences between the British system and the French model of a parliamentary republic steadily came to be reduced. The gap between them was above all the legacy of

⚜ 3 ⚜

The Age of Rehabilitation

A T THE BEGINNING OF the twentieth century, executive power was gradually recovering from the disfavor in which it had mostly been held in the nineteenth. There were three reasons for this in Europe. First, the advent of an age of mass democracy with the spread of universal suffrage. The ruling classes, pillars of an oligarchic style of parliamentary liberalism, came to see that the sudden need to cultivate popular support could be met if the role of the executive were suitably revised. The old fear of "the many" thus gave way to a new imperative, of managing crowds, and led to a new approach to the problems of governing. Second, the war of 1914–1918 brought about a decisive change in the way political life itself was conceived, with parliamentary deliberation being devalued in favor of a novel emphasis on decision making and efficiency. Third, new methods for achieving the purposes of governmental policy (culminating in the triumph of Keynesian economics) had the effect of dramatically enlarging the responsibilities of the state. All these things, taken together, amounted to a new regime of political will. An age in which the nation's intents and purposes were imagined to be wholly expressed by legislation of a very general kind had been left behind, and a new age marked by the more immediate and particular action of the executive now came into being.

Crowds and the Strengthening of the Executive

Beginning in the 1890s, a great many books appeared in Europe in response to the perceived menace of social disruption in what soon came to be called the "age of crowds." In Italy, the work of Scipio Sighele enjoyed immense success. Translated into almost every European language, it proposed a way of interpreting various popular outbursts—revolutionary riots, of course, and more recently the bloody scenes of the Paris Commune—whose memory still haunted the bourgeois imagination.[1] In France, Gabriel Tarde advanced a theory of "interpsychology" to account for violent collective phenomena of this type.[2] Already in Germany three decades earlier, in 1859, a new journal called the *Zeitschrift für Völkerpsychologie und Sprachwissenschaft* had been founded to encourage studies by historians, legal scholars, and anthropologists in the new field of "folk" (or "ethnic") psychology. But it was unquestionably the later work of another French author, Gustave Le Bon, that attracted the widest attention among educated readers. No matter that Le Bon was little more than a popularizer of doubtful science, the lasting influence of his book *La psychologie des foules* [1895] can hardly be overstated.[3]

This new fear of crowds marked a departure from the earlier prejudice against the masses that had obsessed liberal and conservative elites throughout the nineteenth century. The old mistrust of the many was connected with the idea that ordinary people were not sufficiently educated, not sufficiently rational, to take part in informed deliberation about matters of public welfare. Insofar as they represented the total sum of such individual incapacities, the many had to be denied the right to vote, or at least prevented from attaining positions of responsibility. Crowds were something quite different. What mattered was not the personal qualities of the individuals composing them, but the collective dynamic they embody. Crowds are not simply aggregates of individuals, Le Bon insisted; they have their own specific character.[4] "[By] the mere fact that he forms part of an organized crowd, a man descends several rungs in the ladder of civilization. Isolated, he may be a cultivated individual; in a crowd, he is a barbarian—that is, a creature acting by instinct. He possesses the spontaneity, the violence, the ferocity, and also the enthusiasm and heroism of primitive beings, whom he further tends to resemble by the facility with which he allows himself to be impressed by words and images . . . and to be induced to commit acts contrary to his most obvious interests and his best-known habits."[5] Tarde, writing a few years later, drew an illuminating contrast between the notions of a crowd and a public.[6] Whereas a public is a virtual group of people, organized around shared ideas and interests that make up a common view of the world, a crowd is a quite present and spontaneous multitude, immediately constituted by its passions and its reactions; whereas a public is a loose association of like-minded individuals, a crowd is a uniquely vital collective being. Le Bon had implicitly made much the same argument, while going further than Tarde in noting the political consequences that flow from it.

Although the reign of crowds seemed to Le Bon inevitable, consecrated as it was by universal suffrage, the new "science" he claimed to have discovered would make it possible at least to control them: "A knowledge of the psychology of crowds is to-day the last resource of the statesman who wishes not to govern them—that is becoming a very difficult matter—but at any rate not to be too much governed by them."[7] The distinctive feature of crowds is that they are irrational, creatures of pure emotion and imagination, and for this reason they are readily manipulated by skillful leaders and agitators. "At the present day," he observed, "these leaders and agitators tend more and more to usurp the place of the public authorities in proportion as the latter allow themselves to be called into question and shorn of their strength. The tyranny of these new masters has [the] result that the crowds obey them much more docilely than they have obeyed any Government."[8]

The solution was plain. Demagogues had to be watched and isolated—this much went without saying. But it was also necessary to invent a new style of government adapted to the new age they heralded. If "the multitude is always ready to listen to the strong-willed man,"[9] the politician must henceforth possess the same power. The idea that he should play a foremost role in forging a novel psychology and economy of will met with an enthusiastic response on both sides of the Atlantic.[10] In America, Theodore Roosevelt was one of Le Bon's greatest admirers. In France, leading parliamentarians flocked to the weekly luncheons he hosted. Aristide Briand, Georges Clemenceau, Paul Deschanel, Édouard Herriot, Raymond Poincaré, and André Tardieu were not alone in seeing his "still stammering science" (as Le Bon himself modestly described it) as the key to modern politics. In the years that followed, not only Lenin, Mussolini, and Hitler, but also De Gaulle were among his most attentive readers.[11]

Le Bon's analysis led him to conclude, first, that the golden age of parliamentarianism had come to an end. Because assemblies were incapable of expressing the type of visible and unified will that was now required, democracies had to be organized around a strong executive that could count on the support of a durable parliamentary majority.[12] This seemed to him all the more necessary as the age of crowds threatened to open the way to an age of dictatorships. He went on to publish a number of articles warning that if new methods of democratic governance were not devised at once, and promptly put into effect, fascism and Communism could not help but prevail.[13] With regard to France, as elsewhere, he was wholehearted in his support of plans for strengthening the executive through the installation of a prime minister who would truly be the head of government. But he did not look at the relative inferiority of the legislature that these schemes implied in the light of any particular constitutional theory. Its inferiority derived instead from psychological and sociological circumstances that he took to be objective and, for this very reason, unavoidable. The terms of the debate had therefore radically changed. The rehabilitation of executive power came now to be seen as both a practical and an intellectual necessity.

The political impact of Le Bon's ideas was also associated with the methods he unapologetically recommended to politicians for winning the support of voters, leading one prominent social psychologist to call him "the Machiavelli of mass societies."[14] In the penultimate chapter of his great work, devoted to "electoral crowds," Le Bon presented what amounts to a short instruction manual for candidates, which in its amoral candor rivals earlier writings on the theory of what were once called reasons of state. Voters, he says, "must be overwhelmed with the most extravagant blandishments, and there must be no hesitation in making [them] the most fantastic promises." Le Bon emphasizes the importance of particular words and phrases that allow an orator to work his will on a crowd, advising candidates addressing an audience of workers, for example, to hammer away at the themes of "infamous capital," "vile exploiters," and the need for a "socialization of wealth."[15] Notwithstanding his keen interest in showing candidates how they might most effectively defeat their opponents, there is no cynicism in Le Bon.

He looked upon the political scene of his time with detachment, urging the adoption of techniques of persuasion that he believed the age of crowds had made inescapable. Nor did he inveigh against universal suffrage. Although he was unsympathetic to it as a matter of philosophical principle, he considered it to be so firmly established in modern societies that there was no longer any point resisting. In this way he was able to satisfy both democrats and all those, then still very numerous, who subscribed to elitist theories. Crowds were now a fact of life, and a scientist does not distrust facts—this much, the gist of his argument, really, was plainly understood on all sides. If they did not wish to see the worst demagogues triumph, politicians had no choice but to learn the art of managing crowds. Furthermore, if the individuals who form a crowd cannot do without a master (as Le Bon says in his final chapter, on parliamentary assemblies), then politicians now had to think of themselves as masters, and not as representatives in the traditional sense.

The Shock of the Great War and the Cult of Leadership

Even though universal suffrage more or less quickly became part of the institutional landscape of European countries and the United States during the late nineteenth century, it was accompanied everywhere by a diffuse sense of popular frustration. The disappointment that historically was indissociable from the triumph of democracy had many sources: indignation at the undue influence of party officials, dismay at the persistence of malrepresentation, a growing impatience with parliamentary incompetence, and, not least, the moral outrage provoked by revelations of widespread corruption. If this disenchantment often gave rise to a longing for more direct forms of civic expression, hardly anyone openly wondered about the objects on which the power of public opinion should be brought to bear. With the exception of France, where memories of Bonapartist culture were still alive (here again one thinks of the Boulanger episode), the idea that democracy could be harnessed to an immediately active executive power did not strike a chord anywhere in Europe. Antiparliamentarian sentiment during the period operated in the manner of a closed circuit, fed by a spirit of cynical disillusionment that in turn it served only to strengthen. All that was suddenly to change with the Great War. Political criticism now came to be associated with a demand for strong government, by what seemed to be both an obvious and an urgent analogy with the conduct of military operations.[16] The shift in mood was particularly pronounced in France, historically the country most reluctant to recognize the special character and importance of the executive.

War, as Tocqueville had noted in *Democracy in America*, "invariably and immeasurably increases the powers of civil government, into whose hands it almost inevitably increases the control over all men and all things."[17] This is what happened in his native land between 1914 and 1918. Yet no particular program of industrial mobilization had been contemplated by the military authorities. All the planning of the general staff was based on the expectation of a short war that could be fought by drawing down the stocks of matériel built up in peacetime. Already by the end of 1914, the prolongation of hostilities had altered the outlook of both generals and politicians. New methods had to be devised for producing arms and munitions, managing shortages, levying requisitions, and ensuring the daily subsistence of the civilian population in the face of supply disruptions. Military strategy had become inseparable from circumstances on the home front. There was no alternative, then, to unified and coordinated action, and for this purpose an executive capable of fortifying the nation's resolve and concentrating its energies was crucial. A fragmented ministerial system subject to the uncertain will of parliament plainly would not do. It was in this context that De Gaulle's thinking about the rehabilitation of the executive began to take shape. "The conduct of war," he wrote in 1917, "consists in a people straining to gather all its strength."[18] The problem facing France, he continued, was that

> [because] we have no sovereign, . . . no person, not even theoretically, can combine government and command. In point of fact, the Constitution of 1875 proclaims that the president of the Republic is the head of the executive, that the army and navy are subject to his orders, that he signs treaties and approves all civil and military appointments; and so, according to the letter of the Constitution, it seems perfectly normal that the president of the Republic should effectively supervise the general conduct of the war. But our customs, our political traditions have in fact denied the president of the Republic executive power in the strict sense, and have made him a permanent member of the Council of Ministers and a representative figure.[19]

In the absence of a strong president, it was widely agreed, the government had to be fundamentally restructured. Léon Blum, in his "Lettres sur la réforme gouvernementale" [1917–1918], presented the case with impressive clarity.[20] He began by noting a grave shortcoming:

> Our Councils [of Ministers] are never capable of a definite decision, very seldom of useful deliberation. For decision, execution, they are too numerous, and too many opposing good wills are paralyzed in them. They possess none of the normal organs with which an executive body must necessarily be equipped. Although the law envisages, on many occasions, that resolutions are to be drawn up in the Council of Ministers, the Council has no secretary, no minutes, no archives. None of its so-called decisions takes a precise and certain form. . . . I do not recall a major law, a long-range reform, a general administrative program being discussed in the Council of Ministers. The most serious questions come before the country in advance of our Councils having debated them or even being aware of them."[21]

The solution seemed obvious to Blum: the Council had to be provided with a true president, responsible solely for directing and coordinating the work of the ministers. Until then prime ministers combined this office with a specific ministerial portfolio to which they devoted the better part of their time. This was no longer a workable arrangement. "A head of government," Blum famously wrote, "is no less necessary than the head of an industrial firm."[22] It was the duty of this official "to have his hand constantly on the tiller, map and compass before his eyes."[23] To the question "Shall this leader be one man or several?"[24] he responded, "In a democratic state, sovereignty belongs, in theory, to the people and to the assemblies that represent it. In practice, it is delegated to one man. Necessity wishes it thus."[25]

This way of talking was totally foreign to the republican tradition. Blum did not shrink from provocation. Of this leader, this first among ministers (the term "prime minister" was just then coming into use), he went so far as to say: "Let us accustom ourselves to seeing him as he is or as he ought to be: a monarch whose main lines of action were drawn beforehand, a temporary and always removable monarch, but nonetheless, so long as he enjoys the confidence of parliament, endowed with the totality of executive power, gathering together and embodying in himself all the nation's energies."[26] Failing that, he argued, the very idea of ministerial responsibility would have no meaning. Although Blum did nonetheless remain an ardent defender of the parliamentary regime, he was adamant that it had to be thoroughly redesigned. Parliament should be no more than a "strict inspector," the "instigator of executive action." And precisely because it was obliged to acknowledge a "single power of control," entrusted to the president of the Council, who was himself recognized as "the leader," it was the leader's duty to be parliament's "guide," perched above it and charged with "regulating the whole of political activity," so that, "from his lofty command post, he may calmly consider it and dominate it completely."[27] Blum, in other words, called upon his countrymen to accustom themselves to a radically different way of thinking about government.

But it was not for all that an entirely new way of thinking. In holding that "the practical means of exercising this mastery have not changed since Louis XIV,"[28] he sought to restore the old conception of executive power as a natural and necessary function of leadership, regardless of political regime. So long as it was not accepted, he maintained, France could not hope to overcome its impotence and eliminate the wasted effort and futile unrest that no country at war can long survive. In the event, an immediate response to the crisis was to appear in the person of Clemenceau. As for Blum, his subsequent involvement with the Socialist Party led him to abandon this stance in large part, and with his conversion at the Tours Congress in December 1920 to the Marxist doctrine of the dictatorship of the proletariat his commitment to parliamentarianism was weakened as well.[29] Even so, the volume collecting his short essays on governmental reform that came out at the war's end vividly and unmistakably testified to a dramatic shift in the thinking of political elites.

With the close of the First World War, then, the democratic ideal had ceased to consist solely in the exercise and realization of legislative will. As a prominent intellectual of the period put it, the time had come "to reduce the distance between two terms that were habitually opposed: authority on the one side, democracy on the other."[30] The idea of command, having become familiar from the conduct of war, was no longer thought to be incompatible in principle with the recognition of popular sovereignty, no longer seen to convey a sense of inherently degrading submission to external authority. Not only did the rhetoric of command take its place once more alongside that of government during this period, the alliance of the two, command and government, soon came to be accepted as a basic precept of the art, essential in times of war, of leading armies and ensuring the means of their support.

In Great Britain, David Lloyd George symbolized this new executive regime with the formation of his famous War Cabinet, equipped with a secretariat, the cabinet office, that for the first time centralized the activities of the different ministries. In France, the onset of war had the effect initially of marginalizing the position of the president of the Republic. Raymond Poincaré, elected to this office on 17 January 1913, had hoped to strengthen it by enlarging the body of *grands électeurs,* only to see its historically limited representative role reconfirmed with the opening of hostilities. "The war was truly a black hole for the president of the Republic," in the words of one contemporary observer.[31] More than anyone else it was Clemenceau who, beginning in the late fall of 1917, came to stand for the break with the tradition of assembly government. While he showed great skill in negotiating with the joint committees of the Senate and the Chamber of Deputies,[32] he was the first to display the boldness and assertiveness that Blum along with many others had called for in a prime minister.

Clemenceau sought above all to put an end to what he called "internal defeatism," the bitter fruit of a parliamentary culture of compromise and risk-aversion.[33] In one of several scathing editorials that appeared in *L'Homme enchaîné* in early 1917, he had attacked the heads of the current government as "leaders of sovereign improvidence," denouncing Briand's "delight in holding forth" and mocking the "pieties" spouted by Poincaré, both of whom he despised for concealing "awkward realities" beneath their verbiage.[34] A few days before being named president of the Council that November, he published what was to be his last editorial under the title "A Government Wanted," calling upon those in power to govern "in broad daylight" and to form "a team of workers who will work."[35] Two months earlier he had asked, "Will we or will we not have a government? There is the crisis, the true crisis, a crisis of character, a crisis of will. For three years we have been waiting for a way out from it to be found."[36] In the same spirit, a few days later, he railed against the witchery of the "lords of official parliamentarianism" who knew only how to brew "batches of groups and influence."[37]

Calls for a strong executive power grew louder after the war, amplified by the new interest in finding ways to manage a society and an economy that were now more complex than before and soon to be buffeted by the turbulent crises of the 1920s and the 1930s. Already during the war, a concern with efficient command and control had spread to all areas of human endeavor. Beyond the military, its influence was felt most deeply in administration, in both the private and the public spheres. Shortly after the turn of the twentieth century, the rational organization of labor under new methods of industrial management had formed the theme of two works by the American mechanical engineer Frederick Winslow Taylor, *Shop Management* [1903] and the classic *Principles of Scientific Management* [1911]. A whole specialized literature grew up in the aftermath of these studies on both sides of the Atlantic. In France, the writings of the mining engineer and executive Henri Fayol made the greatest impression. Though both Taylor and Fayol were chiefly concerned with the role of efficiency in industrial organization, their analysis turned out to have a much wider impact, in large part because it was understood in ruling circles to deal with the problem of command in its most general sense. For Taylor, administration was ultimately a matter of getting human beings to obey orders;[38] Fayol, for his part, made "government" the grand unifying concept of command regimes of all types. It is hardly surprising, then, that each of them should have found an enthusiastic audience in the political world. Both Blum and Lenin expressed admiration for Taylor's work. In the French case, experts trained at the prestigious École Polytechnique played a pivotal role in developing a deeper understanding of command by extending it from military affairs, first to industry and business administration, and then to politics.[39]

In the interwar years the leader came to be generally regarded as a positive and necessary figure of the modern world. In America, the notion of leadership was now a central part of thinking about social organization. In Germany, the idea of a *Führerprinzip* gained currency. In the Soviet Union, Stalin was called *Vojd'*, which is to say both leader and guide; Lenin had earlier emphasized the importance of good "leadership organization" under the Party's supervision.[40] This was a real revolution. The old identification of good government with anonymous rule endorsed by liberals and revolutionaries on both sides of the Atlantic was now a thing of the past, no less than the slogan "Down with the bosses!,"[41] a rallying cry not only for syndicalists and socialists during the nineteenth century, but also for republicans. Until the First World War, the

leader had exclusively been a figure of traditionalist-authoritarian culture. Even at the war's end, the Russian philosopher Nikolai Berdyaev
could still be heard vehemently denouncing the link between democracy
and what he saw as a rising tide of "depersonalization" throughout the
world.[42] But events had caught up. The figure of the leader was now
celebrated on all sides, having finally emerged from the age of impersonality as the indispensable condition of good government.

There was a polemical aspect to this as well. For some, and most
noticeably in France, the cult of leadership revived a preoccupation with
the place of "aristocracies" in democracy that had persisted throughout
the nineteenth century. In conservative circles, which constantly fulmi-
nated against modernity and called for a return to the traditional values
of order and authority, it was apt to have a frankly archaic air.[43] For many
others it carried a managerial connotation, often with antiparliamentarian overtones in political contexts. These various sensibilities were
nonetheless united in agreeing on the need for a renewed appreciation of
the virtues of executive power. The age of leadership had arrived.

The Rise of Executive Action and the Decline of Legislation

After the First World War the scope of public policy everywhere found
itself enlarged, as much with regard to the economy and industrial pro-
duction as to social problems. This had three main consequences. First,
governing was no longer a matter of laying down rules but of achieving
concrete results. The important thing now was to be seen to be "taking
measures," which is to say implementing effective strategies. Here again
events conspired to promote the ascendency of the executive. Bertrand
de Jouvenal described this development as marking a transition from
"supremacy of the law" to "supremacy of the end," with the result that
a *teleocracy* was substituted for a *nomocracy:*

> A government today is at fault if full employment is not maintained, if
> [gross] national product does not increase, if the cost of living goes up,
> if the balance of payments slips into deficit, if the country falls behind
> others in technological innovation. If educational institutions do not
> supply specialized talent in a quantity and a proportion corresponding
> to the needs of the social economy. Economic and social policy is a wager
> on the future that calls for a constant revising of calculations and the

consequent readjustment of measures taken. But this task requires a
more subtle and more flexible modus operandi than passing laws.[44]

Second, with the advent of a new age of voluntarism, and the novel
techniques of policy making that accompanied it, the economy came to
be regarded as a system of variables corresponding to flows of various
kinds that needed to be optimized.[45] This represented a radical departure
from earlier ideas of what it meant to govern. For liberal governments
of the nineteenth century, an interventionist approach to economic
policy made no sense, since all adjustments of supply and demand were
supposed to be automatically regulated by the "natural" laws of the
market. Their sole concern was to ensure that the state did not abuse its
institutional prerogatives, limiting itself to administering a sound monetary policy while keeping budgets balanced. The Marxist position was
not very different. Owing to the fact that the "iron laws" of capitalism
imposed implacable constraints, no reform of the system was possible, as
Marx himself had famously asserted in his 1865 speech on value, price,
and profit. The ideas of "reflation" and "stabilization" therefore had no
place in either liberal or Marxist doctrine. Liberals accepted, at the very
most, that the state can counteract cyclical unemployment by investing
in public works projects when recession threatens to tip over into depres-
sion. Marxist economists, for their part, held basically the same view.
Crises were inevitable in capitalism: only a change of regime, giving up
capitalism for socialism, could alter this state of affairs.

Furthermore, once the economy was considered to be a system of
variables needing to be optimized, it became something that could be
acted on and modified. In principle, at least, all such variables were now
amenable to intervention: not only the supply of money, but government spending and revenues, consumer prices, aggregate supply and
demand, and so forth. The new language of economics itself expressed
this change, the term "policy" having been broadened to include all such
measures of economic activity in the wake of the Keynesian revolution.
Thus one learned to speak of monetary policy, fiscal policy, incomes
policy, and the like. In the meantime, cyclical corrections and structural
adjustments became both complementary and indissociable, and the
scope and effect of governmental action further enlarged with the appearance of a new and scarcely less essential activity: regulation. To say

that it upset the usual assumptions about the nature of public administration would be an understatement. It rendered obsolete a whole style of thinking about what governments should or should not do, whether in relation to practical questions concerning state intervention in the private or public sectors (Should the government act to alleviate poverty, for example, or to build transportation networks or improve education?) or to fundamental philosophical principles (Under what circumstances, if any, should the government's interest supersede the claims of individual citizens? Does the government have an obligation to promote social justice? Must it seek to ensure equal opportunity for all?). In order to have its intended effect, the notion of regulation demanded the existence of a central agent, the executive, buttressed by the police power of the state. Keynesianism, in utterly changing how the most traditional elements of governmental action were regarded, was more than a theoretical system. As Pierre Mendès-France noted, because it "implied a set of practical solutions . . . all financial institutions, the budget, credit, money, taxation received a new meaning and a new function."[46]

This functional expansion of the scope of executive power was also associated, in the third place, not only with a new method for producing legislation, but also with a transformation of the form and the very content of laws themselves. Their form changed because laws became more and more an executive prerogative as a result of new procedures for submitting bills and setting parliamentary agendas. The content of the laws themselves changed because, far from being the general rules imagined by the men of 1789, simple and few in number, they now consisted for the most part in a great many regulations and directives bearing on increasingly specific objects. Making laws had become just another means of governing. The old distinction between legislative power, identified with generality, and executive power, identified with particularity, had by the same token been completely erased. In the 1920s and 1930s, most spectacularly in France, the multiplication of laws in the form of decrees demonstrated the growing power of the executive at the expense of the legislature. In effect, reliance on legislation by executive decree represented a new system of government—as though the legislature had abandoned its historical functions.[47] Beyond this specific technique, however, it was the nature of law itself that had been

⚔ 4 ⚔

Two Temptations

T HE GREAT REVERSAL THAT we have just examined, though it did
bring about the rehabilitation of executive power, was not enough
to give it a secure place in democratic life. When the need for a strong
executive became evident at the turn of the twentieth century, the first
attempts to adapt it to existing institutions soon came to naught. In Europe, the failure of the Weimar Republic, which I consider in Chapter 5,
was the most dramatic example. And yet almost everywhere it was as
though a reinvigorated executive could be conceived only by depriving
it of any real democratic character. This was done in either of two
ways. On the one hand, through a trivialization and depoliticization
of executive power, which was thereby reduced to its managerial and
administrative aspect. The technocratic ideal that arose in this way was
to be most fully realized in the United States and, to an even greater
degree, in France. On the other hand, through a radicalization and an
autonomization of executive power—the only available course of action
in a world in which states of emergency were considered to be the permanent condition of politics. This view was to underlie the coming to
power of Nazism in Germany, where it was brilliantly expounded by one
of the regime's most eminent jurists, Carl Schmitt. To be sure, these two
methods for abstracting the executive from democracy cannot be placed
on the same level, for in relation to a parliamentary-representative

system they stand opposed: whereas the technocratic view is not incompatible with such a system in principle, the doctrine of decisionism elaborated by Schmitt absolutely rules out any form of coexistence. The fact remains, however, that each in its own way had the effect of preventing executive power from being established in a democratic setting.

The Technocratic Ideal

The perceived necessity of a strong executive initially assumed the form of a trust in the virtues of public administration. Antiparliamentarianism and the reaction against the influence of parties over political life gave rise to a situation after the First World War where the effective exercise of executive power was seen to depend on the independence of the administrative machinery of government. This view was informed by two overriding concerns, which must be distinguished even if they are closely bound up with each other: first, a managerial interest in rationalizing the functions of the state; second, a political and institutional interest in establishing an administrative capability whose force and legitimacy would derive from its depoliticization. Together they characterize what today we are accustomed to call a "technocratic" style of governing, nowhere more completely developed than in France and America. Let us begin by examining why its earliest proponents imagined they were advancing a scientific purpose.

In America, the aim of rationalizing public administration on behalf of an efficiently assertive executive branch was associated toward the end of the nineteenth century above all with the names of Woodrow Wilson and Frank J. Goodnow. Wilson, a professor of jurisprudence and political economy who was to become the nation's president in 1913, had published a pioneering article some twenty-five years earlier on the study of what he called "practical government."[1] In a modern industrialized society, Wilson argued, democracy cannot limit itself to constitutional debate about methods for promulgating laws and holding elections. Acting in the general interest requires going directly to the heart of complex problems and dealing with them without delay. This in turn requires that the executive be assigned a central role. In theory, administration is only a means for giving effect to political decisions. Wilson stressed that this had become a much more complicated business than before. Defining the objectives of government could no longer be separated from the difficulties encountered every day in trying to carry them out. It was therefore necessary to develop a pragmatic science of administration, not only out of a concern for efficiency but also because the needs of democracy itself had changed.

Goodnow, a legal scholar sympathetic to the progressive movement, sought to meet this challenge by proposing a new way of looking at public administration in America.[2] He emphasized, first, that real executive power was exercised for the most part by the organs of administration, many of them government agencies that had only recently been created. In *Politics and Administration* [1900],[3] Goodnow revisited the classical theory of the separation of powers with an eye to reformulating it in the light of current practice. The sphere of politics, he maintained, is confined to the legislature and the judiciary; administration is the province of the executive branch. If the essence of politics consists, by hypothesis, in trying to express a general will, the essence of administration resides in the pursuit of efficiency and rationality. From this it follows that whereas administration can achieve "executive perfection" only by *internal means,* "legislative perfection" is wholly dependent on an *external* will, popular sovereignty. Accordingly, there are two kinds of generality at work: substantive generality in the case of administration, which is dedicated to excluding particular exceptions of any sort; procedural generality in the case of politics, dedicated to including the greatest possible number of citizens in the most unanimous possible expression of a collective intent.

What was new was that administration had become an autonomous profession that answered a legitimate public interest in promoting efficiency and expertise. As against the messiness of subjective democracy, with its crude methods for forcing a general will to emerge from the ballot box, changing times demanded something cleaner and more precise—objective democracy. Hence the necessity of devising a style of administration that would be both guardian and servant of the common good,[4] whose efficiency and rationality were bound to guarantee its objectivity. Hence, too, the rationalist mystique cultivated by American progressives at the turn of the twentieth century, with the result that reason and efficiency were raised to positions of prominence in the pantheon of democratic virtues.[5] Finding the right way forward, they believed, depended on handing over power to disinterested experts, for

democracy was not "government of the majority, but of those who deliberately place themselves in the service of all."[6] Mary Parker Follett, a
leading progressive management theorist with close ties to the English
Fabians, regarded "democracy as a method, a scientific technique for expressing the will of the people," and spoke of the advent of a new age of
both public policy and democracy.[7] A scientific approach to government
would therefore impose greater order while at the same time protecting
democratic values.

In France the triggering event was the First World War, though
Taylor already had many enthusiastic readers before it broke out (one
scholar, looking back on the period, spoke of a "Taylorian turning point
of French society").[8] "We have been saved in spite of the state"[9]—a famous phrase that well expressed the mood of the time, with government
intervention now being regarded in a new and positive light. The twin
imperatives of reorganizing administration and industrializing the state
were urged most strenuously after the war by Taylor's principal French
disciple, Henri Fayol. His book *L'incapacité industrielle de l'État* [1921], followed two years later by an influential lecture on the new doctrine of
the administrative state, set the tone of what was to become a widely
shared attitude. Having made an intensive study of the postal and telecommunications service (PTT), Fayol delivered a damning verdict on its
operation, overseen by a succession of incompetent undersecretaries of
state, with little or no long-term planning, few if any performance indicators for management, and woefully inadequate incentives for em-
ployees. But the PTT was only a symptom of a deeper illness that affected
the whole of the state apparatus. It could be cured only by "introduc[ing]
in the state the [same] practices that favor the success of industrial
firms,"[10] which is to say by organizing public administration according
to the new principles of rational management, of which Fayol had already made himself the foremost theorist in Europe with the publication of *Administration industrielle et générale* [1916].

The ideal of competence thus came to be established on each side of
the Atlantic, and with it the technological view of reason as a progressive form of social generality by comparison with the unruly emotions
of the masses. The emphasis on efficiency and scientific administration
revived an old prejudice, that a capacity for rational deliberation is the
basic condition of political life, which French doctrinaires had been the
first to insist on in the early nineteenth century. It was for want of being

able, or perhaps even for not wishing in the first place, to conceive of government democratically that administrative-executive power once more came to be accepted in both France and America as a central element of governmental organization in the guise of technocracy.[11]

In each country this acceptance was indissociable from the rise of antiparliamentarianism, and indeed of antipolitical feeling, as a consequence of popular anger at the corruption of public officials. In France, scandals such as the one that grew out of the bankruptcy of the Panama Canal Company in 1889 and came to light three years later contributed very largely to a widespread sense of revulsion. In the United States, the influence over public affairs exerted by political parties was denounced on all sides. Almost all the large cities were controlled behind the scenes by bosses, men who ran the local political machines of the party in power. The elected mayor was in most cases no more than an underling. It was the boss who filled administrative offices, gave and took away jobs, made the important decisions. Corruption was present at every level of the system. By the turn of the twentieth century, municipal malgovernment had come to symbolize the dysfunction of American democracy, however much it may have exaggerated its main features. The only solution, it was felt, was to depoliticize executive power in the great urban centers.

The ineptness and venality of the political class was no less vigorously objected to in France, and led many there to the same conclusion. "Since anyone is qualified to do anything," Charles Benoist famously pointed out, mocking the routine confirmation of ministerial appointments, "he can be put anywhere any time."[12] This form of "ministerial amateurism" was constantly deplored in France before and after the Great War. A whole way of being and acting in the political world, which Émile Faguet had accused of observing a "cult of incompetence," was sharply criticized at every opportunity "What is a politician?" Faguet asked. "Someone who has no ideas of his own, and little in the way of education, sharing in the main the sentiments and the passions of the crowd; someone who has no other occupation than to concern himself with politics, someone who, if his political career were to be taken from him, would die of hunger."[13]

The same complaint was heard in the United States. There the progressive movement sought to eradicate the "virus" that fueled corruption and demoralized the citizenry. This meant dethroning the city bosses, identified in the public mind with all manner of political evil. There was general agreement on the need, first, to clean up municipal elections by removing them from the control of the parties and democratizing them—for example, by introducing a system of primaries. But it was also necessary to restructure municipal authority, concentrating effective control in the hands of a commission equipped with expansive prerogatives and made directly accountable to the people. Doing this, it was believed, would help to reduce the opportunities for abusing administrative power, which was scattered among a large number of specialized departments whose work was directed by the bosses. This system of government by commission (or commission government, as it was also called)[14] was widely adopted, in many places as the first phase of a larger reform program. Often it was augmented by the appointment of a city manager having executive powers, with the local commission limiting itself to setting forth the main objectives of public policy. Recruited on the basis of professional qualification and hired by elected officials, these managers were considered to embody that *objective power* which alone was thought capable of ridding democracy of the "partisan poison" that threatened to destroy it. By narrowing the scope for political influence and increasing administrative and managerial power, it would once again become possible to promote the general interest, only now more effectively than before.[15] It was during this period, just after the First World War, that the term "technocracy" was coined to designate a system of government in which the resources of the nation were marshaled and deployed by experts for the common good.[16] Just so, administrative power was considered to be fundamentally democratic in nature—though democracy in this sense no longer had any need for popular participation!

A similar state of mind prevailed in France after 1918. There, however, calls for a nonpartisan administrative-executive form of government were inspired more by lessons drawn from the war than by a desire to give new life to democratic ideals. The work of Henri Chardon, a member of the Council of State and one of the most ardent early twentieth-century French advocates of administrative power as an antidote to political power, provides a striking example. It was just this, an excess of political power, that seemed to him the "organic vice" of the French Republic. "The exaggeration of what we call politics," he

wrote, "has eaten away at France like a cancer: the proliferation of useless and unhealthy cells has stifled the life of the nation."[17]

Already before the war, in *Le pouvoir administratif* [1911], Chardon
had argued that a parliamentary regime, divided by partisan conflict
and interrupted by frequent elections, could not act effectively in the
general interest. "Administration," he emphasized, "exists and must
exist in its own right, outside politics."[18] For only administration can
embody the qualities of permanence and generality necessary for the
realization of the common good. Chardon agreed with public-service
theorists that civil servants have a special "interest in being disinterested," but he laid greater stress on the legitimacy of the authority they
exercise on their own account as experts: "A government official ought
to be considered not as a ministerial delegate charged with rendering a
public service, but as the technical representative of a permanent interest of the nation."[19] Indeed, even the most minor official, in the performance of his duties, "is himself the government."[20] Political power
remains useful and legitimate, to be sure, but it can play its role only if
the legitimacy and independence of administrative power are also recognized; the function of political power has to be limited to "sovereign
control" of government action. Thus, for example, Chardon recommended stripping ministers of their old authority and reassigning them
to an office of "comptroller general." The health of a democracy, in his
view, depended on maintaining a balance between these two powers.

State of Exception

The perceived need to provide the executive with emergency powers
also influenced thinking about this branch of government after 1918.
The rule of law presupposes the existence of a stable and predictable
world. But events never unfold in a perfectly smooth and repetitive way.
To the contrary, they are often complicated by the sudden appearance
of the unexpected. It is exactly this that justifies granting executive
power, conceived as distinct in its character and purpose from legislative power, its own sphere of application. From a theoretical point of
view, as we have already seen, this point was long disputed. But once
the particular case assumes an extreme form, as an unforeseen and

imminent danger, and the normal rhythms of public life are disrupted by extraordinary circumstances, the need to act promptly and forcefully becomes inescapable. The very abruptness of the moment condenses and precipitates events, producing an exceptional and immediate reaction, as when armed conflict breaks out or catastrophe strikes. In that case the supremacy of the executive inevitably imposes itself: ordinary rules are swept aside; decision supplants the norm. There is, of course, great danger in this as well. A government is apt to find itself either paralyzed, incapable of reacting, or tempted to enlarge its prerogatives unilaterally, suspending the rights and liberties of its citizens.

To forestall an usurpation of power, the only option is to entrust executive authority during a state of emergency to a special magistracy. This is what the ancient Romans sought to do by supplementing the regular institutions of state with a unique public office, dictatorship, when confronting an urgent threat made it necessary to cast off the yoke of customary law.[21] The etymology of the name for this office must be taken into account if we are to fully appreciate the originality of the institution. In Latin, the term does not carry any connotation of despotic or tyrannical power. Our word "dictator" comes from the verb *dictare*, which reminds us not only that his authority derived from the fact that it was his words that were obeyed, but also that the orders he gave were given orally, not in the form of *written laws*. The powers of the dictator, though they were considerable in Rome, were nonetheless strictly circumscribed.[22] The management of exceptional circumstances, in other words, was specifically contemplated as part of the normal functioning of permanent institutions; the republican legal order was neither abolished nor suspended by the state of emergency that established the dictatorship. The flexibility of this arrangement, amounting to an informal constitution, made it possible to cope with threats to the state of several kinds in a remarkably efficient way without the system itself ever being called into question.[23] Machiavelli and Rousseau both praised classical dictatorship on precisely this ground.[24]

The failure of the moderns to develop a theory of executive power had the consequence that they were incapable of constitutionalizing emergency rule as the Romans had done.[25] *As a practical matter* they were able to consider how exceptional circumstances should be managed, but only in a purely finalist sense, with irregular measures of every sort being licensed by appeals to "public safety" and the need to "restore order," ensure the "security of the state" and "protect society." The American Constitution, while it does make reference to such circumstances, only very vaguely suggests the possibility of authorizing special powers; in France, article 14 of the Constitutional Charter of 4 June 1814 no less obliquely permitted the king to make "the necessary regulations and ordinances for the execution of the laws and the security of the state."[26] Here and elsewhere, throughout the nineteenth century, there was much wavering and irresolution. This was on the whole a century of peace in Europe, and it was mainly in response to revolutionary threats that emergency legislation was resorted to. The French law of 9 August 1849 decreeing a state of siege unavoidably made a strong impression everywhere on the Continent. But it was not until the conflict of 1914–1918 that a turning point was reached, particularly in Germany, where the profound disruptions of the postwar period threatened to upset the legal order. Although the question was to remain unresolved from both a theoretical and a juridical point of view,[27] the Weimar Constitution did nonetheless represent the first modern attempt to democratically constitutionalize emergency rule. Its fatal defect was the exceedingly vague wording of its article 48, used from 1930 to 1933 to justify a change of regime, which opened the way to Nazi domination.[28] It is against this background that a wholly different interpretation of emergency rule suddenly gained terrifying force. Not content to operate within a legal framework for the management of exceptional circumstances, Hitler moved at once to institute in normal times the extraordinary powers of an executive whose authority was now effectively immune to challenge, signaling the end of the parliamentary order. Decisionism, as the new doctrine of state was known, had found its great theorist a decade earlier in the person of Carl Schmitt.

"Sovereign is he who decides on the exception"—thus Schmitt's famous dictum in *Politische Theologie* [1922],[29] a work that announced a radical departure from the traditional ideals of representative government and deliberative democracy. Ten years later, in *Der Begriff des Politischen* [1932],[30] he criticized liberalism for what he saw as its antipolitical character. In limiting government merely to the routine supervision of civil society, liberal democracy had forgotten that the harsh realities of a state of nature—conflict and the chronic struggle for existence—are inescapable facts of social life. Politics therefore had to be reconceived, by frankly admitting the brutal implication of mankind's fall from grace, that human history is a record of the shifting fortunes of friend and foe, constantly recast in the crucible of war.

Schmitt's vitalist conception of politics led him to glorify executive power as the decisive form of political authority, not merely by virtue of its unrivaled capacity to produce immediately tangible effects but also, and most importantly, as the agent of world-historical change. The true character of executive power manifests itself under exceptional circumstances, because it is then and only then that "the decision frees itself from all normative ties and becomes in the true sense absolute. . . . Unlike the normal situation, when the autonomous moment of the decision recedes to a minimum, the norm is destroyed in the exception."[31] Exceptional circumstances were understood to have a revelatory function, laying bare the essence of politics and exposing executive power for what it really is, a sovereign exercise of the will. There may seem to be an air of absolutism about this; indeed, some commentators have insisted upon an indissoluble link between decisionism and absolutism.[32] Schmitt himself sought to parry the charge by framing his view of politics in terms of a democracy of embodiment. If the sovereign *is* the people, the indivisibility of sovereignty and the unity of its exercise are consistent with a type of order that can plausibly claim to be democratic. Whereas from a liberal-parliamentary perspective democracy is considered to be stronger the more executive power is restrained, from a decisionist-identitarian perspective the opposite is true.

The exaltation of executive power thus came to be extended to embrace a theory of sovereign dictatorship. In an appointive dictatorship of the classical Roman type, the declaration of a state of emergency instituted a special and temporary authority for the purpose of maintaining the existing order. Schmitt, by contrast, conceived of dictatorship as a means of creating a new order.[33] "From the perspective of sovereign dictatorship," he emphasized in *Die Diktatur* [1921], "the entire existing order is a situation that dictatorship will resolve through its own actions. Dictatorship does not *suspend* an existing constitution through a law based on the constitution—a constitutional law; rather it seeks to create conditions in which a constitution—a constitution that it regards as the true one—is made possible. Therefore dictatorship does not appeal to an existing constitution, but to one that is still to come."[34] Dictatorship in this sense is the highest form of executive power, because the exceptional circumstances to which it is meant to respond are just the ones in which the state reveals its essential mission: "War against the external enemy and suppression of internal rebellion would not then be states of exception, only the norm in which the law and the state would exercise their inner purpose with direct force."[35]

Does sovereign dictatorship, unlike Roman dictatorship, therefore stand outside the law in its constitutionalization of exceptional powers? As a jurist, Schmitt could hardly avoid the question. He justified his position in two ways: by advancing a theory of constitutional authority, on the one hand, and by redefining the very notion of a norm, on the other. Schmitt was an attentive and enthusiastic reader of Abbé Sieyès. He quotes Sieyès several times, not only in *Die Diktatur* but also in a work on constitutional theory published seven years later, *Verfassungslehre* [1928]. He was particularly impressed by Sieyès's impassioned plea on behalf of constituent power as a radically creative force, the pure expression of an immediate will: "Reality is everything, form is nothing."[36] Elsewhere he identified constituent power with a "national will that cannot be subjected to any form, to any rule."[37] Raw and unconstrained power of this kind was therefore distinct from a constituted power, which consists merely in the ordinary exercise of collective sovereignty by elected representatives. The very fact that such a distinction could be made amounted to an implicit recognition of the superiority of constituent power. This was a language that Schmitt instinctively understood. Because nothing prevents the nation from continually giving itself "new forms of political existence," the nation is a " 'formless formative capacity,' "[38] and the people, as the possessor of constituent power, "are superior to every formation and normative framework."[39] It is therefore in the exception that this power shows itself to be fully sovereign, magnificent in the naked truth of its creative potency.

Schmitt's revival of constituent power in exceptional circumstances was ultimately a celebration of decision, which is to say of execution. But he did more than analyze the political implications of the sort of paradoxes of action one finds in Machiavelli's political philosophy or Weber's sociology of domination. He went so far as to hold that the most important social and legal norms have always been established on the basis of a decision, and not of deliberation, whether among citizens or in parliaments. He developed this argument from two considerations, one etymological, the other historical and constitutional. In *Der* Nomos *der Erde* [1950], Schmitt maintained that "the meaning of [the word] *nomos* [has] its origin in land-appropriation,"[40] which is to say an act of taking, with a secondary sense derived from the act of sharing and distributing. To begin with, then, a norm was the product of a decision whose result it recorded; it had a directly active dimension, prior to any regulative function. Laws, in the political sense of the term, ought therefore to be understood as issuing from a definite will, a commandment—in short, from an act of sovereignty (which is why Schmitt laid emphasis on constitutions that, in determining "a people's form of existence," embody the fundamental presupposition of all later prescriptions).[41] Accordingly, a state of exception is simultaneously the moment at which the constituent sovereignty of the people is realized and the moment at which the essentially decisional character of politics is affirmed. The idea that it is in their interaction and communion with executive—that is, dictatorial—power that the people actually assert their sovereignty and that their will is carried out contradicted the basic principle of a representative regime, namely, that the general will is expressed by a parliamentary system of legislation. Executive power in Schmitt's sense therefore required the categorical rejection of liberal democracy.

Continuities and Discontinuities

It scarcely needs to be said that these two temptations, as I have called them, technocracy and decisionism, are still with us today. The appeal of technocratic rule is undiminished wherever the impotence of a partisan executive has led to popular disenchantment with democracy. France is perhaps the outstanding case. Following the Second World War, the discredit that the Third Republic had brought upon itself created from the ranks of the Resistance a whole generation of high-ranking civil servants who came wholeheartedly to commit themselves to something very much like a priestly calling, with the mission of governing the country behind the scenes on behalf of the general interest and in opposition to governments whose chronic instability they saw as the inevitable consequence of partisan maneuvering and the pursuit of short-term advantage. Faith in the ability of technical expertise to compensate for the narrow self-interest of incompetent politicians has periodically reappeared since, particularly in response to the financial crises of the first decade of the twenty-first century.

As for the temptation to impose unilateral executive authority under the pretext of a state of emergency, again we find it persists in more or less aggravated form in all parts of the world. One thinks especially of Latin America in the 1960s and 1970s, where an obligation to protect public safety was frequently cited as a justification for installing dictatorships. From Brazil to Chile and Argentina, reasons of "national security"[42] were invoked by military officers to legitimize coup d'états. In Russia and other countries of the former Soviet bloc at the beginning of the 2000s, the notion of "sovereign democracy" was adduced in support of a new type of authoritarianism.[43] In the United States, in reaction to the events of 11 September 2001, emergency powers have been added to the standard inventory of executive prerogatives. Barack Obama, weakened in domestic affairs by resistance from the Congress, which withheld its approval of certain key elements of his legislative program, finally decided against rescinding the mechanisms of emergency government put in place by George W. Bush, and in some cases even strengthened them. In France, an embattled president looked to assert military force in hopes of restoring his sagging fortunes. Without concluding, as some have done, that emergency government has now become the rule rather than the exception,[44] one must nonetheless acknowledge its enduring fascination.[45]

The idea that the executive forms a natural part of democracy in what may be thought of as its regular form, by contrast with the technocratic and decisionist deformations to which it has been and still remains liable, achieved broad acceptance only with the advent of presidentialization. Let us therefore take a closer look at the history of this phenomenon.

⇥ PART II ⇤

THE PRESIDENTIALIZATION OF DEMOCRACIES

◁ 5 ▷

The Pioneering Experiments: 1848 and Weimar

THE PERSONALIZATION of presidential government was so prominent a feature of the political life of the last decades of the twentieth century that the choice of a head of the executive branch by means of universal suffrage has now come to be seen as one of the most obvious characteristics of a democratic regime. But the break that it represented with earlier conceptions of good government occurred only very gradually, over the course of more than a century, beginning with the presidential election of 1848 in France, which led to a return of Caesarism; then with the Weimar regime in Germany, swallowed up by the onrushing tide of Nazism; and finally, again in France, with the first steps, thought by many to be steps backward, taken by Charles de Gaulle as head of the Fifth Republic. I treat the first two moments here, and the Gaullist episode in Chapter 6.

1848, or the Triumph of Thoughtlessness

In France, the direct election of the president of the Republic by universal suffrage was approved in November 1848 without having been the subject of any real debate. At the meeting of the small constitutional committee charged with considering various methods for selecting a leader of the executive branch,[1] two options were contemplated from the very outset: direct exercise of executive power by the Assembly, or the assignment of such power to delegates of the Assembly; and the formation of a collegial executive, consisting of consuls or directors. Both of these models were borrowed from the Revolution. In the end, however, and with virtually no substantive discussion, a new procedure was decided upon—voting for a president. It was a negative choice in the main. The instability and chronic conflict created by the collegial institutions of Year III and Year VIII were still vividly recalled by many, no less so than the dark moments of which the committees of 1793 and 1794 were an indelible reminder. The American example, by contrast, was crowned with the prestige of a new type of republic that at the time was ritually opposed to a conventional republic, which is to say one with Robespierrist overtones.[2] The presence of Alexis de Tocqueville and Gustave de Beaumont on the constitutional committee had counted for much in this regard. The president's eligibility for another term of office was a matter of greater disagreement; it was finally approved, following the committee's recommendation, on the condition that on completing his term the outgoing president not present himself again as a candidate before a period equivalent to the proposed term (four years) had elapsed. Consensus was less easily achieved with respect to the manner of selecting a president. Jules Dufaure had proposed election by the Assembly,[3] Armand Marrast a selection of candidates by the Assembly who were then to be submitted to a popular vote. Eventually the principle of direct election by the people, without any limitations on candidacy, won general acceptance. The only restriction was that the winner had to obtain a minimum of two million votes—any number beneath this threshold being thought to diminish national sovereignty.

Most of the provisions suggested by the committee were adopted in the final version of the constitution, though not without bitter differences of opinion in the Assembly that need to be recalled if we are to fully appreciate the circumstances of this extraordinary constitutional innovation.[4] On the extreme left, Félix Pyat, a future communard, had argued against the very institution of a presidency on the ground that there cannot be two distinct expressions of the popular will; indeed, the idea of a division of powers is fundamentally unrepublican. "In a republic," Pyat maintained, "there is only one law, the law of the people, only one king, the people themselves, represented by an elected assembly, the National Assembly. This assembly must therefore be sovereign like the people it represents; it sums up all powers, it rules and governs by the grace of the people, it is absolute like the old monarchy and can likewise say: *l'État, c'est moi.*"[5] To his mind, democracy and the republic consisted in the transfer of the old royal power *to an elected body.* This was a classically and radically monist view, unalterably opposed to notions of balance and counterweights. But it was a liberal view as well, to the extent that the existence of a collective direction through a representative authority was seen to provide the people with a guarantee that political power would remain subject to the law. The election of a single man, by contrast, above all if he were permitted to exercise real authority, would make him a force that Pyat reckoned to be not only immense but effectively irresistible, and therefore potentially threatening. Such an election, he warned, would be "an anointing much more divine than the holy oil of Rheims and the blood of Saint Louis."[6] From two things one, Pyat insisted: if the president is weaker than the Assembly, the way will be open to impotence and ungovernability; if he is stronger, his strength will be overwhelming and he will have a power far greater than that of an unaccountable constitutional monarch. The danger of the proposed system, then, was that it was inherently unstable. It is true that Pyat neglected to mention the equilibrating function provided for by the draft constitution in the form of a Council of Ministers answerable to the parliament. But his basic argument, having to do with conflicting sources of legitimacy, remained a formidable one, and all the more as he ruled out any comparison to the United States as irrelevant for French purposes. The situations of the two countries, he pointed out, were very different; in America, the office of the presidency was indispensable in holding together a federal system of states whose unity had yet to be securely established. As a democrat of the extreme left, Pyat could hardly take exception to the idea of election by universal suffrage, but he could without inconsistency object to following the American example in the case of the presidency. At all events he was unquestionably right to identify this as the chief dilemma facing French democrats. Nevertheless, in failing to inquire into the specific character of executive power and its operation in a democratic setting, he did not manage to go to the heart of the matter.

The socialists, for their part, feared the specter of monarchy. Pierre Leroux accused the proposed constitution of trying to "preserve the monarchy under the name of presidency, thus giving licence to every kind of ambition."[7] Proudhon expressed the same view. "Presidency is monarchy," he warned in the fall of 1848. "Arouse an insatiable desire in the land for monarchy and the land will answer you with a monarch . . . your president will be king."[8] For Proudhon, the danger was also connected with the fact that, in the minds of the people, true power—power that is perceptible and visible—resided with the executive,[9] and that, for the same reason, they would turn to men capable of subjugating them, not to men of actual talent. "Do you seriously imagine," he asked the members of the committee, "that the people, having an unmarried daughter, the Republic, would consent to give her to a boor such as you or me—to Cavaignac, Lamartine, Ledru-Rollin, or Thomas Diafoirus? Really? A soldier, a versifier, a bachelor of laws, [a doctor of medicine]—president of the Republic! You must be mad! Do the people know such persons? Do they care about their ranks and their diplomas? . . . What the people require for the Republic, what they ask for, is a good male, a sturdy man of noble breeding."[10] For Proudhon, the very idea of a presidency had to be dismissed out of hand. Like Leroux, he believed that the representative system needed instead to be fundamentally reformed, so that an organized proletariat could exercise power.

For conservative republicans, the most important thing was to retain parliamentary power in the monist form given it by the republican tradition (on this point they were to find themselves in agreement with the extreme left). The representative system from which such power had issued seemed to them to have the cardinal virtue of taming popular passions while placing authority in the hands of the nation's elites. Nevertheless they did not go so far as to reject outright the idea of a presidency—further evidence of the broad appeal of the American model at the time. Jules Grévy, in his first notable parliamentary speech, pleaded for the Assembly to be given preeminence, and called upon it to assist in electing a head of government who could also be turned out of office by a vote of the Assembly should the need arise. His greatest concern was to guard against a resurgence of the Bonapartist menace:

> Do you forget that it was the elections of Year X which gave Bonaparte the strength to raise up the throne again and seat himself upon it? That is the power that you would establish. . . . Are you sure that it would never find a man of ambition tempted to use it to establish himself? And if this ambition belongs to a man who knows how to make himself

popular, if he is a victorious general, surrounded by the prestige of military glory that the French are unable to resist, if he is the offspring of one of the families that have ruled France and he has never expressly renounced what he calls his rights, if commerce languishes, if the people suffer, if they find themselves in one of those moments of crisis in which misery and disappointment deliver them to those who hide plans to deprive them of their liberty beneath promises, do you reply that this man in his ambition will not end up overturning the Republic?[11]

The fear of losing their traditional privileges, combined with a dread of Bonapartism, therefore led Grévy and like-minded conservatives to reject election through universal suffrage. But there was little or no political or constitutional argument brought to bear in support of their position. In this respect they resembled the socialists: their critical intelligence was not equal to the intensity of their loathing.

It is partly for this reason that reservations about the proposed constitution, even steadfast opposition to it, proved to be of little consequence. No careful legal reasoning, no appeal to basic political principle was needed in order to sweep such criticisms aside. It was not a matter of two distinct conceptions of democracy being opposed in an intellectually substantive debate. Tocqueville, to whom it fell to defend the committee's draft before the Assembly, had to do no more than assure his listeners that fears of a new Bonapartism were misplaced and that the risks associated with competition among the several branches of government arising from a separation of powers were overstated. Above all he was at pains to minimize what was at stake, maintaining that the power of the president "came to little, even with popular election."[12] His confidence in this regard derived from the fact that provision had been made for a Council of Ministers having comparable authority (though he omitted to say that these ministers were to be appointed by the president). For the author of *Democracy in America*, the prospect of electing a president gave no cause for alarm whatever. It served only to add a bit of color to an office that otherwise was rather drab. That "so weak a figure" could command respect only by virtue of the "great shadow of the people" that hung over him as a result of the mandate they had conferred upon him showed how insubstantial he really was. "Take that away from him," Tocqueville observed, "and, by the terms of the Constitution, there will be nothing left of him."[13] Popular election, mere crutch or burnishing tool though it may be, was nonetheless one of those inventions of civilized life whose progress could not be interrupted, however much one might be inclined to deplore it.[14] Gustave de Beaumont, for his part, was convinced that "it is *self-evident* that the election of a president can be accomplished only by universal suffrage."[15]

The great orator of the period, Lamartine, had defended the procedure more ardently. An "anxious and jealous" democracy needed to be shown the respect she deserved. It was necessary, then, "to give generously, amply, sincerely, not withholding anything, the whole of her privileges."[16] The risks of reviving dynastic memories? He brushed them aside with the back of his hand: "The Republic fears nothing." What of the passions of the many, the workings of partisan manipulation, the campaigns waged by demagogues? To skeptics and all those who felt uneasy he memorably replied, "One poisons a glass of water, one does not poison a river. . . . A nation is incorruptible like the ocean." Constitutional arguments over conflicting powers and the problem of dual legitimacy? He had made it clear at the very beginning that he intended to leave to one side these "secondary, as it were scientific" considerations. Nor did the dreaded leap in the dark, to which British liberals had famously likened universal suffrage in general, trouble him in the least: "Power, in a republic, is in the populace or nowhere at all." Thus the lesson of history, he proclaimed—and the conclusion to which it inevitably led: "*Alea jacta est!* May God and the people decide! One must leave something to Providence." And then, at last, to hearty and prolonged applause, he called upon the Assembly to inaugurate by means of this novel institution a "Republic of enthusiasm . . . a splendid dream for France and the human race."[17] In Lamartine's telling, it was the triumph of man's better nature.

Many conservative deputies, only recently converted to republicanism, sought to reassure themselves by imagining that universal suffrage favored moderate candidates. At all events, their overriding fear of socialism made them desire an executive-repressive power that could be sure of its legitimacy once the voters had spoken. Lamartine's rhetorical nimbleness and Tocqueville's casual fatalism came to be combined with these political calculations in such a way that a major innovation in the history of democracy was approved without ever having been carefully considered. At the same time it had to be something that could easily be reversed if circumstances required. And so it came to pass, with the rejection of the Caesarism of the Second Empire and the return to the old system, which, as it turned out, was to have no need of being closely examined in advance either. It is in this dual sense that one may speak of 1848 as a false start. The emergence of presidential democracy would have to wait, as the adoption of a strict assembly regime by the Third Republic not even twenty-five years later made abundantly clear.

The Weimar Constitution

The German constitution devised by Otto Bismarck in 1871, in the aftermath of victory in the Franco-Prussian war, set up a dualist system under which power resided mostly with the executive. In creating a constitutional monarchy with a parliament, the Reichstag, that was elected by universal suffrage, Bismarck managed to satisfy the demands of both liberals and socialists (with the ulterior motive of weakening parliamentary power through the political division that was bound to arise from a system of proportional representation). There was nothing parliamentary about the new regime. The emperor could dissolve the Reichstag, but the Reichstag could not remove the chancellor, the head of the executive, who answered only to the emperor. From a functional standpoint, with the exception of budgetary affairs, the parties represented in the parliament had available to them solely the power of monitoring and oversight; moreover, their fragmentation prevented the *political* formation of a majority voice having a legitimacy of its own that could offset that of the executive.

Following Germany's defeat in 1918 and the departure of the emperor, a new constitution once again installed a dualist regime, but one that was structurally more sound than its predecessor, in which both executive and legislative powers were strengthened. On the parliamentary side, in addition to the prerogatives in legislative and budgetary affairs it formerly enjoyed, the Reichstag was granted real political autonomy (in particular, it could pass a motion of no confidence regarding not only the chancellor of the Reich but individual ministers as well). At the same time executive power was fortified by the direct election of the president of the Reich through universal suffrage. More than anything else, it was this particular innovation that distinguished the

Weimar Constitution, adopted on 31 July 1919.[18] Nevertheless it was bound up with a set of other democratic arrangements that in combination gave this document its pioneering character in Europe in the early twentieth century: the institution of women's suffrage (though Germany was not alone in approving it); a mechanism for removing the president of the Reich, through a popular vote authorized by a two-thirds majority of the Reichstag; and the countervailing power of the president of the Reich to call for a popular referendum to reverse a decision of parliament with regard to the budget, taxation, or the salaries of civil servants, as well as for a referendum on a proposed law submitted by petition of a tenth of the eligible voters.

There is no need to analyze the constitution of the Weimar Republic in detail. It nonetheless will be instructive to take a closer look at the circumstances under which provision for the popular election of the head of the executive came to be agreed upon, and what is more—this is the remarkable thing in retrospect—agreed upon in a relatively harmonious fashion. There was nothing obvious about such an outcome beforehand. The Social Democrats, for example, had started out by objecting to the president of the Reich as a mere substitute emperor (*Kaisererat*), charging that election of a president by the people was "a truly Napoleonic trick."[19] Their instinctive preference was for a parliamentary regime under which the government would depend for its survival on popular support. Gradually they came to accept the idea of a chief of state, but on the condition that he would be nothing more than a figurehead. Then, on realizing that a Social Democrat might occupy this office, they relented (Friedrich Ebert, their leader, did in fact become the first president, serving from 1919 until 1925). The liberals, for their part, saw the type of dualism that was envisaged as a modern form of the sort of constitutional monarchy they liked. On the right, as a whole, it was felt that a president could not help but balance and limit the effects of popular opinion in its parliamentary expression. It was also believed that only such a figure could prevent the Reichstag from becoming just another "talking shop," a common term of derision synonymous with impotence. Indeed, the diffuse antiparliamentarian mood of the period made an increase in executive power more or less welcome on all sides.

Everything considered, electing a president by universal suffrage pleased some without upsetting others. Contrary interests eventually converged, ensuring the measure's adoption. But its success concealed a certain ambivalence that later was to prove explosive. Although the Social Democrats had accepted an elective presidency, they sharply rejected the idea of a plebiscitary president of the Reich as a counterweight to parliament; and while they naturally regarded election by universal suffrage as democratic, they remained fundamentally committed to the principles of a parliamentary regime (amended nonetheless by the provision for referendum procedures).[20] In this they remained ardent defenders of a *multiparty democratic system*. Others, as we have seen, were rather more comfortable with the expansion of executive power that the new constitution enshrined.

The decisive issue, though it played little part in public debate about the role of the executive and, in particular, the nature of presidential power, concerned the federal organization of the country in the form of individual states (Länder) under preponderant Prussian influence. The prospect of Prussian hegemony was deeply disturbing to the two main architects of the constitution of 1919, Hugo Preuss and Max Weber. Even if they did not agree on what needed to be done to prevent a dangerous disequilibrium from emerging (Preuss wanted to cut up Prussia into ten Länder, whereas Weber, more realistic in reckoning with the resistance that such a move was likely to encounter, envisaged institutional safeguards instead), both saw the limitation of parliamentary power as a key element of any possible solution. Pure parliamentarianism, which is to say a Reichstag elected on a strictly proportional basis, was bound to open the way to the very imbalance of power they sought to block.[21] For the same reason it was essential that the president not hold his power from the Reichstag. It could only be conferred directly, by a vote of all the people.

Max Weber and Plebiscitary Democracy

Beyond these narrowly constitutional considerations, Max Weber sought to design a plebiscitary democracy [*plebiszitäre Führerdemokratie*] in which charismatic legitimation, a "basically authoritarian principle," would be amenable to "an anti-authoritarian interpretation."[22] Weber's insight was that the mechanism of popular recognition could be made to operate in reverse. In the classical model of the charismatic leader, the fact of ruling is taken to be primary, with the recognition of his authority by those subject to it *subsequently* validating, which is to say legitimizing, their state of domination. But if such recognition were to be granted beforehand (by casting a vote, for example), then it could be considered a source of legitimacy rather than the consequence of it. In that case it would be possible to speak of a properly democratic form of legitimacy. Whence Weber's definition: "In its authentic form, plebiscitary democracy—the principal type of *Führerdemokratie*—is a kind of charismatic rule whose legitimacy derives from the will of those who are ruled. The leader (demagogue) rules by virtue of the devotion and trust his political followers place in him personally."[23] By way of example he cited ancient dictators as well as Cromwell, Robespierre, and the two Napoleons. The modern instances seemed to him no more than expedients, however, mixing old and new elements in response to particular circumstances. What was needed for present purposes was a revised conception of plebiscitary democracy that would serve as a model for stable government in an age of mass democracy.

Weber set out to do just this in a series of newspaper articles first published in 1917 and collected the following year under the title *Parlement und Regierung im neugeordneten Deutschland*.[24] To follow his reasoning one must keep in mind what, as a sociologist, he took to be the point of departure for all political reflection at that time. Three structural factors in particular needed to be taken into account. First, bureaucratization and the self-guiding tendencies of administration to which it gave rise, both of which were signs of efficiency and sclerosis. Second, the central role played by political parties, together with the growing influence of local machines and professional politicians (on this point Weber adopted the arguments of James Bryce, Robert Michels, and Moisei Ostrogorski, to whom he often referred). Third, the danger in an age of mass democracy that the "emotional element" would prevail in political deliberation. Accordingly, Weber thought it necessary to do the following things: channel the energies of public administration and direct its course, since otherwise it would be inclined to obey its own internal dynamic; find a good use for parties, now an inescapable fact of political life (he had, in any case, already acknowledged their value in helping to restrain the wilder expressions of popular feeling); and, finally, considering that universal suffrage was now no less irreversibly established than parties themselves, show respect for popular sovereignty while at the same time holding it in check.

Electing the Reich's chief executive by universal suffrage seemed to him a way of achieving all three objectives at once. He therefore urged that the new Weimar Republic be founded on two complementary principles: constitutional-parliamentary legitimacy, on the one hand, and what he called the revolutionary legitimacy of a president elected directly by the people, on the other. Revolutionary legitimacy represented a position of both subservience and empowerment: while it ceded to the parties the right to determine which candidates were qualified to hold the highest office, it also granted the right of choosing among them to the masses, who in this way affirmed their sovereignty. A new age of democracy was at hand, displacing the previous party-dominated system. "Active democratization of the masses," Weber wrote, "means that the political leader is no longer declared a candidate because a circle of notables has recognized his proven ability, and then becomes leader because he comes to the fore in parliament, but rather because he uses the means of *mass* demagogy to gain the confidence of the masses and their belief in his person, and thereby gains power. Essentially this means that the selection of the leader has shifted in the direction of *Caesarism*. Indeed, every democracy has this tendency. After all, the specifically Caesarist instrument is the plebiscite."[25]

In this regard Weber was not interested in whether one form of democracy could be said to be more "advanced" than another. He had always been a highly skeptical democrat; the idea of an active general will, for example, made no sense to him.[26] As a sociological realist he was accustomed to regard power as something that was bound to be exercised by an oligarchy.[27] One might say that he took a purely instrumental view of democracy, not at all a philosophical one. Rather paradoxically, as it may seem, he used the plebiscitary model to work out a minimalist conception of democracy[28] (clearly Schumpeter was influenced by it, even if he does not cite Weber, in holding, for example, that "acceptance of leadership is the true function of the electorate's vote").[29] Nevertheless it was a conception of democracy that took into consideration the link, which seemed to him apparent everywhere, between the democratization of the masses and the personalization of politics.[30] In this sense one might say that he intended to make only limited use of Caesarism.

It is important to remember that Weber did not fear that a modern plebiscitary democracy might deteriorate into charismatic dictatorship (though he recognized there was no reason in principle why such a thing could not happen). For him the present danger was quite different, namely, that the mounting influence of party machines would interfere with popular support for strong leadership by inducing an "increasing bureaucratic rigidification of voluntary political action."[31] At the same time, however, he counted on the major parties to keep the masses in line, even in the event that new plebiscitary procedures were to be authorized.

Weber died in 1920. Probably he would have been surprised to discover that one of his most attentive readers a few years later would be Carl Schmitt, but of course Weber did not live long enough to see how problematic the hybrid character of the 1919 constitution would turn out to be. Schmitt, for his part, took from Weber only the idea that democratic-plebiscitary legitimacy superseded the authority of both political parties and acts of parliament, and used it to redefine democracy in a radically illiberal fashion while at the same time stripping it of the constitutional safeguards that Weber had devised for the purpose of forcing the president to continually "live up to his charismatic leadership endowments."[32]

Weber's view of the tendency to Caesarism was inseparable from his understanding of political power as essentially executive in nature. To his mind, the executive had the dual characteristic of being a directly *active* power (it consists in *making decisions*) that is exercised by individuals. "This inevitable circumstance," he wrote, "means that mass democracy, ever since Pericles, has always had to pay for its positive successes with major concessions to the Caesarist principle of leadership selection."[33] Legislative power, by contrast, he saw as *collective* and for the most part essentially *negative*.[34] A realist in matters of political theory, as we have seen, Weber utterly rejected the legalistic assumptions of the liberal democratic regimes of the late eighteenth and nineteenth centuries. He also recognized that *political will* was perceived, no longer as a body of statutes expressing a "general" will, but as a set of specific, immediately apprehensible decisions. This is why popular antiparliamentarianism declared its opposition to the sort of "will to powerlessness"[35] it detected in the activity of parliaments and parties, united in their indifference to the daily needs and expectations of ordinary citizens.[36] The

Caesarist perspective was part and parcel of a new age of agency and the will, as these things were now understood by the masses, the unmistakable mark of a fundamental rift between the governed and their governors that had somehow to be repaired democratically. All of this was, in any case, very far removed from the old revolutionary utopia in which the people themselves legislated directly.

Laboratory of Disaster

How did it come to pass in the space of a few years that the Weimar Republic, which sought to lay the foundations of plebiscitary democracy, should have given way to Nazi dictatorship? The total concentration of power in the executive, and the cult of personality that accompanied it sprang from a radicalizing impulse whose motivations have been endlessly debated. Everyone will agree that it was crucially connected with the disrepute into which the Reichstag had fallen. Yet this antiparliamentarian sentiment was not very different from what one encountered everywhere else in Europe at this time. Not only was it of a piece with the popular mistrust that was already widespread in imperial Germany, the atmosphere then was less acrimonious than what one found in France, for example, in the late nineteenth century. There was no equivalent in Germany of the Panama affair or the influence-peddling scandal several years earlier involving decorations for prominent persons.[37] The image of representatives profiting from the system was also less vivid there than in France, where the vote of an allowance of 15,000 francs for deputies had provoked a public outcry and jibes about potbellied parliamentarians (*les ventrus*) feeding at the public trough. Members of the Reichstag, by contrast, received no compensation before 1914. Scandals did, of course, break out at the beginning of the republican period (one thinks especially of the famous Barmat affair in 1924),[38] but there was no peculiarly German predisposition to antiparliamentarianism.

There were other reasons for the upsurge in antiparliamentarian feeling from the mid-1920s onward as well, beginning with what may be called functional causes. Many members of the Reichstag also held a local seat in a state parliament (Landtag), and their strong provincial loyalties often led them to attach greater priority to their work in the Länder than in Berlin. Parliamentary life in Germany had none of the sparkle and excitement it enjoyed in France and Great Britain. Party discipline was strict, and it was the party leaders who decided on voting and strategy, not the elected representatives. Nor was there any of the brilliant oratorical jousting and interpellation that elsewhere attracted the public's attention and gave parliaments their political prominence. In short, there was nothing that in any way resembled a *parlement de l'eloquence* in the French or English style.[39] The Reichstag's sessions amounted to little more than a succession of long, boring speeches read out from the floor of the chamber. Few people paid any notice.

There were also purely partisan reasons for the disfavor with which the parliament was now regarded. They were linked in the first place to the rapid loss of support for the Republic's founding political parties, due not only to dissatisfaction with the government on the part of a section of the electorate but also to the lukewarm endorsement of new regime by those whom Friedrich Meinecke called rational republicans (*Vernunftrepublikaner*). At the same time, beginning in the mid-1920s, several parties with significant parliamentary representation were less and less willing to conceal their scorn for the Reichstag. One of these was the German National People's Party (DNVP in its German acronym). In 1928 its leader likened the Reichstag to a mire into which the German people were being dragged down and smothered, and called for the overthrow of the Republic and democratic institutions.[40] The Communist Party (KPD), which had come into existence at the same time as the regime, bitterly denounced the parliament as a laughingstock and advocated a revolutionary strategy of disruption. As for the Nazis (NSDAP), their growing power was accompanied by an increasingly hostile display of utter contempt for the Reichstag. Even before their electoral breakthrough in September 1930, they constantly railed against the institution. Adolf Hitler had spoken of it in *Mein Kampf* as a "vacillating majority of individuals," attacking the deputies as "moral shirkers" and "narrow-minded dilettantes" who constituted "a demi-monde of intellectuals of the worst sort."[41] Joseph Goebbels, later to be put in charge of the NSDAP campaign in the federal elections of 1930, had noted during his first successful attempt to win a seat in the Reichstag two years earlier that its sessions put one in mind of a "school of rabid Jews," and went on to say: "Parliamentarianism has long been ready to fall. We are going to sound its death knell. I have already had enough of this comedy. They will not have occasion to see me there very often, in their High Assembly."[42]

Finally, constitutional reasons for the demotion of the Reichstag counted for a great deal in the collapse of the Weimar Republic. The hybrid character of the 1919 Constitution, a combination of presidential and parliamentary systems, suggested to some that it might contain its own alternative. Article 48, which permitted the president to issue emergency decrees, seemed to offer a way out from the difficulties created by the absence of a majority and the corresponding paralysis of the chancellor. The effect of this perception was to put all " 'consciousness of parliamentary responsibility' to sleep."[43] Gradually at first, then more quickly, the conviction grew that presidential power could be freed from legislative constraint altogether, further aggravating the decadence of the parliamentary order—and this all the more as neither the president nor the chancellor had commanded a majority since 1920. Even outside the procedures authorized by Article 48, beginning in 1919 the Reichstag passed a series of framework laws ("skeleton bills") that granted the government the right to act directly by means of decrees in certain areas. The president, for his part, relied on the authority of Article 48 to issue a series of emergency decrees (from October 1919 until January 1925, Friedrich Ebert issued no fewer than 136 decrees of this type). Carl Schmitt's authoritarian vision, expounded first in *Die Diktatur* and then, two years later, in *Die geistesgeschichtliche Lage des heutigen Parlamentarismus* [1923], was well suited to a set of circumstances that Weimar had created almost from the beginning.

The critical moment in the transition from presidentialism to dictatorship, which nonetheless had been only very vaguely foreshadowed in the early years of Weimar, was suddenly hastened in March 1930 with the appointment of Heinrich Brüning as chancellor. Lacking a clear majority, Brüning now sought to govern as independently of the Reichstag as possible. Parliament thus found itself effectively supplanted by an executive-legislative power that was bound to rely even more heavily on Article 48 than before.[44] Ultimately it was owing to the tolerance of a slender majority, made possible by the Social Democratic Party's refusal to join forces with the two extremist parties, the KPD and the NSDAP, in an effort to bring him down, that Brüning was able to bring into existence an "explicitly antiparliamentary presidential government."[45] If its authority could be sustained, it would amount to nothing less than a change of regime. The turning point came finally in July of that year, as President Hindenburg began to rule almost exclusively by emergency decree. From 1930 to 1932, a time when the Reichstag had already shortened its sessions and did still less than before, he issued 116 such decrees. The steady dissolution of parliamentary responsibility only worsened a chronic imbalance. Under Franz von Papen, appointed chancellor in June 1932, this course of events gathered additional momentum, with the result that the new form of government came to be irreversibly established. The general sense of quasi-permanent crisis was further encouraged by the economic turmoil of the period (deflation, massive unemployment, bank failures), which the Nazis were able to successfully exploit at the polls in March 1933. The longing for bold executive action at a moment of paralyzing confusion, the sense of humiliation that the crushing weight of reparations imposed by the victors of 1918 had made only more painful to bear, the promise at last of enduring national unity ("Ein Volk, ein Reich, ein Führer")—all these things allowed a transient disequilibrium of presidential power to be converted into a permanent dictatorship, with the acclamation of a *Führer* now replacing customary mechanisms of legitimate succession.

The reason for the catastrophe, according to Friedrich Meinecke, was that "the German people were simply not ready for parliamentary democracy."[46] It is very difficult to say whether a people is ever ready for democracy, if by that one means that all voters behave as rational actors concerned with the common good. But it is plain that the divisions of German society, as they were expressed in the party system, played a decisive role. The thing that needs to be emphasized above all is that democracy during the Weimar period was primarily conceived of as an *authorizing procedure,* a granting of permission to govern, and not as a constant process of adjusting the balance of powers between government and society, in the manner of what I have called a permanent democracy. German history has shown us, tragically, what is likely to happen when democracy is turned back against itself.

And yet the return to parliamentarianism of these years was not without its critics. In France, for example, the various movements of the Resistance were united in emphatically denouncing the crisis of authority from which they believed the country had suffered under the Third Republic and calling for the executive to be strengthened and principles of sound government to be acted upon.[1] Above all this meant modernizing the apparatus of the state, as we have already remarked. Yet the technocratic augmentation of executive authority, at a time when the classic style of parliamentarianism was once more in vogue, raised a great many questions to which there was no ready reply. The striking change of position on the part of someone like Léon Blum testifies to a peculiarly French quandary in thinking about democracy.

We saw earlier that at the close of the First World War Blum had advocated a thorough reconstruction of executive power, this with a view to creating what he came close to calling a republican monarchy. After the Tours Congress in December 1920, having inherited leadership of the Socialist movement in France, he had to choose his words more carefully. Presenting the constitutional program of the French Section of the Workers' International seven years later, he nonetheless said much the same thing, only now even more firmly: "We do not confuse parliamentarianism with political democracy."[2] On this point his opinion never changed. In an essay written in his prison cell at Bourrassol, in 1941, Blum insisted that "democracy and parliamentarianism are not at all equivalent and interchangeable terms"; indeed, "parliamentarianism is not essentially democracy." From this he drew the conclusion that "the parliamentary or representative regime does not constitute the form of democratic government exactly adapted to French society, and so it is necessary to search for forms that better suit it." He went on to praise the Swiss and American models, recommended that an important place be given to the device of referendum, and argued in favor of equipping the executive with "an independent and continuous authority."[3] He was troubled, too, by one inadequacy of French parliamentarianism in particular, that the absence of highly structured and disciplined parties had led to an increase in disruptive personal rivalries. All these reservations were to be swept away soon after the Liberation. In early 1946, in response to de Gaulle's warning against the danger of a return to parliamentarianism and a party-based system, he categorically disagreed: "In France, for the time being, there is no viable and stable democracy outside a parliamentary regime, and there can be no viable and stable parliamentary regime outside an organized party system."[4] Blum's striking reversal reflected the state of mind of many people during this period.

The drafting of the constitution of the Fourth Republic left no doubt that at least a rough consensus had been reached on this point, the essential features of which are worth recalling. The first version (adopted on 19 April 1946 by the National Constituent Assembly) was wholly parliamentarian in spirit, providing for the election by a simple majority of the president of the Council of Ministers by the National Assembly itself. The procedure's staunchest defenders, the Communists and the Socialists, were able to turn aside the strong objections brought against it by René Capitant, an eminent constitutionalist.[5] While the office of president was retained, its occupant was clearly meant to serve only with the express consent of the people's representatives, since approval by a two-thirds majority of the Chamber of Deputies alone was needed (once again without having to consult its companion body, the Council of the Republic). Significantly, the minutes of the meetings of the Constitutional Committee record no speaker proposing election by universal suffrage. The president's prerogatives were dramatically reduced as well. Only after debate was it accepted that he should preside over the Council of Ministers, the High Council of National Defense, and the High Council for the Judiciary, while nonetheless being denied the right of reprieve. All these arrangements, by means of which a pure assembly regime was established, were regarded as the ultimate expression of democratic progress, particularly on the left. The apprehensions of the Popular Republican Movement (MRP) were widely enough shared, however, that a referendum on the draft constitution, held on 5 May 1946, resulted in its rejection by 53 percent of the votes cast. Work therefore began on a new version with the aim of moderating the most extreme features of the original proposal. Now the president was to be elected by both chambers. And although the old practice was revived of entrusting the appointment of a President of the Council to parliament as a whole, the prime minister still found himself deprived of the right to dissolve parliament.[6] Narrowly approved in a second referendum on 13 October 1946, the Constitution of the Fourth Republic looked to the past for inspiration, not to the future.[7] The institutions it put in place were not very different from the ones then found in most other European countries. As in Italy, the fragmentation of the party system made it impossible to create clear and durable parliamentary majorities.

In the 1950s and 1960s, the Western democracies by and large formed a system of assembly regimes. The Weimar experiment with presidentialism was now a remote interlude, and the name "Weimar" itself had become a shorthand for democracy's most abysmal failure. The great exception to this system, of course, was the United States. In Europe only two countries, Ireland and Finland, elected the head of the executive branch by universal suffrage.[8] In Ireland, the procedure was bound up with the winning of independence from the British crown in 1917; more than anything else, it symbolized the fact that the people were now citizens of their own country. In Finland, following the proclamation of independence from Russia in 1917, the Constitution of 1919 provided for popular election, but with the final outcome being settled indirectly through the ballot of an American-style electoral college. The eccentric customs of two small countries could hardly be supposed to supply the basis for a general model, however, and therefore they were the object of no larger debate.

The American Exception

The American presidential system, in spite of its earlier prestige, did not seem to Europeans after the Second World War to constitute a universalizable model either. Nor was the indirect method it stipulated for electing the president thought to represent a step in the direction of democratic perfectibility. It was regarded instead as a sort of aberration, the product of particular circumstances and, above all, the result of a negative choice. When the Constitution was ratified, in 1787, the idea of direct election by all the citizens had been explicitly rejected, as had the further suggestion of congressional appointment. Agreement on selecting a president by the vote of a small body of electors from the individual states—an electoral college, as it was called—emerged as an alternative to these two failed proposals. In the event the practical difficulties of holding a general election (bringing a great many people to Washington was no easy thing in those days) and a rather aristocratic view of suffrage[9] combined to ensure the adoption of this arrangement. It was therefore something very different from popular election, and all the more so because the state legislatures were free to designate their electors by a method of their own choosing. In some states the legisla-

all, a structural element: the vigorous assertion of the powers and pre-rogatives of the executive. This lay at the heart of the Gaullist under-taking. As Capitant, an advisor to the regime on constitutional matters in 1958 and later a Gaullist member of the National Assembly, put it, "I believe that a strong state is suited to democracy in the twentieth century, rather than the weak and divided state to which the liberals aspire."[13] This view had a positive aspect, which consisted in affirming the preeminence of that *directly active power* which was believed to be necessary in a modern and constantly changing society. But the Gaul-list determination to exalt the executive, in the dual sense of the inde-pendent exercise of this power and the display of preeminence that it implied, was also associated with a demeaning opinion of the legisla-ture, in the first place because of its reflexive obedience to sectarian impulses. A parliament, in de Gaulle's famous phrase, "convenes a del-egation of special interests."[14] The natural function of the executive, by contrast, on account of its unified structure, is to represent the general will and unity of the country. This entailed two things: first, attrib-uting to the office of chief of state a capacity for embodying the nation; second, giving it a type of legitimacy that raised it above partisan ri-valry. In 1946 de Gaulle had called for the chief of state to be chosen by an electorate much larger than the French parliament. It will be recalled, too, that he severely criticized the American system on just this ground, that the electoral process in the United States was largely subservient to party organizations[15] (while at the same time lacking a sufficiently solemn character, in part because of the journalistic fascination with the boisterous side of political competition). But he had not seriously con-templated the idea of election by universal suffrage. It needs to be kept in mind that none of the many constitutional schemes drawn up by the various Resistance movements had envisaged such a procedure. The specter of Caesarism was once again widely dreaded, and authorities on nineteenth-century history could be counted on to remind one and all that the experiment of 1848 had not ended happily.[16]

Twelve years later, in 1958, the situation was essentially unchanged.[17] It was not until 1962 that direct popular election of the president was approved by referendum. How are we to explain the delay in instituting a procedure that now seems in retrospect virtually synonymous with the Gaullist view of democracy? There were, first of all, technical ob-stacles. In 1958 the chief of state was simultaneously president of the

French Republic and president of the French Union, an alliance of fran-cophone nations created by the Fourth Republic to replace the old colo-nial system. Formally, then, the Constitution of the Fifth Republic had a federalist dimension (some experts, Capitant among them, actually spoke of a "Franco-African federation"). Election by universal suffrage would have posed the problem of determining the population of eligible voters. Would all Union nationals be qualified to cast ballots on the same basis? Or would it be necessary to devise different modes of election, one for Metropolitan France and another for the confederated territories? The case of war-torn Algeria presented still more perplexing difficulties.

But these were not the only reasons the issue was not broached in 1958. Even if de Gaulle was subsequently to say more than once that he had "long" believed that universal suffrage was the only possible method for electing a president,[18] he could not help but recognize that both tactical and strategic considerations counseled caution. He was, of course, well aware that many of his adversaries feared him as a poten-tial dictator, and therefore thought it prudent to take into account the "passionate prejudices" that for more than a century had held sway in France.[19] "Furthermore," he was to later emphasize in explaining his frame of mind in 1958, not without a certain hauteur, "I had intended to assume the duties of head of state myself at the outset, in the belief that, by reason of past history and present circumstances, the manner of my accession would be a mere formality having no consequence with regard to my role. On further consideration, however, I resolved to com-plete the edifice in this respect before the end of my seven-year term."[20] There is a sense, too, in which the four referendums conducted between 1958 and 1962 amounted to a substitute for direct popular election, by effectively sanctioning the bond between the people and the Gaullist regime.[21]

By 1962, decolonization had mostly been accomplished and Algeria had won its independence. The technical obstacles having now been re-moved, de Gaulle was able to turn his full attention to the task of se-curing the future of the Republic he had founded. His successors, he felt sure, would not enjoy the advantage of what he grandly called his "per-sonal equation."[22] The time had come at last to place the constitutional reform authorizing direct election of the president before the people. Re-action was swift. The left was adamantly opposed. The indignation of the Communist Party, which had already hinted at a coup d'état, was redoubled with the announcement of the referendum, but in hopes of attracting broader support it was content to issue vague warnings against the dangers of "personal power"[23] while at the same time presenting itself as the most resolute defender of classical parliamentarianism. The Socialists, for their part, revived the charges that Léon Blum brought against the General in June 1946 after the second Bayeux speech: "What General de Gaulle calls a true leader," Blum had written then, "is a president of the Republic who, without being responsible to the Assembly, would yet possess real power of his own, a president of the Republic of whom the principal ministers and the president of the Council himself would be the representatives and the emanation. . . . Such a conception is not viable. . . . Not only does it create a personal power, its implementation would require that all public life be dominated by this personal power. What republican could consent to that?"[24] And he went on to say:

> All sovereignty necessarily emanating from the people, one would have to go back all the way to the source of sovereignty, which is to say restore election of the head of the executive branch by universal suffrage, as in the American Constitution, as in the French Constitution of 1848. There lies the logical conclusion of the system. . . . But in France, where the passage from presidential power to personal power is one of the tried and tested perils that threaten democracy, the granting of executive power to one man by universal suffrage is called a plebiscite.[25]

Non au plebiscite—thus the slogan urging a vote against de Gaulle's plan that was to be painted on walls throughout the country in 1962.

Pierre Mendès-France, though he had been highly critical of the Fourth Republic, threw all his energies into the fight and inveighed against the increase in authority, great enough to crush any opposition, of a "governing president" elected by universal suffrage. In a widely noticed book that came out in early October 1962,[26] only weeks before the scheduled vote, Mendès-France expressed alarm at the prospect of an "elective monarchy . . . [a] centralization of power in the hands of a man who deliberates alone, orders alone, decides alone."[27] Such a mode of election, he argued, "cannot provide any real political control; it risks depoliticizing the electorate, forces it to neglect its democratic duties, to become accustomed to alienating its sovereignty. . . . It also gives adventurers an unexpected opportunity."[28] For these and other charges he cited the authority of the General himself, in a passage of the Bayeux speech two decades earlier on the subject of dictatorship.[29] François Mitterrand showed still less restraint. In a polemic of exceptional vehemence that appeared a year and a half after the referendum, Mitterrand took oblique aim at the Stalinist overtones of the constitution of the Fifth Republic,[30] railing repeatedly and at great length against "completely domesticated executive power," "dictatorship," "a monarch surrounded by his personal servants," even "totalitarian propaganda." In the eyes of a man who was himself preparing to go before the voters in the 1965 presidential election, de Gaulle was nothing less than an "enthusiast of absolute power"—living proof that there was still "a strong remnant of Bonapartism" in many parts of the land.[31]

Conservative opinion was no less harshly critical. Raymond Aron, though he had himself been an active member of the Rally of the French People (RPF) from 1948 to 1952, condemned a "despotic constitution" and the "invocation of a mysterious legitimacy superior to legality";[32] describing de Gaulle as a "monarch" given to a "typically Bonapartist style of acting," he concluded that such a form of government could "in its essence [be] only provisional."[33] Those on the right who lamented the loss of French Algeria were for their part violently opposed to a mode of election that put the crowning touches on a despised regime. On both the left and the right, at least two-thirds of the political class called for a vote against the referendum of 28 October 1962.[34] In the event, 62 percent of the French people approved the proposed reform. A majority of the electorate, in other words, did not see the man who had issued the appeal of 18 June 1940 as an apprentice dictator.[35]

The referendum's result was evidence, too, that most people welcomed this reform as a step forward, for they now enjoyed an important additional civil right. And because its opponents could not be troubled to say exactly what they considered democratic government to consist in, whether they were content to circulate nebulous insults (Mitterrand ridiculed a "trompe-l'oeil democracy")[36] or whether they did no more than recycle old and increasingly less persuasive arguments that founded parliamentary authority on an implicit hierarchy setting representatives above those whom they represent, the presidential system—whose great virtue, from the point of view of the people, was that it confided responsibility for electing the head of state to them—steadily gained acceptance in France. Minor political movements on the left that had been alone at first in defending this type of regime saw the major parties

be dissociated from any form of pluralistic competition. Fifty years after emancipation from colonial domination, the situation in a part of the world where civil wars and coups d'état continue to be commonplace still remains unstable. Nevertheless, setting aside the case of the Moroccan monarchy, the presidentialization of regimes elsewhere in Africa redefined what was considered to be both normal and desirable in a democratic order. By the beginning of the twenty-first century, its place had been widely and securely established.

In Asia and Latin America, disappointment of varying kinds with parliamentarianism in the aftermath of dictatorship produced a similar response. On these continents, as in Africa, election of a head of state by universal suffrage was adapted to a broad range of circumstances, from authentically democratic regimes to variants of Caesarism and charismatic-populist styles of leadership. In all these cases, however, presidentialism came to be seen as the general form of good government. Latin America is perhaps the most striking example: in the early 1980s there were only three countries where the president was elected by popular vote in a competitive election (Colombia, Costa Rica, and Venezuela); thirty years later, with the notable exception of Cuba, the practice was universal. In Europe itself, the situation changed considerably during this period—not in the west, to be sure, the parliamentary model having remained dominant in the lands where it had been invented; but in the east, where the collapse of the Soviet Union unleashed a wave of presidentialization, both in former republics and in countries that had belonged to the Soviet bloc.[38]

Personalization Beyond Presidentialization

In 1974, Maurice Duverger, another leading French constitutional expert, published a work with the provocative title *La monarchie républicaine*.[39] He argued that the power of governing in France belonged to a person invested with supreme legitimacy, by virtue of his selection by universal suffrage, who took or inspired all important decisions and who presided over the conduct of the nation's policy. In short, a monarch—but a republican monarch because he had been elected in an open ballot, exercised a mandate limited to a fixed term of office, and was subject to some measure of parliamentary scrutiny. At a distance of almost sixty years, Duverger spoke in terms similar to the ones Léon Blum used in 1917 to describe the type of efficient and structured government that in his view all democracies ought to aspire to. In the early 1970s, however, there was nothing novel about this way of looking at the matter; the Gaullist regime, after all, had been severely criticized for having assumed just such an aspect. But Duverger's purpose was not to add his voice to a chorus of opposition. It was to suggest that, beyond their formal differences, all the major democracies were now evolving in the same direction. The heads of the executive branch of government at the time were not, of course, directly elected in West Germany, Canada, the United Kingdom, or Sweden. Nevertheless, Duverger maintained, it was owing to a "disguised election" that the prime ministers of these countries had come to power, legislative elections having become, *at bottom*, the equivalent of presidential elections. "When one considers the assemblies of these countries," he wrote, "one describes their regimes as [examples of] majoritarian parliamentarianism; but, when one looks at their governments, one must speak of republican monarchy."[40] Several years earlier the Irish political scientist Brian Farrell had made the same observation in *Chairman or Chief?*: "In almost all political systems, executive dominance and the personification of this domination in a single leader is a central fact of political life."[41]

Four decades after the publication of these two pathbreaking works, what might be called a sociopolitical tendency for executive power in democracies to become personalized has effectively been realized everywhere, above and beyond a constitutional tendency to presidentialization. But it must also be emphasized that these first attempts to analyze the convergence of the different manifestations of executive power, as distinct from the functional properties of particular regimes, went farther than earlier expressions of concern in the face of personalization,[42] which often amounted to little more than nervousness about the uncertain effects of the increasing power of audiovisual media in enlarging the traditional scope of political leadership. The notion of personalization, it needs to be remembered, had never been mentioned before in connection with democracies. Historically, it was considered mainly to be a structural aspect of despotic regimes, superimposed on the fact of an *individualization*—that is, an undue privatization and illiberal concentration—of power. Applying the concept of personalization to the study of democracy therefore represented a sharp break with the prior emphasis on impersonal authority.

The phenomenon of presidentialization-personalization assumed a great variety of forms,[43] as much on account of differing constitutional frameworks as because there are as many individual personalities as there are chiefs of state. If the figure of the great man came to be associated with it in the first instance (in this regard the persona of General de Gaulle functioned as both image and screen), over time persons holding a nation's highest office came to seem more like the people who had elected them, and expectations regarding presidential stature were correspondingly lowered. Even in France one spoke of "Caesarism without genius" in describing the Fifth Republic after 1969.[44] In this way there opened up a divide, which has not ceased to widen in the meantime, between the *political form* of presidentialization-personalization and its *social incarnation*. The former has continued to expand, whereas the latter was bound to shrink with the advent of "normal" presidents. The gap between the two has also been sustained, as we will see, by the ever more pronounced distinction between the political qualities required to win election and those that make a good governor.

All these considerations suggest that the notion of a presidential-governing model must be set in a broader perspective. The model comprises three dimensions: functional, institutional, and constitutional. The first two are common to all modern regimes: personalization (functional dimension) and preeminence of the executive (institutional). In strictly constitutional terms, however, the differences between specific cases are much greater, since the institution of the presidency does not exist everywhere and, where it does, the forms it assumes vary both with regard to the powers of the office and the manner in which it is established. But if the constitutional aspect is understood more generally to include the notion of a *head of the executive branch,* and if the phenomenon of disguised elections is taken into account, then it becomes possible to detect a tendency to constitutional convergence as well, which in turn permits us to speak of a standard presidential-governing model.

⚝ 7 ⚝

Unavoidable and Unsatisfactory

The Democratic Motives of Presidentialization

Beyond the creation by the media of a personalized style of politics, which has been analyzed in great detail since the 1960s,[1] the phenomenon of presidentialization-personalization sprang from specifically democratic impulses of three kinds. First, presidentialization answers a social demand for accountability. On this view, democracy is primarily a regime in which the government is to be held responsible for its actions, election being only one of the methods available for doing this. Responsibility, because it implies judgment, places governors in a subordinate relation to the governed. It therefore can be meaningful only under a personalized form of government, for responsibility must be attributive in order to be exercised, which is to say assignable to an individual; an assembly, by contrast, cannot properly be said to be responsible. This is a point on which Jacques Necker, finance minister to Louis XVI and the first true theorist of modern executive power, had laid great emphasis. "How," he asked in respect of the revolutionary assemblies, "could one fail to be frightened by the unlimited authority of a collective being, which, passing in the blink of an eye from a living to an abstract nature, has no need either for compassion or pity and for itself has no fear either of condemnation or censure?"[2] Louis Fréron, editor of *L'Orateur du Peuple* and a man of opposite political views, had arrived at much the same conclusion, calling upon his parliamentary colleagues in 1795 to loosen the grip of their "inviolable hands" and allow executive power to be confided instead to "responsible hands."[3] For Fréron, this sort of responsibility was necessarily associated with popular election. Objections to the assembly regime fell on deaf ears at the time, however, so strong was the hold of the principle of impersonality on people's minds. Eventually the spell of dogma was broken and critics gained a hearing. Over the course of the following century the belief grew that the exercise of power had become a monopoly of traditional representative-aristocratic governments, with no corresponding obligation of civic responsibility, since everything was played out behind the closed doors of partisan scheming and parliamentary deal-making. Popular election of the head of the executive had the opposite effect of radicalizing and polarizing responsibility. This is what made it attractive to the masses, who yearned to be able to influence the course of immediate events. No more forceful proof of this ability could be given than the act of turning an incumbent out of office.

Presidentialization responds in the second place to a social desire, which the personalization of politics furnished with a visible object, that became more powerful as the revolutionary urge receded. No matter how it was expressed, the idea of revolution sought to embed dreams of changing the world in a larger vision of historical development. In its fully elaborated Marxist version, which was long to dominate the thinking of much of the left, history could be seen to have brought forth a demand that lay at the heart of democratic modernity, arising from the will that each person be an actor by taking part in movements devoted to assisting and accelerating the course of history itself. With the waning of revolutionary fervor, hope gave way to a sense of loss and dislocation, which in turn caused the deep-seated longings of the people to be projected onto the figure of the person elected to the highest office in the land.

Third, and finally, the presidentialization-personalization of democracy corresponds to a demand for greater transparency—what I call legibility—of institutions and decision making. In an age marked by the growing complexity of government and by the increasing anonymity of large bureaucracies, it gratifies a desire for simplification. The head of the executive branch, whose face is seen everywhere and whose words are heard by all, stands in the sharpest contrast imaginable to the ambient opacity of the politico-administrative system. It is above all for this reason that a presidential system appears to ordinary citizens to hold out the prospect of reclaiming politics for themselves.

These three democratic impulses, acting in combination, have given presidentialization an irreversible momentum. At the same time they are apt to be regarded with suspicion, since each one can be turned back against itself. Responsibility is now more readily assigned, while simultaneously assuming the form of a blank check. The more directly the will of the people is brought to bear, the greater the risk that it will be permanently degraded into a form of spectacle, with the result that the confusion of words with action becomes intensified still further. What is imagined to be superior institutional transparency turns out to be only a mirage, a delusory effect of modern communications technology. It is plain to see, then, that the presidentialization of democracy is at once deeply unsatisfactory and altogether unavoidable. But we cannot be content to leave matters at that. We need to look more closely at what makes this state of affairs so fraught with difficulty. The first step will be to distinguish between the method used to select and legitimate a chief executive, which is election, and the very nature of presidentialism itself, which consists in the supremacy of the executive over the legislative branch.

Legitimation by Election

The classical theories of legitimacy were theories of the *authorization* of power, of how command over others is made acceptable to them. It was on just this understanding that Max Weber constructed his famous typology distinguishing legal, traditional, and charismatic forms of legitimate rule.[4] Guglielmo Ferrero approached the subject from the same perspective, in a work that likewise came to fruition amid the turmoil of a global conflict. "The principles of legitimacy," Ferrero held, "are justifications of power, which is to say of the right to rule. Of all human inequalities, none has greater need of reasoned justification than the inequality established by power."[5] Whereas power comes from above, legitimacy in modern societies, he argued, always comes from below, for it requires in one way or another "the consent—active or passive, but [in either case] sincere—of the governed."[6] In a democracy this consent is expressed by means of election. As Weber had put it more than two decades earlier, "A popularly elected president . . . is the palladium of genuine democracy."[7] This may well be the most concise definition that can be given of a democracy of authorization. A whole tradition of thinking about democratic leadership has grown up since, amounting in effect to a commentary on Weber's theory of the relation between Caesarism and popular choice. The worldwide adoption of election by universal suffrage as the preferred method for choosing a chief executive testifies to the force of an idea that has come to acquire a sort of intuitive obviousness, at least as a practical matter. As a theoretical matter, however, it has not ceased to arouse disagreement, for it appears no less evident that election is not by itself enough to determine the proper relationship between the governed and their governors. For want of any better alternative, it has nonetheless managed to establish itself as accepted wisdom, even if only in a mood of fatalistic resignation.

The problem is that the limitations of legitimation by universal suffrage alone are particularly pronounced in a presidential system. A popular vote exacerbates four basic structural tensions that are inherent in a democratic election. The first is a consequence of the fact that an election tries to accomplish two things, selection and legitimation, by applying a single principle, majoritarianism, that determines its outcome. Here the difficulty is that these two aims do not stand in the same relation to the majority principle. The usefulness of such a principle in identifying the winner is plain, for simple arithmetic is enough to produce agreement on all sides. But it is a different matter with regard to legitimacy, which cannot be fully conferred by a result that has been arrived at on a majoritarian basis. Whereas the selection procedure has been satisfactorily carried out, legitimation remains yet to be accomplished. The discrepancy between the two is limited in the case of the election of a representative assembly, for the number and diversity of its elected members constitute an expression of a plurality of interests and opinions, though not of a truly general will (which moreover does not exist prior to its being expressed by the citizens themselves). In a presidential election, by contrast, the choice of a single person does not bring about the sort of *representative correction* that to one degree or another an assembly election inevitably produces.[8] The person selected to be president therefore suffers from a correspondingly greater deficit of legitimacy.

This deficit may be measured, as a first approximation, by subtracting the number of votes won from the total number of votes cast; in elections where abstention rates are high, however, the number of voters received by the winner may in fact represent no more than 20 to 25 percent of registered voters. Note, too, that any divergence from the state of public opinion, however difficult it may be to measure opinion accurately by polls or through social networks, is immediately apparent because the population as a whole unambiguously expresses its feeling by these means. There is liable to be a difference, then, between the will of the people considered as a society and the will of the people considered as a smaller population of voters.

Secondly, there is a tension between the qualities a candidate needs to have in order to be elected and those that are required in order to govern effectively. The successful candidate must be attractive to voters. What matters is his ability to charm people, to make people believe that he is one of them, no matter how diverse the communities they belong to may be. This means having to make more and more promises, at least some of them contradictory, and saying more or less different things to different people. Governing, on the other hand, is a matter of deciding. This makes it difficult to keep conflicting promises for very long. To govern is to make decisions that must more or less often rend the veil of calculated imprecision that political rhetoric constantly endeavors to weave. The failure to keep promises is bound to cause disappointment; in the extreme case, it leads people to turn their backs on politics. This often poses less of a problem for a parliamentary representative than for a president, however. If representatives are in opposition, they can go on speaking as they did when they were candidates for office. If they are in the majority, their individual views are subsumed within a collective position, though they can also keep a certain distance from the decisions of any government that may be formed out of the majority they jointly constitute.

An election exhibits, in the third place, a tension between principles of similarity and distinction. On the one hand, it embodies a sort of finality, in the strict sense of the term, since elected representatives serve the purpose of standing for society. They must therefore be like those who have chosen them, as though they had been made in their image, sharing their concerns, speaking in their place, and acting on their behalf; they must, in short, be their doubles. In this respect their outstanding quality is that they are absolutely *ordinary*. And yet, on the other hand, an election is expected to bring forth experts, persons possessing unusual talents that set them apart from everyone else. In this respect representatives make up a sort of "elective aristocracy," to recall an expression that was often employed during the French Revolution. Opposite and apparently incompatible things are wanted of election, in other words, so that it may function both as a representative sampling or random drawing (technical ways of expressing ordinariness) and as a competition or examination (selective procedures for ranking candidates).[9] The two principles, similarity and distinction, can nonetheless achieve something like equilibrium in a sufficiently diverse representative assembly; and it is possible, moreover, to devise procedures and institutions that will simultaneously strengthen each of them.[10] Popular election of the head of the executive, by contrast, is characterized by the fact that it has practically nothing to do with representation as figuration. A president can claim to embody the nation, but he cannot be just anybody.[11] It is for this reason, too, that critics are encouraged to identify the government's response to social demands with him personally, for it is easier to attack someone who stands out from the rest. He is automatically set up, against his will, as a supreme savior, a deus ex machina; and this in turn only magnifies the consequences of his earlier words as a candidate, which promised that he would be able to change things. Under these circumstances, the perception of the relative powerlessness of whomever may be chosen to govern at the end of an election campaign cannot fail to be reinforced.

A presidential election therefore differs structurally from local elections and the election of a representative assembly in three ways. But there is a fourth difference as well, arising from the provision that a president may be reelected. All theories of election consider this question, which in its general form has classically has been regarded as a crucial element of the relationship between the people and their representatives. The prospect of reelection leads a representative to anticipate voters' future judgment and therefore to take it into account in deciding on a present course of action.[12] It has the virtue of encouraging representatives to remain faithful to their commitments, since voters make up their minds on the basis of a candidate's past behavior—a phenomenon known as *retrospective voting*.[13] The role played in a democracy by the prospect of reelection and the retrospective character of voters' motivations is well established, no less than the advantage an incumbent usually enjoys over a challenger.[14] But these factors, which exert a very perceptible influence in municipal elections, where a record of competent management in local administration can often prolong a political career, have much less weight in presidential contests. The latter kind of election is more purely political, chiefly because voting in that case has a mostly negative character. One consequence of this is that first-time candidates, whose campaign rhetoric cannot be contradicted by a prior history of government service, may sometimes have a considerable advantage. Once again, whereas the political effects of retrospective judgment and anticipation in assembly elections can be aggregated and evaluated in a statistical fashion, the possibility this implies of correcting for specific variations or deviations from a mean in parliamentary balloting, for example, is not available in the case of the election of a chief executive.

Presidentialism and the Propensity to Illiberalism

Finally, popular election of the head of the executive places a special emphasis on the personal distinction that such a ballot confers, through the unique position that it authorizes the successful candidate to occupy. The winner's elevation to the highest office brings with it another kind of distinction as well, a legitimacy above and beyond that of other branches of government. By establishing a direct bond with the voters, which is to say one that henceforth will be free of the organized mediation of parties, the successful candidate is endowed with a sort of super-legitimacy that cannot help but encourage a certain illiberalism. This implicit hierarchy—in which the weak legitimacy of the legislative branch, an expression of partisan disagreement and therefore by its nature divided, is subordinated to the strong legitimacy of the executive, by its nature unitary—was at the heart of the Gaullist vision. De Gaulle himself succinctly explained the reason for it: "The spirit of the new Constitution, while keeping a legislative parliament, consists in arranging matters in such a way that power is no longer something partisan, but proceeds directly from the people, which implies that the chief of state, elected by the nation, is the source and holder of it." This was intended as a criticism of the American presidential model, which implied a strict separation of powers that he considered impossible to achieve in France owing to the intractability of political divisions. De Gaulle, in other words, understood presidentialism to be synonymous with a legitimate concentration of power. On this point he was unequivocal. "It must be clearly understood," he said, in words that were to be etched in the nation's memory, "that the indivisible authority of the state is wholly confided to the president by the people who have elected him, that there exists none other, neither ministerial, nor civil, nor military, nor judicial, that is not conferred and maintained by him." The distinction made between the duties and the scope of action of the chief of state and those of the prime minister was only a matter of managerial convenience, "in ordinary times."[15]

The illiberal potential of presidentialism derives from just this—not from the phenomenon of polarization-personalization by itself, but from the link between this phenomenon and a narrowly majoritarian conception of democracy. The problem of majority rule in practice, as we saw earlier, is that it conflates a *principle of justification* with a *technique of decision*, two quite distinct things that do not entail the same consequences. From a procedural point of view, the point of the majority principle is readily grasped in simple arithmetical terms: since everyone will agree that 51 is greater than 49, its adoption makes it possible to conclusively decide the outcome of an election, thus giving democracy its definitive aspect. From a sociological point of view, however, the majority cannot be said to speak for the people as a whole, for it designates only a fraction of the people, even if it is a dominant fraction. Now, the legitimation of power through voting always comes back to the idea that a *general* will is expressed in this fashion. But in fact one only behaves *as if* the greatest number expresses such a will. It is on this fiction that democratic election rests—a pretense that may be said to be justified in a technical sense, but whose presumptive character must always be kept in mind.[16] It is what leads the legitimacy of a power sanctioned in this fashion to be regarded as being limited, for example, by a recognition of the inalienable rights of individuals. This kind of limitation reflects the fact that the license to govern conferred by election, in constituting the legality of a government, does not thereby validate the actions and decisions of this government. The distinctive feature of election of the head of the executive by universal suffrage, then, is that it exaggerates the democratic fiction by creating a super-legitimacy, which might be said to be strictly functional in nature, as a result of enlarging the scale of the electorate. Caesarism, for its part, is based on a confusion between a functional super-legitimacy of just this sort (which leads to a hierarchical ordering of powers) and democratic justification, seen as the expression of a general will, whose fictitious character is not merely preserved but actually aggravated in the case of presidential election. It then compounds this error by judging all forms of social expression according to a numerical criterion of representation. Napoleon III justified curbing the freedoms of the press by saying that, unlike the government, it had no representative character: journalists expressed only their own personal ideas, because they had not been elected to any office, making the press an "illegitimate rival of the public authorities."[17]

Explicitly illiberal arguments of this sort were to have relatively little support a century later in France, which under de Gaulle remained a nation of laws. But they are still apt to be used to justify openly authoritarian government today. One thinks of the doctrine of democratic sovereignty defended by Vladimir Putin in Russia, Recep Tayyip Erdoğan in Turkey, and all those other elected strongmen who now have come to power on several continents.

On the Impossibility of Turning Back

The specter of Caesarism encouraged a certain fatalism as presidentialization gathered impetus in democracies around the world, in the sense that it has come to be seen as an irreversible phenomenon. "There is no turning back"—thus the defense invariably resorted to by those who deplore what they consider to be the disease of presidentialism, while at the same time justifying their resignation in the face of an institution as well established as the popular election of the head of the executive. But this is a way of sparing oneself the trouble of seriously examining the matter. What exactly is the nature of the impossibility in this case? Is it merely the result of habit, something one has gotten used to? Does it depend on arguments that artful demagoguery makes it very difficult to challenge? This would amount to saying that there is no point criticizing universal suffrage once it has been granted, because immediately it somehow becomes an irresistible force, a fact of life with which there is no choice but to make one's peace. Recall that it was in just this light that conservatives ended up regarding universal suffrage in the last decades of the nineteenth century in Europe. The appeal to irresistibility permitted them to malign a disliked form of election as a matter of principle, while as a practical matter coming to terms with something that could not be gotten around. This attitude—a sort of prudence of powerlessness, as it might be called[18]—is no longer an option today. Presidential election must be justified in theory, and not only as a reluctant concession to the accidents of history. Justification must proceed in turn from the fact that such a procedure mobilizes citizens, confers importance and dignity upon them,[19] and interests them in politics—even if simultaneously, as we have seen, it heightens the dangers, the pathologies, and the limitations that every election exhibits in its own way. The true remedy is twofold: first, presidentialism must be made to operate as a *regime* in such a way that its propensity to illiberalism is controlled; and then it must be conceived as constituting a democratic form of *government*.

⚞ 8 ⚟

Limiting Illiberalism

H OW CAN THE IRRESISTIBLE presidentialization of democracy be regulated in order to curb its inherent tendency to authoritarian rule? Three possibilities suggest themselves: improved supervision of elections; reparliamentarization; a return to impersonal forms of authority.

Electoral Controls

No competition for public office is more strictly controlled in most democracies than the election of a chief executive. Constitutions typically limit the number of posts that may be held concurrently, and fix the conditions for serving consecutive terms—rules that are invariably more constraining in the case of a president than the ones that govern the election of members of parliament or of local officials. The lapse into authoritarianism often occurs when sitting presidents endeavor to introduce constitutional modifications suppressing this type of limitation.[1]

Recourse to procedures for removal from office has often been recommended as a way of encouraging elected representatives to remain faithful to their campaign promises. Debate over such procedures has a long history, going back to antiquity. In modern times it was renewed

or by seeking a judicial remedy in the event that citizens brought an action against their elected representatives for failing to honor their commitments, in which case the political mandate was treated as a civil mandate. There was much parliamentary debate on this subject in France, particularly in the 1880s and 1890s,[6] when bills that would have imposed such sanctions were rejected not only in the name of a classical conception of representative government, which allowed deputies a certain freedom of maneuver, but also on grounds of impracticality.

Finally, a demand for removal may arise from an unfavorable political judgment concerning the private or public conduct of an elected official. One form it can take is a type of ballot measure known as an initiative, as in the case of the American recall procedure of that name, instituted in fifteen of the states, the District of Columbia, and three territories since 1908. Only seven of the states require specific petition requirements to be satisfied in order for an initiative to be brought before the voters.[7] Almost all elected officials in these states are eligible for removal; two governors have so far been forced to step down before finishing their term of office. It is generally at the state level that recall is now contemplated. Here, as with regard to popular referendums on legislative matters, the general principle counts for nothing; everything depends on how a particular removal mechanism is designed. If the mechanism could be activated on the petition of only a very small proportion of registered voters (5 percent, for example) and the corresponding ballot measure brought before the electorate as a whole at any time, even shortly after an election, then elections would lose all meaning. Conversely, if the conditions for a measure to be placed on a ballot and voted on are very difficult to meet, that would make it an instrument of last resort, to be used only under exceptional circumstances. This was the fate of Article 43 of the Weimar Constitution, for example, which provided that the president of the Reich could be dismissed by the people, but only if a recall referendum had been approved by a prior two-thirds majority vote of the Reichstag. Two countries, Belize and Venezuela, currently have a mechanism of this nature in place. In Venezuela, the procedure can be set in motion after half of the president's term of office has elapsed if 20 percent of registered voters file a petition for a recall referendum. Removal from office is then authorized if the number of votes in favor is greater than the number received by the president in the first place, so long as at least 25 percent of registered voters took part in the original election. In 2005, an attempt to overturn Hugo Chavez's election that met these very strict conditions nonetheless failed. The conditions in Belize are stricter still.

The French procedure for the removal of a chief of state, in the form given it by the constitutional revision of 2007 (Articles 67 and 68), constitutes a minor variant of this latter political approach. According to the report of the commission established to advise on the matter, the aim was to go beyond the old monarchical doctrine that the king can do no wrong, which was felt to license an "intolerable" impunity.[8] The authors spoke of introducing a "safety valve," but the precise legal nature of the removal procedure they had in mind was not clearly defined. And while emphasizing that their purpose was not to create "a sort of political responsibility, like the one to which a government is subject," they also disavowed any intention of imputing criminal responsibility, settling instead for the curiously vague alternative of "situating the responsibility of the chief of state in a political register." What this amounted to, in effect, was instituting an exceptional procedure in order to deal with situations that were themselves exceptional.[9] It therefore could not in any way be regarded as treating the pathologies of presidentialism by ordinary means.

Whatever its modalities may be, a recall procedure involves correcting the outcome of an election, which in turn requires holding a further election. Recall must therefore be seen as part of a democracy of authorization, since demanding responsibility in the performance of the duties of elective office ultimately depends on election itself.

Reparliamentarization

The presidentialization of democracy has almost everywhere been accompanied by a *rationalized parliamentarianism*.[10] This term refers to attempts to regulate parliamentary behavior by means of arrangements designed to eliminate the risks of chronic governmental instability inherent in assembly regimes, which in the nineteenth century, and again in the interwar period of the twentieth, were thought to constitute the ideal type of parliamentarianism. These arrangements make it more difficult for legislators to challenge ministerial conduct, on the one hand by putting in place restrictive procedural mechanisms (time limits for introducing a motion of no confidence, with larger majorities being required in order to pass such a resolution, and in the extreme case the right of the executive to dissolve parliament) and, on the other, by imposing electoral rules favoring the emergence of clear majorities (limits on proportional representation, strict conditions for proceeding to a second round of voting, and so on). The point of all this was to protect the executive against undue legislative interference, which is to say, in plain language, to reduce as far as possible the ability of parliament to topple a government. Germany was among the first European countries to take steps in this direction after the Second World War, by placing very stringent conditions on the use of motions of no confidence, which moreover could be sponsored only by opposition members capable of forming a viable majority. In the United Kingdom, the executive's right of dissolution carried with it the decisive power to schedule elections. France, by contrast, under the Fourth Republic (and, to a still greater degree, Italy during this period), continued to practice a traditional style of parliamentarianism.[11] In this respect the Fifth Republic marked a clear break with the preceding regime. Article 49 of the Constitution of 1958, setting forth the government's responsibility before parliament, recalibrated the balance of power between the two branches by requiring the approval of a majority of the Chamber of Deputies in order for a resolution of no confidence to be adopted. This had the effect of adjusting the burden of proof to the advantage of the government, which now ruled as a divided minority: since the abstention of undecided deputies was not taken into consideration (only those votes cast in favor of the resolution being counted), the opposition was obliged to put together a proportionally greater majority of the remaining total if it hoped to prevail. This also forced parliament to abide by a principle of responsibility (paragraph 3) that enabled the government to pass a bill without having to bring it to a vote unless a motion of no-confidence, placed on the agenda within twenty-four hours, was carried by the chamber.[12] Completing the reversal of the executive's relationship with parliament, it now enjoyed a right of dissolution as well. Under these circumstances, the government had indeed become the preeminent political authority in the Fifth Republic, as it is also, through reliance on similar methods, in most countries.[13]

The question arises whether the Fifth Republic did not set a particularly worrisome precedent in this regard, establishing a sort of ultra-presidential model. Vivid memories of Caesarism had, of course, made the French especially alert to the danger that direct popular election would produce pathological outgrowths; and the arrogance of Gaullist rhetoric did nothing to assuage fears of creeping authoritarianism. Considered in international comparative perspective, however, the widespread adoption of the French presidential model can be seen to have occurred without deleterious consequences, at least not in France itself.[14] There, as elsewhere, the political role of parliament in governing the country was plainly diminished[15] and the ascendancy of the executive consolidated; but at the same time the parliamentary functions of oversight, evaluation, and interpellation were reaffirmed and fortified. The major constitutional reform of 2008, which amended forty-seven articles of the 1958 Constitution, was undertaken in just this spirit.[16] The Balladur Commission, in its advisory report, had spoken of the "need for a rebalancing of institutions through an enlargement of the functions and the role of Parliament," and explicitly emphasized the necessity of "loosening the stranglehold of rationalized parliamentarianism."[17] Nevertheless the new powers granted to parliament did little more than expand somewhat its supervisory authority, approve a mandatory consultative role with regard to appointments and financial matters, allow greater freedom of internal organization, relax external controls on the legislative process, and broaden the scope of opposition prerogatives. All of this amounted to a reparliamentarization of the way government operates, obliging the executive branch to explain itself more fully and enabling the legislative branch to exercise greater vigilance. But it did not alter the basic fact of the political preeminence of executive agencies in relation to parliament; indeed, the president found his own position vis-à-vis the prime minister actually strengthened.[18]

Where ultra-presidentialism of an authoritarian and / or populist type does in fact flourish today, there is a dominant narrow majoritarian electoralism whose institutions and rhetoric can be traced back directly to the French model of the Second Empire, as we saw in Chapter 7. Democratic monarchies, of which seven still exist in Europe, are no less obviously different from ordinary presidentialism. In these systems, even if the head of the executive is determined through what is sometimes called a disguised (or "hidden") election, the presence of a hereditary sovereign transforms the nature of government, notwithstanding that he or she is a constitutional figure holding no real power. Here the tendency to identify power with the figure of the prime minister is restrained by the fact that the monarch concentrates the regard of society upon his or her person.

No one should suppose that such distinctions in any way absolve presidentialism of its failings. But it is important to understand that it is not by "reparliamentarizing" democracies—here I use the term in a political (rather than a functional) sense—that they will be delivered from them. This is what all those who call for the establishment of a Sixth Republic in France assume. The idea of modeling a successor regime to the Fifth Republic on an "English-style prime ministerial regime"[19] springs from a desire not merely for a more active parliament but for a system in which parliament would actually be the center of gravity. In this scheme the president would appoint the prime minister, but in so doing he (or she) is obliged to "take into consideration the national will and the majority of the National Assembly" (per Article 9 of the draft constitution),[20] which is to say, to name the head of the coalition that prevailed in the legislative elections, who furthermore cannot be dismissed. The prime minister, enjoying greater autonomy than before, would have correspondingly greater powers, including the authority to choose and appoint ministers, and to set the agenda of the Council of Ministers, even if he (or she) does not preside over it. To avoid the pitfalls to which the assembly government of the Third and the Fourth Republics was vulnerable, he would be allowed greater independence in carrying out his cabinet's policy: he would have the right to dissolve parliament, to submit any item of proposed legislation to a referendum, and to take advantage of the expedients authorized by the third paragraph of Article 49 of the present constitution, especially for the purpose of forcing adoption of a finance bill. Finally, although the prime minister is not elected by the people, he would nonetheless be responsible to the National Assembly. The proposed constitution retains election by universal suffrage of the president (whose term of office would be fixed once again at seven years), but he would be limited to performing the duties of an umpire or referee and would no longer have prerogatives of his own in governing (even in respect of foreign policy, since there he would merely be informed by the government of any negotiations entered into for the purpose of concluding an international agreement). He would thus become a sort of constitutional monarch—but an elected monarch. It is here that the difficulty presents itself. A scheme of this sort says nothing about the conflicts over legitimacy that would inevitably arise in a situation where a relatively weak president is chosen by direct popular vote and a relatively strong prime minister is appointed as the result of a hidden election. This is why the most cogent critics of contemporary presidentialism recommend either a return to the practice of choosing a figurehead as president by means of parliamentary election or to the creation of a comparably weak (because hereditary) monarchy.

New Forms of Impersonality

If the break with the tradition of impersonality is one of the main features of presidential-governing democracy, new forms of impersonality have nonetheless appeared in the meantime. The growing constitutionalization of democratic regimes is perhaps the most notable expression of a concern to limit the tendency to illiberalism, amounting to something like a revival of the venerable idea of the rule of law. The articles of contemporary constitutions—concise, immutable, few in number—exhibit the same qualities that were desired of laws in the eighteenth century. There is one major difference, however. The branch of government responsible for adjudicating disagreements over the meaning and application of the language of a nation's constitution is no longer conceived of as a sort of passive bystander. Modern constitutional courts, though they have a collegial structure (in this respect recalling an older conception of the executive), are eminently active bodies. And it is the independence of the judiciary and allied regulatory authorities that today constitutes one of the surest safeguards against a drift toward authoritarianism on the part of executive agencies.[21]

The democratic character of independent bodies charged with regulatory and oversight functions, first set up in the United States in the late nineteenth century, has so far been unexamined for the most part.[22] They are nonetheless increasingly responsible for superintending the management, not only of economic and social affairs, but also of political life (especially with regard to the conduct of elections and campaigns for public office). These institutions represent another aspect of the reversion to impersonal rule. Organized on a collegial basis, like the courts, they respond to a social demand for impartiality. They anticipate and remedy shortages or oversupply of key resources, monitor the functioning of financial and other markets, and protect basic freedoms against the harmful effects of favoritism, coercion, discrimination, monopoly, and indeed any form of influence that undermines equal treatment under the law or compromises the public character of certain goods and services. Such authorities operate wherever society has an interest in objective and unbiased scrutiny, with the aim of satisfying two conditions of generality, fair and open competition, on the one hand, and consensus, on the other. With the establishment of what may be thought of as desubjectivized authorities having specific functions and well-defined powers of intervention, as the result of a combination of citizen pressure and government acquiescence, another rampart has been erected against illiberalism. In an age of presidentialized democracy, their continuing vitality is no less essential than a robust and vigilant judiciary.

The importance attached to such institutions is in no way a consequence of depoliticization. Far from being external to democratic political life, constitutional courts and independent regulatory bodies are at its heart. But they represent other ways of giving effect to democratic purpose than the ones produced by the judgment of a majority of voters. In this sense they may be said to be part of a regime of "competitive articulation" of the general interest.[23] Both types of institution monitor and regulate government agencies, but they do not replace them. These agencies will continue to be reserved a considerable freedom of action so long as problems of economic management, social policy, and the administration of justice, to name only three of the most prominent areas of executive responsibility, require clear-cut choices to be made in a timely fashion.

Nor is the sort of impersonality embodied by independent authorities to be confused with the frankly antipolitical and antidemocratic sensibility that underlies the notion of *economic constitutionalism,* particularly in the form given it by James Buchanan in extending the work of Friedrich Hayek.[24] Both Buchanan and Hayek hark back to the eighteenth-century utopia of a world governed uniquely by the market, which is supposed to express laws of nature, the most objective rules of all. Hayek had elaborated the concept of "demarchy" as a rival order to democracy in which human will, condemned to arbitrariness on account either of incomplete information or partisan bias, plays no role. The same perspective inspired the researches of Finn Kydland and Edward Prescott, who claimed to have shown that the mechanical application of a stable rule always produces better results than political decisions.[25] In their work, as in that of Buchanan and Hayek, automaticity recommends itself as a generative principle because it eliminates the very possibility of entertaining alternative choices. What one is dealing with here, then, is a totalizing impersonality, not the merely functional impersonality of independent regulatory agencies and constitutional courts.

Functional impersonality must also be distinguished from two other concepts, "government by numbers"[26] and governance. In Europe, the quantitative analysis of fiscal policy stipulates numerical criteria according to which budget deficits in those countries that are signatories of the Treaty on Stability, Coordination, and Governance in the Economic and Monetary Union, which came into effect on 1 January 2013, are judged to fall within admissible limits. Any citizen of a ratifying eurozone state is familiar with the figure 3 percent. This is the authorized budget deficit ceiling, expressed as a fraction of gross domestic product. Scarcely a day goes by when a news report does not mention it. The mechanical character of the correction mechanism brought into play when the ceiling is exceeded (the phrase "automatic pilot" is often used in this connection) has been sharply criticized, and the precise circumstances under which it is to be triggered are the object of incessant negotiation.[27] But none of this rises to the level of economic constitutionalism in the sense intended by Buchanan and Hayek. Government by numbers amounts to no more than the barest substitute for a concerted approach to budget management, which in the absence of a European Constitution and a unified political space has no hope of existence. Automatic piloting is the minimum that can be agreed upon when there is no agreement on anything else.

The same is true for the notion of governance. Governance is a transnational phenomenon of still broader scope, aimed at providing policy guidance and building consensus for decisions on matters of worldwide urgency (global warming is no doubt the most conspicuous example today), that engages a variety of actors (states, nongovernmental organizations, private corporations) in interlocking and continuous processes of negotiation and compromise that do not fit into the normative framework of traditional diplomacy. It is the equivalent, at the microeconomic level, of decentralized and participatory management; at the international level, it takes the place of a nonexistent world government, posing as a cooperative attempt to cobble together more or less satisfactory solutions (often, alas, with very modest results, as in the case of recent climate conferences). Governance therefore has nothing to do with impersonality in the sense we are interested in. Like government by numbers, it is an intermediate form, prepolitical and predemocratic.

The value of the different ways of limiting the illiberal potential of presidentialism that we have just looked at very quickly just now cannot be underestimated. But they do not tell us under what conditions democratic authority can be properly exercised in everyday life. It is to this question that I turn in Part 3.

PART III

A DEMOCRACY OF APPROPRIATION

9

The Governed and Their Governors

LET US START FROM the fact that no theory of democratic government exists today. The historical reasons for this state of affairs are well known. But one may go further: there has never been any real theory of government, period. To be sure, what we call "executive power" has always existed. But it was invariably understood in practical terms by those who exercised it. Power for those who held it was its own justification. They had to know how to command obedience, to impart motivation, to defuse discontent, to manage imbalances of power, to eliminate rivals. Governing for them was the art of combining force with cunning and charm in order to conquer a position and then to keep it. For that, a theory was of no use. The experience of leading men and directing their minds sufficed to guide them in this ambition—together with the counsels of those who had served alongside the powerful and observed the causes of their successes and their failures. A practical literature on the exercise of power, composed for the instruction of princes, soon came into being. Anyone who hopes to formulate a democratic theory of government today must take this literature into consideration, if only to appreciate the magnitude of the task.

Let us begin, then, by looking at the classic analysis of reasons of state inaugurated by the writings of Machiavelli and Commynes in the early decades of the sixteenth century, a tumultuous time when the upheavals accompanying the advent of the nation-state in France and the spread of rivalry among the emergent principalities in Italy aroused a growing sense of insecurity. In addition to external threats, there were domestic sources of vulnerability, connected in Italy with the problem of controlling a population that had grown restless under the rule of the great families in the major cities and in France with the royal administration of an expanding territory. At the same time, the counsellors who whispered in the ears of the mighty were looking for ways to exploit new possibilities, to bring into play novel "expedients" and "subtleties" that would permit princes to consolidate and perpetuate their domination. For this purpose neither laws nor grand principles held any interest. For them what mattered was the reality of governing, which is to say the circumstances under which mastery of an *art of execution* could be achieved.[1]

The Reason of Princes

From the middle of the sixteenth century onward, the Wars of Religion divided societies and weakened established rule everywhere in Europe, not only on account of the scope and intensity of internal conflicts, but also for reasons of an almost anthropological nature. For the clashes arising from resistance to the reformist movement that had swept over the continent were to profoundly alter the relationship of individuals to authority, to subvert the habit of obedience by insisting on the freedom of personal conscience, in short, to deny the obviousness of an obligation to submit to the powers that be. Jean Bodin, in *Les six livres de la République* [1576], sought to resolve the issue by means of a constitutional theory of the state as sovereign power. In this conception, sovereignty is a method by which the governed may be kept apart from their governors, and public order made to depend as much on regulating the distance between them as on the concentration of authority. Perpetual and absolute, sovereignty makes it possible to guarantee internal order and peace by reducing all subjects to a uniform state of subordination. The modern state, equipped with greater powers of coercion that enabled it to exert control over a clearly defined territory and the people within it, was thereby provided with its fundamental principle. But the idea of sovereignty was not enough by itself to settle the question of command and obedience as a practical matter. What was needed in addition was a way of justifying government so that its effectiveness no longer rested on the routine threat of force or a belief in the sacred character of power—a way of proceeding, in other words, further along the path opened up by Bodin. Justus Lipsius, a philosopher in Leiden, in the Netherlands, was the first to grasp what the dawning of a new age of politics implied. "What heavy labor it is," he remarked only a little more than a decade later, "to hold back and restrain so many heads with a single head, and gently to bring under some common yoke of obedience this great restless, disunited, and unruly multitude."[2] Like Bodin, he saw the need for an apparatus of state capable of ensuring order and safety. But to his mind the prince's ability to command involved a specific kind of practical knowledge: he had to be capable of acting prudently. This meant having an understanding of situations, knowing when to strike and when to hold back, when to cajole, when to reassure, when to insist.

A few decades after Lipsius, *raison d'État* theorists began to develop a systematic approach to the question. No one expounded their leading idea better than Daniel de Priezac in *Des secrets de la domination* [1652], a title that by itself constituted an entire program. "In the art of governing peoples," he wrote,

> there are always reasons hidden and unknown to the common people, without the aid of which states would have been able neither to preserve their form, nor to acquire their perfection. Whatever grandeur, and whatever power kings may possess, yet they do not enjoy the privilege of the most insignificant sculptors, who can give to the matter they work on such form as seems to them good; but men, often harder and more stubborn even than marble, make plain enough that they are born to a liberty so great that rather than obey they oppose obstinacy to reason, and rebellion to authority. It was therefore necessary to have recourse to some secrets of state, and to inventions that Aristotle named sophisms, which through a plausible deceit would confine the mind of the people and fascinate its eyes.[3]

Gabriel Naudé, in *Considérations politiques sur les coups d'État* [1639],[4] gave the new art of governing its canonical formulation. Naudé likewise urged that politics be conceived in terms that went beyond the need for stronger laws. The political science that he hoped to create encompassed the relationship not only between states, but also between governed and governing. This science rested on what would later be called a realist view of human affairs. Naudé endorsed the judgment of Jean-Louis Guez de Balzac, that there exists among men only a "commerce of cheats and fools,"[5] and approved the rebuke addressed by Nero to his advisors, that they "gave their opinion as if they were in the Republic of Plato, and not among the base and despicable rabble of Romulus."[6] The art of governing implied a strict separation between politics and morality that was fundamentally incompatible with the idealism of most earlier authors on the subject. On this view the security of the state was paramount; what is more, the rules for its protection belonged to a primary sphere of responsibility that overruled the claims of all others. Accordingly, he defended both the Saint Bartholomew's Day Massacre of 1572 and the practices of the Inquisition, for in each case it was a matter of "going beyond the common law in the service of the public good," of attaching the highest priority to the "bold and extraordinary actions that princes are obliged to carry out in difficult and sometimes desperate circumstances against the common law, without regard for order or any form of justice, risking individual interest for the public good."[7] The essence of politics, in other words, was seen to reside in the conquest and the keeping of power, considered as ends in themselves.

The mainsprings of this realistic art of government, whose theoretical foundations had first been laid in early sixteenth-century Europe, were pretense and deception. "Who does not know how to dissemble does not know how to rule"—thus the essential maxim.[8] In the *Breviarum politicorum* [1684], Mazarin summarized his message to those who aspire to govern in the same terms: "1. Feign. 2. Deceive."[9] It was not by immersing oneself in books that one could learn to govern in this fashion,[10] but in understanding human motivations so that they might be more easily manipulated. The "royal science" that Naudé sought to construct was a *practical and realistic art of ruling* by means of which it would be possible to exploit passions, superstitions, and fears for the sake of holding on to power. Only through constant vigilance, he believed, could the state endure. Like Commynes and Machiavelli before him, Naudé had a keen sense of the precariousness of circumstances. "All the things of the world, without any exception," he emphasized, "are subject to revolutions. . . . Sciences, empires, sects, the world itself is not exempt from this vicissitude."[11] Insofar as governing was a form of interaction, always shifting and unstable, between the prince and society, maintaining the position of the state required an unending series of specific and exceptional acts intended to ensure the continuity of power—coups d'état, in the most literal sense of the term.

The secrets of Naudé's science were reserved, of course, for the exclusive use of those who held power. By its very nature, knowledge of this kind had to be kept hidden from the common people. It is hardly surprising, then, that Naudé should have contented himself with a printing of twelve copies for the first edition of his *Considérations politiques;* it would have been dangerous to give broader circulation to a work devoted to "unmasking the action of Princes and of laying bare what they attempt every day to conceal with countless artifices."[12] The methods used to shape opinion and the techniques for misdirecting credulous minds could on no account be divulged to the masses—the very people who were to be reduced to subservience. Precisely because the exercise of power resided in creating a distance between the prince and his subjects, the stratagems employed for this purpose, the *arcana imperii,* could not be spoken of, for if they were, the people would not come to regard their subjugation as the result of a natural superiority. But at the same time these secrets of state had to be known to a privileged few, an inner circle of illuminati who not only stood apart from the common and the vulgar but actively colluded with one another in order to perpetuate their rule over them. Treatises on reasons of state were meant for their eyes alone.

The type of rule that *raison d'État* theorists sought to institute was justified in these works with reference to a prejudice that was implicit in the need for secrecy. Precisely because the masses were looked down upon as rabble, an almost subhuman breed liable to the most immediate passions—a "very cruel beast . . . having an inconstant, rebellious, quarrelsome, covetous disposition," to recall Naudé's phrase[13]—it was both necessary and just to govern by dissimulation and manipulation. This sociological assumption, as it might more charitably be called, was shared by learned freethinkers, exponents of an aristocracy of reason that was to play an essential role in winning wider acceptance among elites for the doctrine of *raison d'État* in the seventeenth century. Indeed, they considered scorn for the common people to be the condition of all progress.[14] This view, however disturbing it may seem to us today, was forcefully argued by the two foremost figures of philosophical ("erudite") libertinism, Pierre Charron in *De la sagesse*

[1601] and François de La Mothe Le Vayer in his four *Dialogues faits à l'imitation des anciens* [1630]. "I have always thought," Le Vayer candidly remarked, "that it was against the torrent of the multitude that we had to employ our principal forces, and that having tamed this monster of the people we would readily overcome the rest."[15] Rationalist contempt for the crowd was seized upon by Naudé and his contemporaries, not least for the excuse it gave them in ruling over the world from their own private Olympus.

The naked cynicism of such works would have made their authors unpublishable in an age of popular sovereignty. Yet political leaders have continued in the meantime to conduct themselves in accordance with these same precepts, as though their wisdom went without saying. The advent of universal suffrage only strengthened the sense of the uncertainty of power in the minds of those who held it, men who found themselves obliged to admit that they served a new master. There thus came about a divorce between what is said in the course of campaigning for public office, owing to the candidate's overriding need to convince voters that he is a man of the people, and what is done once one has been elected to office, which depends on having recourse, now and forever more unmentionable, to quite ancient methods for holding on to power and manipulating the many.

The Age of Seduction and Manipulation

The manner in which the governed were dominated by their governors was henceforth bound up with techniques of appeal and persuasion, methodically refined by modern public relations experts, that find their most perfect expression in the election campaigns we know today. The *Commentariolum Petitionis,* supposed to have been written in 65 or 64 BCE by Quintus Tullius Cicero, younger brother of the great orator, and addressed to Marcus as he contemplated embarking on a political career as a candidate for one of the two consulships of the Roman Republic, is the first systematic statement that has come down to us of the art of conducting a successful campaign.[16] Strictly speaking, Quintus's handbook on electioneering is a treatise on manipulation. From it one learns how to acquire influential friends, how to flatter voters and advertise one's devotion to them, how to sway public opinion and ensure that "as many ears as possible are filled with the highest praise" regarding one's fitness to hold office. Quintus recommends discrediting rivals, in the best case by encouraging "scandalous talk of the crimes, lusts, or briberies of your competitors, depending on their character." Above all he urges his brother to mount a dazzling spectacle, a "brilliant, resplendent, popular campaign" that will set him apart from the other candidates, captivate the masses, and establish his reputation as a man of stature who must be reckoned with. Last, but not least, he reminds Marcus that his eloquence is a decisive weapon, for "this is what holds the attention of men in Rome and wins them over, and deters them from hindering or harming you."[17]

The rules of allurement in this domain have scarcely changed. They still aim at bewitching voters, only now with the assistance, witting or dumb, of the media. Maurice Joly, one of Napoleon III's fiercest adversaries, was the first to warn against the manipulation of opinion in the modern media age in his *Dialogue aux enfers entre Machiavel et Montesquieu* [1864].[18] The interest of this work today has less to do with the fact that it harshly attacked the authoritarian character of the regime, as many others did at the time, than with the light it cast on the novel relationship the emperor had created with the press. Apart from the dangers posed by censorship, what attracted Joly's notice was the rise of *journalism as a power in its own right.* "Since journalism is so great a force," he has Napoleon III say in the name of Machiavelli, "do you know what my government would do? It would make itself a journalist, it would become journalism incarnate."[19] And he goes on:

> Like the god Vishnu, my press will have a hundred arms, and these arms will stretch out their hands to every shade of opinion over the entire surface of the country. Everyone will be of my party without knowing it. Those who think they are speaking their own language will be speaking mine, those who think they are rousing their own party to action will be rousing mine, those who think they are marching under their own banner will be marching under mine. . . . Aided by the hidden loyalty of these public prints, I will be able to say that I direct opinion at will on all questions of internal and external policy. I awaken people's minds or lull them to sleep, I reassure them or confuse them, I plead for and against, the true and the false.[20]

From this it naturally followed that "making use of the press, using it in all its form—thus today the law of governments that wish to survive."[21] A century later, Hannah Arendt was to denounce the manipulation of public opinion by governments seeking to turn the "inventiveness of Madison Avenue" to their own advantage.[22] The charge has lost none of force since.

While representative institutions and modes of participation have evolved and gained in sophistication since the founding revolutions of the eighteenth century, the art of governing still relies on methods that are as monotonous as they are primitive. The same schemes, the same subterfuges, the same rhetorical evasions continue to inform the conduct of rulers obsessed with holding on to power. With the emergence first of print journalism on a massive scale, and then of its electronic variants, the instruments of control and deception have only been multiplied. Unless we make a concerted effort to break the spell of princely enchantment, we will never succeed in grasping the reality of the relationship between the governed and the governing in a modern democracy.

The Problem of Self-Government

The governed-governing relationship, as it really exists, is characterized by an imbalance. However many individuals may aspire to set themselves up as a legislature (by means of the referendum mechanism), the people as a whole cannot govern itself. There is a *structural asymmetry* between the governed and their governors, distinct from the asymmetry that exists between the represented and their representatives, which in the absence of complicating factors is merely functional. Let me elaborate on this crucial point.

In a democracy it is the people, either directly or, more often, through their representatives, who make the laws they are obligated to obey. "The people, being subject to the laws, ought to be their author," as Rousseau put it in the sixth chapter of the second book of *Du contrat social* [1762]. Is this to say that democracy amounts to obeying oneself? More to the point, is it actually possible to govern oneself (where "governing oneself" is understood, of course, in the *political* sense of the term, and not in the restricted sense of personal self-control)? This question may be answered in two ways, from either a sociological perspective or an institutional perspective.

In sociological terms, the question of self-government runs up against the fact that the people who make the laws do not exactly coincide with those who ought to obey them. The former is the *people as a civic body,* which in its essence is one (even if it is constituted only by the fiction of majority power); the latter is the *people as a social body,* which is characterized by the diversity of its conditions and the variety of its individual behaviors. The two classes of people are not congruent, and may even be opposed to each other. This is a point on which Rousseau laid great stress in the chapters of *Du contrat social* devoted to the question of government. One thinks of the closing words of the fourth chapter of the third book, on democracy: "Were there a people of gods, they would govern themselves democratically. So perfect a government is unsuited to men." These sentences must be properly understood. They do not mean that Rousseau finally confessed to his skepticism regarding to the possibility of political emancipation. The point he wished to make was that the generality of the law would be fatally compromised if the legislator were permitted to modify it at the moment he applied it. In modifying it, he would in effect be renouncing the civic body's solemn allegiance to generality for the sake merely of ministering to particularity; no longer a priest, he is now no more than a manager, and therefore constantly tempted to favor specific interests.[23] The gods, for their part, are not vulnerable to such a temptation, for they forever persevere in their essential being. This is why Rousseau called for the separation of sovereignty—the unchallengeable sovereignty of the people—from government, which in his eyes ought to be exercised by one man or by a small group of men considered incapable of being corrupted. Sovereignty should therefore be democratic, whereas government, firmly subordinated to the executive, gained nothing by being democratic. In effect, then, he solved the problem by demoting executive power to a secondary position and placing it outside the sphere of popular sovereignty.

But even if one does not follow Rousseau in this, there remains a gap between the people as a social body and the people as a civic body. A government is not only the authority that enforces the laws, mechanically, as it seemed to political thinkers of the eighteenth century. It must supply a means of bridging the gap between these two aspects of the people. Indeed, one might well suppose that this is the first object of government in its managerial capacity (making choices and acting as a referee). A people cannot govern itself, politically, for it exists in two ways that do not coincide, as a body of citizens (thus expressing a principle of generality) and as a body of individuals (expressing a principle of particularity). Individuals, because they are never immediately citizens, must therefore always be governed. Accordingly, political authority must always stand outside and apart from individuals. Functional considerations pull at sociological reality from opposite sides, as it were, thereby establishing the requisite separation between executive power and its structurally reflexive dimension.

There is another aspect of the asymmetry between governed and governing that needs to be taken into consideration. Whereas parliamentary deliberation implies the existence of a collective body, decision must be concentrated. Executive power, no matter how it may be justified and instituted, is by its nature one;[24] society is always multiple. It is for just this reason that initiative is concentrated in the executive. Functionally, the many are always subordinate to the one; but the one is only the idealized or finished form of the many. A reflexive dynamic is inescapably at work, by which the one and the many act upon one another.

Self-Management, Self-Government, Self-Institution

The operation of reflexivity in this sense leads us to make a clear distinction between self-management and self-government.[25] A *specific group* is always capable of managing itself. Co-owners of a property or business, members of a labor union or a civic group or a neighborhood association—all such people can organize themselves for the purpose of jointly taking decisions that concern them all. There are many examples, past and present, of general-assembly regimes of this type. Their viability is subject only to strictly physical limitations, the size of the group, for example, or other impediments to meeting in plenary session. But there is another essential feature, their strictly functional character. The purpose of groups of this kind, known as horizontal groups, is to manage a good, an activity, or a plan. Each participant stands in the same relation to the others and on the same level: they are all producers, or consumers, or co-owners, or users, or neighbors. There is an element of immediacy, in other words, that unites them. In political life, by contrast, the common fact of citizenship coexists with the multiplicity of roles that each citizen plays. From this inevitably follow contradictions between competing interests, which give rise in turn to tensions between taxpayers and users of public services, between producers and consumers, and so on. Looked at in this way, individuals are not merely units, as it were, of public accounting. Hence the need for reflexivity in the form of action by public authorities: beyond the range of strictly managerial tasks that fall to it, a government must endeavor to conciliate the various segments of society and negotiate whatever compromises are necessary among them.

A further distinctive characteristic of democracy is that, in addition to the deeply problematic notion of self-government, it is founded on the self-institution of society.[26] This principle expresses the fact of popular sovereignty in the most elementary possible fashion. Historically it has assumed two basic forms. The first arose with the adoption of constitutions by universal direct suffrage. Here the pioneering innovations occurred in the aftermath of the French Revolution, when the Constitutions of 1793, Year III, and Year VIII were ratified in this fashion.[27] In an age that regarded the representative system as the last and most perfect stage of political evolution, the exceptional symbolic power of a ballot of this nature was unsurpassable. The practice of ratification by the constituent people was later to be extended following the First World War by international recognition of the principle of *self-determination*,[28] which is to say the right of peoples to decide their own political arrangements. But self-institution may also appear in a more permanent fashion in the guise of deliberative democracy. The underlying assumption is that society has an interest in allowing citizens to take part on a regular basis in public debate on the great questions facing every nation in respect of social solidarity, the administration of justice, separation of church and state, and so on. Here the power of the people as citizens is not a consequence of voting; it issues from the freedom of all to speak openly about political issues, so that each individual may enter into dialogue with every other.

The asymmetry that obtains between the governed and the governing therefore in no way implies unresisting submission to external authority. It has a strictly functional dimension that is compatible with the active and unconditional affirmation of the principle of self-institution and the practice of self-management.

The Impossibility of Doing Away with Exteriority

The functional character of the asymmetry between the governed and the governing may also be interpreted negatively, by showing that philosophies based on the idea of abolishing government lead to impasses of one sort or another. Historically, as we have seen, the refusal to conceive of the executive as a governing authority in the strict sense derived originally from the cult of law in the form given it by political theorists in the eighteenth century. But it also reappeared in another form in the nineteenth century: anarchism, understood in the etymological sense of the term as the absence of rule. Proudhon was the first to have formalized its principles. The point of departure for his analysis was not very far removed from the classical revolutionary view, as his commentary on the events of 1848 in France makes clear. "It is for the National Assembly," he says in a typical passage, "through the organization of its committees, to exercise executive power, as it exercises legislative power by its joint deliberations and its votes. Ministers, undersecretaries of state, division heads, etc., uselessly duplicate the representatives, whose idle and dissipated lives, given over to intrigue and ambition, are a continual cause of difficulties for [public] administration, of bad laws for society, of wasteful expenditures for the state."[29] But Proudhon was not content to leave it at that. He rejected the very principle of political subordination. Socialism, to his way of thinking, was the "contrary of governmentalism,"[30] for the aim of revolution must be to banish any and all political institutions of an overbearing or imperious nature. "We no more accept the government of man by man," he declared, "than the exploitation of man by man."[31] Property and government were the two principal ways in which social exteriority is institutionalized: "What in politics is called *Authority* is analogous and equivalent to what, in political economy, is called *Property;* these two ideas are synonymous and identical with each other."[32]

Proudhon therefore had to socialize property and at the same time "anarchize" power.[33] By this latter term Proudhon meant doing away with the gradations of status that power is bound to create, and substituting for them radically decentralized forms of cooperation and association. This was something quite different from advocating direct government, as the Democratic Socialists were to do in 1851. "The revolutionary formula,"

Proudhon objected on that occasion, "can no longer be direct legislation, or direct government, or simple government: it is *no more government*."[34] One might almost say that he had rediscovered for himself the outlook of the philosophers of the Scottish Enlightenment, who sought to replace traditional political organization by the unmediated activity of civil society.[35] But whereas these thinkers sanctified the mechanism of the market, which they believed would bring about an objective, neutral, and anonymous order, Proudhon laid greater stress on what he saw as the necessity of making the *producer* the central figure of society. He proposed therefore to substitute *"rule of contracts,* that is, economic and industrial rule [for the] old system of rule of laws. . . . The idea of contract excludes that of government."[36] But if political rule had thus been decreed to be abolished, it could not avoid being sustained and disseminated by the rules of the economic system, with the result that social bonds among human beings would now consist solely in the self-management of their various activities. What Proudhon refused to recognize was that the political sphere has an autonomy and a specific character of its own, connected with the existence of a shared civic life. The public institutions on which society in this fundamental sense is based cannot be reduced to a set of private and unrelated cooperative arrangements.

The dream of a society exempt from any external form of political rule lived on during the twentieth century under the impetus of anthropological research. In France, the work of Pierre Clastres, an observer of the Guayaki Indians in what is now Paraguay, did much to shape the antiauthoritarian ethos of the post-1968 period from this perspective. In a number of influential essays, collected for the most part in *La Société contre l'État* [1974] and *Recherches d'anthropologie politique* [1980],[37] he worked out the implications of what he took to be the most important result established by his fieldwork among the Guayaki, namely, that their leader had no real power. Leader he was, by virtue of the respect shown to him on all sides and the splendor of his dress and ornament; but a leader whose prestige had no coercive effect, who enjoyed no independence of decision, and who gave no orders, at least not in the sense of injunctions meant to be obeyed. Political power, in this culture, combined uncontested legitimacy with very restricted authority. Clastres conjectured that this absence of power in the usual sense was not the sign of any lack or failing due to the embryonic state of political development in Guayaki society; instead it was the consequence of a conscious and deliberate collective will that no figure be set over the community as its master.[38] More generally, he suggested that so-called primitive societies were not somehow incomplete, having been prevented by their archaism from constructing an autonomous political sphere with a formal apparatus of state; to the contrary, they had shown the wisdom to resist such a temptation—making them a model, or something very much like one, for a liberal order yet to be devised by advanced societies. Hence the enormous appeal of his first collection of essays among nonspecialist readers of a certain temperament.

Among anthropologists, Clastres's thesis has been the object of much debate.[39] He was criticized in particular for having concluded too much from his observations on the Guayaki, overlooking the fact that many primitive societies had been ruled by chiefs or priests who were as authoritarian as they were brutal, some asserting a right of life or death over all those subject to their absolute power (in which case the relationship of master to subject, so far from having been dispensed with, assumed its most extreme form). Of greater interest for our purposes, however, is the fact that commentators invariably emphasized the role of law in Guayaki society. The leader's power to rule was limited, they pointed out, because the law laid down the rules by which the community lived. The law's authority in this respect was incontestable by virtue of the fact that it proceeded ultimately from a divine source, the transcendent supremacy of the gods having been superimposed on the sacred legacy of the community's ancestors. Human beings were therefore obligated, in the eyes of the Guayaki, to act in strict conformity with these inherited rules. They were rules, moreover, that could not be violated without endangering the very existence of Guayaki society, for they were the fruit of past experience, itself rooted in a primordial and supernatural creation. There was nothing new, then, that human beings had to invent in order to live well. A primitive society taking this view was the most conservative society imaginable. What is more, in a society opposed in principle to change in any form, the very notion of politics had no place. Politics consists precisely in a permanent reevaluation and adjustment of the rules of social life. To exercise power is to be capable of modifying these rules and adapting to what cannot be foreseen; to rule is to impose one's own law in a certain way.

The situation of the Guayaki chief was exactly opposite. He did not have to dictate to the community, only to recall an immemorial law that was inseparable from the founding myth that gave the group its identity. He was the spokesman of this law, in the strictest sense of the term. "From the mouth of the leader," as Clastres himself puts it, "spring not only the words that sanction the relationship of command-obedience, but also the discourse of society about itself, a discourse through which it proclaims itself an undivided community and proclaims its determination to continue in this undivided condition."[40] If there was neither a properly political sphere nor a state, this was because society excluded conflict and division from its midst. It could conceive of itself only as homogeneous. If disagreement emerged among the Guayaki, it was dealt with at once by expulsion. The law of the gods and ancestors was a law of obligatory unanimity. The leader could not issue commands that were the result of any personal decision; the words he spoke were sacrosanct, for "the leader, when he speaks, never expresses a personal whim or asserts a personal law, but only articulates a sociological desire, that the society remain undivided, and pronounces the words of a law that no one has laid down, for it is not a product of human decision."[41]

The Guayaki thus escaped domination by a leader only at the cost of blind submission to a law about which they had no say. Their emancipation from human political power was purchased at the price of absolute conformity to divine and ancestral tradition. This dependence was literally engraved, moreover, on the bodies of youths submitted to unimaginably cruel initiation rituals. "Society inscribes the words of the law on their bodies for all to see," Clastres notes. "For the law is the foundation of the social life of the tribe, something no one is meant to forget."[42] By means of these rituals the permanence of the law was established, and the equal dependence of all persons on it. Rule was totally internalized, and hidden beneath the outward appearance of a society having no government. Human liberty was therefore nothing more than a purely intellectual apprehension of necessity, the will having been identified with unfailing obedience to the commandments of nature and the gods.

Proudhon on the one hand, the Guayaki on the other—two utterly opposed ways of rejecting the idea of government by embracing the law, in the one case through its ceaseless propagation by means of contractual agreements and other forms of self-management, in the other by virtue of its superhuman authority. Together, they show that the demons of political domination and the asymmetries of power are exorcised only in the illusion of their denial.

Domination and Asymmetry

The challenge facing us now is to demonstrate that it is possible for the governed to escape domination by their governors, while at the same time recognizing the inherent asymmetry that obtains between the two. It requires that we have a clear understanding of the various ways in which power may be taken away from the governed, and a keen awareness of the constant risk that such confiscation will come to be institutionalized. The whole difficulty of giving a satisfactory definition of democratic government consists in just this. Some political thinkers have considered it to be an impossible task, particularly in view of the problem of democratic oligarchy. Historically, the analysis of democratic oligarchy has assumed two main forms: theories of aristocratic democracy, on the one hand, forged during the French Revolution and based on the assumption that voting operates as a technique of differentiation; and elite theory, on the other, which holds that in every political regime the exercise of power ends up being reserved to a small leadership group.[43] Robert Michels, for example, held that there is an iron law of organizations ("Whoever says organization says tendency to oligarchy"); Vilfredo Pareto, for his part, reckoned that the life of societies is chiefly marked by the constant transformation of dominant groups ("History is a graveyard of aristocracies").[44] Realist theories of this type have generally been understood by their authors as establishing the existence of objective laws from which no escape is possible. But they can also be seen in another light, as drawing up a map of tendencies threatening to undermine democratic life. Realist theories have their place in a theory of democracy, for to minimize such risks, or even to imagine that they can be wholly eliminated by pronouncing the equivalent of magic spells, always amounts in one way or another to obscuring them, thereby rendering domination illegible or invisible.

To have some idea of what the attempt to make government a part of democracy involves, we need to be able to say exactly how domination can be grafted onto the governed-governing relation. The first step is to distinguish it from the types of domination analyzed by Max Weber and Pierre Bourdieu. Following Weber, one may speak of *status domination.* The different cases he describes—traditional, rational-legal, and charismatic—involve forms of rule [*Herrschaft*] that are recognized and legitimized by individuals.[45] In each case there is a relationship of willing obedience to authority. This kind of consent is implicitly linked, in Weber's view, to the assumption that there exists an irreducible distinction between the masses and elites. Bourdieu, for his part, is primarily interested in the mechanisms by which a dominant class imposes its norms and values on some larger population. Here one may speak of a *conditioning domination* that causes such norms and values to be internalized as "natural" and "objective," and therefore to be legitimated.[46] Whereas Weber examines domination in an institutional context, Bourdieu treats it as a social and cultural phenomenon.

The governed-governing relationship in a democracy does not fit into either of these frameworks. It does, of course, rest on an asymmetry. But the domination relations that arise from it have no constitutive character; they do not give government one form rather than another. It is therefore necessary to speak instead of domination *effects,* which appear as various forms of dispossession, alienation, and exclusion, and which change the nature of the asymmetry by giving it the character of subjugation. What we find at work here are practices, behaviors, modes of organization, mechanisms of decision: an opaque institution produces a domination effect, even if the holder of its office was elected; demagogic appeals demean citizens while pretending to exalt them; a lack of attention to people's daily lives is equivalent to a negation of the representative principle; decisions taken in secret amount to a revival of arbitrary power.

The notions of domination elaborated by Weber and Bourdieu necessarily imply a structural relationship. The governed-governing relationship, by contrast, produces real domination effects in a democracy only in the event of its dysfunction, in the same way that the representation relationship comes to be distorted—so that representatives exercise power over their constituents—only as a result of deliberate manipulation. Furthermore, unlike what occurs in the situations characterized by Weber and Bourdieu, there is no consent on the part of the governed to the improper or unlawful conduct of their governors. In a democracy, citizens do not accept that a government can act as a father, or a master, or a god. The forms of practical rule they recognize do not entail acquiescence in a hierarchy. There is a sense, too, in which the position of a government is always precarious. Its decisions are often contested. The governed, skeptical of authority, are unwilling to bow down in submission, and therefore cannot be made to feel that they are naturally or in any other way inferior to their governors. Indeed, it is often with barely disguised contempt that they look upon those whom they themselves have nonetheless elected to public office.

In a democracy, then, it is idle to say that the governed take power for themselves, since it has already been taken away from them, in a manner of speaking, once they select their governors. Nor can they imagine taking it back through some more or less impossible form of self-government. It is only by regulating the conduct of those who govern them, and supervising the acts of government that are performed in their name, that power can truly be reappropriated. What is needed, then, is a practical way of thinking about democratic emancipation.

What Makes Democratic Government Democratic?

If democracy is a way of governing, and not only a regime, it must be defined by a way of exercising power that is peculiar to it. The distinctive characteristic of executive power is that it is determined by its own activity. Executive power cannot be understood in terms of its state and its function alone, however, as in the case of institutions. This point is crucial. A state specifies a set of initial conditions, a law of composition, and rules of operation; a function specifies operation over a bounded domain. Taken together, state and function determine the particular nature of an institution or kind of authority. Legislative power and judicial power can both be adequately characterized on the basis of such criteria. But they are not enough to account for the nature of executive power. To be sure, the manner of its formation, the conditions under which it may be exercised, its scope of authority in relation to other powers, and the principle of its function are all laid down in constitutions. But the practical application and influence of executive power also depend on things that are more difficult to formalize, matters of custom and habit that are shaped by the passage of time.

In order to understand the way in which executive power is exercised, we must consider not only the content of decisions, but how they are reached. At the same time we need to keep in mind that the legitimacy of those who govern, and of public agents in general, depends on how their performance is judged. Many studies have shown that ordinary citizens need no instruction in this regard.[47] Voters want to be heard, to be taken seriously, to be kept informed, to be treated with respect, to be involved in making decisions. If these conditions are met, they will be more readily disposed to accept public policy choices that may be unfavorable to them personally. They will, however, instinctively doubt the soundness of decisions by government officials that appear to be poorly thought out and then put into effect without any meaningful consultation beforehand.[48]

Voters are not asking for direct democracy, in the technical sense of the term, even if they do favor referendums being held from time to time on particular questions. What voters really want is that government officials do their jobs competently and diligently, in the belief that their first duty is to serve the general interest, not to further their own careers. Voters accept the division of labor between governed and governing, but only on the condition that their desires in this regard are fully satisfied. In that case they are prepared to tolerate having only intermittent electoral sovereignty ("stealth democracy," as it is sometimes called). But they despise nothing more than elected officials who regard themselves first and foremost as representatives of their parties,[49] unless it is their tendency to shut themselves up in their own little world, apart from the people who have elected them. What voters want, in other words, is that government be as transparent as possible.

We need therefore to describe the essential elements of this relationship, between the governed and their governors, in order to determine what makes democratic government democratic. In what follows I discuss three such aspects: legibility, responsibility, responsiveness. Then, in Part 4, I turn to the main qualities required of democratic leaders themselves: truthfulness and integrity. Let us begin by examining the qualities of good government, which sketch the contours of a *democracy of appropriation*.

10

Legibility

WITH THE ADVENT OF modernity came new methods for making human activities legible and measurable. Nowhere did they have greater consequence than in the economic sphere. Double-entry book-keeping was invented in the fourteenth century, making it possible for debits to be put into correspondence with credits; its spread followed the worldwide advance of the market economy and capitalism. Beyond its usefulness as a management tool, this form of accounting made the activity of a merchant or a manufacturer legible. Prospective dealings with lenders or borrowers of funds could now be objectively examined as well, and the soundness of their financial positions monitored and evaluated.[1] Very soon the term "accounting" acquired a dual meaning, so that the passive idea of bookkeeping came to be bound up with the more active, relational view of a rendering of accounts. Etymologically, the notion of *accountability* had this dual meaning from the very beginning. The word itself derived from an Anglo-Norman expression of old French origin that had been used in the eleventh century by agents of William the Conqueror, who sought to establish the new royal government in England, and therefore also the power to levy tax, on the basis of an itemized inventory of the assets of the kingdom's landed proprietors.[2] The historical roots of this key word in the modern political lexicon clearly bring out the relationship between power and the auditing of accounts.

If power is action, whoever controls action exerts power to the same extent. Indeed, it was on just this principle that the democratic impulse first began to take shape. Already in ancient Greece one finds alongside magistrates a whole series of appointed officials—a special class of inspectors known as straighteners (*euthynoi*), accountants (*logistai*), comptrollers, public advocates—who played an essential role in examining the handling of money by elected officials.[3] In the parishes and urban communities of medieval Europe, the auditing of accounts was not infrequently a source of considerable power. Later it was to be at the heart of the modern parliamentary system.

The Eye of Parliament on the Government

England was the major laboratory in the development of parliamentary institutions. Even before the cycle of revolutions that began in the mid-seventeenth century, the publication in 1610 by the king's first minister of an accounting of receipts and expenses marked a decisive innovation. The need to increase state revenues in periods of conflict led finally to the crown's acceptance of more systematic supervision of the use of public funds by Parliament. With the end of the second Anglo-Dutch War of 1665–1667 an Accounts Commission came to be established, the first of its kind.[4] One must be careful, of course, not to take an overly simplistic view of this chapter in the history of parliamentarianism. Quite apart from the reluctance of the king's ministers, many members of Parliament were no less hesitant to embark upon this path. For conservatives, the idea of accountability could not help but have a revolutionary resonance as an outgrowth of the forced modernization of the state during the Civil War (1642–1651).[5] A preliminary proposal for an Accounts Commission, equipped with strongly augmented powers by comparison with earlier draft versions, had been put forward in 1644, and the Commission's prerogatives were subsequently to be enlarged in stages over the rest of the century. Other members of Parliament feared more generally that a monitoring of public accounts would strengthen the government's ties with the two Chambers, and encourage it to make greater financial demands in the future. It was for this reason that the prospect of greater accountability came to be associated in many people's minds with the idea of big government. And they were not wrong, at least in relative terms, since taxation in England over the course of the eighteenth century was twice as high as in France. Nevertheless the burden was tolerated, for the establishment of a parliamentary regime allowed public expenditures to be examined by the people's representatives and made known throughout the country,[6] whereas the secrecy of French absolutism gave rise to incessant tax revolts.

Even so, and notwithstanding that the first experiments with accountability were made in England, the first manifesto arguing for the virtues of financial transparency came from France. In January 1781 Jacques Necker created a sensation by publishing a record of royal finances, the *Compte rendu au Roi*, which clearly assembled for the first time all the information needed to assess the balance of state revenues and expenditures and the composition of public debt. Though it was illustrated with a forbidding array of tables and figures, Necker's work aroused immense curiosity; it was the great best-seller of the period, with more than 80,000 copies finding readers in every corner of the kingdom. In the "Letter to the King" that serves as an introduction to the volume,[7] Necker points to the benefits that would accrue to the country from publishing such information on a regular basis. "An institution of this sort, were it to be made permanent, would be a source of the greatest advantages," he maintained. "The obligation to display the whole record of his administration would influence a minister of finances from the very beginning of his career in office." At the same time, while the dissemination of public accounts promised to exert a positive constraint on administration, it should also make it possible to protect administrators against unscrupulous critics. "The hope of this publicity," Necker noted, "would make [the people] still more indifferent to these obscure writings, with which one seeks to disturb an administrator's peace of mind, and whose authors, sure that a man of lofty spirit will not descend into the arena to respond to them, profit from his silence in order to unsettle some opinions by means of lies."[8]

More generally, transparency would have a beneficial political and social effect, he felt, because to "constantly make a mystery of the state of finances" breeds mistrust.[9] The need to instill public confidence was to be a recurrent theme of Necker's writings, not least in his major work published three years later, on the administration of the finances of France. He was the first to emphasize the cognitive and intertemporal dimension of confidence, "this precious sentiment which unites the future to the present, which gives some idea of the permanency of the goods [people enjoy] and of the term of the difficulties [they endure]."[10] He likened nations in this respect to "old men whom a long experience of the errors and injustices of mankind has rendered suspicious and distrustful." When transparency rules, however, "difficulties disappear, and credit is then given to the [benevolent] intentions of ministers."[11] Necker was an Anglophile, and his admiration for British institutions was sharply criticized by opponents at home. In a single stroke, however, he had managed to go further than reformers across the Channel, as the procrastinations of the Accounts Commission there during the 1780s testified. For this reason Necker's treatise was to have an enormous impact in Europe, foreshadowing the modern practice of presenting a government's budget. Necker also stressed the importance of printing a document of estimated revenues and proposed spending, so that it could be read and freely commented upon. In giving a theoretical explanation of the benefits that might be derived from such an enterprise of "public notoriety,"[12] he anticipated the first formulations of a *democracy of the public* in which the notion of publicity enlarged that of representation.

A few years later, the French Revolution set forth the basic principles of such a democracy. The Declaration of the Rights of Man and the Citizen stipulated that "society has the right to require of every public agent an account of his administration" (article 15), and that the people have the right, by virtue of their contribution to state revenues, "to know to what uses it is put" (article 14). Both these provisions were to be adopted by the Constitutions of 1791 and 1793, and an agency responsible for inspecting official accounts, the Commission de la comptabilité, was set up in 1792. Although it fell far short of fully realizing revolutionary ambitions in this regard, an impetus had nonetheless been imparted and a direction indicated.[13]

Parliamentary oversight of government did not come to be actively exercised until the nineteenth century. The increasing financial transparency of the state was accompanied everywhere by the rise of representative government and democracy, with liberals identifying their struggle on behalf of a more robust parliamentary regime with the improvement of procedures governing budgetary deliberations. In France, under the Bourbon Restoration, the practice of approving ministerial appropriations on the basis of specialized "budget chapters" did much to stimulate debate on the meaning and purpose of representative government. The principle of drawing up the state budget on the basis of separate accounts, one for each category ("chapter") of government expenditure, was established in 1827 and put into effect four years later with the adoption of a systematic procedure for voting by chapters. Whereas appropriations had been authorized for seven ministries in 1814, and for fifty-two sections in 1827, in 1831 there were votes on 116 chapters—a number that grew to 400 in 1877, and 933 in 1911. These figures testify by themselves to the growing maturity of the French parliamentary tradition. Under the influence of this authorization procedure, a modern system of public finances was gradually put in place, and the budget, in the form of a finance law, now provided deputies with a quantitative picture of the state's activities. It symbolized the advent of a fiscal regime that was regular, not only in the technical sense that it constrained government through the institution of a set of clear and enforceable rules, but also in the political sense that the annual publication of a record of actual and projected expenditures made the approval of a government's budget a central element of public debate outside parliament itself. Discussion of the finance law in the Chamber of Deputies provoked comment and caused questions to be raised throughout the country, where the interest aroused in the first place by newspaper reports and editorial opinion was carried on by a flood of booklets and pamphlets. All of this in its way represented a reappropriation of the state by society.

Popular Oversight of Parliament

The call for parliamentary supervision of government was coupled from the earliest days of the French Revolution with a demand for a public record of the activities of the people's representatives. Even before the Estates-General gave way to the National Assembly, men such as Brissot urged the adoption of a mode of deliberating "such that the public can always watch over its representatives,"[14] publicity being equivalent in their eyes to a form of participation. When a member on the right side of the chamber had suggested that "strangers be removed,"[15] so that the deputies might deliberate among themselves in peace, he was sternly rebuked:

> Strangers! Are there any among us? Has the honor you received from them when you were named deputy made you forget that they are your brothers and your fellow citizens? Have you forgotten that you are only

their representative, their proxy? And is it your intention to withdraw yourself from their gaze, when you owe them an account of all your proceedings, of all your thoughts? Would that our fellow citizens surround us on all sides, that they press up against us, that their presence may inspire us and encourage us.[16]

This indignant response calls our attention to a revealing point of terminology: the term "strangers" (*étrangers*) was long to be used in the rules of procedure of parliamentary assemblies, both in France and Great Britain, to refer to the members of the public admitted to watch debates from the gallery—a habit suggesting that a certain esprit de corps had characterized parliamentary life from its very beginnings.

The justification of a public presence in the chamber was connected with a newly enlarged conception of representation, in which the holding of office was meant to be part of a permanent conversation with society. Already at the outset of the Revolution, then, the concept of *representative democracy,* a form intermediate between strict representative government and direct democracy, had been worked out in some detail. It is significant that women, who did not vote, were often seen in the visitors' galleries during the Revolution—proof of the symbolic and political importance of galleries in helping to extend the reach of representative procedures. The question of galleries was at the heart of debates over the architectural design of the meeting hall of the National Assembly during the revolutionary period. Robespierre, in his famous speech of 10 May 1793 on representative government, regarded "the admission of a few hundred spectators crammed into a narrow and uncomfortable place" to be inadequate.[17] Arguing that "the entire nation has the right to know the conduct of its mandatories,"[18] he went so far as to say: "Were it possible, the assembly of the people's delegates ought to deliberate in the presence of all the people. The meetings of the legislative body should take place in a vast and majestic edifice, open to 12,000 spectators. Under the eyes of so great a number of witnesses, neither corruption, nor intrigue, nor perfidy would dare show its face; the general will alone would be consulted, the voice of reason and of the public interest would be the only one heard."[19] To give the principle of publicity still greater effect, Robespierre spoke rather picturesquely of a *physical responsibility*. In the event, however, for practical reasons, the capacity of the galleries during this period ended up being limited to a few hundred spectators.

Whereas the Revolution had in many respects made the imperative of publicity more urgent in France, progress had slowed in Great Britain ever since the seventeenth century. A strict prohibition against entry by outsiders, explicitly declared in 1650 in the midst of civil war, was renewed on seven occasions during the following two centuries.[20] The public was not allowed to attend the debates of the House of Commons until 1845, when a fixed quota of places equal to half the number of members was finally approved. It is true that the architecture of the Palace of Westminster presented an obstacle to larger attendance. Women were long excluded from the chamber itself, being restricted to a ladies' gallery with limited visibility up until a few years before they first gained partial suffrage in 1869.[21]

The arrangement and dimensions of galleries were discussed at great length in all democratic countries during the nineteenth century. At the time it was generally accepted that parliamentary architecture ought symbolically to reflect the people's primary sovereignty. Reconstruction of such buildings in Australia and Germany toward the end of the twentieth century testified to the permanence of this preoccupation, even though in the meantime the televised broadcast of debates had practically everywhere modified the fashion in which it was felt necessary to accommodate a public presence. In Canberra, in the early 1980s, the architects had been asked to keep two things uppermost in mind.[22] It had first been decided, for strictly functional reasons, that the executive and the legislature should reside under the same roof in view of the growing convergence of interests between the two branches of government. At the same time a greater share of the space was granted to the executive as a way of emphasizing that Parliament was to be thought of not so much as a body meant to supervise the executive, which was responsible to it, as a body meant to maintain the executive in power.[23] It was also desired, in the second place, that Parliament should be made to display as fully as possible its character as a place of the people. Thus the architect who won the competition crowned the building with a vast roof terrace where the public could freely move about, above the representatives sitting beneath their feet. Still more important, large interior floor spaces were designed in such a way that visitors could make their way to the physical heart of the building—proof of the openness of parliamentary proceedings to public view.

A few years later, the return of the German capital to Berlin following reunification inspired plans for reconstructing the old Reichstag. The imposing shell of the Wilhelmine building was preserved, with the addition once again of a roof terrace accessible to the public by elevator. But here the striking feature was that the debating chamber is surmounted by a great glass cupola rising from the terrace, so that visitors can look directly down upon their representatives. The visual impression of transparency was intensified by the placement at the center of the cupola of a cone of convex mirrors directed downward to the center of the hemicycle, offering every spectator a panoptic view of the workings of the chamber below. The German and Australian models have been imitated several times since, notably in the case of the Parliament of Flanders in Belgium and the National Assembly for Wales in the United Kingdom. In both these cases, the commissioning organs of government had expressly asked the architects to give material expression to the idea of open government.

Beyond the physical accessibility of representative assemblies, publication of parliamentary debates was also considered to be essential. In France, the principle of publicity had been accepted since the earliest days of the Revolution. *Le Moniteur universel* introduced itself in its first issue (November 1789) as a "historian of the workings of the Assembly."[24] But the appearance of a complete record of its sessions lay yet far in the future. Publication did not assume the form of anything even approaching full-length quotation until 1835; and it was only in 1848 that the Assembly equipped itself with a stenographic department capable of producing faithful reports of parliamentary debate. From the beginning of the Third Republic, two decades later, all documents circulating within the two chambers (draft legislation, reports on members' bills, inquiries, and so on) were simultaneously published in series of *Annales parliamentaires.*

Across the Channel, it was not until the end of the eighteenth century that parliamentary debates became the object of detailed public accounts. Documents concerning parliamentary activity had circulated before then, to be sure, but they were concise, seldom containing more than summaries of votes and the daily order of business, and passed only among members of the houses. In the seventeenth century, staff of the two chambers were strictly forbidden to take notes of official business. Bits and pieces of the private record, mostly having to do with personal indiscretions of one sort or another, nonetheless began to leak out into the press in the early eighteenth century, but without the reported remarks ever being attributed to a specific speaker. The House of Commons reacted sharply to these early forms of publicity in 1738, reserving the most severe sanctions for members who wrote down what was said in debate—and with some success, it would appear, since one Parliament of the 1760s is actually described as an "unreported Parliament."[25] The hostility to publicity was not connected with politically reactionary sentiment, as it was during the same period in France, where *raison d'État* theorists openly praised the virtues of secrecy. Parliamentarians, whether they were members of the House of Lords or of the House of Commons, regarded it in the first place as an expression of their independence.[26] The two chambers considered themselves to be *privileged bodies,* which is to say assemblies endowed with specific prerogatives that were theirs and theirs alone.[27] Their autonomy—primarily in relation to the power of the throne, of course, but more broadly in relation to anything that threatened to restrict their own power—was sacred, having been won by force of arms during the revolutionary period. It was therefore not the principle of publicity in itself that was objected to, but rather the way in which it was acted on by the press. And yet representatives also considered themselves to be responsible above all for fulfilling a *constitutional function,*[28] without any corresponding obligation to answer to their constituents.

The two principles were plainly in conflict. It was a question not so much of a tension between a right to secrecy and a right to publicity, however, as of a tension between a privilege claimed by the two chambers and a right to publish asserted by newspapers that had become used to printing whatever information they were able to gather from various sources. The great debate on the question took place in 1771 in the House of Commons. John Wilkes, an intrepid champion of expanded liberties, defended the freedom of printers to publish accurate accounts of parliamentary debates. Wilkes did not succeed in winning the approval of his colleagues on this occasion, but the controversy nonetheless marked a turning point, and printers were rarely taken to court afterward. Even so, many decades were to pass before verbatim reports were allowed to openly circulate. It was only with the Reform Act of 1832 that the public character of parliamentary activity was affirmatively recognized, this at a time when the principle of representation was beginning to be reconceived. Both houses then took practical steps to enable the press to do its job (a private arrangement having been negotiated with the *Hansard* for an official transcript to be made publicly available). Finally, in 1909, the two houses resolved to publish their proceedings themselves. Respect for their privileges and the democratic concern for publicity now at last coincided.

Bentham and the Eyes of Democracy

Jeremy Bentham was the first to compose a genuine treatise on the publicity of parliamentary affairs, included as part of his posthumously published *Essay on Political Tactics*.[29] As a young man, Bentham had drawn up designs for a novel type of prison, the Panopticon, with a view to improving the rehabilitation of criminals. His thinking on this subject attracted fresh interest almost two centuries later with the appearance of Michel Foucault's book *Surveiller et punir* in 1975.[30] Foucault saw this "eye of power" as the original model for a new kind of government-enforced discipline.[31] But Bentham himself attached still greater importance to creating an *eye of the people,* which he saw as the essential element of democratic modernity. In this connection he advanced five main justifications for the principle of publicity.

The primary function of publicity, Bentham held, is to bring popular pressure to bear on representatives so that they will feel obliged "to perform their duty." For the incentives to neglect this duty are many: "The greater the number of temptations to which the exercise of political power is exposed," he concluded, "the more necessary is it to give to those who possess it, the most powerful reasons for resisting them. But there is no reason more constant and more universal than the superintendence of the public. The public compose a tribunal, which is more powerful than all the other tribunals together."[32] For Bentham, no institution can be its own judge, not least because the unavoidable effects of partisan division deprive it of impartiality. The monitoring of government by public opinion would introduce a mechanism of *compensatory continuity* in the representative system, since it operates on a permanent basis, whereas elections are by their very nature intermittent.

The second aim of publicity is to "secure the confidence of the people, and their assent to the measures of the legislature." In this respect Bentham regarded it as a means of strengthening the government's credibility and helping it to conduct its affairs more efficiently: "In an open and free policy, what confidence and security [there is]—I do not say for the people, but for the governors themselves!" Publicity served this purpose in two ways. First, by eliminating the poison of mystery, and with it public suspicion. "Suspicion," he emphasized, "always attaches to mystery. It thinks it sees a crime where it beholds an affectation of secresy; and it is rarely deceived. For why should we hide ourselves if we do not dread being seen? In proportion as it is desirable for improbity to shroud itself in darkness, in the same proportion is it desirable for innocence to walk in open day, for fear of being mistaken for her adversary." Second, publicity gives everyone a clearer view of where matters stand once contrary positions have been vigorously stated in open debate. In that case, "objections have been refuted,—false reports confounded; the necessity for the sacrifices required of the people have [sic] been clearly proved. Opposition, with all its efforts, far from having been injurious to authority, will have essentially assisted it. It is in this sense that it has been well said, *that he who resists, strengthens:* for the government is much more assured of the general success of a measure, and of the public approbation, after it has been discussed by two parties, whilst the whole nation has been spectators."[33]

In the third place, publicity serves a reciprocal function. "In the same proportion as it is desirable for the governed to know the conduct of their governors," Bentham observed, "is it also important for the governors to know the real wishes of the governed." Furthermore, publicity is an essential condition of the proper functioning of the electoral system, for it "enable[s] the electors to act from knowledge." If to elect is to choose, the only good choice is an informed choice. In the absence of publicity, hazard and caprice rule. This, then, is the fourth reason: a lack of publicity would sever the bond between reason and democracy, and "add inconsequence to prevarication." The fifth, and final, reason is that publicity would provide representatives and those who govern "with the means of profiting from the information of the public." Bentham readily conceded that "[a] nation too numerous to act for itself, is doubtless obliged to entrust its powers to its deputies." But that begged the crucial question. Will these representatives "possess in concentration all the national intelligence?" he asked. "Is it even possible that the elected shall be in every respect the most enlightened, the most capable, the wisest persons in the nation?—that they will possess, among themselves alone, all the general and local knowledge which the function of governing requires? This prodigy of election is a chimera." Bentham was alert to the underlying sociological problem of representation, sensing that few of the most intellectually distinguished persons of his time had an interest in entering politics or, if they did, had the means to do so. Only through publicity would the political sphere be able to benefit from their ideas and their experience, for it was "a means of collecting all the information in a nation, and consequently for giving birth to useful suggestions."[34] The enemies of publicity in politics therefore comprised three categories, all of them disreputable: *malefactors,* who seek to escape the notice of a judge; *despots,* eager to smother public opinion, whose force they dread; and, finally, *incompetents,* who constantly justify their inaction by the supposed irresolution of the public.

The Triumph of Visibility over Legibility

Where do matters stand today from this point of view? The principles Bentham laid down seem to be universally accepted in democracies, except for one difference of vocabulary (to which I will return in Chapter 15), namely, that the word "transparency" is now commonly used to express a desire for what is called open government. The scope of this latter notion has come to be considerably enlarged in the interval. Whereas the imperative of legibility was historically restricted on the whole to budgetary and financial questions, it is unfettered access to information that is now insisted on in all spheres of public policy, including matters of foreign affairs, defense, and education that were long considered to be governed by reasons of state. Exposure of what in the United States are called state secrets is demanded and justified on grounds of accountability, both to parliaments and to society.[35] Citizens wish to be able to penetrate the "black boxes" of decision making, whether these conceal the functioning of ministries or the activity of representative institutions. Today the democratic ideal of transparency finds itself more and more urgently called upon to combat opacity in all the many forms that threaten its very existence.

But at the same time it is apparent that we are dealing not solely with a binary opposition between secrecy and transparency. The problem also has to do with the legibility of things, which implies an act of interpretation. Here it is plain to all that the world may often be illegible, even as we find ever larger quantities of instantly accessible information at our disposal; and furthermore that there is a widening discrepancy between legibility and the ever greater visibility of political figures. Whether this constant increase in visibility is a consequence of celebrity culture and its various vehicles, or of the waves of images driven onward by the development of new communications technologies, or of the reciprocal compulsions of seeing and being seen,[36] it has had the effect of making citizens feel closer (usually in superficial ways, it must be said) to those who hold power. Yet at the same time public institutions have become more opaque in the eyes of ordinary people, decision making more impenetrable, policies more difficult to evaluate. The comprehensibility of the political world, in other words, has diminished. But there is a deeper problem, that the tensions produced by rising visibility in an age of receding legibility aggravate mistrust and disenchantment, and feed a growing sense of alienation from public service. This situation is the opposite of what was long true of democracies in the past, when the motives of public policy were readily interpreted, at least by comparison with today, and public figures were seldom seen.[37]

What is taking place now is a kind of return to the ancien régime in France. Royal power then was carefully displayed, even as the business of the King's Council was conducted with the greatest secrecy, away from public view. Legibility and visibility were already dissociated in those days, and deliberately so. Louis XIV embodied this distinction with surpassing brilliance. Never had a monarch been so public a figure. No moment of his day, from getting up in the morning until going to bed at night, was private; even his mistresses were openly acknowledged. "We are not a private person," he said of himself. "We are wholly devoted to the public."[38] To be sure, the people looked on from a certain distance, but they were nonetheless bound all the more closely to the object of their fascination by what Pascal called the "cords of imagination."[39] The important thing to keep in mind, however, is that this artfully managed spectacle existed side by side with the most complete discretion regarding how decisions of state were reached. The king was frequently seen but rarely heard. In the person of Louis XIV, ostentation was inseparable from silence, light from mystery.[40] The way in which the sovereign's doings were reported by the most influential newspapers of the period, *Le Mercure de France* and *La Gazette de France*, replicated this dualism. What was made public concerned only the incidental details of his daily schedule, described as concisely as possible: "the King heard morning mass"; "the Court went to Marly"; "the King, Queen, and such-and-such a member of the royal family came to Paris and did this and that"; and so on. There was never any mention of his foreign policy or the management of the kingdom's finances, still less of meetings of the King's Council.

The historical roots of this dissociation between visibility and legibility should remind us of the importance of a *politics of legibility* in democratic life. Policies, and the institutions that carry them out, must be generally understood if citizens are to be able to claim ownership. Democracy consists in just this possibility. Illegibility, by contrast, amounts to a form of confiscation. Understanding power, the mechanisms and procedures by which it operates, is one of the modern ways of "taking power" (to use perhaps the most misleading of all political expressions—for power is not a thing, but a relation). To be ruled, on the other hand, is to be put in one's place, made subject to institutions whose opacity and complexity effectively strip people of their citizenship. In the aftermath of the two first historical stages of publicity, parliamentary oversight of the executive having been extended by popular oversight of parliamentary activity, a third, more exacting way of promoting publicity began to take shape as citizens *themselves* took it upon themselves to inquire into the functioning of public institutions. This initiative, which may well be seen as an expression of the contemporary demand for direct democracy, requires not only information but also legibility. This, in turn, as I have already had occasion to emphasize, implies an ability to interpret events and grasp their implications. Legibility in this active sense has now established itself as a cornerstone of the republican ideal.

Its opposite, illegibility, inevitably creates disenchantment and rejection. Consider the situation of European institutions today. There can be no doubt that the growth of Euroscepticism, of which the spectacular increase in rates of abstention in elections to the European Parliament in Brussels and in Strasbourg is only one of the most obvious signs, is directly tied to the feeling of dispossession that illegibility produces. It has been sustained by the fact that political talk about Europe typically refers to an entity that does not exist, but on which are projected all those desires that no longer seem able to be satisfied at the national level: the desire for a Europe that would provide social protection against the adverse effects of globalization; for a Europe that would wield power abroad at a moment when the medium-sized nations composing it struggle to influence foreign affairs; for a Europe that would regulate markets and curb their excesses. In the eyes of the continent's citizens, as a result, Europe appears much smaller than it really is. "Europe" is a name associated with the disillusionment that comes of seeing these desires not realized, and of having only a very partial view of a vast bureaucracy whose sole occupation appears to consist in issuing an ever larger volume of rules and requirements, interrupted from time to time by tedious summit meetings. This is not what Europe actually is, of course, any more than it is a sort of unfinished parliamentary democracy. A great edifice has in fact been built around three central institutions: a Commission, a Court of Justice, and a Central Bank. But for the ordinary citizen these organs of government might as well *literally* be black boxes, so completely do they appear to occupy a world of their own, their inner workings hidden from view.

Power is exercised for the most part by the experts, judges, and technocrats who preside over these nominally independent institutions, making new law and promulgating regulations and standards in a constantly growing number of fields. But what may be described as an "implicit" European model has been devised behind the scenes, gropingly, one step at a time, without having really been thought through. One rightly speaks in this connection of a "stealth strategy," a "cloak of invisibility."[41] European institutions constitute an almost purely negative expression of impersonality that lies outside anyone's control. Hence the pervasive sense that there exists a "democratic deficit." And yet for want of legibility, for want of any clear idea how the powers of the institutions housed in Brussels—the European Commission, Council of the European Union, European Council, and one of the two official seats of the European Parliament—are actually exercised, it is a feeling that has been able to express itself only in the form of a demand that classical parliamentarian democracy operate at this supranational level. To be sure, reforms have been made in this direction, notably with the enlargement of the European Parliament's prerogatives by the Treaty of Lisbon in 2009. They have nonetheless run up against the fact that the power of arbitration remains in the hands of the Council formed by the heads of state of member nations, and that the question of who should serve as the head of an executive branch therefore cannot be put to a vote by the citizens of Europe. The result is that democratic expectations formulated in traditional electoral-representative terms,[42] which cannot truly be said to apply in this case since Europe is not advancing toward the formation of a federal state,[43] are bound to remain unfulfilled in the shadow of three great autonomous and opaque institutions holding real power.

Democratizing the European Union would mean honestly acknowledging this discrepancy and making the actual functioning of its institutions comprehensible to the Union's citizens. Here legibility implies a concerted effort to encourage debate about the missions of these institutions and their mandates, to hold them responsible for their conduct, make their deliberations and their ways of governing more transparent, oblige them to explain and justify proposed courses of future action and to tolerate the public expression of dissenting opinions.[44] Plainly, democratization in this case does not require the election by universal suffrage of the officials of these institutions. It requires that citizens have the ability, through analysis of readily available information and public discussion, to monitor the activity of these institutions and to have a say in their decisions. Only once they have a thorough and critical understanding of the real power these institutions exercise will citizens be able to decide on the uses to which it should be put, by making it a subject of national debate in every member country.

The present state of the European Union is a particularly illuminating case of the political costs of illegibility and the problematic implications of impersonality. Many other examples exhibiting these same features could be cited, whether they concern government institutions proper or the public policies they design and implement. But opacity has still more perverse consequences. To the extent that it favors the spread of a conspiratorial outlook on the world, it poses a distinct threat to democracy.

The Demons of Opacity

Both Jeremy Bentham and Benjamin Constant laid emphasis on the importance of eliminating the poison of suspicion by means of publicity. I have already referred to Bentham in this connection. Constant, for his part, argued that an official act performed outside of public view can never be completely justified and that decisions taken in secrecy by those in power are liable always to have "the appearance of connivance and complicity." What is more, he added, "perils are not averted by concealing them from view. On the contrary, they multiply in the darkness that shrouds them. Objects grow larger in the night. In the darkness of night, everything appears hostile and gigantic."[45] The terms of this problem have changed considerably in the intervening two centuries. In a world in which information, and the disinformation, revelations, and scandals to which it gives rise, are broadcast continually, suspicion of those who govern finds new sources of inspiration on all sides—and this all the more as the old habit of respect for authority has been given up and, with the decline of the other two "invisible institutions," converted into an attitude of instinctive mistrust.[46]

The sense of powerlessness that weighs on many people is apt to provoke what may be thought of as compensatory attempts at imaginary rationalization. Conspiracy theories, as they are more often called, seek to restore coherence to a world that is experienced as incomprehensible and threatening.[47] They claim to show that, behind the obscurity and apparent complexity of events, a perfectly simple and rational kind of power is at work. They allow people who feel they are at the mercy of circumstances, reduced to the condition of pawns and helpless spectators, mere playthings, to reestablish order in a chaotic world and thereby make sense of it. They promise a way of reappropriating the course of events by exposing its hidden engines. Illegibility is thus taken to be the sign of an organized enterprise of dissimulation in the service of a plan to dominate and / or exploit ordinary people. The enterprise itself is usually understood to be worldwide, in order to explain its exceptional influence; in the extreme case, it is regarded as the motive force of human history.[48] Concealed by the smoke screen of legal institutions are a small number of powers (Trilateral Commission, CIA, Illuminati, Elders of Zion, and so on) that pull all the strings. The revelation of a few cases of manipulation, alas quite genuine, suffices for all situations to be interpreted in the same light. On this view, citizens need to be made aware of the vast schemes hatched by mysterious elites so that they will no longer be fooled by the democratic façade of modern politics.[49] One may speak in this sense of conspiracy theories as having a dual *cognitive and political function,* that is, of dispelling a widespread sense of dispossession and of attributing responsibility for the misfortunes of humanity. It is supplemented, moreover, by a *psychological function,* of making it possible for anyone to find simple answers to the problems he faces. Tocqueville

had noted in this connection long before that "a false yet clear and precise idea will always have more potency in society at large than a true
but complex one."[50]

Periods of change and moments that mark a sharp break with the past
are particularly auspicious for the growth of conspiracy theories and
the spread of rumors, as though events must always outrun our powers
of understanding. This state of affairs has been very well studied in the
case of eighteenth-century France. Arlette Farge has shown, for example, how popular rumors of the age sprang from a tacit but very real
desire on the part of the most humble members of society to involve
themselves in matters of state, hoping in this way to gain some insight
into the mysteries of power and the secrets of the Court.[51] Rumors often
had the effect, then and later, of crystallizing and amplifying collective fears, hopes, and hatreds.[52] Marc Bloch analyzed the false news
that circulated during the First World War in the same fashion, observing that it invariably arose from widely held ideas that predated its
appearance, forming a sort of mirror in which the collective consciousness could contemplate its own features.[53]

Conspiracy theories flourished during the French and American
Revolutions as well. In France, freemasons, aristocrats, speculators, and
Girodins were all stigmatized by turns in order to account for the revolutionaries' failure to achieve their objectives, on the one hand, and the
horrifying excesses to which it led, on the other. By placing blame all
around it became possible for the country's difficulties to be given a
simple explanation, and for the doubtfulness of democratic ideals to be
safely ignored. On the other side of the Atlantic, in the 1760s and 1770s,
the belief gained currency that the mounting tensions with the British
crown could proceed only from the covert designs of diabolical forces
plotting against liberty in the two countries.[54] Even Burke entertained
the possibility that a "double cabinet" was intriguing against the people
behind the scenes, as a way of explaining the discontent that was keenly
felt by many in England at the time.[55]

Conspiracy theories flourished once more at the turn of the twenty-
first century. Considering the basic points I have just briefly mentioned,
it is not difficult to see why. Wars, financial crises, and terrorist attacks
had made the world an unpredictable and menacing place. History was
now harder to make sense of than when East-West rivalry structured
and guided the course of geopolitics. The progress of globalization had

moreover instituted a faceless unification under the dominion of anonymous market forces and the ascendancy of unelected authorities of one kind or another. All this made events even less legible than before, responsibility less easily assigned, and the true sources of power more difficult to discern. Opportunities for action seemed at the same time to have become fewer, feeding a vague feeling of abandonment, of having been left behind. Together these things helped to bring about a vigorous resurgence of the old styles of magical thinking and paranoid suspicion.

Today the increased availability of uninterrupted streams of information, especially via the Internet, has further strengthened the credibility of conspiratorial rationalizations by permitting alternative views of reality to emerge. Objective and verifiable data coexist with mere opinions and rumors in a state of cyber chaos that allows them all to be treated on an equal basis.[56] There is no more urgent task, then, than improving the transparency of institutions and decision making in order to ward off the demons of opacity, which rob citizens of the power to see clearly and think critically as actors in a history of their own making.

Legibility and the Right to Know

For individuals in their relationship to institutions, gaining access to information has always been of decisive importance. Here again the question of power has not only to do with what is rightfully one's own, one's personal property, but also with the nature of the relation that obtains between those who hold authority and those who are subservient to it: the relation of worker to boss, of constituent to representative, of the governed to the governing. In the economic sphere, for example, the labor movement, formed with the ultimate aim of abolishing wage labor (objected to as a form of subordination), set about mobilizing support not only for the right of industrial workers to higher pay, social security, and improved working conditions, but also for the public disclosure of information about how businesses are run. The campaign for workers' control had made this last point a central element of its demands since the early part of the twentieth century. "Open the books" was the watchword in Great Britain. At the same time a parallel movement was led by shareholders and investors who wanted to be able to evaluate a company's real present situation and its prospects for the future (a 1930 law in the United States marked the first great step forward in this connection). Later, beginning in the 1960s, citizen monitoring groups appeared in various spheres of social life. Innovations were again particularly notable in the United States, with the advent of so-called good government organizations and litigation in the public interest ("cause lawyering"). In 1971 Ralph Nader launched his Public Citizen movement, with special emphasis on protecting the rights of consumers. Another nongovernmental organization, Common Cause, having recruited and trained some 400,000 supporters in citizen advocacy, achieved considerable success with regard to campaign finance reform and disclosure requirements. On a smaller scale, The People's Lobby used techniques of direct democracy authorized in California to reform certain aspects of local politics in that state.[57]

No such movements existed on the same scale in Europe during these years. The reasons for this are straightforward. Political parties were closer to citizens then than they are now, and took an active role in defending their interests; they were thus more representative than in America, where parties functioned chiefly as machines for getting out the vote. Furthermore, the idea that radical social change was still possible in Europe caused priority to be attached to mass demonstrations and other broad-based displays of political will at the expense of concerted attempts at reform, which, being more narrowly focused, were considered to be of secondary importance. Demands for greater transparency first gained traction in Europe with pressure from consumers to obtain accurate information about product ingredients, reliability, and safety. Businesses eventually came to accept that it was in their own long-term interest not only to cooperate with regard to product labeling, but also to publish more detailed accounts, develop internal auditing standards and rating systems, publicize executive pay, and prepare social balance sheets. The constraints under which companies are now obliged to operate in this regard are quite strict—though evidently not yet strict enough, to judge from the emergence of fresh scandals concerning working conditions and problems of various kinds related to the quality of information currently being furnished by manufacturers. Nevertheless, the battle lines are clearly drawn. It is a quite different matter with regard to political institutions, however, and public administration generally.

The extent to which transparency in politics lags behind transparency in business is all the more apparent as candidates for office are exclusively concerned with getting elected (and elected officials with getting reelected), and as no one any longer expects capitalism to be overthrown. There are several reasons for this. The first is sociological, and has to do with the prevailing balance of forces in the two domains. The acceptance of information requirements in the economic sphere was a consequence of the pressure brought to bear by the various groups concerned—labor unions, consumer groups, shareholders (especially through their meetings), the business press, certified auditors, departments of taxation and finance—all of whose interests converged in the same direction. The situation is different in politics. Parties, being alternately in power and in opposition, do not stand together with the people on whose support they depend. To the contrary, as structuring forces of the political class they are the principal agents of opacity. The same thing, unfortunately, is true of civil service unions: their members typically regard the obligation to share information with the public as a minor duty, indeed one that threatens their very independence. The unspoken hostility to what are perceived to be encroachments on the authority of public administration works simultaneously to strengthen a corporatist bias and obscure what institutions actually do.[58] Individuals are therefore even more alone than they were before in fighting to obtain information from administrative agencies and elected bodies. Only recently, and hesitantly at that, have ad hoc associations begun to emerge for this purpose in Europe.

All the more striking, then, is it to recall that access to administrative documents was initially thought of as an individual right almost everywhere, beginning with the United States, where the pioneering Freedom of Information Act (FOIA) was signed into law in in 1966 and took effect the following year. It laid down the principle that citizens' access to information is a right, and that refusal to grant such access constitutes an exception needing to be justified. The FOIA has subsequently been amended, and its provisions strengthened, on a number of occasions, notably under the Obama administration. In Great Britain, in 2005, a prior legislative enactment came into force that guaranteed a very broad public "right of access" to information pertaining to the functioning of administrative and political institutions. In France, although a Commission for Access to Administrative Documents (CADA) had been established by a law of 17 July 1978, its scope long remained limited and it was not until a ruling by the Council of State (the Ullmann decree of 29 April 2002) that this right of access was considered one of the "fundamental guarantees granted to citizens for the exercise of public liberties."[59]

But what is at stake today is something greater than this. It involves a *right to know*,[60] which cannot help but enlarge the very idea of citizenship. This right has two aspects, one associated with *open government*, the other with a *legible society*. The question of open government is today the more disputed of the two. However much the corollary principle of "open data" may be celebrated as marking the dawn of a new age, both of a right to information and of democracy itself, the demand for unfettered access has been fiercely resisted everywhere. For a democracy of appropriation, the battles now being fought on this terrain are the equivalent of what the campaign for universal suffrage was for a democracy of expression in the nineteenth and twentieth centuries. The success of the present campaign will depend on legislation and court rulings, of course, but also on how completely, or with what modifications, they are put into effect. It will be generally agreed that greater openness is needed in communicating with public institutions. Most people's experience is limited to replying to official correspondence, standing in line at city hall, and waiting for someone to answer their telephone call. As for strictly political institutions, their workings are still too often hidden from view. Take, for example, the National Assembly in France: its sessions are a matter of public record, partially televised, and its official documents are all available; but at the same time the crucially important work of its committees remains largely unknown.

The notion of a legible society, for its part, is a response to the problem of how ordinary citizens can hope to acquire a practical understanding of the mechanisms of government. A legible society ought to permit individuals to enjoy what might be called *real citizenship*, which is to say to gain insight into the difficulties encountered in trying to bring into existence a society of equals through the informed design and implementation of redistributive measures. This will only be possible if we are able to see the world around us as something more than the mere availability of information.

Attempts to realize open government and a legible society are two complementary methods of citizen reappropriation. Alongside exercises in participatory democracy that seek to diversify, and thereby enrich, opportunities for individual expression and involvement in order to correct the shortcomings of the electoral-representative system, the idea behind both these methods is to reduce the distance between the governed and their governors, as well as the distance separating the governed from one another, through greater knowledge. Under both methods, the right to know also has the property of going beyond the traditional division between human rights (which protect the individual) and civil rights (which organize participation in a political body). It creates a right of personhood, allowing individuals greater control over the world in which they live, while at the same time giving tangible effect to citizenship, so that the reality of social ties will be immediately apparent.

A civic undertaking of this nature requires that new citizen groups be formed for the purpose of doing those things that political parties have left undone. Parties were initially the means by which universal suffrage was established. Later they came to have the functions of stimulating public debate, expressing social identities, giving meaning to events, illuminating the future. The fact of the matter—as I have already insisted at some length—is that they are now solely concerned with the business of getting candidates elected to public office, where they will alternate between submission and opposition to the government in power. Parties form the pivot, in other words, on which a democracy of authorization turns. It therefore falls to organizations of some other kind to help build a permanent democracy.

To have some sense of the magnitude of the task remaining to be accomplished, we will need to say more precisely what a right to know involves. It has two dimensions. It may refer, on the one hand, to the idea of lifting the veil of secrecy, of gaining access to documents that previously were kept hidden or considered to be confidential; or else, on the other hand, to the accessibility of information about the routine operations of government. In the first case one is dealing with whistle-blowers, computer hackers, guilt-ridden insiders, skillful journalists—all of them trying in their various ways to obtain and disseminate information that had been concealed for reasons of state or of economic interest. If it is generally agreed that public awareness of such information is indispensable for understanding how the state really functions, whoever is responsible for disclosing it will be praised as a defender of democracy. Perhaps the most momentous instance in the twentieth century was the publication of the Pentagon Papers in the United States. Transmitted to the *New York Times* by Daniel Ellsberg, this huge mass of government documents (classified as "top secret—sensitive") about American involvement in Vietnam threw a harsh light on the gap separating official accounts of the war from realities on the ground.[61] Hannah Arendt, in a long article devoted to the affair, emphasized that "the basic issue raised by the papers is deception."[62] They showed that the management of the war had largely been dictated by objectives of domestic policy and shaped with an eye above all to the repercussions of the conflict on the president's image; that the extent of the country's combat engagement was much greater than had been admitted; and that the advice of military strategists and intelligence services was often considered to be less valuable than editorial opinion and purely political considerations. In our own time, the revelations due to Edward Snowden with regard to activities of the National Security Agency, along with others published on the WikiLeaks site by Julian Assange, have played a comparable role.

But the main point to be emphasized is that, even with regard to "pure" revelations of this kind, the ability to analyze documents is what matters. Information has value only if it can be properly interpreted. This condition is still more obvious when the right to know finds itself confronted by ever higher mountains of administrative directives and government statistics. The problem then becomes one of "data smog"— unmanageably dense and disordered flows of information that, by generating a new kind of opacity, create an almost irresistible temptation to selectively edit and assemble facts under the influence of arbitrary assumptions of all sorts.[63] Of the new forms of despotism that have arisen in recent years, none poses a greater threat to undermine democratic societies from within than overinformation. The right to know therefore is meaningful only if there is also the possibility of understanding. This means that legibility must also be synonymous with intelligibility. Whistleblowers are rightly honored today, and doing more to protect them against misguided prosecution is a vital safeguard of democratic integrity. But it is no less imperative that we call attention to the problem of intelligibility. Schools and universities can offer assistance in this connection, the media as well. Indeed, it is not unreasonable to suppose that the democratic function of these institutions may soon be crucial. In a world saturated with information, the task of filtering and deciphering has assumed a new urgency. What is more, by teaching the principles of sound qualitative analysis these institutions stand to regain the central place in public debate that the Internet has caused them to lose on the merely quantitative level.[64] For much the same reasons, at a time when experts and specialists enjoy unrivaled prestige in both the academy and society, it will be necessary to reconsider the role that generalists can play in educating the electorate. In parallel with this, citizen groups will need to be formed in all walks of economic, social, cultural, and political life, but they will be able to advance the cause of intelligibility only if they are sufficiently impartial to have credibility. Public interest research groups (PIRGs) of the sort that have long existed in the United States may furnish a model in this regard. In time the reputations of these various organizations for scientific and critical rigor[65] will come to be established, and the usefulness and relevance of their respective contributions ranked accordingly.

A Social Preference for Opacity

If the right to know has been accepted, at least in principle, by democratic governments with regard to the functioning of the state and the management of public policy,[66] it is important to note that society, either as a whole or in one of its parts, may sometimes nonetheless display an implicit preference for opacity. This occurs when a consensus forms in favor of overlooking one or another of the black boxes that are customarily left unopened in examining fiscal and social policy. Take the case of taxation in France, for example. The entire system operates by relying as far as possible on indirect taxes (less noticeable than the direct kind), creating new tax brackets, and multiplying special exemptions, all with the aim of inducing a sort of "fiscal anesthesia."[67] The result is that any attempt to make tax burdens more equal meets with determined resistance, and not only from the privileged classes. The problem is that the consequences of reform are apt to appear threatening to all because they cannot be known in advance.[68] Here it is plain to see that an improved understanding of how the world really works will have a positive effect only so long as it is able to disarm the opposition that uncertainty is bound to provoke, by doing much more to level the incidence of taxation across society as a whole.

One must also take into consideration the fact that many social systems find it to their advantage to operate behind a "veil of ignorance," to use John Rawls's famous phrase.[69] The welfare state, for example, regards the problems for which it primarily takes responsibility (illness, unemployment, work accidents) as objective risks. It therefore concerns itself, not with the behavior of individuals, but with the situations in which individuals are statistically apt to find themselves. An objective approach of this kind helps to legitimize the welfare state itself, for the system of redistribution that it administers—a form of social insurance, in effect—is generally considered to be fair. But if the veil of ignorance were to be lifted, in an attempt to link the individual situations with individual behaviors, the whole system is liable to be destabilized. Might it sometimes be better not to know, then, in order to preserve social harmony and to minimize the chance that some people will be wrongfully neglected? Myself, I am inclined to say no, while at the same time admitting that the challenge of achieving greater equality and fairness is particularly daunting, and arguing that we must therefore explore how societies function in even greater depth than ensuring political legibility might otherwise be thought to require. This is not only the very essence of democracy in its reflexive aspect; it is also precisely what seeing the whole enterprise through to the end means, for citizenship and social knowledge go hand in hand. Realizing citizenship in its fullest sense will be possible only if political activism is harnessed to clear-sightedness. But the revolution that one day will come of combining lucidity and understanding has yet even to begin. It summons and awaits its actors.

⊿ 11 ⊾

Responsibility

RESPONSIBILITY HAS BEEN DEFINED as "the liability that offsets the asset of any government."[1] This rightly emphasizes that responsibility must be understood in the political sphere as the counterpart to the exercise of authority. In introducing the idea of a debt that representatives owe to their constituents, it compensates for the element of relinquishment inherent in the act of delegating a task, by insisting on a corresponding obligation that must be fulfilled. The principle of responsibility is analogous to what in physics is called a balancing or countervailing force: it accustoms a government to having to act within certain limits, causing it periodically to revert to its point of origin. Responsibility therefore needs to be seen as part of a democratic economy of power and vulnerability. It is a way of ensuring that, whereas the holding of an office proceeds directly from election, the exercise of authority is linked to other mechanisms of ratification and review, which, by contrast with elections, are permanent. In giving back power to the governed while at the same time requiring those who govern to submit to a certain measure of control, responsibility plays a major role in shaping the relationship between the two. To be responsible is to accept being subject to procedures that enforce such a limitation.

Responsibility in the sense that concerns us here has two objects. It applies first to the very fact of holding power, by allowing governments to be challenged and, in the extreme case, brought down. This, strictly speaking, is the domain of *political* responsibility. Second, responsibility determines the circumstances under which power may be said to be properly exercised. In this case it can be understood in two ways, both as an obligation owed to the past, by virtue of an official having to explain and justify his actions by means of a *rendering of accounts*, and as a commitment to the future, so that to be responsible for something "means that one makes a concerted effort to ensure that the thing is successfully accomplished."[2] Here responsibility involves a *test of ability*. History shows that practical experience with responsibility in all of these senses preceded the achievement of universal suffrage almost everywhere. Governors have often found it expedient to accede to the sort of dependence that responsibility implies, the more readily to obtain the consent of the governed. I have already mentioned the principle of budgetary review, which associates legibility with a rendering of accounts (from which, as we saw earlier, the term "accountability" derives). Now, however, we need to go further. We need to try to work out the deeper implications of political responsibility by examining the primitive form it first assumed in England with recourse to a criminal procedure, impeachment, designed to sanction acts of misgovernment.[3]

An English Invention

From the close of the Middle Ages onward, the procedure of impeachment was meant to punish abuses of power. Along with the doctrine of habeas corpus, it was regarded as one of the main bulwarks of English liberties, civil and political alike. Burke saw it as "that great guardian of the purity of the Constitution."[4] The accepted view was that the king could not himself ever be directly accused: whether power was considered to be his by divine right, or simply derived from customary rules of succession, the principle that "the king can do no wrong," to recall the familiar expression of the period, was generally admitted. The targets of impeachment were therefore his ministers, members of the Privy Council, and high officers of the crown. Since there could be no question of contesting the sovereign's right to make such appointments, it was a matter instead of bringing an accusation (the primary sense of the verb "to impeach") of misconduct against one or more persons in a criminal trial. Individual behavior was prosecuted, in other words, not political convictions; the high crimes chiefly aimed at to begin with were acts of corruption and treason. The usual procedure, by which the House of Commons drew up a bill of indictment for judgment by the House of Lords, sitting as a tribunal, grew out of the ancient conception of Parliament as a High Court. From the earliest times, then, representation was considered to be indissociable from the duty to ensure good government. William, 4th Baron Latimer, chamberlain of the royal household during the reign of Edward III, was the first to be sentenced under this procedure, in 1376.[5] Over time, along with popular consent to taxation, it came to be regarded as one of the two principal means for the supervision of executive power in England.

By the early seventeenth century resort to impeachment had become rather frequent, and its character steadily changed as a result of two things. First, it began to be employed in prosecuting figures of lesser stature, such as judges and ecclesiastics. Second, and more important, the class of indictable offenses had grown larger. To the high crimes of treason and corruption that impeachment had originally been meant to address was now added the much broader and more vague category of high misdemeanors. Eminent persons close to the king, such as the Duke of Buckingham and Francis Bacon, found themselves accused of abuse of official power, neglect of duty, misapplication of funds, and contempt of Parliament's prerogatives. Other kinds of misconduct, not necessarily criminal in the legal sense of the term, came instead under the head of political crimes or mismanagement. William Blackstone, the great commentator on English law, forged the notion of "mal-administration" for the purpose of bringing together in a single class a range of offenses committed by persons in the service of the nation, emphasizing that even if they are not violations of established law, they nonetheless warrant punishment insofar as they depart from a certain conception of the public good and public trust.[6] Edward Coke, another towering figure of English law, noted that the House of Commons, in bringing these charges against public officers, acted as an "Inquisitor-General of the grievance of the kingdom."[7] That gave Parliament the right to dismiss ministers without thereby appearing to challenge royal authority. The procedure of impeachment thus came to be used as an instrument of political control wielded by the people's representatives over the executive.

and less a matter of his own choosing. In this context the emergence of political responsibility amounted to acceptance of a kind of vulnerability that acted as a counterweight to a government that was stronger, more independent, and more concentrated than it had been.[10] If it was now more exposed to parliamentary reprimand, the executive was at the same time also less feared than before and could, up to a point at any rate, assert its will without encountering resistance. Moreover, the notion of political responsibility had yet to be incorporated in an automatic mechanism of any sort. Giving it effect still depended on the prime minister's assessment of the state of parliamentary opinion and possible threats of impeachment, as well as on his perception of the risk of provoking an irreversible crisis—in the worst case, resumption of civil war. The modern conception of parliamentarianism that was to flourish in the nineteenth century therefore emerged only gradually.

The English experience stands in singular contrast to that of the French parliamentary monarchy of 1814–1848. Cabinets in France were not constituted to begin with as an organized group of officials jointly deliberating under the guidance of a prime minister. The notion of ministerial solidarity did not exist, and no one imagined that ministers could form a unified and autonomous body. Each minister was conceived to hold an office directly confided to him by the sovereign, and each one felt himself to be bound by this primary loyalty before considering his relations with parliament. Seldom, if ever, did any of them contemplate resigning after a negative vote of the Chamber of Deputies on legislation that he had proposed. The situation that existed under the Restoration did not last, of course. With the advent of the July Monarchy in 1830 the deputies became more restless and more demanding, and Louis-Philippe paid closer attention than his predecessors had to changes in parliamentary opinion. During this period three ministers (out of fifteen) stepped down following a crisis provoked by a negative vote in the lower chamber. But these resignations were in fact due more to disagreements over policy among the ministers themselves than to acceptance of a principle that being overruled by parliament should automatically bring about a minister's departure. The idea that there could be a parliamentary prerogative of this nature had not yet occurred to anyone. The very reversion to monarchy after the Revolution and the Empire seemed to amount to recognition of an implicit royal prerogative in respect of the appointment and dismissal of ministers,[11] even if the Chamber of Deputies was determined to exercise a right of supervision over the conduct of ministers and the management of affairs of state.[12]

The idea of political responsibility was regarded at this time only in purely tactical terms, as the ultraroyalists had done at the beginning of the Restoration in taking up arms against the liberals. Vitrolles, a prototypical man of the ancien régime, expounded the ultras' view of the obligations incumbent upon a cabinet of ministers in a regime of representative government. He distinguished five: ministerial responsibility, extended by a right of dissolution; the necessity that the cabinet have the support of a majority of the Chamber of Deputies; the advantage for the king of choosing as ministers men held in esteem by the deputies; the principle of cabinet unity; the division of the representative body into two chambers. Of these five requirements, the first was paramount: "It is necessary, for the guarantee of his authority, that [the king] consent to exercise it only through intermediaries who, in accepting this honorable mission, are always ready to sacrifice themselves in the event that the principles and the acts of their administration come under attack by opinion, supported by the force of the laws. This is what is called the *responsibility of ministers*, that first condition without which no representative government could exist."[13] In this way the ultras, then in the majority, sought to govern the country, by putting pressure on the king to listen to them. The liberals had a field day, denouncing the ultras' cynicism and their "stunning conversion." As Royer-Collard famously answered them, "The day when the government will exist only through a majority of the Chamber . . . we will be in a Republic."[14] It is striking to note, by the way, that one of the principal liberal theorists of the period, Benjamin Constant, did not grasp the true meaning of political responsibility as it had been experimented with in England for almost a century. He continued to understand ministerial responsibility as something that could be only individual, and its abuse only criminal in nature,[15] not imagining that it might be seen in a different light under a monarchy, even a liberal one.

For want of any generally accepted principle of political responsibility, it was left to riots and revolutions to reconcile government with majority opinion in France—first in July 1830, following the enactment by Charles X of ordinances that contradicted popular sentiment (to say nothing of the civil liberties they suspended); and again in February 1848. It was not until the Third Republic that the cabinet's political responsibility to parliament was recognized and acted on in something like the English manner.

From Rule to Irrelevance

The essential criterion of a parliamentary regime, as it has been understood since the middle of the nineteenth century, is that ministers bear a political responsibility to elected assemblies. "Political responsibility," as one author has well summarized it, "implies an obligation on the part of those who govern to respond to parliament for acts performed in the discharge of their duties, according to a special procedure determined by the Constitution."[16] It was in England that this way of linking accountability with responsibility was given its earliest modern form, the "Westminster model,"[17] on the basis of the practical experience of the eighteenth century. The power of parliamentary oversight and censure was first openly acknowledged there in the wake of the electoral reform of 1832, which more clearly aligned public opinion with its parliamentary expression. The prime minister had not become a mere puppet of Parliament, however, since he still enjoyed a certain freedom of maneuver by virtue of the fact that he could choose when to step down and therefore was able to control the timing of new elections in accordance with established rules. A government's resignation, in other words, was not necessarily an immediate consequence of parliamentary defeat.

This was the first way in which the Westminster model differed from the system of assembly government that operated in France under the Third Republic, where the cabinet was a comparatively passive instrument in the hands of parliament. But it also departed from the French model in two other ways. First, English political life was organized around two great parties of government, each one capable of constituting either a majority or an opposition. This functional distinction, and the alternation of roles it implied, exerted a stabilizing influence, whereas the fragmentation of the French system of assembly government, consisting of a number of smaller parties, inevitably produced coalitions that were as fragile as they were transient. In England, the opposition explicitly saw itself as aspiring to power; more than this, because it enforced real voting discipline among its members, it was able to present a sort of reverse image of the government—hence the institution in the twentieth century of a "shadow cabinet" embodying and articulating the dissent from official policy.

Second, relations between the legislative and executive branches in England profited from a greater willingness to accept the autonomy and the legitimacy of the executive than in France. John Stuart Mill considered them to be founded on a distinction between "ultimate controlling power" and "active power,"[18] according to which the government enjoyed a *practical* preeminence, whereas Parliament had a *democratic* preeminence (he said that the people must "possess [controlling power] in all its completeness," considering Parliament to be "at once the nation's Committee of Grievances, and its Congress of Opinions").[19] "Instead of the function of governing, for which it is radically unfit," he concluded, "the proper office of a representative assembly is to watch and control the government: to throw the light of publicity on its acts: to compel a full exposition and justification of all of them which any one considers questionable."[20] Plainly this view of parliamentary duties and authority stands in sharp contrast to the one that then prevailed across the Channel. And yet, despite the marked discrepancies in both theory and practice between assembly government and the Westminster system, the two shared a certain general idea of political responsibility common to all modern representative governments. Moreover, as a practical matter, they devised identical techniques of parliamentary supervision of the executive, including censure, calling ministers to account, discussion of speeches from the throne, and formal inquiries.

Beyond these points of difference and resemblance, the details of which I cannot elaborate on here, the important thing to emphasize is that this notion of political responsibility, as it was understood, institutionalized, and practiced for two centuries, has today lost all its force. Several factors combined to bring about this change over the course of the twentieth century, evidently in variable proportions depending upon the particular case. These factors were political and constitutional in nature, since they worked chiefly to strengthen the executive, but there was a structural implication as well, for they had the effect of reinforcing the intrinsic legitimacy that arose from direct election of the head of the executive, which by itself makes a president more independent in relation to the parliaments that established the principle of direct election in the first place. The presidentialization of democracies attaches importance to an electoral responsibility that is owed to the voters at the expense of a political responsibility that is owed to parliament (while at the same time altering the circumstances under which political responsibility is exercised). In parallel with this, the role of parliamentary majorities in giving political support to the government achieved new prominence, a state of affairs that the mechanisms of rationalized parliamentarianism served only to consolidate. The effect of all this was to gravely undermine the constitutional implementation of political responsibility, at least in Europe, where parliamentary challenges to governments have become very rare since the 1970s.[21] Even when such challenges do occur, they are typically the result of defection by members of a majority rather than formal invocation of a principle of responsibility.

The breakdown of the idea of political responsibility, beyond these strictly political and constitutional factors, was also linked, in a diffuse but nonetheless decisive fashion, to what may be called a *crisis of imputation*. The notion of imputation is at the very heart of the traditional conception of responsibility. To impute is to ascribe an action to someone, to give it an author.[22] To be responsible is to have to justify whatever action may be imputed to one. In its political aspect this obligation has been subverted by the increasingly opaque character of government decision making and the growing complexity of public administration. It is now more and more difficult to know who is really responsible for a decision. There are too many parties involved in any given matter, too many agencies and departments having a hand in the management of routine business, for the average citizen to be able to see clearly what is going on and for misconduct, when it occurs, to be justly imputed.[23] The increasingly frequent substitution of the managerial notion of governance for the political notion of government is proof of this. Governance, in its modes of regulation and decision, exhibits two distinctive characteristics. First, it involves a plurality of *actors* having different attachments and status. Public and private agents from government, business, and the nonprofit sector circulate and interact with one another, each exercising in his own fashion a "governing" function in the sense that he is able to exert pressure or otherwise make his influence felt one way or another. Here, then, a heterogeneous and interactive network of participants, the nature of which is partly captured by the expression "civil society," stands in contrast to a uniquely legitimate actor-decider. Second, the so-called decisions of this network do not assume the form of a deliberate choice made at a clearly identifiable moment. They are the result of complex iterative processes. The very term "decision" is all the more inappropriate as these different actors all participate in a continuous process of consultation, negotiation, adjustment, and compromise.

The advent of what the late German sociologist Ulrich Beck called a risk society has only intensified this crisis of imputation. "In contrast to all earlier epochs (including industrial society)," Beck noted, "the risk society is characterized essentially by a *lack:* the impossibility of an *external* attribution of hazards."[24] Hence the search for new methods of assessing and assigning responsibility that we see today. Increasingly citizens have placed their hopes in justice, the forms and proportions of which evidently differ markedly from country to country, sometimes with a view to obtaining compensation for a wrong or injury or other damage, but mainly in order to unravel a tangled skein of causes and effects so that one or more culpable persons may be identified and punished. This is the source of the growing tendency to criminalize the acts of elected representatives, cabinet officers, and senior civil servants.[25] The infected blood scandal in France, at the beginning of the 1990s, testified dramatically to this change of perspective.[26] What might be thought of as a preference for penalization accelerated the decline of strictly political responsibility by providing an alternative to it, that is, by making it possible to prosecute public officials in the event that taking a fatalistic view of the accidental character of a given event appears to be morally and socially unjustifiable. Judicial decisions are now expected to bring about a collective catharsis by convicting, and whenever possible sentencing, the "guilty," which is to say those members of the governing class who fail to fulfill their political responsibility. If public officials neglect this responsibility, it is not only because they disregard other responsibilities as well; it is because they no longer even perceive the true meaning of responsibility, which goes beyond any imputation of personal misconduct. The outstanding characteristic of persons who are responsible is that they willingly assume the consequences of a situation in which they do or did not play a direct role. It is from this point, then, that we must make a fresh start.

A New Basis for Political Responsibility

It needs to be understood first of all that the principle of political responsibility has nothing to do with any mechanical procedure of imputation. It has to do rather with a *democratic fiction* that makes it possible to maintain public trust by dispelling the aura of impunity created by the opacity and complexity of modern decision making and banishing the feelings of powerlessness to which it gives rise. This pretense is both psychologically and politically necessary, for it is rooted in the very purpose of democracy, namely, to establish a regime in which people control their destiny. It is therefore at the level of the individual person that the fiction now takes on its deepest significance. When an event of real or symbolic importance profoundly shocks public sensibilities, the resignation of a minister in his or her capacity as a *responsible figure* restores meaning and nobility to political action, and gives back dignity, not only to the official concerned, but to the ideal of public service that this official represents. As one recent commentary put it, it allows an official "to take upon himself the sins of his administration in grave circumstances," thus bringing about a "democratic purification."[27] Such a gesture, however rare, rests on a personal commitment, and gives citizens the feeling that their distress and their anger have been recognized. Enlarging the notion of political responsibility in this manner is indispensable if faith is to be maintained in the capacity of democracy to involve ordinary citizens in public life. But it is not only the exercise of individual responsibility that matters. It is also the fact that what is at issue is a responsibility to the governed, which is to say to the opinion of the people, and not the classical notion of responsibility to a parliament (though this, too, unavoidably has a collective aspect).

Unlike the old form of responsibility, what might be called a direct responsibility to popular opinion cannot be constitutionalized. Its purpose is to defend and preserve the three great invisible institutions of trust, authority, and legitimacy. So long as the ability to act increasingly depends on the nature of the relationship between the governed and their governors, the role of these institutions can only continue to grow. Direct responsibility in the sense I have in mind has at the same time a dimension that might be described as moral, for it requires that ministers feel themselves primarily responsible for strengthening democracy rather than putting their careers first (which is apt to have the contrary effect of causing them to overlook the misdeeds of their subordinates). This conception of political responsibility occupies as central a place in the current presidential-governing model of democracy as the notion of representation did in the old parliamentary-representative model. The extent to which the democratic ideal may be said to have been achieved

exactly this, to question what the government in office does, to challenge its acts and decisions; this, one might say, is the very purpose of opposition in a democracy.[30] The difficulty is that opposition operates for the most part by assembling a mass of particular criticisms in order to contest the validity of a government's policy in its whole thrust and tendency. There is a widespread perception that this way of exercising responsibility needs to be depoliticized—the term "depoliticize" being understood here in the sense of depriving political parties of the exclusive control they have long enjoyed. This can be done in several ways. First, by enlarging the forum of debate to include public opinion in its various forms, by analogy with the online forums of many social networks, only in a more organized fashion, while also incorporating advice from ad hoc watchdog groups. The exercise of responsibility in this expanded form will attract all the greater interest as citizens have the impression that it is not, or at least not any longer, through elections and party competition that matters have to be judged and punishment meted out. Henceforth civic initiatives of many different kinds may convene the court of public opinion and arraign a government.

The great problem confronting us today has to do with the role that opinion should play now that it has become an omnipresent actor in its own right. Opinion is the contemporary expression of direct democracy, understood not in the usual procedural sense of collective decision, but sociologically as the directly active and expressive form assumed by an entire political community in all its diversity. The problem itself is not at all new. More than two centuries ago the first theories were formulated of opinion as a rival to representation; indeed, this was one of the great *topoï* of the late eighteenth century, and more specifically of the revolutionary period in France.[31] But the difference today is that public opinion now has a *material existence*, whereas before it existed only in the form given it by notables and other prominent persons, by political organizations, associations, unions, also by the press (in its capacity as a mediator between governed and governing). This direct material existence is due to the Internet, which therefore must be regarded as a social institution and not merely as a medium—only an institution that appears as something monstrous, multifarious, contradictory, throwing the most insane rumors together with the most carefully considered accounts; as an accurate expression of real life and at the same time a fevered projection of every imaginable fear and fantasy. It is tempting to say that this institution is none other than the *people,* in the sometimes negative sense given to this word in the eighteenth century.[32] In that case we need to renew an old line of inquiry and ask how the people are to be represented, given an audible voice and the power to intervene, so that they may become an attentive and critical examiner of government. Right away one meets with a difficulty that is symmetrical to the one we encountered earlier in connection with the conditions for imputing responsibility, when there are too many hands taking part in a decision. Here the problem is that there are too many voices.[33] In order to give the exercise of responsibility-as-justification its full effect, ways will have to be found to formally constitute opinion, in the proper sense of the term. Here again patience and determination are required, for it is a question of forming citizen groups of a new kind, dedicated to channeling and structuring social expression. This is a matter of some urgency, to which I will return in due course.

The third form of accountability, responsibility-as-evaluation, involves a public assessment of both the efficiency and the effectiveness of government policies. It seeks to measure the gap between intentions and results when words and deeds diverge; to discover why, for example, an educational policy aimed at promoting equal opportunity has failed, or why the expected redistributive effects of an economic policy have not been fully realized. Understanding the reasons for disappointments of this kind, particularly when the consequences are unforeseen and harmful, is crucially important today. Considerable effort is now devoted to monitoring the implementation of government programs and evaluating their performance.[34] It is a complicated business, however, requiring quite detailed technical analysis in order to be properly carried out.[35] Even if the complexity of the matters under review makes it necessary that such monitoring and evaluation draw upon all relevant expertise, the quantitative methods of the social sciences unavoidably occupy a preeminent place. Making sure that this type of analysis will be the servant of democratic ideals, and not their master, is essential. Here again the media have a major role to play alongside researchers.

These three forms of responsibility-as-accountability have historically been a part of the role reserved for parliaments. We have nonetheless seen how the manner in which they are exercised has gradually come to express a more direct relationship between governed and governing, not only as a consequence of the demand that accountability be made more democratic—on this point there is no turning back—but also because the nature of parliamentary activity has changed, with the result that it is now governed exclusively by the logic of partisan rivalry. This competition has had a positive effect in rationalizing the function of opposition, but at the same time it has debased the quality of debate by systematically politicizing it, which is to say by limiting members of the opposition to a single purpose—opposition—and none other. This in turn cannot help but lead to an impoverishment of everything that may be thought of as intrinsically parliamentary, not least by denying the ineliminable vagueness and indefiniteness of any definition of the common good. We have a duty today to rediscover for ourselves the spirit and form that parliamentary life used to have, animated as it was by independent-minded representatives and devoted to the tasks of over-sight, inquiry, advice, and assessment, by setting it in a broader, more democratic framework. One step in this direction, in France, has been the recent interest in reforming institutions created in the early years of the Fifth Republic, such as the Economic, Social and Environmental Council. This interest is wholly consistent with the idea that public opinion must now be seen as an essential element of an *organized civil society*. Together, they open up a path that will need to be explored if we are to understand what the exercise of responsibility really involves.

Responsibility to the Future: Commitment

Responsibility to the future is ultimately a matter of will, which assumes an ability to change things. For one cannot be held responsible if one does not have the power to act on the world. The notions of power and responsibility are therefore closely related. Under the classical parlia-mentary system this dimension was embodied by a *vote of investiture*, which had the function of avowing trust in a government's ability to weather political storms and to carry out its program. Hence the resort from time to time to a general vote of confidence. This is an essential aspect of responsibility in its political sense, strongly emphasized by Max Weber.[36] In the modern era of rationalized parliamentarianism, cer-tainly in France but elsewhere as well, the earlier obligation to be formally invested in an office before taking up its duties is often considered to be of little or no importance, a mere formality, as though the faith placed by the people in their representatives to confront the future bravely and honestly no longer has to be solemnly acknowledged and sworn to. It is scarcely an exaggeration to say that today "ministers treat parliamentarians, to whom they owe nothing, as perfect strangers."[37] The president's blessing is all they need.

The nature of political will is no longer the same either. Whereas its assertion used to be connected with the alternation of governing parties and a certain attitude toward social change, as part of a more general conception of the ability to act on the world, it is now understood in a more prosaic and more immediate way. Just as there is a crisis of imputation today, it may also be said that there is a crisis of will. One has only to consider the sense of powerlessness that causes citizens everywhere to doubt the capacity of governments to influence events. If we recognize ourselves as having a responsibility to the future, we must grant this feeling, which is at the root of contemporary democratic disenchantment, our full attention. Beyond the facile stigmatization[38] of a political class considered to be insufficiently concerned with serving the common good or blindly submissive to neoliberal ideology, there is a deep problem here. How ought we address it? The two most familiar answers to this question could not be more different. One is to engage in a rhetoric of optimism and uplift, and to pretend, as is generally done, that there really is no problem ("Don't worry, everything is under control"). The other is simply to throw up one's hands and acknowledge defeat ("We have tried everything, there's nothing more to be done"). The manner in which governments deal with employment is remarkable for illustrating both of these attitudes and ways of talking. But there are other possibilities. Sometimes will is ignored altogether, or else treated in a negative fashion. One thinks of the old reactionary traditionalism, which combined acceptance of the existing order of things with a hatred of any attempt to change it. This sentiment continues still today to inform the thinking of neoliberals and other conservatives, as well as certain biopolitical and ecological ideologies on the left that urge human beings to forsake their technological pride and embrace instead a politics of life and nature, enjoining them, in effect, to be docile disciples of a kind of objective knowledge that implicitly rejects the democratic ideal of a world-transformative will.

But there is yet another way of conceiving responsibility, as a capacity for commitment in relation to the expression of a will. On this view, "projective" will is to be distinguished from "reflexive" will. Projective will is understood to arise from energy and imagination, a determination to overcome resistance, to triumph over adversity, to persevere. It is appropriately applied to individuals, as a description of moral character. Its archetypal figures in history are the warrior and the rebel: Napoleon, on the one hand, the *ogre de volonté*, the man of 18 June 1815 who set himself against fate; but also all those anonymous outlaws, insurgents, and dissidents who have forced the powerful to yield by bringing to bear an energy disproportionate to their numbers and strength. Their example has lost none of its inspirational force in a modern world torn between selfish enjoyment of personal happiness and the aspiration to change the course of history. Among the disenchanted and debilitated democracies of Europe at the turn of the twentieth century, the march toward what was to become the Great War was hastened by the transposition to a collective level of an individual desire for salvific vitality. No one had more penetrating insight into this phenomenon than Robert Musil, not only in his great novel *Der Mann ohne Eigenschaften* [The Man without Qualities], but also in a great many essays. In response to the question of how the European continent managed to derive psychological and moral satisfaction from going to war, he laconically replied: because we had had our fill of peace.[39] "The War, it seems to me, erupted like a disease in this social organism; an enormous pent-up energy, without access to our collective soul, finally dug itself this gangrenous fistula channel to it."[40] At the same time war imposed itself as a remedy for the mediocrity of bourgeois society, as a way of escaping the tyranny of narrow self-interest and the trivialization of human existence. For Musil, the problem of modernity consisted in just this, that it made recourse to a "new doctrine of the will"[41] inevitable, and with it a return to a way of living that would be "uninterrupted activity, a sort of combustion like breathing."[42] After the war, Hitlerism whipped up the tides of history and irresistibly swept it onward by presenting itself as a regime of the will incarnate. With the Nazis, he wrote, it is "the will that has assumed power in Germany."[43] And so it was that remedy became poison. After 1945, Western nations sought to stave off a resurgence of totalitarian voluntarism by celebrating the virtues of a more modest conception of democracy. In this they were greatly aided, it is true, by the thirty years of strong economic growth that followed the second war, which compensated for the exaltations of the past by cultivating a new taste for consumerist materialism.

But in a world that was no less unstable than before, despite being more interdependent, and now much less sure of its values, the question of will and the capacity for commitment was bound to reappear. It will generally be conceded today, except by those who are inclined to extremism, that the old projective will can no longer have the place it once did, when it was associated with the exercise of unrestrained sovereignty in a closed world—politically closed, that is, for this type of will retains all of its power as an individual moral quality. What is needed now is reflexive will. Whereas projective will, applied to politics, looked upon society as an individual writ large, unified and therefore homogeneous, capable of being mobilized and commanded like an army, being directly amenable to authority and able to be shaped in the same way that a person creates a personality for himself, reflexive will operates on the assumption that social division is the fundamental fact and proper object of politics. It therefore shines a light on the conflicts, inequalities, disagreements, and prejudices that infect society, in order to lay them bare, to make them visible to all, and to submit them to public debate. A commitment to the future on the part of those who govern then becomes linked to the collective action of society on itself with the aim of establishing a freer, more just, and more peaceful world. The power of this will is linked in turn to the ability to *reshape* (etymologically, the meaning of the word "reform") society by making it perceive not only its true nature, but also the reasons for the impasses into which it is constantly led. The exercise of this will therefore also depends on being able to think clearly.

⤞ 12 ⤝

Responsiveness

TODAY, IN ALL PARTS of the world, people feel they are heard less and less—and represented less and less well—by those whom they have elected to public office. Even if the words they have spoken at the polls do not quite vanish into the thin air of parliamentary debate, the governing class gives every sign of being afflicted with deafness. Making matters worse, the views of ordinary citizens are now expressed only fragmentarily on social networks, where they are subtly manipulated to support the interests of organized pressure groups or else confined to vague and ineffectual noises of protest. An unwillingness to listen on the part of those who govern is therefore compounded by an atrophied capacity for expression on the part of the governed. Historically, there are two main reasons for this. First, a growing reliance on elections as the primary vehicle of civic expression, virtually complete by the end of the nineteenth century and an abiding influence throughout the twentieth. Second, the professionalization of political parties, which likewise began in the nineteenth century and, with the desocialization of politics toward the end of the twentieth century, had the effect of almost wholly detaching them from real life. We will need to examine the sources of our present predicament more closely in order to understand what must be done if a true *democracy of expression and interaction* is to be established that will bind citizens and representatives together in a permanent and dynamic way, so that the governed may at last assert their sovereignty over the governing.

Listening and Governing: A Lesson in Regressive History

The idea of obliging government to take notice of public opinion is not new. It was formulated at the beginning of the nineteenth century by the first modern theorists of governmentality, Jacques Necker and François Guizot. To be sure, it was not as democrats that they thought about such matters. Yet as men who had experience in the exercise of power, they understood that the American and French Revolutions had ushered in a new era. If political discourse in general, and the language of election campaigns in particular, were still enrolled in the old school of the arts of seduction and manipulation, governments now had to take into account the existence of an emancipated civil society in which citizens had the means, not only of expressing their interests and their opinions, but also of defending them. It was therefore no longer reasonable to suppose that it might still be possible to manage a people through a combination of harshness and cunning, as Naudé and Mazarin had done. Nor did Necker and Guizot feel the least sympathy for the classical liberal orientation of thinkers such as Constant, who dodged the question of the executive in arguing on behalf of a weak government. This is why they undertook to publish original intellectual work— Necker in *Du pouvoir exécutif dans les grands États* [1792], Guizot with a whole series of writings during the first years of the Restoration that culminated in *Des moyens de gouvernement et d'opposition dans l'état actuel de la France* [1821]. These two books expounded the first practical philosophies of executive power in an age of popular sovereignty.

Necker had been quite alone during the Revolution in holding that executive power, far from being a matter of minor importance, played an essential role in political affairs. The attention of the men of 1789 was concentrated almost exclusively on the problem of how to constitute a legislative body and how to interpret the principle of representation. Necker regarded these questions as secondary, or at least amenable to a range of equally satisfactory solutions. In his eyes, the purpose of a parliament in its legislative function, which is to say its essential purpose, was simply stated: to lay down norms. And this purpose was not in any substantial way affected by the number of its members, the manner of their appointment, or the length of their term of office. A parliament's function, in other words, is wholly independent of its form. But with regard to the problem of constituting an executive branch, which he described as "the principal and perhaps the sole difficulty of all systems of government,"[1] it was exactly the nature of its function that he found problematic. The executive he considered to exercise a directly active power; more than this, it is defined by the content of its actions, being entirely reduced to them. By contrast with a legislative body, then, its function is wholly dependent on its form. "One can easily describe its duties, and separate them from those that belong exclusively to the legislative body," he observed in this connection. "But when one wishes to compose this power; when one wishes to choose the elements suited to constituting its force, one perceives the difficulties of such a theory; and one would perhaps pardon the National Assembly for having failed to understand them or for having diverted its attention from them, if all our misfortunes, those that we have suffered, those that we suffer now, those that we fear yet, were not to be ascribed to this first error."[2] Necker's prescience in asking under what conditions a government might be at once efficient and liberal could not be more plain in retrospect.

It was one of his closest readers, François Guizot, who twenty years later advanced the first coherent account of governmentality in its modern form. Whereas Necker had examined executive power in its essence and function, Guizot considered it mainly in terms of its practical effectiveness. The liberal theory of governmentality he sought to develop took as its point of departure the idea that "every government, in order to assure its survival, must satisfy the needs of the society that it governs and seek to discover its roots in the moral and material interests of its people."[3] For Guizot, the exercise of power was indissociable from social knowledge. "One must have a firm grasp of society, study everywhere what it desires," he emphasized.[4] One must "study [its] needs and examine their nature."[5] In *Des moyens de gouvernement et d'opposition,* one of the major political works of the nineteenth century, he gave systematic form to a very novel conception of the appropriate role of government. "Political power," he remarked, "is often prey to a curious illusion. . . . Ministers, prefects, mayors, tax collectors, soldiers, these are what are called means of government; and when it possesses them, when it has entangled them together over the face of the country, it says that it gov-

of a nation. This insight was to be elaborated as the main argument of *Des moyens de gouvernement et d'opposition:* the real means of government reside in these interests, these passions, these opinions, which together comprise the "needs" of society; they are the handles, so to speak, by which those in power need to take hold of the masses and guide their movements. The task of government, then, is to insert itself into this system of needs with the aim of conforming to it as closely as possible. From Guizot's analysis of political instruments and means of government there also followed a social critique. If the government of the day was an idle machine, powerless to accomplish its aims, this was because the ruling dynasty was, "if not foreign, at least too external to public existence, too little anchored in the needs and the forces that seem bound to decide the fate of all."[11] It was incumbent upon his fellow liberals to learn how to govern otherwise, in anticipation of the day when they would come to power.

At this point in Guizot's career, of course, these were the words of a fierce opponent of the regime. But he had nonetheless done something no one had done before, in conceiving the relation between government and society in positive terms. This led him to think in unaccustomed ways about the nature of representation as well. He proposed going beyond the idea of an electoral mandate and the exercise of surrogate authority, regarding representation instead as a kind of cognitive process. On this view, representation is inseparable from publicity, which is superimposed on it. Already in 1818, two years before inaugurating an ambitious course of public lectures on the origins of representative government, he was clear on this point. "Properly considered," he wrote, "what characterizes the institutions to which Europe aspires is not representation, nor is it election, nor is it deliberation; it is publicity. The need of publicity, in the administration of public affairs, is the essential mark of the social state and the spirit of [our] time. . . . Where publicity is lacking, there may be elections, assemblies, deliberations; but peoples do not believe in them, and they are right not to."[12] Publicity, he insisted, makes it possible to set in motion a process of "reciprocal revelation" between government and society. On coming back to this question in 1828, having been permitted by the government to resume his lectures after a suspension of six years, he was to recognize the importance of the separation of powers and of election; but he did not abandon his earlier opinion that, from a theoretical standpoint, "publicity is perhaps the most essential characteristic of representative government."[13]

Election, he held, "is, by its nature, an abrupt act scarcely admitting of deliberation: if this act is not bound up with habits of every sort, with everything the voters have previously reflected upon, if it is not, in other words, the result of a long prior deliberation, the expression of their habitual opinion, it will be very easy to catch their will by surprise, to make them to listen only to the passion of the moment; then election will be lacking in sincerity and reason."[14] Publicity, by contrast, made it possible to maintain a permanent communication between popular opinion and government.

At the very outset of his career in government, having been named secretary general of the Ministry of the Interior in 1814, Guizot took part in compiling a volume issued under the title *Statistique moral du royaume* [Moral Statistics of the Kingdom] that carried on research published earlier as *Tableau général de l'esprit publique* [General Description of Public Feeling]. These initial studies of popular opinion, conducted on the basis of very detailed questionnaires,[15] marked a radical departure from other inquiries of the period that at first sight may appear to be similar. During the Revolution, in 1792, Jean-Marie Roland, then minister of the interior, had created an Office for Correspondence Relating to the Formation and Propagation of Public Feeling that was chiefly responsible for furthering the Girondin cause in the provinces.[16] And for two years under the July Monarchy, from 1837 to 1839, there was a Department of Public Opinion, mocked by Balzac, who accused it of using secret funds to pay journalists to furnish provincial newspapers with articles favorable to the government as the occasion demanded. Guizot's purpose was entirely different. What he sought to put into effect was a new way of thinking about government.

Notwithstanding their focus on contemporary events in France, the writings of Necker and Guizot might have been expected to be generally welcomed for providing a broader definition of the active sovereignty of the people and relied on as a preliminary guide to the problem of creating a virtuous relationship between governed and governing. In the event, however, they were to remain little known and all but deprived of consequence, even though other works by both of these authors found a great many readers in France and abroad. It was not until Habermas revived interest in Guizot's great work on the means of government and opposition more than a century later that it came to be recognized as the "classic formulation of the 'rule of public opinion.'"[17]

Throughout the nineteenth century, liberals' obsession with the concept of a minimal state caused them to limit their political ambitions to the defense of traditional parliamentarianism. In republican and socialist circles, by contrast, priority was attached to finding ways of improving the representativeness of elected officials in relation to their constituents. On both sides, then, the problem of executive power was sidestepped.

Only by developing and sharpening the intuitions of Necker and Guizot, and then giving them institutional form, will it be possible to create a democracy of interaction between government and society that gives power back to citizens by obliging all those who govern to be more responsive to their expectations. But at the same time it is no less important to rehabilitate the prevailing modes of political expression, atrophied under the corrosive influence of a merely negative democracy and enfeebled by the oversimplifications of opinion polls and the divisive effects of social networks. This debilitation has a history, which it will be useful to recall in order once more to appreciate the magnitude of the citizens' revolution that needs to be carried out.

Polarization and Contraction of Political Expression

The growing power of populist movements is one of the most notable political phenomena of the early twenty-first century, in Europe and well beyond. Anything so massive and far-reaching cannot help but have many causes. By no means the least of these, as we have seen, is the sense of abandonment felt by people who no longer consider themselves to be represented by traditional parties. Let us briefly review the circumstances under which these parties, as well as unions and other such large organizations, came to be established as virtually the only spokesmen for society. This polarization, which beginning in the late nineteenth century led to the rise of what might be called monopolistic forms of representation, was marked by a dramatic reduction in the number of outlets for popular feeling that had existed only a hundred years earlier, at the time of the American and French Revolutions. Perhaps the most striking example of the spirit of direct participation in civic life that once flourished on both sides of the Atlantic is the importance, nowhere more pronounced than in France, attached to the right to petition government for redress of grievances.

The right of petition has, of course, a predemocratic origin. In both England and France it had been granted so that personal complaints might be heard at a time when private individuals had no court or representative body to turn to. This motivation was to endure. From the earliest days of the French Revolution, however, petitions increasingly assumed a collective and political character, demanding the adoption of a certain law, the reform of an institution, or a new approach to public prosecution. In this respect petitions accompanied and extended citizen activity by bringing into existence a form of direct democracy alongside a representative mechanism. Thus, for example, a decree of 1789 establishing a right of suffrage explicitly mentioned the granting of the right of petition as a sort of compensation for the confiscation of electoral authority implied by the prohibition of imperative mandates and by the freedom of action accorded to representatives.[18] In addition to relaxing the strict adherence to formal procedure associated with electoral representation, the practice of petition also made it possible to counterbalance the restrictions that were placed on voting rights, above and beyond what a two-round system of election entailed in this regard. For disenfranchised members of the population, petition functioned in effect as a "substitute for the right of political suffrage."[19] Those who failed to satisfy the property qualifications for active citizenship could make their voice heard by this means; the same was true for women. Whereas suffrage was limited in several ways, petition was truly universal.

It is hardly surprising, then, that the right of petition should have been widely exercised during this period. Moreover, it was an integral part of parliamentary life, since provision was made for deputations of signatories to plead their case at the bar of the Assembly.[20] One has only to consult the record of its proceedings to note the considerable place then occupied by the announcement of these requests in the daily order of business (they were in fact introduced and discussed in open session). As late as the July Monarchy, Cormenin, one of the great Republican pamphleteers of the period, was pleased to observe that, through petition, "any proletarian is able to go up to the tribune and speak publicly, before all of France. Through it, the Frenchman who is disenfranchised, neither voter nor even citizen, can initiate an action, as the deputies are able to do, as the government itself does."[21]

The remarkable thing is that the practice of petition was also severely criticized, from the time of the Revolution onward, by the most conservative theorists of representative government. Some held that those who had won distinction by the fact of their election should rightfully enjoy a monopoly on representation. "To act or speak for others," one of them insisted, "is to represent, and citizens holding no office have no [duty of] representation to exercise."[22] Others were influenced by the fear, no less social than political, of seeing petitioners "elevate personal wishes to [the status of] political votes," thus "substituting democratic anarchy for the representative system."[23] The republicans were eventually to end up, for doctrinal reasons, thinking along the same lines. A man such as Ledru-Rollin, now remembered as the father of universal suffrage in France, had praised petition during the years of struggle to obtain voting rights as equivalent to a "press of the masses," a "publication of public thinking";[24] but after 1848 he changed his position entirely, now maintaining that the ballot box sufficed to express the opinions and demands of society. No one in the republican camp expounded this reductionist point of view more forcefully than Émile de Girardin. "The right of petition," he noted bluntly, "is a democratic misconception and a republican anachronism. The sovereign commands and does not petition."[25] Petition, for Girardin, was only a primitive and unfinished form of the sovereignty of the people. A right of petition had no reason to exist unless the people had been dispossessed of it. "The right of petition is part of monarchical law," he reiterated, "it has no place in a democratic regime. Restore universal suffrage, genuinely restore it, and the right of petition will become perfectly useless."[26]

The republicans of 1848, like their successors under the Third Republic, thus sought to regulate and minimize a right that was now considered to be obsolete. They expected that the habit of voting, once it had taken hold everywhere, would make its effects felt throughout the entire sphere of politics. A society could therefore be imagined to express itself only in one of two ways, either through a wholly institutionalized and formalized political procedure or through the absolute privatization of opinion. Hence the gradual extinction of the right of petition. Once parliament limited itself to recording petitions without ever discussing any of them, beginning in 1873, the right had been brought down once and for all from its "constitutional pedestal."[27] In the following decades the new disjunctive attitude toward social expression became a characteristic feature of parliamentary democracies everywhere, not only in France, and the main cause of a corresponding contraction in civic participation. This outlook came to be reinforced by an equally restrictive understanding of the place that politics ought to have in a democracy. The great debate that took place in the late nineteenth century on the right to demonstrate on public thoroughfares, which in France opposed what was then called the extreme left to the political establishment, is exemplary in this regard. Not only did it embody the historical and theoretical distinction between polarized institutional representation and multiform social representation that I have just emphasized; in setting the people against parliament, the debate gave this distinction an immediacy it had not had until then, and provided a remarkably sensitive instrument for analyzing the type of limited democracy that the founders of the Third Republic wished to institute.

Public demonstrations, to their way of thinking, could be justified only under exceptional circumstances—rising up against a despotic regime, for example—that amounted to something like the equivalent to the old "right of insurrection" celebrated during the Revolution.[28] Apart from rare events of this kind, however, the direct and unavoidably disordered form of democracy that such demonstrations implied seemed to them inadmissible. Why should there be any need to take to the streets if the nation were represented in the Chambers? "I see no utility in duplicating in this manner a discussion that would take place in the meeting hall," as one leading radical republican put it.[29] Even taking to the street in protest of unjust treatment was not considered to be legitimate, as disapproving commentaries in the republican press of the period regarding strikers' processions made clear. "The caravans that go past chanting refrains . . . may be suitable for street vendors, but not for republican workers," one columnist complained. "They are useless and lamentable."[30] Pierre Waldeck-Rousseau, for his part, went so far as to speak of such protests as a "usurpation of public thoroughfares," amounting to an act of confiscation, by "orchestrators of outside demonstrations"—outside, that is, the authorized parliamentary-representative space.[31] For the left, by contrast, demonstrations were part of an enlarged view of representation. Édouard Vaillant, a leading figure in the Socialist Party, went straight to the point during parliamentary questioning in January 1907 of Georges Clemenceau, who had become prime minister three months earlier: "There will be no true

Republic so long as the working class is unable, through its demonstrations, to display its will directly," he told Clemenceau. "So long as it is obliged to rely on the presentations of its delegates and its representatives, it will not enjoy complete and perfect expression. This is why we consider that along with freedom of assembly and association there is a necessary complementary freedom, the freedom of demonstration, the freedom of direct and public display [of opinion] by workers and socialists."[32] There was, in other words, a "right to the street" that needed to be recognized.[33] Traditional republicans had no patience for the popular longing for plural democratic expression. In this matter, as with regard to petitions, their conception of democracy remained narrowly circumscribed by a monist view of politics. From the banning of trade guilds by the Le Chapelier law of June 1791 to the rejection of a right to petition and demonstration, one finds the same logic at work.

The negative effects of this restrictive impulse, particularly marked in the French case, were partly offset by the representative character that the mass parties had come to acquire toward the end of the nineteenth century. The emergence of labor unions, creating a specific form of representation for the working classes, provided public opinion with another outlet.[34] For almost a century, from the 1880s until the 1970s, this representative dualism furnished a stable framework for the expression of interests and opinions. Finally it broke down, as much for institutional as sociological reasons. The institutional reasons had to do with the decline of the social function of representation once performed by political parties, which had now become satellites of government agencies, and the simultaneous retreat of unions, weakened by the new regulatory environment in which labor relations were negotiated. The sociological reasons were connected with the changing nature of political demands, now no longer a product solely of collective social identities (which unions, to a greater degree than parties, used to express in a more or less satisfactory fashion). The course of individual lives is more and more affected today by the challenges, the trials, and the fears of everyday existence; and the need to respond to them has led people to form new types of communities based on something other than social identity. But these communities have not yet found their own means of expression, the absence of which encourages the organs of government to withdraw into themselves, making it still harder for people to make their voices heard.

Atrophied Democracy

Simultaneously confronted with the decline of parties and unions, on the one hand, and the fact that new forms of social experience have no forum of their own, on the other, citizen expression finds itself more impoverished than ever before. For the most part it assumes the form of one or another species of protest, under the reductive and fragmenting influence of opinion polls.

The right to demonstrate eventually triumphed by force of circumstance, in France as elsewhere, overcoming the pompous apprehensions of the staunchest republican defenders of the parliamentary system of representation. At first demonstration was part of a larger repertoire of means of political assertion and collective action. Today it is something different, primarily as a result of having been universalized. Taking to the streets used to be one of the only ways for the downtrodden and oppressed to draw attention to their plight. Now people from all classes of society take part in public protests. Marches organized by the well-off and people on the right have become commonplace.[35] If demonstration has now become a standard form of political advertisement, it is also in large part because it is the simplest mode of expression of a negative politics, in an age when uncertainty about the choices voters face makes the formation of positive majorities more difficult.[36] It is an age, too, when the best organized interests find it much easier to attract the notice of those in power than the many invisible members of society.

In the meantime opinion polling has assumed an unprecedented importance, though now it serves a purpose different from the one it was originally supposed to have. When polling was first developed, it was regarded as an auxiliary technique of representation. This was the view of George Gallup, the pioneering figure in the field during the 1930s. Gallup imagined that polling would permit him to resolve the difficulty Abraham Lincoln had described: "What I want is to get done what the people desire to have done, and the question for me is how to find that out exactly."[37] At about the same time, in France, the General Confederation of Labor (CGT) spoke of "a new instrument furnished to democracy."[38] During the Liberation, one editorial writer noted the appearance "of other means of expressing public opinion than the voting paper"[39]— this at a moment when the mechanisms of democracy were broken and in need of repair everywhere in Europe. Polls rapidly came to be occupy a central place in political life, albeit typically as mere barometers of personal popularity or improvised mini-referendums. Without entering into the debate over the problems posed by treating public opinion as an entity in its own right (often a pointless debate, it seems to me), the important thing to emphasize is the binary political use of opinion surveys. Whatever cognitive value they may have, in revealing what people actually think, it is for the most part secondary by comparison with the part they play in the media's orchestration of political rivalry. At all events the original purpose of enriching political participation has now all but been lost.

Today, even though social networks have given society a fragmented look that is almost impossible to interpret, the governing class tends to react only with a wary eye to the street and the polls. This distant and distrustful relationship to the governed is the natural counterpart to an atrophied capacity for social expression. A more democratic—that is, a more responsive and interactive—government implies a society that makes its presence felt in a more vigorous and more diversified fashion. Misgovernment and malrepresentation are in this sense inseparable companions.[40]

The Forms of Interactive Democracy

Finding a way out from our present predicament requires in the first place that representation be set in a plural and enlarged perspective. This has become all the more necessary as the party system no longer has any representative function to speak of, with the result that populist movements are able to turn the situation to their advantage by presenting themselves as antiestablishment and yet at the same time as spokesmen for all members of society, especially the most forgotten among them, who are supposed to form a homogeneous mass. The divorce of representation-as-figuration from representation-as-delegation must now be considered to be irreparable. If the latter function still follows mechanically from election, which thus plays a role of arithmetic selection, the former has to be reconceived as an autonomous phenomenon. Representation-as-figuration in respect of social issues must take as its point of departure the fact that the word "people" can be understood only in terms of the diversity of social conditions and life experiences that give it practical meaning. "People" in this sense is also the plural of "minority," the echo of all forms of invisibility. To be represented is therefore not to be expelled to the outer darkness of an indistinct mass or consigned to a category that caricatures and obscures reality by means of a shorthand phrase concealing prejudice or stigmatization (suburbs, public housing projects, bobos, outcasts, and so on). What are called "the people" have life in the same way an animated film does, as a result of the rapid succession of a series of still images. To immobilize them, as though they were a block of marble, is to denature them. It is also to forget that "the people" is the name given to a shared way of life that remains to be constructed, that has not yet been achieved.

It is this diversity that must be represented, which is to say constituted as a social world in which each person will have a feeling of belonging and of being recognized by others. How can this be done? Making political participation immediate and real for all requires imagination. I have tried for my part to sketch the outlines of a "narrative democracy" in my recent book *Le Parlement des invisibles* [2014], which served as a manifesto for the "Ordinary Lives" project I mentioned earlier. This attempt to describe and to learn must also rely on stories and other accounts from literature and the social sciences, whether they are told in words or images, in printed works or via the Internet. In this way the "terrible ignorance we have about one another" that Michelet deplored long ago, in 1848, may be able at last to be remedied. But mine is only one initiative among many others that will have to be developed further in order to give substance to so vast a program. It is hardly a coincidence that more powerful ways of making individual voices heard by electronic petition should have emerged just as new forms of democratic expression are being devised and put into effect.[41]

Beyond this narrative and cognitive dimension, the problem of institutionalizing new forms of representation-as-figuration cannot be avoided. One might think of organizing special forums devoted to examining the most pressing matters of public policy, for example, or to designing permanent institutions of a novel type. For the moment let us confine our attention to the first approach, reserving a discussion of the second for the Conclusion. Such events might take the form of ad hoc meetings convened for the purpose of studying a range of major social issues (from the functioning of the welfare state, for example, to the future course of intergenerational relations) in a neutral setting free from partisan influence. Participants in these conferences might be asked to agree on a framework and a method for enlarging the sphere of public debate, with a national commission being set up to act on their recommendations—thus extending to so-called transversal questions what the National Commission for Public Debate in France attempts to do with regard to environmental policy as well as city planning and land use, the government having first been invited to publicly take a position on the findings of the relevant study groups. Again, it goes without saying that this is only one suggestion for how such a system might work. For when it comes to improving relations between the governed and their governors today, everything remains to be invented.

I should make it clear, too, that the imperatives of legibility, responsibility, and responsiveness both amplify and revitalize the old notion of a mandate. Today the social appropriation of power can be achieved by other means than the submission of the governing to the will of the people that a mandate was supposed to mechanically accomplish (and, of course, never did). The constraints of justification and the unimpeded circulation of information combine to oblige public officials to deliberate in closer consultation with members of society, who in turn feel they are in a stronger position when they are better equipped to understand what is going on around them and able to express their personal experience in a meaningful way. The feeling of being deprived of a voice, of being an exile in one's own land, derives from the ignorance that comes of being kept in the dark. A government that is forced to operate more openly and to provide a clearer and more detailed account of its actions, by contrast, loses its haughtiness. The more transparent it is, the less arrogant it is. What is more, citizens who feel they are no longer cut off from the flow of information and knowledge now stand in a new and more productive relationship to those who govern. They have obtained power for themselves, not by "taking" it or "seizing" it or "controlling" it, but by redefining it and making it function differently than it had in the past. What is at work in a democracy of interaction is a new political economy of social expression—what in English is called "empowerment."

One of the first to have thought of democracy in these terms was Émile Durkheim. He started out from two observations. First, that a merely arithmetic conception of democracy is entirely inadequate, because in the absence of unanimous elections it is inevitable that some individuals will go unrepresented and because, as he put it, majorities are liable to be "as oppressive as a caste."[42] Second, that a purely administrative conception of the state is no less inadequate, because the state is also the "organ of social thought."[43] These two considerations pointed to the need to create a form of democracy in which government and society continually interact with each other (unlike despotic or aristocratic regimes, where the outstanding fact is the government's isolation). "The closer communication becomes between governmental consciousness and the rest of society, the more this consciousness expands and the more things it comes to comprehend, the more democratic will be the society's character," Durkheim urged. "The notion of democracy is therefore to be understood as a maximum extension of this consciousness."[44] He explicitly contrasted this view of the matter with the idea of an imperative mandate, at the time very much favored in extreme left-wing circles as a solution to the crisis of representation. Durkheim considered the separation between government and society to be a fact of life, not something detrimental or harmful in and of itself. Accordingly, the proper role of government was not to passively reflect the state of society, but to actively help carry out the task of self-reflection in which society must engage in order to assume a truly collective form. The counterpart to this functional distinction was a state of affairs brought about by the combined effect of social deliberation, on the one hand, and the increased attention paid by government to society, on the other. For Durkheim, it was on account of this dual character that democracy has to be seen as both a mode of government and a form of society.[45] The preceding pages are intended in a similar spirit, only one that the urgencies of the present day have unavoidably given a rather sharper edge.

PART IV

A DEMOCRACY OF TRUST

⫸ 13 ⫷

The Good Ruler in Historical Perspective

I N THE parliamentary-representative era of democracies, politicians tended to disappear behind programs, individuals behind classes. In the presidential-governing age, by contrast, the importance of personal leadership is reaffirmed. The character and abilities of political actors weigh heavily in the judgment of voters, who see them as reliable indicators of the effectiveness of political action. When ideologies fall into decline, when the definition of the general interest proves to be more elusive than it once was, when the future appears uncertain and threatening, the talents and the virtues of rulers (to use the language of an earlier time) reassert themselves and serve as points of reference for public debate. In France, for example, François Hollande's claim to be an ordinary person was thought to raise questions about his steadfastness and resolve, and more generally his fitness for high office.

While the character of a good ruler is a matter of unusual interest today, it nonetheless has a long history, of course, which allows us to construct a typology of the various forms it has assumed. Over the past 800 years or so there have been four main conceptions: the medieval model of the *virtuous prince;* the model of the *representative as the product of pure election* that emerged with the French Revolution; the Caesarist model of the *man as a people* embodied by Napoleon; and the model of the *politician by vocation* described by Max Weber. To these I propose adding a fifth figure, the *trustee*, in the broad sense this term has in Anglo-American law, which in my view ought to serve as a model for us today, looking to the future.

The Virtuous Prince

The title I have given to the present volume, *Good Government*, itself has a long history. It recalls the name commonly given to the celebrated series of fresco panels *(The Allegory of Good and Bad Government)* that adorns the Council Room, the Sala dei Nove, in the Town Hall in Siena. Painted by Imbroglio Lorenzetti in 1338–1339 for the edification of the nine members of the city council and the people of Siena, these paintings illustrated the virtues of the good prince as well as the sources of peace and prosperity and the misfortunes resulting from their neglect.[1] But the idea of good government belongs to a larger medieval philosophical tradition of thinking about politics, based on the moral qualities of the sovereign. From the Early Middle Ages one spoke of "mirrors of princes" *(specula principum)* in describing a genre of books of advice and instruction for the rising generation of dynasts that reflected the image of an exemplary ruler.

The earliest writings on the virtues required to govern well evidently do not date from this period. The authors of these so-called mirrors were strongly influenced by the great works of antiquity. One thinks, in particular, of the *Meditations* of Marcus Aurelius, Cicero's *On Duties,* and Plutarch's *Parallel Lives.* But the outstanding characteristic of mirrors is that they laid much greater emphasis on ethical questions than their classical models had done. They were also published at a time when the authority of the clergy among secular rulers was at its height. European sovereigns of the period were surrounded by bishops and clerics, and the idea that temporal power was useful only because spiritual power did not enjoy the means necessary to rule on earth came to be widely accepted.[2] It was a time, too, when saintliness was considered the supreme personal ideal, and even kings were primarily concerned with assuring their own salvation. In France, Louis IX (after his death, Saint Louis) undertook a whole series of initiatives aimed at repairing harms and injustices caused by his administration in order to secure the redemption of his soul prior to departing on the seventh crusade in 1248.[3]

The first mirrors appeared in the Carolingian period. But it was not until the twelfth century that they began to play an important role, not only in the practical education of princes but also for the purpose of elaborating a political philosophy in which the legitimacy of governing others is combined with an ability to discipline oneself. All these works were agreed in insisting that a man is unfit to be king if he cannot command obedience through his virtues. The first one to have an impact throughout Europe was the *Policraticus* composed by John of Salisbury in about 1159, a moment when the question of tyranny dominated theological and political thought. In order to drive out the absolute evil incarnate in a regime unbound by any constraint, it was the vehicle of such a regime, the faithless and lawless ruler, that had to be removed. Salisbury had been deeply affected by the assassination of his friend Thomas Becket, Archbishop of Canterbury, in Becket's own cathedral, an event that he himself had witnessed. Salisbury was haunted by the thought that a sovereign as unworthy as Henry II, who had armed the murderers, might one day reappear. For this reason he regarded moral education as the central problem of politics, and set out in the fourth book of the *Policraticus* (dedicated to Becket) to describe the qualities of the good prince.[4] If the modern concept of sovereignty had not yet been forged at the time, the idea of a power to command was, of course, generally admitted. But it was a power that was understood to be governed by a moral obligation of conformity to the principle of equity (*aequitas*), which is to say a power subject to the divine justice of natural law, superior to the positive laws of men. The prince was therefore called upon to exercise self-discipline. Salisbury demanded not only that he have the public good uppermost in mind; he also required that the prince be indifferent to personal wealth, show magnanimity, be chaste, and combine piety with humility.

A century later, Giles of Rome's treatise *De regimine principum* [On the Guidance of Princes, ca. 1279], conceived in the same spirit and composed for the benefit of the young man who was shortly to become king of France as Philip IV (Philippe le Bel), gave rise to a vast secondary literature on the necessary virtues of rulers, arguing that "the moral perfection of the sovereign is, if not a condition of his power, at least a justification."[5] Such excellence was considered to be the surest guarantee against royal arrogance and high-handedness, and the basis for all attempts to ensure enlightened government at a time when the first signs of a concentration of power portending the advent of nation-states had cast the proper use of authority in a new light. The juridical aspects of sovereignty and the theoretical foundations of secular power were not yet thought to be of crucial importance. It was morality, not law and constitutional arrangements, that should direct political thinking. Giles of Rome even went so far as to call jurists "ignoramuses" (idiotae politia). "Those who know politics and the moral sciences are more to be honored," he advised his royal pupil, "than those who know laws and privileges."[6]

This view was also to inform the argument made by Thomist thinkers on behalf of a paternalistic government founded on a love of the people, which they held to be the only true rampart against tyranny.[7] Christine de Pizan, in her Livre du corps de policie [1404–1407], developed in great detail the idea of the king as "father of his subjects," central in the political philosophy of Aquinas. On this view, all the requisite qualities of an admirable ruler—his goodness, his simplicity, his humanity, his magnanimity—sprang from "the love that the good prince must have toward his subjects."[8] Closely related to this was the theme of the "good prince [who] must resemble the Good Shepherd,"[9] adapted from the biblical parable.[10]

Concern for the moral education of princes was to continue to nourish a considerable literature until the end of the eighteenth century.[11] One thinks in the French case of Pierre Nicole's Traité sur l'éducation d'un prince [1670; subsequently reprinted as part of his Essais de morale] and Bossuet's Lettres sur l'éducation du Dauphin [1679]; also of Fénelon, who wrote Les aventures de Télémaque [1699] in his capacity as tutor to the Duke of Burgundy. But the influence of these writings was to be limited to the persons for whose teaching they were composed. They aimed at making the future king a good Christian in his personal conduct, but no longer told him how he should govern.

The Elect

For the men of 1789, breaking with the ancien régime meant being done once and for all with a form of government ruined by corruption. Talent and virtue were now summoned to take its place. The revolutionaries did not, of course, dream of going back to the good prince of the mirrors;

the Middle Ages, as far as they were concerned, were destined to remain a part of the Dark Ages. But they had been brought up on the
classics (Saint-Just was famously to say that the world had been "empty
since the Romans"), and most of the members of the Constituent Assembly had Plutarch's *Lives* and Abbé Barthélemy's *Voyage du jeune
Anacharsis en Grèce* [1788], a best-seller of the late eighteenth century, in
their personal libraries. The representatives in whom they sought to
invest all power and authority were to be, in Sièyes's phrase, "the most
upright, the most learned, and the most zealous for the well-being of
the people."[12] How were such men to be identified? By means of election.
But election had a quite different meaning for them than it does for us
today. In addition to the original and primary sense of choosing someone,
there still survived then the theological overtone of the Latin *electio*, with
its suggestion of an "inspired" choice. "It is just," Sièyes wrote, "that the
men charged with representing the nation be drawn from the number of
those who have done it the greatest honor and who are most deserving of
its recognition."[13] To elect was thus *to distinguish*, in the proper sense of the
term: to confer distinction on the basis of exceptional qualities. It was not
a matter of deciding between competing programs or rival political figures. "The assembly of the representatives of the people," as one contemporary observer put it, "is composed of elite men because they have
been chosen."[14]

    After 1789, the tendency of representatives to disregard their popular
mandate and to form an aristocracy of a new kind was frequently criticized. Election, as it was then understood, had been intended to forestall any such deviation from a fundamental principle of revolutionary
government. Representatives did indeed comprise an elite, but one that
was conceived as nothing more than a sum of pure individuals, persons
who did not jointly constitute a body. The term "elite" had meaning only
in the singular, designating a representative recognized solely for his
own distinctive virtues.[15] The idea that election ought to have the unique
purpose of detecting personal talent and virtue is implicit in Article 6
of the Declaration of the Rights of Man and the Citizen. These qualities
therefore could not be aggregated in order to create a group or a caste.
There were elite individuals, but not *elites;* nor were there "capacities,"
in the sense of a competence or qualification, as liberals were later to
contend in justifying property-based suffrage. Men distinguished by
election formed at the most a de facto group, wholly changeable, always

variable.[16] The eminence recognized by election was not a differentiating kind of superiority, it did not injure equality. Thomas Paine had made exactly this point in talking about the distinction of wise men. "Whatever wisdom constituently is," he noted, "it is like a seedless plant; it may be reared when it appears, but it cannot be voluntarily produced. There is always a sufficiency somewhere in the general mass of society for all purposes; but with respect to the parts of society, it is continually changing its place. It rises in one to-day, in another tomorrow, and has most probably visited in rotation every family of the earth, and again withdrawn."[17]

The "pure" conception of election, as it may be called, was expressed during the French Revolution by a prohibition against presenting one-self as a candidate for elective office. This arrangement, which cannot help but seem surprising to us, so strongly is voting now associated in our minds with campaigning, was not a residue of some archaic system. To the contrary, it had been carefully considered as part of an elaborate and sophisticated philosophy of election.[18] It reflected, in the first place, an almost obsessive aversion toward anything that threatened to undermine the idea of equality. Canvassing for votes was seen as a disguised assertion of personal superiority and a worrisome sign of unhealthy ambition. One caught a whiff of aristocratic pretension in the sort of eminence that actively seeking public office seemed unavoidably to imply—a quite different eminence than the one conferred by election. Election—what Quatremère de Quincy called "true candidacy"—was conceived above all as a method of identifying those persons who were the most capable and the most worthy of assisting in the expression of the national will.[19] It therefore involved no contradictory debate, no political choice in the sense in which we ordinarily understand this term. But election was also, and perhaps above all, a matter of rejecting everything that soliciting popular support entails: the temptation to represent one's record in a way that is calculated to mislead voters, the premium placed on rhetorical skill, the tendency, in other words, to favor deceit and dishonesty. Many recalled that in republican Rome the crime of intrigue, broadly construed to include all attempts by a candidate to influence the outcome of elections through underhanded maneuvering, was severely punished.[20] This is why revolutionary legislation placed voters under a solemn obligation, before casting their ballot, to respond affirmatively to the oath administered by the presiding officer of their polling station:

"You swear and promise to name only those whom you will have chosen in your soul and conscience, as the most worthy of the public trust, without having been influenced by gifts, promises, solicitations, or threat." Indeed, this oath was frequently reproduced on the voter's registration card, a sign of the importance that was attached to it.

Although the idea of pure election is almost completely outmoded today, a certain idealistic presumption persists, that a good representative or a good leader should be chosen in a manner free from the distorting pressures of excessive partisan competition. It can still be met with from time to time in local politics, and also, though less commonly perhaps, at the strictly political level. The way in which General de Gaulle stood before his fellow citizens, refusing to wear the civilian uniform of an ordinary candidate, reminds us of the abiding public appeal of a person of talent sincerely devoted to pursuing the general interest, by contrast with the self-serving cleverness of a mere politician.

The Man as a People

It is sometimes held that if a political figure were the absolute incarnation of society, that is, if someone were to perfectly represent all interests and opinions, all expectations and fears, he or she would be unanimously elected and the various contradictions and tensions that plague election would vanish at the same time. To this it will immediately—and rightly— be objected that the implication holds only if certain assumptions about the mind of the voter are granted, and that embodiment in this sense simply has no meaning in a complex and divided society. History is nonetheless filled with grandiose claims to popular universality. In France, as we saw earlier, supporters of the First Empire spoke of a "man-people" in asserting the legitimacy of Napoleon's right to rule. The same expression was revived in connection with his nephew some fifty years later.[21] Napoleon III himself, in a volume setting forth his political ideas, maintained that "the nature of democracy is to personify itself in one man."[22] Both formulas were denounced by the respective adversaries of these regimes, who saw them only as vulgar slogans aimed at masking a craving for personal power and at justifying a fundamentally illiberal form of government. The term "Caesarism" that then came into use as a shorthand for such pretensions implicitly reduced them to a specifically French pathology having its source in the excesses of the Revolution. This failed to notice that Caesarism undeniably enjoyed broad popular support because it had in its own way responded, however unsatisfactorily, not only to a widespread sense of malrepresentation but also to a deep-seated longing for strong-willed and assertive leadership. Caesarism assigned a central place to executive power while at the same time purporting to achieve democratic ideals, by uniting a principle of incarnation with an imperative of responsibility. Far from coming under the head of a mistaken French exceptionalism, this conjunction was later to recur in the guise of a great many totalitarian and populist regimes throughout the world.

Among those that embraced one-man rule in the twentieth century, communist governments were perhaps the most prominent. The concentration of all powers in the executive was only their most visible emblem. Such regimes claimed to have established nothing less than the government of society over itself, since the Party, made homogeneous and unanimous by the liquidation or expulsion of its domestic enemies, is the perfect expression of society.[23] This is why democracy was measured in terms of the "class nature" of a government and not by conformity to certain selection criteria. In the Communist world, the general will was not supposed to be the result of a calculus of individual preferences and opinions, freely expressed (or so bourgeois democracies imagined); it was an objective social fact and historical datum, the will of a united, harmonious, and self-governing community—and therefore capable of being expressed by those who possessed a knowledge of both the present and future state of society. "Representing" society in this sense amounted to a purely cognitive task, not a procedural exercise of some sort. Once the people were really and truly one, there was no longer any difference between representation and social knowledge: the positions of individuals now being completely absorbed by the objectivity of situations, what was true for one and what was true for all were identical.

From this the justification of a one-party state naturally followed, inasmuch as it was only the "form" of an objectively homogeneous class. As Lenin put it, "Proletarian class=Russian Communist Party=Soviet government."[24] These interlocking equivalences led Solzhenitsyn to call Stalin an "Egocrat."[25] Claude Lefort, commenting on this neologism, rightly emphasized that Solzhenitsyn had sought to suggest that such a ruler could not be understood by means of the usual epithets—autocrat, dictator, despot. "With the egocrat," he observed, "the unity of a purely human society is fantastically achieved. With him the perfect mirror of the *One* is established. This is what the word *Egocrat* suggests: not a master who governs alone, free from laws, but one who concentrates social power in his person and appears as though he had absorbed the substance of society, as if, absolute *Ego*, he could expand indefinitely without encountering resistance in things. . . . Even entrenched in the citadel of the Kremlin, it is with the whole of society that he is conjoined."[26] Whereas Louis XIV imagined he embodied the state, Stalin dared to assert something much bolder: "La société, c'est moi." There was therefore no distinction any longer to be made in this case between individual power and social power. The two perfectly coincided. Having merged a completely personalized form of government with the impersonality of the law, the egocrat managed to have it both ways: he could oversee his own cult of personality while at the same time pretending that he was only the anonymous voice of all. At once absolute master and a man embodying an entire people, he never said: "I wish . . ."; always "The Party thinks that . . .", "The Party has decided . . .", "The masses expect that. . . ." Once a government is considered to be the pure incarnation of society, it is the people who govern themselves. In this way the pyramid of identities uniting the leader with the masses succeeds in establishing the only type of regime that can claim to have instituted self-government (known in the Soviet case, literally, as government of and by workers' councils).

Populist movements, particularly in Latin America, exploited the same themes on a smaller scale. "I am not a man, I am a people"—these words, emphatically repeated over and over by the Colombian leader of the 1930s and 1940s, Jorge Eliécer Gaitán, set the tone for populist rhetoric throughout the continent in the decades that followed.[27] Gaitán's background is worth recalling. As a student in Rome, in 1926–1927, he wrote a doctoral thesis under the direction of Enrico Ferri, a famous criminologist who had given up socialism for fascism, and became his protégé. Gaitán attended a number of National Fascist Party rallies and later acknowledged that he had been impressed by Mussolini's ability to dominate a crowd and to channel its energies. He studied *Il Duce*'s gestures with particular care, also the way in which he varied the intonation of his voice to hold the attention of his listeners—techniques that Gaitán faithfully imitated during his subsequent political career in Colombia.

At once anticapitalist, an opponent of oligarchy, and conservative, Gaitán was proclaimed the "people's candidate" in the 1946 presidential elections, in which his party was defeated. Two years later he was assassinated. Since then his name has symbolized both the spirit and the ambiguities of Latin American populism. For his oratorical gifts as well as his ideological fervor he was admired by Fidel Castro; also by Juan Perón, who likewise saw himself as a man-people and who spoke of a sort of depersonalization in describing the profound change that revolution had worked upon him,[28] so that his individuality came to be swallowed up by the collective identity of the Argentinian people. It was this fusion of man and nation of which Eva Perón was to make herself both the interpreter and the guardian,[29] making it clear that everything she possessed in her role as Evita, the daughter of the people (as opposed to Eva, the president's wife), belonged to the people. When her enemies reproached her for her jewels and the magnificence of her wardrobe, in order to discredit her in the popular mind, she proudly retorted to the applause of the crowds that flocked to see her: "Do we, the poor, not have as much right as the rich to wear fur coats and pearl necklaces?"[30] The *we* said it all!

In the present century, during the 2012 presidential election campaign in Venezuela, Hugo Chávez, referring explicitly to Gaitán, repeated the magic formula over and over again: "When I see you," he said to cheering audiences at his rallies, "when you see me, I sense it, something says to me, 'Chávez, you are no longer Chávez, you are a people.' I am in fact no longer myself, I am a people and I am you, this is how I feel, I am incarnate in you. I have said it before and I say it again: We are millions of Chávezes; you also, you are Chávez, Venezuelan woman; you also, you are Chávez, Venezuelan soldier; you also, you are Chávez, fisherman, farmer, peasant, shopkeeper. Because Chávez is no longer me. Chávez is a whole people!"[31] Thus was reborn the old idea of *representation as a mirror.*[32] In his inaugural address as president of the Republic in 1999, Chávez went so far as to tell his audience: "Today I convert myself into your instrument. I scarcely [any longer] exist, and I shall fulfill the mandate that you have confided in me. Prepare to govern!"[33] Here the desire to legitimize a phantasmically democratic presidentialism could not be more frankly stated.

Caesarism, totalitarianism, populism: these categories are evidently not the same, and the regimes falling under them have historically displayed a broad range of tendencies to repression and the restriction of civil liberties. But beyond the very considerable differences among such regimes, one finds the same urge to break free of the constraints of election and put in its place something thought to be fundamentally more democratic, a personalization of power. The politics of identity, on the rise everywhere in the world today, favor the spread of this way of understanding executive power, joining a vision of social homogeneity to an expression of the nation's will embodied by presidential election.

The Politician by Vocation

Analyzing the new situation created a hundred years ago by the reign of modern political parties, far removed from the universalist pretensions we have just been considering, and still further from the eighteenth-century utopia of pure election, Max Weber brought to bear a tough-minded realism on the question of political leadership in the twentieth century. Weber suspected that with the presidentialization of democracy, in contrast to the preceding culture of parliamentary impersonality, the viability of political regimes would increasingly depend on the personal qualities of those who occupied its highest offices.[34] As an alternative to both the ineffectual dilettantism of leading European political figures and the corrupt wheeling and dealing of their American counterparts, he sought to encourage the view of politics as a vocation,[35] a calling that could be answered only by men who were the opposite in every respect of professional politicians. Weber had witnessed the bureaucratization of parties and noted with alarm the growing power of their officials, especially in the case of the best-organized one of the day, the German Social Democratic Party. On all sides he had seen the emergence of political figures without qualities of their own, a whole class of men who were parasites on politics, whether they held public office or were part of a party apparatus or wrote about politics as journalists, men without strong convictions, having only a weak sense of responsibility, if any at all, men whose world was ordered by the infighting of party conferences and the overriding need to win the next election. The great challenge facing democracies at the dawn of the presidentialist era, he believed, was the recruitment of genuine leaders. The challenge was all the greater as history, he feared, was beginning to take another direction.

Referring to the parliament of his own country, Weber wrote that Germans had to make up their minds whether it was to become "a place

for the selection of leaders [or a place for the selection of] people striving
after careers as officials."[36] From the depths of his skepticism he was
nonetheless able to draw a portrait of the type of committed politician
democracies required: persons having a keen awareness of their responsibilities, in the understanding that the exercise of power implied a
duty of accountability; persons capable of displaying independence, ig-
noring partisan influence and serving instead the general interest; persons prepared to devote themselves passionately to a cause; persons
having, finally, good judgment—what he called a "sense of proportion,"
that is, the ability to take a detached view of the present moment, seeing
it against the turbulent background of historical change and complexity
while at the same time "maintaining an inner calm and composure."[37]
But would persons endowed with such qualities, even if in addition they
possessed a certain charismatic charm, really be able to assert themselves under pressure from powerful political machines and escape
their clutches? One may doubt it. Weber described an ideal type of which
history has furnished us with very few examples. We have no choice,
then, but to look beyond perfect leaders in seeking to come to terms with
the presidentialization of politics, this new fact of democratic life
everywhere.

Senior civil servants were sometimes opposed to politicians in We-
berian terms during the twentieth century, particularly in France. Apart
from its rationalizing impulse, the technocratic culture of the age owed
its legitimacy to a similar claim of moral and intellectual superiority,
with the result that technocrats came to see themselves as modern versions of the medieval prince, servant of his subjects, or of the monk-ruler.
"One joined the administration as one might have taken religious
orders, to carry on the fight," as one of the archetypal high officials of
the period, Simon Nora, an inspector of finances, summed up the state
of mind of the cohort that took over after the war.[38] A vocation for public
service, the mystique of the state, a magistracy in the name of the general interest, even a priesthood—these were the sort of images that spontaneously came to mind when such officials were asked to describe their
reasons for serving the state.[39] Nora himself expressed the motivations
and sense of entitlement of his generation with unusual candor: "We
were the finest, the most intelligent, the most honest, the ones who enjoyed legitimacy. It must be recognized that, for thirty or forty years, the
feeling that I express somewhat ironically here is what inspired the tech-

nocratic class."[40] Nora and his colleagues had their own mirrors, a body of writings that came out of the Resistance whose principles they did their very best to live up to. They therefore illustrated an exception—inevitably a transient one as well, for the aristocratic sensibility that animated the *grands corps de l'État*, sure of their duty as the sole legitimate custodians of the general interest,[41] was incompatible over the long term with the advent of a self-consciously democratic society.

Persons for whom politics is a vocation are, as I say, few and far between today. Weber would have been bitterly disappointed, though probably not surprised, to learn that almost a century later careerists in elective office and at the highest levels of the state remain the best-equipped battalions of the political class. Apart from technical reasons having to do with the functioning of parties and the electoral system, certain patterns in the distribution of elites help to explain why this should be so. In every society there are hierarchies among professions, positions, and activities, and corresponding to these are different ways of assigning social status, all of which shape individual ambitions. In Imperial China the bureaucracy attracted the most brilliant minds, whereas science and technology held less appeal; and it was in just these domains, where previously it had been ahead of the West, that China ended up falling far behind. In Renaissance Europe, Jews and other religious minorities, finding themselves barred from holding public office, concentrated their energies in commerce and finance. Intellectual life, for its part, has flourished whenever great intellects have had only a limited choice among careers. In every historical period, the political, economic, military, intellectual, and artistic worlds have exerted varying powers of attraction.

Today it is plain that politics holds little interest for young people by comparison with the arts, business and finance, and the life of the mind. Polls confirm that the social prestige of public office has fallen to new lows. This is perhaps the most regrettable aspect of contemporary political life, for in an age of diminishing social cohesiveness, when critical choices need to be made with regard to the future of the planet, we are more than ever in need of vibrant democracies—and therefore of good rulers. It is not a problem that can be made to go away by waiting for the coming of a providential leader or a supreme savior, someone capable as if by magic of exorcizing the demons of impotence and mediocrity that paralyze democracies today. We must take a more sober view of what the present situation requires, in the hope of being able to discover effective and durable solutions. The broken relationship between society and its rulers is where we will have to start.

The Trustee

Reestablishing a sound relationship between the governed and those who govern depends in the first place on repairing bonds of trust that have been very badly damaged. Trust is what allows us to count on someone. In sociology it has been defined as a disposition toward others making it possible to form a "hypothesis for future behavior."[42] Trust depends on having sufficient knowledge of another person to be able to take for granted his ability to pursue an objective, his sincerity, and his devotion to the common good.[43] It economizes on explanation and justification (a person whom one trusts to accomplish something enjoys an initial presumption of competence and faithfulness) and allows a relationship to be solidly and lastingly established without any need for formalized verification procedures (a verbal agreement has the force of a contract and, in the political sphere, once concluded continues to have effect indefinitely). The importance of the role trust plays between governed and governing is made all the more important today by the fact that the representativeness of the governing class has been severely degraded, as we saw earlier.[44]

Here the value of the old notion of a *trustee,* someone who personifies trust, in describing the qualities of a good ruler becomes clear. Formerly used to characterize and essentialize representation in its most archaic form, as a total delegation of the power to act on behalf of others (with the dual aspect of absolute confidence and unconditional faith in a person's ability to perform the tasks confided to him), this notion paradoxically finds renewed relevance in a post-representative political world,[45] only now in a strictly functional manner since it is in the very nature of executive-governing power to render the notions that originally structured the modern concept of representation, mandate and figuration, effectively obsolete. As a means of intervening in the realm of the unforeseen and the particular, executive power can now be democratically approved, beyond its primary authorization through election, only if it acquires a dimension of intertemporality of the kind that characterizes the position of the trustee. This is what is aimed at in practical terms by the attempt to construct a permanent democracy. In Chapter 12 we considered the problem in connection with the obligation of responsiveness that those who govern owe to the governed. Now, through the notion of trust, creating a robust and sustainable relationship between government and society can be seen also to depend on the character and qualities of governors themselves.

Two things are essential for this purpose. First of all, integrity. By providing valuable information about the character of candidates and their moral fitness to hold public office, integrity makes it possible to judge how well they meet the responsibilities that election confers upon them. Second, truthfulness, which is to say speaking plainly, frankly, and, above all, honestly. In the absence of truthfulness, no relationship of trust can be created. I now take up these qualities in turn, beginning with the second one.

☲ 14 ☲

Truthfulness

"Public speech has become a dead language," a leading political figure recently noted.[1] He had in mind a kind of language that, because it is no longer comprehensible, goes unheard. Once it had been a living language. As a living language, it did two things: it created social bonds and served as a vehicle for mutual understanding, on the one hand, and, by producing meaning and knowledge, made it possible to efficiently explore reality, on the other. The atrophy of these two functions brought about its demise. Words such as "people" and "solidarity" seem now to echo in a void, having been deprived of all substance by politicians, male and female alike. They do not talk about life as it is experienced by the citizens they represent. The feeling that ordinary people have of not being listened to is only strengthened by the emptying out of these words.

This is a very serious problem, for to govern is also to speak—in order to explain oneself, to look forward, to set a course, to account for one's actions. To govern is to speak because language is, quite simply, the instrument we use to make sense of the world. A genuinely democratic politics gives voice to the lives people actually live, makes the purposes of public policy legible and the obstacles to successfully carrying it out understood, finds the words to express the nation's feeling at moments both of trial and triumph. To speak truly helps to give people more con-

is to say a method of posing a question, marshaling arguments and ex-
pounding them effectively by means of a balanced periodic style, and
creating a sense of drama and expectation that give the peroration the
force of triumphant obviousness.[6] It therefore required a competence
that could be taught and eventually mastered through training and
practice. Rhetoric was an intellectual discipline, for it was founded on
the idea that the power of reasoned argumentation is what wins support
and carries a decision. But it was also an art of seduction, for it convinced
the listener by acting upon his passions and his instinctive beliefs. The
orator sought to control the minds of his listeners, to impose his authority upon them, to make them prisoners of his eloquence. Speech
was no more than an instrument, then, a means of achieving an end, a
way of obtaining approval. An audience's deepest and most considered
convictions played no part in the matter.[7] In Athens, a city where vir-
tuosos of the spoken word presided over a permanent festival of eloquence, orators were admired as artists of a particular kind, theatrical
performers whose feats of verbal skill dazzled their listeners.[8] For a
practitioner of *parrēsia*, by contrast, it was the truth of the message that
mattered before all else. One identified oneself with it to the point of
making oneself speech incarnate. In personally committing oneself to
one's audience, however, so that speaker and speech were wholly united,
there could not help but be an element of danger. "The orator," Foucault
observed, "can perfectly well be an effective liar whom others find convincing. The *parrèsiaste*, by contrast, will be the courageous sayer of a
truth in which he risks himself and his relationship with others."[9]

A person who spoke truly and forthrightly was therefore the exact
opposite of someone who aimed to charm and flatter. He consciously
ran the risk of arousing opposition, of exposing himself to reprimand
and rejection. He had no fear of going against the prevailing view
because he had fully armed himself in the very act of saying what he
believed to be true. A person who spoke plainly in this sense found himself fortified by a kind of moral, sometimes even physical, courage. Demosthenes, in the *Philippics,* memorably recalled that he had "narrowly
escaped being torn to pieces" several times for having directly challenged
popular opinion,[10] making it clear that he had accepted in advance the
troubles that his words might bring him.[11] Demosthenes stood up to his
audience. He reproached it for allowing "its self-satisfaction to be flattered by listening only to pleasing speeches," and charged that by their

indolence and their indifference the Athenians had given the advantage to Philip of Macedon.[12] Reading these extraordinary orations today, one feels sure that Demosthenes must in fact more than once have been physically assaulted by his fellow citizens, with grave risk to his life. A more vivid illustration of how completely *parrēsia* differs from trying to please and get ahead can scarcely be imagined. Politics is not a trade to be taken up by careerists, for it demands total commitment. Truthfulness is the outstanding characteristic of a person for whom politics is a vocation in Weber's sense.

One finds an echo of this conception in the thinking of certain figures in France during the Revolution. Camille Desmoulins, who represented the best of the journalism of the period, insisted that "what distinguishes the republican is the frankness of his language."[13] The character of a republic, he maintained, consists "in concealing nothing, in going straight to the point, openly, in speaking plainly, as to men and things alike."[14] But the problem during the Revolution had been a lack of just these things—what was called an "abuse of words." The obstacles to plain speaking did not arise solely from an excess of demagoguery. They had their source also in the indefiniteness of the language as it was spoken and written, in its ambiguities, whether deliberate or otherwise, which had the effect of muddying public debate by giving different, sometimes quite opposite meanings to the same terms. The discrepant uses of the word "people" had testified to this from the very beginning, and nowhere more clearly than in the debate that took place at Versailles on 14 May 1789 regarding the composition of the new national assembly. A return to the term "Estates-General" had initially been suggested, but it was quickly rejected as having too much of an odor of the ancien régime about it. The alternative put forward by Sieyès, "Assembly of the Known and Verified Representatives of the French Nation,"[15] was discarded not only because it seemed overly legalistic but also because it did not appear to have any usefulness beyond the needs of the present moment. Mirabeau, renowned for his way with words, felt that "Representatives of the French People" would have the advantages of both forcefulness and simplicity. Nevertheless, he was rebuked by several men who were to take their place among the most influential members of the Constituent Assembly. "If by the word 'people,'" Target objected, "you mean what the Romans called *plebs*, you then admit a distinction among orders; if this word answers to *populus*, you extend the right and intention of the Commons too far."[16] Thouret, for his part, regretting that it is "a word that lends itself to all things," abruptly settled the matter by saying: "The word 'people' does not express what we have in mind."[17]

The problem of verbal ambiguity did not end there. From the beginning of the Revolution it was clear that a new vocabulary was needed to describe the motives and principles of the new political order that was being established. One no longer spoke of subjects, for example, but of citizens; not of a kingdom, but of a nation; and so on. It was a time of extraordinary inventiveness in this connection, and a novel political language did in fact emerge. But not only was it a language in flux, it was liable to be corrupted as well. Some of the most bitter recriminations expressed during the Terror concerned just this point. Thus Sieyès, the father of the first French Constitution, scathingly denounced "the infamous prostitution of the words most dear to French hearts, Liberty, Equality, People," considering "the abuse of what once was a common language" to be by no means the least source of the misfortunes of the age, words having now lost their natural meaning and been made to "conspire with the enemies of our country."[18] One of the most acute observers of the new France, the poet Heinrich Heine (whose great talents as an essayist and a journalist are largely forgotten today), was under no illusion as to the power wielded by the *Moniteur universel* in 1793: "This is a book of magic that you cannot put in chains, for it contains conjuring spells much more powerful than gold and rifles, words with which the dead can be awakened in their tombs and the living sent unto the shades of death, words that turn dwarves into giants and with the aid of which giants are crushed, words that can destroy your power with a single stroke, as an axe lops off a king's head."[19] Detached from reality and harnessed to an ideology, employed as weapons, words were no longer placed in the service of public debate and democratic discussion. They had become instruments instead for policing thought and manipulating minds, in order either to overthrow a government or to keep it in power.

False speech of this sort has a more pernicious influence on democratic life even than the orator's indifference to truth. For now not only does language work to seduce and dissemble, it creates a factitious and caricatural world that outlaws all opposition and banishes the very possibility of inquiring into the conduct of public affairs. It has the effect, in Cochin's famous phrase, of "eliminating reality in the mind instead of reducing unintelligibility in the object."[20] This effect is never more

language," which stood accused of having "stabbed" the Revolution of 1848. And Blanqui himself, well known for his loathing of those whom he called "artists of speech," railed time and again against "the deplorable popularity of bourgeois disguised as tribunes" with all their "high-sounding lawyerly phrases."[25] Quotations of this sort could be endlessly multiplied. The interesting point for our purposes is that the denunciation of fine words that cajole and deceive the people led not to a demand for plain speaking, but instead to a glorification of direct action, of immediately effective insurrection. Bringing about a revolution, for Blanqui as for Lenin after him and others of their type, was not a matter of inciting society to deliberate in order to agree on a common plan of action; it was a matter of acting from the very first, not of talking (a prejudice that naturally went hand in hand with a reverence for the revolutionary vanguard). "Whoever has the sword has bread," as Blanqui, the prisoner of Belle-Île-en-Mer, put it in his famous toast of 25 February 1851. For these leftist agitators, as for right-wing proponents of decisionism,[26] speech itself was the enemy. First, because it distracted from the goal to be achieved, but also because it was associated with a positive view of discussion that implicitly endorsed an unacceptable form of relativism. One finds the same belief among all these enemy brothers in a truth, whether historical or religious, that imposes itself on humanity and makes debate of opposing ideas both useless and dangerous. "Man is born to act," the conservative Spanish political theorist Juan Donoso Cortés declared, "and perpetual discussion, incompatible with action, is altogether contrary to human nature."[27] Parliamentarianism, which did nothing more than grant power to a debating society, was evidently a hopeless cause. Executive power, by contrast, recommended itself because it held out the prospect of getting on at once with the business of governing, without interference or delay. Lenin in particular defended this position and all that it implied, amounting to a veritable hatred of speech. The Party had to be on its guard against becoming a "discussion club," he warned; there was no place in it for "freedom of criticism." For speaking (pejoratively referred to as mere "talk," "whining," or simply "hysteria"), Lenin was determined to substitute the sole authority of the *slogan*.[28] In the Soviet dispensation, the slogan was not a useful shorthand, something that helpfully condenses a complicated idea, but a watchword, in the strict sense of the term—an order for something to be done, about which there was no room whatever for argument or second-guessing.

The slogan, in other words, expressed both a military and a militant necessity.

If to speak truly is, by definition, not to lie, plain speaking nonetheless cannot hope to aspire to a perfectly direct connection between speaking and being. Kant, who believed that lying is fundamentally responsible for the corruption of human nature, had asked in *Anthropologie in pragmatischer Hinsicht* [1798] what would happen in a society in which people could only think out loud, which is to say in which all their thoughts were immediately and fully expressed.[29] While he unreservedly rejected lying, Kant held that inevitably there are things that one thinks and yet at the same time would not dare say, even to one's best friend, for fear of upsetting or annoying him, for example. Whereas Kant thought it both desirable and possible to undertake never to say things that one does not think, he felt one is justified in sometimes refraining from saying things that one does think (Jon Elster, extending this line of argument, has gone so far as to speak of the "civilizing force of hypocrisy").[30] To a psychologically impossible ideal of openheartedness [*Offenherzigkeit*], Kant opposed the more feasible aim of sincerity [*Aufrichtigkeit*]. Well adapted though it is to an ethics of personal relationships, plainly this distinction cannot be transposed to political language. In a democracy it must be possible to say everything, at least as far as the functioning of society is concerned.

Finally, in order to understand the historical context within which a devotion to plain speaking first took shape, we must take into account the French revolutionary ambition of devising what might be called an absolute language. One of the earliest responses to the "abuse of words" that often hampered public discussion during the French Revolution had been to try to settle the meaning of the words making up the vocabulary of politics, in order to remedy the confused state of debate resulting from semantic ambiguity. This was notably the case, as we saw a moment ago, with the word "people." Indeed, the suggestion had been made that misuse of it should be punished on the ground that the effects were far more dangerous and long-lasting than was commonly suspected. "If the false use of the word 'People' has been for the spiteful a pretext and a means," urged Adrien Duquesnoy, writing in *L'Ami des patriotes* in July 1791, "it has been an excuse for the simple-minded and the credulous. It is time that the National Assembly put an end to this cause of confusion, and anyone who uses the word 'People' in any other acceptation than the one it ought to have should be very sternly called to order."[31] A remarkable note addressed in Year III to the Committee of Public Safety on "the true meaning of the word *people*" was inspired by the same concern. It is worth quoting at length:

> A confusion of words necessarily entails a confusion of ideas; and up to now most writers, journalists, even chairmen of our Committees, have spoken to us of the *people* of such-and-such a commune, or department, or region, and so on. It is not surprising that popular Societies also believe themselves to be a *people* and that several of their members, whether malevolent or misinformed, draw from this absolutely false principle the very correct conclusion that *wherever is the people, is the sovereign. . . .* The Convention should forestall the recurrence of like errors, by teaching those who do not know or who affect not to know in order to mislead their fellow citizens: first, that the true meaning, the only acceptation of the word *people* is the general collection of all the individuals who form a social body and who live under the same laws; second, that the word *people,* which one is almost forced to use in many circumstances to express the totality of the citizens who compose such-and-such a commune, assembly, etc., is in fact only a *section of the people,* in whatever number these citizens may be, and that it can be understood only as a vernacular and habitual expression; third, and finally, that true sovereignty belongs to the people alone, taken collectively; from which it results that the sovereign is essentially one and indivisible, that it is only a purely metaphysical being, which is to say the expression of the general will, and that, were it otherwise, we would have forty thousand sovereigns in France, as many as there are communes.[32]

A note, one imagines, that had little influence.

Condorcet's purpose in founding the *Journal d'instruction sociale,* in 1793, was more pedagogical than punitive. Its objective was to "combat political charlatans" by elucidating the key terms of an orthodox political lexicon and thereby limit variant and illegitimate interpretations.[33] The journal's motto was simply stated: "Reason is one, and has only one language."[34] In the same spirit, Sieyès proposed that an attempt be made to "fix the language," giving it a stable and permanent form by means of conventions, and thus to provide politics with a "proper language" uncontaminated by the imprecision of "natural language."[35] Sieyès was seconded in this by Destutt de Tracy, author of the five-volume *Élémens d'idéologie* [1815–1818], who sought to create an "analytic language" that would help modify and improve the practice of democracy.[36] The utopian conception of linguistic purity as the condition of plain speaking came to nothing in either case, but there was no getting around the necessity of confronting fundamental questions arising from the indefinite character of political semantics. Democracy is, after all, a regime that unavoidably involves continual and perpetual debate over its basic concepts and terminology.

The Wellsprings of Plain Speaking

We must go back again to Demosthenes, and to the notion of *parrēsia*, in order to see that speaking truly and forthrightly depends above all on wholehearted personal commitment. Whereas the Athenian statesman Aeschines had insisted on the necessity of forming an alliance with Philip of Macedon, Demosthenes called upon his fellow citizens in a series of immortal speeches to oppose the conqueror's designs. "The monster"—this was the insulting epithet Aeschines used to refer to his great rival; and monstrous indeed in his eyes must have seemed the resources of a supreme eloquence united with unsurpassed conviction, which he could only envy and fear in equal measure. Twenty-three centuries later, Georges Clemenceau published a penetrating study of Demosthenes's singular power, whose sources he showed to have been no less anthropological than political. The man responsible for France's resurgence in 1917, himself known as "the Tiger," whose speeches and writings galvanized wavering resolve both at home and in the trenches, had constantly read and meditated upon the *Philippics* during those dark years. After the war he summed up his reflections in an impassioned essay that, curiously, has been all but forgotten since.[37] Clemenceau sought to discover what it was ultimately that had given such extraordinary force to his words by comparison with those of Aeschines. To his way of thinking, the discrepancy could not be understood in terms of technique alone. While recognizing each one's special talents, he found the two men evenly matched. Their attitudes toward speaking, by contrast, were quite different. It was on this point that Clemenceau brought his own expertise and personal experience as an orator to bear.

He laid particular emphasis on the fact that, in moments of crisis, "the crowd seeks to be swayed less by a speaker than by a man, one who is truly a man." For "it is not [the orator's] art that wins our admiration. It is the unreserved offering of will in its pure form. So understood,

234 A DEMOCRACY OF TRUST

speech can be seen to acquire the power of action."[38] In Demosthenes,

the practitioner of *parrēsia*, word and action were joined together,

forming a kind of speech that was the highest possible expression of

temperament and determination. This for Clemenceau was the essen-

tial thing. Whereas Aeschines presented his arguments with exceeding

brilliance, Demosthenes was able to do this and much more. He was able

to reach down to the "depths of his being" and bring forth the most pro-

found emotion, so that his listeners could not but feel that he had given

everything of himself to them. What one saw in Aeschines was an ex-

ercise in virtuosity; in Demosthenes one saw "his life bursting forth at

the will of an impetuous fortune." From this, Clemenceau concluded, it

follows that "the orator persuades an assembly less by the soundness of

his reasoning . . . than by the impression he creates of pouring his heart

and soul into the contest."[39] True communication with an audience, in

other words, springs from a *giving of oneself.* For then the spoken word

has been made indivisibly one with an irrevocable and unshakable per-

Truthfulness in this sense therefore goes well beyond what Kant

meant by sincerity (to which, it seems to me, the English word "candor"

corresponds) and the related notion of authenticity; it signifies a radical

form of involvement in public life, a profound link between personal

existence and collective destiny. Nearer our own time one is put in mind

of De Gaulle's Appeal of 18 June 1940 and Churchill's great speeches

promising blood, sweat, and tears. These moments do not belong to the

class of routine appeals and promises. Clemenceau likened them to "cat-

apults that crush the obstacle with a single blow," calls that inspire citi-

zens to rise above themselves. This is the plain speaking that is required

at times of extreme crisis, when circumstances can only be exceptional.

It is a kind of speech of which only a very few are capable—those very

few whose commitment has never failed.

Plain speaking in ordinary times is less heroic, and in such times it

is indeed closely connected with sincerity. But it is not only a product of

personal virtue; it is also the result of a certain quality of democratic

life. On this point it is necessary to start out from the fact that truthful-

ness is undermined by the structural dualism of political language in a

democracy that we noted earlier. Political language is deployed in two

registers that correspond to distinct objectives: on the one hand, there is the language of getting elected, whose purpose is to help win the greatest number of votes; on the other, the language of governing, which aims at justifying a policy or a course of action. Electoral language relies on seduction and accusation. A candidate seeks not only to discredit or to disqualify his adversaries (particularly by casting their record in an unfavorable light), but also to set himself apart from them (with regard to values, ideologies, or programs) while at the same time aligning his own positions with public opinion as nearly as possible. On the one hand, then, there is a polemical and censorious way of talking about the past, on the other a kind of speech that encourages voters by means of promises and blandishments to look forward to a better future. The discourse of those who govern, by contrast, emphasizes the constraints on action, the many different interests that government must conciliate, and the gravity of the events with which it must deal. Whereas electoral language is founded on both an art of compromise (in order to enlarge a candidate's core support) and an art of avoidance (in order to sidestep awkward subjects or postpone difficult decisions),[40] governmental language must arbitrate and decide—and, by virtue of just this, divide—under the pressures of a daily imperative of *survival,* of having to sustain parliamentary and public confidence from one day to the next, that takes precedence over all else. Even on the implausible assumption that electoral language is animated by a genuine intention to speak truly, it cannot help but turn out in practice to be more or less distant from plain speaking in the fullest sense. This discrepancy is at the root of much that harmfully interferes with democratic life.

What is more, it is a discrepancy that inevitably is aggravated by two tendencies. First, the immediacy and urgency of a given program, which serve to link the language of campaigning with the language of governing, at least in a relatively closed and stable system, tend to fade over time. Second, the presidentialization of democracy, combined with the growing media coverage of politicians, widens the gap further not only by giving a personal face to promises but also by establishing a much more visible way to assign responsibility and apportion blame. Add to these two things the fact that ongoing debate between an opposition minority and a governing majority has the effect of instituting a permanent election campaign in which the two languages are inextricably entangled, and it will be evident that any attempt to eliminate this dual aspect of democratic discourse, essential if truthfulness is one day to become the norm, must come from outside the hermetic world of professional politicians. This will be possible only if citizens themselves understand and embrace the role that is theirs alone to play—something that is far from being the case today. There is, of course, a certain psychological comfort in refusing to accept this challenge, since then one remains free to criticize politicians as harshly as one likes while at the same time feeling justified in doing nothing to change what appears to be an unalterable situation. But it is a false and dangerous comfort. Just as there can be no demagogue without a crowd wanting to be flattered, so a double political language cannot prosper without a schizophrenic electorate.

Finally, truthfulness has a reflexive dimension. This is not only because there is a truth that speaking truly expresses. Speaking truly also implies a recognition of the intrinsic indeterminacy of democracy, from which the ambiguity of its language largely derives. Democracy is indeterminate in its subject, for the very notion of the "people" can be understood sociologically, politically, and juridically; in each case it is associated with specific modes of expression and procedures of representation, with the result that the people is at once a civic body, society in a general sense, and a group of distinct populations considered as one. Democracy is no less indeterminate in its object, for the idea of social emancipation may be interpreted as both a means of autonomy and a means of power. Finally, democracy is indeterminate in the forms it assumes, since representative procedures, for example, can be understood functionally (as a set of techniques for managing popular demands and social problems) or substantively (as a constitutive element of a specific regime type). Hence the recursive character of truthfulness, since democracy consists fundamentally in the unremitting examination of its own indeterminacy. This means having to clarify its underlying tensions and contradictions as well.

The Battlegrounds of Plain Speaking

The struggle on behalf of an obligation to speak truly and forthrightly is waged on three fronts. The most obvious one is that of falsehood and lying. But it must be pressed with equal vigor on two others, in order to

The battle for plain speaking must, secondly, take the form of an attack on political monologues, which is to say a kind of autistic speech, the rhetoric of reasoned nonconfrontation with others. By reducing public debate to a succession of pointless outbursts, on the model of trench warfare, the lifeblood of democracy is drained away. Debate of this kind contributes very little in the way of information; and because it avoids subjecting arguments to any real scrutiny, it very seldom helps to state problems clearly, much less to propose workable solutions. This aspect of political discourse has a long history. It first attracted attention in the context of parliamentary debate, which was once supposed to constitute the archetype of civilized discussion. With regard to a crucial point of order—should interventions in the chambers be improvised, in order to promote a spirit of give-and-take and, by their spontaneity, encourage the lively exchange of ideas, or should they take the form of speeches composed in advance and then read out by their authors, with the risk that they will form an incoherent and unproductive sequence?—the English and French models were diametrically opposed.

In England, from long tradition, speeches were on the whole improvised, with speakers being allowed only to rely on a few brief notes as an aid to memory. The arrangement of the two houses, and their intimate atmosphere, made this a rather natural way of proceeding. Because each member stood up to speak in his place, in the absence of a rostrum, interventions preserved an air of informality enlivened by extemporaneous invention, and, as a consequence, debate often rose to the level of genuine discussion. The French experience was altogether different. From the time of the Revolution, for reasons of both principle and habit, oral presentation of prepared speeches had been the rule. The preference for formal composition was associated in the first place with the view, inherited from the Enlightenment, that it was conceptually superior as a method of communication.[46] "The art of making written speeches," Condorcet was to say, "is the true rhetoric of the moderns, and the eloquence of a speech is precisely that of a book made to be understood by all minds on a quick reading." Hence the necessity of substituting "reasoning for eloquence, books for speakers."[47] Some years later, Sismondi made the same point with even greater assurance: "Serious discussion, that which fills every thinking mind with light and truth, is supported by books."[48] To these considerations, founded on a critique of ancient rhetoric, was added a democratic argument: because speeches were written down to begin with, they were readily printed and therefore could hope to find an audience beyond the chambers of parliament. This was a backhanded way of criticizing the British parliamentary tradition, still marked by a strong sense of belonging to a private society, a sort of gentlemen's club. The architectural plan of the French chambers gave physical expression to the departure from the English model as well. Having to mount a rostrum looking out over a hemicycle could not help but give the orator's performance a more solemn character. His position was rather that of a professor lecturing to an audience seated in an amphitheater than of a debater answering his opponent from the same platform. The presence of a large lectern also permitted the orator to comfortably lay out his papers. The French system was almost designed, one might say, to produce an endless stream of monologues.

This system, despite several attempts at reform,[49] has persisted until the present day. Jeremy Bentham sharply criticized it,[50] and Benjamin Constant devoted an entire chapter of his *Principes de politique* [1815] to showing how troublesome its implications were from a democratic point of view. One point he felt worthy of particular emphasis:

> When orators limit themselves to reading what they have written in the silence of their Study, they no longer discuss, they amplify. They do not listen, for what they would hear must change nothing in what they are about to say; they wait for the speaker who comes before to finish; they do not examine the opinion he defends, they count the minutes he takes up and which seem to them a delay. Since there is no longer any discussion, each one reproduces objections already refuted; each leaves to one side anything he has not anticipated, anything that would interfere with his prearranged address. Speakers succeed one another without meeting; if one refutes another, it is by chance; they are like two armies on parade in opposite directions, each marching alongside the other, scarcely aware of its presence, avoiding even to look at it, for fear of departing from an unalterable course.[51]

Two decades later, in his *Livre des orateurs* (published under the pseudonym "Timon"), Cormenin vividly described the difference between the two ways of delivering a speech, comparing the *récitateur* unfavorably to the *orateur:* a speaker who reads from a written text "does not look at the assembly, [he] retreats and disappears into himself and takes up residence in the houses of his mind, where his sentences are all arranged in their proper place. . . . [A reciter has] the eloquence of the day before, whereas the orator must be the man of the moment."[52]

The shrinking of debate to a series of monologues has since been extended to encompass every aspect of political expression, with the same effect of impoverishing democratic society. A monologue is a way of speaking that takes no risk and that, because it can never be challenged, lives on without fear of contradiction inside a fortress of pure assertion. It serves to further harden already entrenched positions by enforcing a particular type of discourse to the exclusion of any other, by encouraging citizens to take sides unreflectively rather than helping them to make up their own minds through the examination of facts and the comparison of arguments. Citizens are thus condemned to passivity. To the question of how this cunning form of slow political death might be counteracted, there is no ready juridical or institutional answer. Fortunately one cannot imagine a law being passed making truthful speech mandatory, except in a totalitarian regime determined to turn it to its own advantage (which is done in various ways, most notably by punishing alleged attempts to subvert the institutions of state). But one might well imagine requiring candidates for public office to take notice of the views of civic groups on all relevant topics in order to promote debate in various settings, at every level, from community councils to nationally televised forums, with the assistance of existing institutions and ones that have yet to be designed. Already a number of broadly representative ad hoc councils and commissions have aided the examination of controversial issues and cleared away obstacles to decision making on sensitive subjects (in France, one thinks of what the Commission on Nationality accomplished regarding citizenship in 1987,[53] of the progress made in clarifying the principle of secularism by the Stasi Commission in 2003, and by the ongoing study of the retirement system by the Pensions Advisory Council, to mention only three well-known examples). The media likewise have a role to play in these areas, with much the same objective of causing partisan verbiage to collapse beneath the weight of its own pomposity, of forcing politicians to come out from behind their protective shell, of helping citizens face up to reality by pulling down ideological barriers. Here again, the democratic function of journalism becomes increasingly vital.[54]

A third front in the battle for plain speaking has been opened up by the sudden emergence of a *language of intentions*. This is a new political development of relatively recent origin. It arose from a general mood of disorientation and powerlessness that, as we have seen, spread in reaction to the impersonal rule of the market and bloated government. Bringing these forces under control will be possible, it is believed, only through an exercise of will in some form other than the one I have called projective. The new language of intentions signals the advent of a kind of political discourse that is less concerned with working cooperatively to change and improve existing policies than with displaying a positive, dignified, yet implacable determination to encourage general resistance to the established order, brushing aside incantatory attempts by conservative forces to co-opt opposition through purely cosmetic reform. The new language restores a feeling of having some measure of personal control over events.

In order to grasp its motivations and purposes, one must have a clear idea of what it is not. It is not the old ideological language, corsetted in certainties; it is not campaign speech, filled with empty promises; it is not monologue, secure in its autism. Nor is it "politically correct" discourse, which smothers reality beneath a thick veneer of self-righteousness, or totalitarian discourse, which imprisons its listeners in an imaginary universe. Nor, finally, is it a matter simply of giving voice to one's convictions. It is something altogether different. It is a language that is bound up with the perception of a world governed by intentions from which all realities issue. Here resistance means taking up arms in order to impose new intentions from which a different and better world may at last emerge. This language is on the ascendant today, not only in social policy but also in economic policy and foreign policy. It cuts society off from its old moorings and retethers it to its own reality, which is to say a determination to remake the world. In this respect it is inherently averse to compromise and practical arrangements, for in the land of intentions everything is in black and white, and good can only be confronted by evil. Politics is thereby reduced to a moral and political choice that does not have to explain where it stands in relation to actual events; good will is enough, having been erected into a cardinal principle. The tenacity with which the Greek government and the institutions of the European Union defended their respective positions after Alexis Tsípras was sworn in as prime minister in January 2015 is a typical consequence of the new language. In placing negotiations on a terrain where no common ground can be found, for want of any objective reality recognized by each side, it is bound to produce stalemate and ill will.

often lags behind popular feeling in such matters, strong pressure has been brought to bear to bring the two into closer alignment. Here the horizon of political integrity coincides with the etymological idea of a complete and unimpaired whole. A person of integrity is someone who has a single-minded devotion to serving the public interest, who is wholly committed to carrying out his responsibilities, and who does not seek to profit from his office. The notion of representation, for its part, has also been modified by the advent of a personal style of politics. Good representation, as it is presently understood, is sensitive to the experience of ordinary men and women. In addition to displaying compassion, representatives and officials are expected to live as their fellow citizens do. In France, an administrative memorandum circulated to members of Jean-Pierre Raffarin's government, laying down rules for the allotment of ministerial housing, reminded them of the "simplicity that is appropriate to representatives of the state" and went into great detail regarding the size of apartments, specifying the maximum number of square meters deemed to be consistent with this principle.[1] Simplicity, it is now supposed, constitutes a self-evident proof of integrity and credibility.

Confidence in government officials is directly related to the credibility they enjoy. It is significant that Philippe de Commynes, one of the fathers of modern political thought, coined the term *crédit* (which he derived from the Latin *creditum*, past participle of *credere*, to believe)[2] in order to define an attribute of government on which the capacity for influence and the freedom available for its exercise depend. Credit in this sense corresponds to a certain capital, namely, the trust that government possesses. Distrust, to the contrary, is nourished by doubt and uncertainty, sometimes founded on objective observations concerning past behavior, sometimes simply on vague suspicions. Let us first consider the latter circumstance. Suspicions of this sort typically arise from a sort of negative halo effect involving an entire professional cohort (the "political class," for example), which is seen to be more concerned with pursuing its own advantage than with promoting the common good. Corruption, conflicts of interest, influence peddling, having a financial or other stake in companies subject to government regulation—all these things, which belong as much to the language of law as the language of public morality, point to a single phenomenon: the subordination of the common good to personal ends. The misdeeds of some, amplified by the scandals they are bound to provoke, feed mistrust of all. Transparency in politics is meant to provide basic information that will make it possible to limit the spread of suspicion, while also exerting a preventive effect by obliging the persons concerned to give a detailed accounting of their financial position, including the sources of investment and other income, annual fluctuations in net worth, and so on. Transparency, in other words, aspires to be a guardian of public integrity. In an age when powerlessness is experienced as a loss of personal control over the course of events, the morality of political leadership—and the prospect of regulating it by means of transparency—are fundamental points of reference in restoring popular sovereignty to its rightful place.

Three Transparencies

Transparency is at once praised and decried. It is praised as an unimprovable remedy for all the defects of politics and a sure means of bringing about the reign of virtue. It is decried as the vehicle of a new form of voyeuristic tyranny, ravenously destructive of the right to privacy, that can only lead to a degraded and degrading opinion of political life. Despite the controversy that surrounds it, transparency plays a similar role today to the one played by publicity in the nineteenth century in helping to usher in an era of liberal-democratic regimes. But it is also distinct from publicity in two ways. First, transparency has a moral dimension that is bound up with notions of purity, honesty, authenticity, and a direct relation between actions and words. Whereas publicity was understood in terms of the availability of information, as a way of giving broad circulation to an objective record of political debate, transparency exposes to view an undecipherable world of obscurity and secrecy populated by reversed images of everything that is plainly seen in the light of day. Transparency is as strangely attractive and redeeming as the night is sinning and fraught with mysterious temptations.

Second, transparency has a wider field of application. Publicity had to do essentially with the relations between the executive and the legislature, as well as between the legislature and public opinion. In an age of transparency, it is *personal behavior* that assumes decisive importance. For want of being able to say what government positively must *do,* the predominant concern now is with what it should *be.* To this extent transparency is part of a larger attempt to transfigure politics. In a time of democratic skepticism and mistrust, when the way in which politicians conduct themselves is more important than any ideas they may defend, it favors a method of analysis and evaluation that substitutes demonstrations of sincerity for what is thought to be the more problematic business of assessing the effectiveness of government. In this context, moral repugnance becomes a decisive variable in the exercise of political judgment on all sides. To fully appreciate the consequences of this transformation for democratic life, we will need to make the notion of transparency more precise. Three senses may be distinguished: transparency as a utopia, as an ideology, and as an instrument.

The utopian view of transparency has historically been associated with Rousseau and, for the most part, with what he had to say about it in the *Confessions*. Describing his ambition for this book, he made a startling admission: "I should like to be able to make my soul transparent to the eyes of the reader, as it were, and for this purpose I seek to present it from all points of view, to show it under all lights, to ensure that no movement occurs in it which he does not perceive, so that he may judge for himself of the principle which produces them."[3] Transparency in this sense defined both a literary method and a literary objective. The *Confessions* was an utterly novel work that brilliantly inaugurated a new genre: the psychological exploration of the self, a fearless plunge into the naked privacy of actions and the secrecy of thoughts. But for Rousseau, transparency was also the basis of all morality. Having a just and proper relationship to others meant banishing secrecy and dissimulation.[4] It was exactly this that he imagined he had done in a famous passage where he speaks of "my heart, transparent as crystal, [which] has never, not for a moment, been able to hide even the faintest sentiment that sought refuge there."[5] Various objections to this conception of morality, and particularly the idea that dissimulation in some form or other may often be indispensable in establishing and preserving peaceable social relations, have been amply commented on and argued about. The essential thing to notice for our purposes is the aim underlying Rousseau's argument, of instituting transparency as a *social state* in such a way that it coincides with a certain *political ideal*.

The problem of transparency had occupied him from the time of his earliest book, the *Discours sur l'origine et les fondements de l'inégalité parmi les hommes* [1755]. In dedicating this work, he described the place where he would have wanted to be born as one "where each person is known to every other, where neither the obscure workings of vice nor the modesty of virtue could escape the notice and judgment of the Public, where this noble habit of seeing and knowing one another makes love of Country a love of one's fellow citizens rather than of a land."[6] The transparency he had in mind was not only a quality of being, a moral disposition; it was also a *social bond*. Individuals came at once to be citizens solely by virtue of their mutual visibility. Later, in the *Considérations sur le gouvernement de Pologne* [1782], Rousseau emphasized that small states "prosper for this very reason, that they are small, and that the rulers can see for themselves the evil that is done and the good that they must try to do, and that their orders are carried out under their direction."[7] Mutual visibility was the "strongest," the "most powerful," indeed an "infallible" means of creating a unified society. It consisted in "acting in such a way that every citizen feels himself constantly regarded by the public, that no one advances and no one succeeds but by means of public favor, that no post, no office is occupied except through the wishes of the nation . . . , that all so depend on public esteem, that no one can do anything, acquire anything, succeed at anything without it."[8]

Transparency he saw both as a form of social existence and as the moral means by which it is brought into being. It is owing to transparency that a group of individuals can be made into a *civil society*, a polity, in which each person immediately becomes a citizen, thus resolving the dilemma Rousseau first perceived in *Émile* [1762].[9] Transparency cannot help but lead each person to deindividualize himself, as it were—to detach himself from his own private interest, to let the mask slip and in this way become *himself*, "without contradiction."[10] The authenticity to which this transparency corresponds causes the individual and the universal to exactly overlap, with the consequence that each person then exists for his neighbor in the manner of one clear-eyed gaze meeting another, a moment of pure communion from which emanates the enveloping light of a silent truth. Jean Starobinski, in a famous commentary, recalling the importance Rousseau attached to the chemical phenomena of fusion, amalgamation, and transmutation, likened his conception of personal transparency to the process of vitrification. In Rousseau, he observed, "the technique of vitrification is inextricably associated with dreams of innocence and of immortality."[11] Rousseau initially became interested in these phenomena while working for several years alongside his first patron, Dupin de Francueil, in an attempt to summarize the current state of knowledge about chemistry. The result of their collaboration was a massive work, *Institutions chymiques* [1747], which gathered a vast harvest of scientific images that Rousseau was to draw upon in his later writings.[12] He showed a particularly lively interest in the ideas of the German physician Johann Joachim Becher, who had developed a whole theory of vitrification according to which, because man himself is "glass," his ashes are capable of being transformed into a "fine transparent glass."[13]

What Rousseau means by transparency, then, is very far removed from the mere idea of publicity. It is inseparable from the ideal of a society that is fully devoted to achieving the common good. By substituting for the vagaries of discussion and negotiation the certainty that comes from making hearts and minds immediately accessible to one another, Rousseau radically essentialized moral and political virtue. In the absence of such transparency, discord cannot help but be insurmountable; in its presence, however, human beings are able to contemplate the divine task of realizing good government on earth. But whereas this task must, by definition, be undertaken on a universal scale, God's knowledge of the world being unlimited (since in His sight the world is totally transparent), Rousseau was led to conclude that only on the comparatively miniscule scale of a small state can human transparency be imagined to produce comparable effects.[14] Many utopian conceptions of social harmony sprang from this perspective in the eighteenth century. But unlike Rousseau, who considered transparency to be indissociably moral and anthropological, thinkers such as Étienne-Gabriel Morelly and Dom Deschamps envisioned a more prosaic destiny, a well-ordered society whose members could be made to conform in thought and speech. Only in the later writings of revolutionaries such as Robespierre and Saint-Just were traces of transparency in Rousseau's sense still to be found. One thinks, too, of the omnipresent symbol of the eye in the iconography of the revolutionary period, which represented as much the eye of popular oversight as the eye in which society is reflected.

Transparency as an ideology is something different. It is thought of as a way of governing, and often today silently substituted for the ancient ideal of bringing forth a new world. The first ones to give the ideal its modern form were the American muckraking journalists who investigated business misconduct and political corruption in the United States at the turn of the twentieth century. Notwithstanding the air of tabloid

Yet if transparency has long been celebrated in this fashion, it is almost always as a means; not until the Progressive era in America did it come to be identified with a political ideal in its finished form, as an end.

In Europe, during the same period, the problem of corruption had been interpreted in a very different way. The Panama scandal is a striking example. Even though the malfeasance in this case was exceptional in its scope, utterly unprecedented, in fact, it did not arouse a popular demand for greater transparency. What Jean Jaurès called the "indelible defects of the social system" were reviled instead, more than the actual dishonesty of corrupt officials; thus Jaurès laid emphasis on the "perpetual scandal of capitalist exploitation."[21] One historian went so far as to say that, considered in relation to the profound historical misfortune represented by capitalism itself, the Panama scandal was only a "minor mishap."[22] Furthermore, if the facts brought to light had exposed the venality of many deputies, it was the parliamentary system *in its essence*—the "rottenness of assemblies," as it used to be said on the extreme right—that was truly responsible.[23] A solution to the problem could therefore be expected only as a result of overthrowing the political and social system, not through any improvement in personal virtue.

In the meantime the appeal of transparency as an ideology—sometimes even spoken of today as a "new religion"[24]—has steadily grown, not only in America but abroad, to the point that it is now held up as a central value of public life. As a consequence, the properly political and social objectives of democratic society have on the whole been neglected. And because the influence of the most zealous believers is disproportionate to their numbers, as in every religion, transparency ever more becomes the cardinal measure of democratic progress. A few years ago, for example, the Sunlight Foundation launched a major initiative, The Punch-Clock Campaign, aimed at forcing members of Congress to put their daily calendars online so that their constituents, now informed about their activity in every detail, would be in a position to draw their own conclusions.[25] Although an ideology of transparency of this sort may well seem impractical (transparency could not itself actually be made into a policy), if not also unwise in principle, *procedures of transparency* must nonetheless be regarded as useful tools for creating an atmosphere of integrity in political life. Here one may speak of an instrumental conception of transparency. The limits of transparency in this third sense will become plain once all three forms are distinguished

fierce, but the forces opposed to one another vary, depending on the case. For this reason an essential distinction needs to be made between *empowering transparency* and *intrusive transparency,* according to whether one acts or is acted upon. It would be absurd to put them on the same level, of course; and to seize on the threat to privacy that intrusive transparency represents as a pretext, in order to disqualify empowering transparency as an instrument for regulating the integrity of politicians, can scarcely be justified. Politicians, for their part, cannot claim a right to privacy equivalent to the one citizens enjoy, since the political part of their personal lives is by its nature public, not private. It is not irrelevant to note in this connection, moreover, that there is an increasingly pronounced resemblance between the situation of celebrities and that of *public-political* figures.[28] The extent of their similarity varies by country, but the tendency everywhere is in favor of giving precedence to a public right to transparency over the right of important persons to protection from public scrutiny. This is particularly evident in the evolving jurisprudence of the European Court of Human Rights, which more and more often now attaches greater weight to protecting freedom of information generally than to protecting individual privacy.[29]

We are now finally in a position to elucidate the nature of instrumental transparency. It is not simply a technique of preventive control. It is also a way of exercising a form of civic power. This kind of transparency institutes a *dissymmetry* between two agents, one subject to a binding injunction, the other occupying the place of an observer.[30] Here the observer has the upper hand. It is when transparency is paramount that the dependence of the representative on the represented and of the governing on the governed makes itself most enduringly felt, much more than in the relationship between candidate and voter, where it is only transitory. The obligations imposed by transparency change the status of representatives and government officials. The former, while they remain unencumbered by any formal mandate, nonetheless find themselves subject to another type of chronic constraint, and the latter now find themselves placed on the same level as representatives. In this sense the obligations of transparency unite the two categories, creating what might be called a community of vulnerability among those on whom they fall, by permanently exposing them to the judgment of the people. Whereas publicity in its classical sense was founded on the idea of exchange between equals, transparency introduces an element of inequality. From the point of view of integrity, then, transparency has become a form of popular sovereignty. It is in this sense that the continual resistance of the political class to calls for greater transparency is to be understood, and the fact that elected officials tend quite spontaneously to see the imposition of such obligations as amounting to a kind of discrimination against them. In this connection it is worth recalling how often they respond to journalists who inquire about their wealth with the same question: "And you, how much do you earn, how much is your apartment worth?"—as if there were something unjust about requiring them, and "only them," to give proofs of their integrity.

The Institutions of Integrity

The institutions responsible for guaranteeing integrity on the part of elective officials have an essentially preventive purpose. In France, the High Authority for Transparency in Public Life is a good illustration. Established by a law of 11 October 2013, in the wake of general outrage over the Cahuzac affair,[31] it represented a great step forward by comparison with the much more limited disclosure requirements previously in force, whether with regard to election campaign spending reports or financial statements filed by elected representatives and other public officials (information that since 1988, at least in principle, had been declared to a Commission for Financial Transparency in Political Life that was equipped with comparatively quite weak powers of review). In compliance with the directives of the new High Authority,[32] headed by a nine-member executive board, nearly 9,000 persons are now required to submit a very detailed annual statement of their income, assets, and corporate interests. Along with ministers and members of parliament and their staff, this requirement applies to a great many senior civil servants as well as officials of various independent administrative authorities.[33] The decision to set up such a body was taken after considerable parliamentary debate, often quite heated. In the end the pressure of public opinion proved decisive, though members of opposition parties did manage to force the government to give way on several points by appealing to the Constitutional Council,[34] which overruled the initial extension of reporting requirements to include children and parents, made public consultation of parliamentary records more difficult by archiving them at the prefectural level, and limited the power to issue injunctions to members of parliament directly (the High Authority having for this purpose to submit a formal request to the Bureau of the National Assembly, in accordance with the principle of separation of powers). These restrictions notwithstanding, the High Authority has already shown itself to be a force for change, notably by making ministerial financial statements available on its website, by forwarding cases considered to be suspect to the Office of the Prosecutor, and above all by creating a new atmosphere with regard to all such matters. Citizen groups dedicated to fighting corruption are now entitled to seek legal remedy or redress from the High Authority, for example, and a special relationship has been established for this purpose with the French section of Transparency International, a global anticorruption coalition. The High Authority hopes to be able to take more far-reaching action in the future as well, not least by expanding legal protections for whistle-blowers.

Presided over since its founding by Jean-Louis Nadal, a man respected for both his scrupulousness and his strength of will,[35] the High Authority moved quickly to assert its claim to political and moral seriousness. Although whistle-blowers are better protected in the United States and Italy than in France, the body of French law concerning declaration of income, property and other assets, and corporate interests by political and administrative officials is currently one of the most complete in the world. In a recent report commissioned by the president of the Republic, Nadal made a number of suggestions aimed at furthering the agency's mission, particularly with regard to more effectively monitoring criminal behavior and enlarging the scope of sanctions applicable to offenders.[36] In addition to discussing a whole set of technical questions having significant consequences for the agency's working relationship with various departments of taxation, jealous of their prerogatives, the report recommends certifying the financial regularity of ministers and candidates for high administrative posts prior to their appointment (particularly with respect to reporting of income and tax compliance), and the good standing of candidates for national elective office well in advance of voting. In all these cases the benefits of proactive auditing will be obvious.

It should be emphasized that the role envisaged for public bodies of this type as guardians of political integrity assumes that oversight will be always exercised by an independent agency. This principle is far from being generally accepted. Many institutions still refuse to wash their dirty laundry in public. The Catholic Church was very slow even to acknowledge the scourge of pedophilia, and the police have long been reluctant to face up to the problem of criminality within their ranks. Both the Church and the police fail to understand what a commitment to transparency really means. It is not only in the interest of a healthy democracy. It is in their own interest. This is a point that Bentham stressed: an institution cannot be considered trustworthy and legitimate if it acts in secrecy as its own judge. "The internal censure," he observed, "will not be sufficient to secure probity, without the assistance of external censure. The reproaches of friends will be little dreaded, and the individual will become insensible to those of his enemies. The spirit of party shut up within narrow limits, equally strips both praise and blame of its nature."[37] A willingness on the part of such institutions to admit their own weaknesses is the clearest possible way of demonstrating that they refuse to close themselves off from the world around them. More generally, transparency strengthens institutions by showing their concern for the common good. This very proposition had been debated and settled in the seventeenth century in England, during the Nine Years' War (1688–1697). Parliament had by then provided itself with an Accounts Commission, as we saw earlier, but in this case it was staff of the various ministerial departments who initially drew the public's notice to evidence of malversation by publishing unauthorized reports based on inside information. They were the first whistle-blowers. A whole series of pamphlets criticized the management of the Commission for the Sick and the Wounded within the Admiralty, for example, reproducing documents proving the corruption of certain officials. In opposition to attempts to deal with such matters internally, there subsequently arose organized campaigns to petition the House of Commons, opening the way to a new type of direct intervention by private citizens with regard to the conduct of public affairs.[38]

Sanctions Regimes

Le Balai—this was the title ("The Broom") chosen by the editors of a short-lived newspaper that first appeared in France in May 1891, even before the shock of the Panama scandal had first been felt. The image

was omnipresent during these years, when antiparliamentarian sentiment had become the prevailing mood of French political life. The
situation in Germany and the United States at the turn of the twentieth
century was much the same. Everywhere voters were urged to sweep
corrupt politicians out of office in order to end the "parliamentary rot"
denounced by the press, then at the height of its influence as an outlet
for political satire and invective. The idea of cleaning house has not
gone away in the years since (the slogan "Let's kick them all out" was
heard on the far left during the presidential election of 2012 in France);[39]
often, however, it has had little or no effect, because not infrequently
candidates widely suspected of corruption, indeed sometimes actually
convicted of criminal wrongdoing, are forgiven by voters. Nevertheless
corruption is now much more actively prosecuted than it used to be in
many countries, judicial resources and specialized police investigatory
powers having been considerably strengthened in the interval. Leading
political figures have been brought to trial and punished, sometimes severely. But are penal sanctions sufficient to deal with these problems?
Following the political philosopher Philip Pettit, one may distinguish between "filters" and "sanctions" in the battle against corruption.[40] Filters
refer to the forms of control and surveillance I have already mentioned;
they have a preventive, dissuasive function. In order to answer the question I have just posed, we need to look more closely at the nature of the
sanctions, or penalties, to which criminal offenders are liable.

In addition to the common offenses of which political figures may
be found guilty, a new type of misconduct is now recognized by the law
to consist in breaches of a duty to defend and promote the cause of transparency. How aggressively these crimes are prosecuted is decisive. But
one must also take into account the moral and political implications of
the injury caused by punishable behavior of this sort. The criminal code
punishes tax evasion, for example, but it makes no distinction among
tax evaders themselves. This, by definition, is the very foundation of a
society based on the rule of law. Considering the moral and political
consequences of such acts, however, their significance for a country will
be seen to vary depending on whether they are committed by a private
citizen or by an elected official. In the first case the sanction redeems
the offense, being proportionate to it. But it is an entirely different matter
if the guilty person is an important political figure. The offense then becomes a reflection on the moral character of the political class as a

whole, and provokes a general feeling of revulsion. It is therefore not only a tax rule that has been violated; a public trust has been abused, with the result that the creditability enjoyed by democratic institutions is undermined. In defrauding the tax authorities, a corrupt political figure shows himself to be *unworthy* of his office. Beyond the offense itself, a crime of *lèse-démocratie* may be said to have been committed, by analogy with the old concept of *lèse-majesté*.[41] How is the idea of an offense against a whole political system to be given its due weight in devising an appropriate sanctions regime? The answer to this question has a long history, having to do with punishments involving a loss of civil rights, whose stages it will be instructive to briefly review.

Two kinds of penalty may be distinguished, one administered for the purpose of *stigmatization,* the other for the purpose of *degradation*. Let us begin with the former. The etymology of "stigma," originally from the Greek, is itself illuminating: the word evokes a visible mark, a tattoo.[42] In Athens, certain types of crimes could lead to banishment or the loss of civil rights; but punishment could also take the form of the impression on the body or the face of an indelible mark meant to permanently recall the guilty person's offense in the eyes of society. Alternatively, a person convicted of such a crime could be publicly shamed by being stripped naked and displayed on a stone block in the middle of the agora, or else by being paraded through the city. The Romans dispensed analogous punishments, adding to them the practice of branding (denoted by the Latin *stigma*). Along with flogging, branding superimposed on the penalty itself a method of physical disfigurement and torture that went beyond mere execution in the case of a death sentence. European ingenuity invented new punitive rituals of unimaginable cruelty, while at the same time providing a justification for them, until the eighteenth century.[43] The history of this barbarousness in its many manifestations, together with the various campaigns to put an end to it, is well known. Yet it should be kept in mind that stigmatizing penalties have not completely disappeared from the contemporary world, notably in the United States. One thinks, for example, of the "perp walks" used by prosecutors to bring arrested suspects before journalists and photographers in a way that is reminiscent of the defamatory promenades of the ancient world. Public shaming in America takes other forms as well, such as obliging people convicted of sexual offenses to post the reason for their punishment on the front door of their homes. While these practices, officially intended to foster popular disgust for certain crimes and to force those who are sentenced for them never to forget following their release from prison what they have done, are often criticized, they also have ardent defenders, even within the ranks of self-styled progressives.[44]

Degradation penalties were different. They were aimed chiefly at ruining a person's reputation, by declaring him to be unworthy. In this sense they fell outside the roster of classical punishments. The Roman censors, whose duties included the supervision of public and private morality, were authorized to examine alleged violations of oaths of office or of matrimony, conduct deemed harmful by its indifference to civic virtue, even displays of luxury that were considered to be excessive. But they could not inflict real punishment, either by imposing a fine or by setting a term of imprisonment. Their jurisdiction extended only as far as a person's reputation, which could be diminished through a reduction of honors or rank, or through a lowering of social status by exclusion from one's tribe.[45] Like stigmatizing penalties, penalties entailing a loss of rank or status were to play an important role until the eighteenth century in Europe. They often strengthened, and symbolically aggravated, penal sanctions applied to persons whose status under the ancien régime was associated with membership in a body considered to be socially influential (the nobility, the clergy, officers of the realm, and so on). Auxiliary punishment consisted in this case in disaffiliating offenders from such bodies. The so-called infamous penalty (*peine d'infamie*) was a way of publicly dishonoring them—and this in an age when honor was often considered a greater good than life itself. Thus a parliamentary councillor convicted of having falsified an inquest might, in addition to being removed from office, be solemnly stripped of his red robe during a public hearing. A priest sentenced to death might be publicly degraded, by being made to divest himself of the chasuble, stole, and alb he had been forced to wear as if he were preparing to say mass, prior to being executed, again publicly. A noble might be made to forfeit his titles and lowered to the condition of a commoner.[46] These penalties, though they were not provided for by law, expressed the determination of such bodies to show themselves worthy of public confidence by expelling those who had showed contempt for their sworn duty to serve the common good. With the French Revolution, honor ceased to be the privilege of a few. But by the same token every person was now liable to be accused of unworthiness in the event of a grave transgression of civic morality, and above all if he had been elected to public office, since henceforth citizens were expected to choose their representatives by giving priority to those who were "the most deserving of public trust."[47] The notions of *trust* and *worthiness* were thus intimately associated at the heart of the revolutionary political ideal. Unworthy representatives were ones who "betrayed the trust of their constituents." Political unworthiness was the subject of much debate during this period, even if it remained difficult to codify.[48] The sanction of civic degradation was instituted by the Penal Code of 1791 in order to curb those failings considered to be most harmful to the common interest, foremost among them the abuse of public trust. It was retained by Napoleon in the Penal Code of 1810,[49] which directed that the convicted person should be led to the public square, where a court was seated, and that in a loud voice the clerk of the court address these words to him: "Your country has found you guilty of an infamous action; the law and the tribunal degrade you from the rank of French citizen."[50] Few elected officials seem to have been sentenced to this penalty in the nineteenth century. Nevertheless the loss of civil rights long continued to be a supplementary punishment accompanying certain criminal sentences. The spectacular degradation of Captain Dreyfus, whose sword was broken in the court of the École militaire on 5 January 1895, served to revive, albeit in isolated fashion and notwithstanding that its basis in law had never been fully settled, the ancient ceremony of dishonor by exclusion from a corps.

In France, the notion of *indignité nationale* enjoyed a stunning resurgence following the Second World War. Support for the idea of sanctioning passive collaboration, which is to say petty instances of moral support for the German occupier, had grown during the Resistance.[51] Special jurisdictions known as civic chambers were created to pass judgment on this kind of unworthiness after the Liberation, with the intermittent assistance of regular courts of justice. Alongside cases of active collaboration brought to trial and punished by imprisonment or death (there were some 1,500 judicial executions), as well as popular reprisals in which some 9,000 people were executed without recourse to lawful procedure of any sort, 95,000 men and women were judged to be unworthy of French citizenship. The unevenness of the sentencing, and the vagueness of the justification given for punishment in many cases, attracted widespread criticism at the time, but its force was blunted by the perceived urgencies of the immediate postwar period.

The accepted view of unworthiness in this sense subsequently evolved, to the point that it came at last to be seen as antiquated. After the abolition of the death penalty in 1981, the new penal code of 1994 effectively eliminated the penalty of civic degradation, retaining only a much weaker version of it in the form of a temporary loss of civil rights. In the process the very category of a *peine infamante* was surreptitiously gotten rid of as well.[52] This situation needs to be reconsidered. At a time when trust between members of society and their elected representatives has all but vanished, the practice of sanctioning democratic unworthiness on the part of officials found guilty of corruption may well deserve to be reinstated in some fashion. Jean-Louis Nadal has courageously reopened the subject to debate by suggesting that both chambers of parliament should have the right to expel a member in the event of grave misconduct as a deterrent measure, and to approve stiffer penalties of ineligibility for reelection,[53] in extreme cases perhaps even a punishment of permanent ineligibility.[54] The question of moral sanctions, above and beyond criminal sanctions, may be expected to stimulate further debate over what needs to be done to ensure greater integrity political life in the years ahead.[55]

CONCLUSION

The Second Democratic Revolution

THE FIRST DEMOCRATIC REVOLUTION, dedicated to the conquest of universal suffrage, sought to make voting citizens the principal agents of popular sovereignty. This revolution is now behind us, even if some countries still look forward to its arrival. But it is far from having accomplished all the things that people assumed it would almost automatically bring about. The words that Flaubert gave to a character in *L'Éducation sentimentale* to say in 1848—"With universal suffrage, we will now be happy"—seem almost risible to us today. The history of this first revolution has thus been one of perpetual disenchantment.[1] For two centuries, as a consequence, societies have been searching for ways to make up for disappointed expectations and correct the mistakes that gave rise to them. We have now finally arrived at the end of this period of exploration. Tinkering with electoral systems, improving the representativeness of elected officials, implementing a principle of parity, limiting the number of offices that can be held concurrently, involving citizens in the selection of candidates, introducing mechanisms of direct (or participatory) democracy—the list of remedial and palliative measures has long been agreed upon. Where they have been put into effect the results have been positive. Yet there still remains much to be done in this connection to combat unrelenting attempts to muffle, or even silence, the voice of the people, whether it is a question, for example, of the role of money in campaigns, or party control over the electoral process, or the persistence, and indeed the worsening, of malrepresentation. Reform in these areas has been limited in two fundamental respects. First, there is an abiding attachment to a majoritarian conception of democracy. This is a problem I discussed in the second book of this quartet, *La légitimité démocratique,* which argued for the need to establish new democratic institutions as part of an enlarged and pluralized approach to expressing the general will.[2] But a second and still more decisive shortcoming has to do with the restriction of citizen expression to choosing a head of the executive branch and other elected representatives, which is to say a simple procedure for passively endorsing the general thrust and orientation of a government's policies.

In the present work I began by noting the many things that a democracy of authorization in this sense fails to do and went on to explore an alternative to it—what I call permanent democracy, founded on a set of principles capable of justly and lastingly regulating the relations between the governed and the governing. Under this regime, citizens are no longer content to be kings for a day. They accept ongoing responsibility for actively monitoring and supervising their governors, who now find themselves subject to a variety of unfamiliar constraints and obligations. In the first book of the quartet, *La contre-democratie,* I had made a start on understanding this "postelectoral" dimension through an analysis of a novel kind of social and political activism that sprang from a distrust of governments.[3] The focus here has been broadened considerably with the presentation of a general theory of democratic oversight, supported by an effort to elaborate the principles of *democratic action* in politics.

Institutions and Actors of a Permanent Democracy

In this book I have briefly described the five principal aspects of a permanent democracy: legibility, responsibility, responsiveness, truthfulness, and integrity. It is no more than a preliminary sketch, to be sure, but the main outlines are now at least clearly drawn. By contrast, I have done no more than allude to the evidently crucial task of describing the institutions and actors that will be responsible for giving practical effect to these principles, calling on several occasions for the creation of "new

democratic organizations." Another book would be required in order to
address the question in detail, taking into consideration also the fact that
what needs to be done will only become fully apparent with the passage of time. It was not until many years had gone by following the initial achievement of universal suffrage, for example, that parties in their
modern form first emerged and then came to be regarded as an integral
part of the electoral-representative system we know today. For the time
being, however, and without having the least desire to engage in political engineering,[4] I would like to conclude the present work by indi-
cating some paths of research and discussion that will reward further
exploration.

A democracy concerned to govern well, and to govern still better in
the future, might be organized around three poles: a *council on democratic
performance*, charged with formalizing the legal basis for principles
underlying a permanent democracy (integrity of elected officials and
transparency of government institutions foremost among them); *public
commissions*, responsible for evaluating the democratic character of public
policy deliberation and of the steps taken by administrative agencies to
put policies into effect, in addition to sponsoring public debate on all
relevant issues; and *civic vigilance organizations*, watchdog groups devoted
specifically to monitoring government performance (especially with
regard to responsiveness, responsibility, and the clarity of political
speech) and working to promote citizen involvement, training, and education. These three types of organization would form the pillars of the
new kind of political system I have in mind. In this context a *charter of
democratic action* could be brought before the public for debate and formal
approval, and perhaps one day be accorded a status in many countries
equivalent to that of the Declaration of the Rights of Man and the Citizen
in France. Without pretending already to have worked out in detail
what a permanent democracy would involve, it may nonetheless be a
good thing, by way of illustration and for the purpose of stimulating discussion, to give at least a rough idea of what its overall architecture
might look like.

The council on democratic performance, under the direction of an
executive board, would be responsible chiefly for intervening on behalf
of each of the two objectives I mentioned a moment ago, integrity and
transparency.[5] It would also serve to strengthen the protections available
to whistle-blowers. To be effective, it should have its own investigative

authority and the power to issue restraining orders to government agencies and individuals alike. It should publish an annual report on the state of democracy, with government officials being obliged to publicly justify their conduct in response to its criticisms and to declare an opinion in respect of its recommendations. All this would require not only that it have more complete jurisdiction than the various independent authorities operating today, but that it be constitutionally recognized as a branch of government in its own right, alongside the executive, legislature, and judiciary. Rallying support for a fourth branch of government is an indispensable condition of being able to bring a permanent democracy into existence.[6] Just as constitutional courts are the guardians of public institutions, a council of this type would be charged with ensuring that the fundamental principles of good government laid down in the Charter are respected. Its democratic character would be warranted by the circumstances of open review under which its members are appointed (including, among other things, public confirmation hearings in both chambers of parliament), the obligation to keep the public informed of its work, and the requirement that its own business be transparent to all (thus itself embodying one of the constitutive ideals of a permanent democracy).

The public commissions I envisage would be continuing bodies set up to scrutinize the formulation and administration of public policy, with a view not only to involving citizens in the work of government but also to making sure that economic and social programs produce legible outcomes. Being few in number, such commissions could be asked to concentrate their efforts on areas of particular concern, such as public health and safety, labor and the economy, culture, education, and research. In this way they would support and extend the activity of government bodies such as the state audit office in France, and by expanding the functions that currently are performed in part by parliamentary assemblies would make such bodies more democratic (acting in this regard with greater freedom and efficiency as well, being shielded from the pressures of partisan competition). Additionally, they would be responsible for encouraging public debate on major issues, functioning in this capacity as the primary sponsor of a truly deliberative democracy. The democratic character of such commissions could be guaranteed by adopting a selection principle that brings together persons nominated by prestigious institutions for their technical competence (thus ensuring objectivity) with persons selected at random (thus promoting equality) and members of citizen groups studying the various topics under discussion (thus furthering the aim of public involvement and what may be thought of as functional representativeness).[7] In the best case, the work of such commissions would succeed also by a sort of pendulum effect in restoring elected assemblies to a preeminent place within the framework of democratic guidance.[8]

The organizations of civic vigilance would include public interest groups and private foundations committed to the advancement of democratic principles. Earlier, by way of example, I mentioned the American organization Common Cause and the various national chapters of Transparency International. Though they are still undeveloped by comparison with larger environmental groups and charitable organizations, they might one day help to bring about citizen involvement of a new type, aimed at combating dishonesty, manipulation, and deceit wherever they stand in the way of open government. Because it is resolved to go directly to the source of a whole range of problems, rather than simply protest their effects, this form of engagement holds greater promise than traditional partisan advocacy. Just as political parties and unions in certain countries receive public subsidies in recognition of their contribution to promoting public and social democracy, a strong argument could be made in favor of granting watchdog organizations similar treatment. As in the case of unions, their representativeness will depend on the size of their membership, their capacity to mobilize support, and the scope of their activity; but such organizations also have a functional character deriving from their original motivation, namely, to create a permanent democracy.[9]

A regime of this sort, around which a second democratic revolution is now beginning to take shape, will therefore need to be equipped with its own agencies. The three categories of institutions I have just discussed would differ in status and have distinct missions, but they would all serve, in mutually complementary fashion, to protect the proper functioning of existing organs of government. Nevertheless they will be able to fully realize their purpose only if citizens come forward and claim responsibility for them. Making the work of such organizations widely known is obviously a first step in this direction. It will be necessary to go further, however, in order to avoid the risk that they may become sclerotic and inward-looking in their turn, incapable of promptly adapting to changing circumstances. Holding an *annual democracy day* might be a way of solemnly reaffirming their importance while at the same time directly involving people in their undertakings. An occasion of this sort might be preceded by public forums, whose various written and oral contributions would form the basis for a series of debates, broadcast by the media, with elected representatives and government officials being invited to indicate how they intend to respond to the criticisms and suggestions expressed in these forums. An annual democracy day would give the people as a whole, not merely the smaller population of registered voters, the opportunity to exercise their right of citizenship.

Functional Democracy versus Competitive Democracy

The permanent democracy I envision has a functional character in the sense that it does not operate over an area already marked out and divided up by ideological disagreements and conflicts of interest. The end it aims at is by definition consensual, and its methods are expressly designed to win the approval of the greatest number. It is for this reason that it cannot be brought into being by means of election. A democracy of authorization, by contrast, is by its nature conflictual, since governing implies a need to make choices, to give a direction to policy, and to set priorities that very seldom are likely to be unanimous. Recourse to a vote then becomes inevitable, in order to decide. This distinction between the two kinds of regime is essential.

The problem is that election does not consist only in choosing a way forward. As a *practical* matter it takes the form of a competitive selection among persons. And it is just this kind of competition that harms democracy. Its effect is first to create an oversupply of campaign promises, and then to feed the disenchantment that inevitably follows when those who are elected turn out to be incapable of honoring the very commitments that enabled them to triumph. This clockwork connection between encouraging electoral rivalry and fueling a machine for generating promises has been strengthened with the decline of the idea of revolution, which formerly had made it possible to link competition with alternating party control, if not actually a change of political system. Apart from an implausible appeal to the personal virtue of professional politicians and the doubtful assumption of efficiency in government, there are few institutional mechanisms that might serve to remedy this state of affairs.[10] The one that comes most readily to mind, a lottery, is better suited to shaping legislative decisions that represent the will of the people than to choosing a head of the executive branch, the chief focus of attention today in an age of presidentialization; what is more, a lottery cannot be a method of setting a direction for policy.[11] The problem must therefore be considered to be structural. Only the vitality of a permanent democracy will be able to limit its harmful effects, in the first instance by forcing public officials to speak plainly and honestly. But it will also be necessary to create a new and more positive type of relationship to the future if the present flood of empty promises is ever to recede.

Looking Forward to the Future

Promising is a by-product of the principle of competition in politics, where it operates in an opposite fashion to the one that regulates markets for commodities. In a commodities market the effect of competition is to lower prices and increase demand. In a political market, by contrast, competition raises prices and lowers demand. The reason for this is that politics is really a futures market. Voters buy options, they wager on the future. In this sense voters are speculators. If a promise is not delivered on, which is to say if reality falls far short of expectations, they pay the difference in the coin of disappointment at some later date. They may go on gambling for a while longer, or they may get up from the table and leave (by abstaining from voting or casting a blank ballot). Bringing citizens back to the real economy of politics means replacing promises by truthfulness. This moreover is what makes promising in politics different from promising in a romantic relationship. Two people in love make a commitment to each other that is put to the test every day; words then exist only in tension with the clear-sighted gaze that is brought to bear upon breaking a promise or failing to keep one ("There is no such thing as love, only proofs of love," as the old expression has it). Politics sustains a different relationship between wishes and actions: the future appears less as something that is built day by day than as something that is awaited—an event, a decision, a change of course that will fulfill all hopes, all dreams.

Finding a way out from this perverse cycle of oscillation between an insatiable appetite for promises and a disenchanted turning away from politics is an essential requirement of democratic progress. But no solution will be possible by submitting to the futile discipline of "con-straints," or yielding to the grim charms of "realism," or pining for a lost paradise that must somehow be regained (which, paradoxically, is what certain critiques of neoliberalism amount to in seeking to rescue a world on the verge of being destroyed, mistaking it for a defunct golden age that can yet be brought back to life).[12] The idea of a world straining to reach the horizon, a world in a state of permanent anticipation, is consubstantial with modernity, and it cannot be made to vanish or go away. There are two ways of regarding this condition of chronic expec-tancy. First, as a secularized version of religious messianism—waiting for a miracle to happen. This attitude has long been dominant on the left, where the prospect of revolution naturally finds an essentially theological-political disposition of this kind a congenial companion. But the future can be conceived otherwise, more positively, as an opportunity to master the world, a capacity for *consciously* making history. On this view, de-mocracy has to be seen in terms of the problems that must be overcome if its potential is to be realized and the constant risk that it will deterio-rate into oligarchical rule successfully avoided. It is a matter, in other words, of looking at democracy as a reflexive phenomenon in which public debate over how it should operate acts on, and is acted on by, a commitment to do what needs to be done in order to produce a stronger and more unified society. This is what permanent democracy means. It is a vision that lies at the heart of the new democratic revolution whose first stirrings are now just beginning to be felt. Just as the spirit of 1789 made it possible to think of society in a new and different way, going beyond what the adoption of an electoral-representative system en-tailed, so too redefining the relationship between the governing and the governed will open the way to a clearer understanding of what must be done to bring about at last a society of equals.

NOTES

INDEX

NOTES

Introduction

1. This was clearly the case in the eighteenth and nineteenth centuries, when "government" and "regime" were taken to mean the same thing. Because the notion of government then encompassed both the legislative and the executive branch, the familiar expression "representative government" signified what below I call the parliamentary-representative form of democratic regime.
2. And this all the more as the form and content of the U.S. Constitution are now for all intents and purposes fixed, it being virtually impossible to set in motion the procedures for modifying it contemplated in Article V.
3. With the difference that, apart from Hungary, the presidents of these new republics were elected by direct universal suffrage.
4. Along with the minor exceptions of Ireland (1938), Austria (1951), and Finland (1988), where the president is not really the head of the executive branch.
5. The distinctive character of the American system derives from the appointment of so-called electors at the state level, with specific rules applying in each case. These electors jointly constitute an electoral college, which names the president. As a result of this second step in the electoral process, the president need not be the candidate who received a majority of the popular votes cast previously.
6. The conditions under which executive power assumed a central place in democracies are examined in Chapter 3.

7. One consequence of this, in the academic literature, is that the manner of appointing prime ministers in the older European democracies is now frequently described as a "hidden election." See my discussion in Chapter 6.

8. I take up these principles, and the constitutions themselves, in greater detail in Chapters 1 and 2.

9. This demand was constantly reaffirmed by labor movements of the late nineteenth century in Europe, when universal suffrage was on the verge of being achieved. In France it was famously formulated by Ernest Roche: "So long as the imperative mandate does not exist, the representative of the people, himself a worker, so humble, so docile on the eve of the ballot, will become the next day a master, an inexorable tyrant." Roche, *Séances du Congrès ouvrier socialiste de France: Troisième session* (Marseille: Doucet, 1879), 590.

10. Otherwise, it was argued, representatives would be paralyzed the moment the circumstances that had brought them to office changed. This is why one of the first decisions of the National Constituent Assembly in 1789 was to prohibit imperative mandates. Without this prohibition, it would not have been possible to do away with the Estates-General, and the chance of political positions being modified by free debate and deliberation would have been excluded as well.

11. The drawing of lots, it must be emphasized, has never been proposed for executive office. The reason for this is simple: a lottery attaches priority to the category of *whatever* (in which the statistical character of a sample is implicit), and by virtue of this comes under the head of procedures associated with representation as figuration; the exercise of governmental functions, by contrast, requires above all a kind of proficiency or skill, which is to say the ability to distinguish and choose between courses of action. The drawing of lots is well adapted to impaneling a jury or assembling a focus group, for example; the precise manner of its operation is liable to vary depending on how the population from which a random selection is to be made has been decided upon.

12. This decisive point in treated in Chapter 9.

13. This, in any case, is its theoretical purpose. "The central institution of representative government," as Bernard Manin puts it, "is election." Manin, *The Principles of Representative Government* (Cambridge: Cambridge University Press, 1997), 6.

14. Inferior, too, because the election of representatives is always plural: it is an *assembly* of representatives that is elected. I shall come back to this point in due course.

15. More or less literal translations of the French term (*démocratie d'exercise*) are unsatisfactory. The underlying notion has two aspects. The first opposes procedural legitimacy (election) to substantive legitimacy (the democratic quality of governmental action and its relation to the electorate). The second involves a temporal dimension, implicit in the contrast between an inher-

ently intermittent electoral democracy and a kind of democracy that is permanently exercised by citizens. At the author's suggestion, I have translated *démocratie d'exercice* simply as "permanent democracy." It should nevertheless be kept in mind that the basic idea of an open-ended civic duty also refers to democracy in its active sense, as a mindful and diligent monitoring of those who govern by those who are governed. —Trans.

16. This state of affairs has led some scholars to engage in what they take to be a form of constructive provocation, declaring themselves to be "against elections." See, for example, David van Reybrouck, *Contre les élections* (Arles: Actes Sud, 2014).

17. See the concluding chapter of my book *Democratic Legitimacy: Impartiality, Reflexivity, Proximity*, trans. Arthur Goldhammer (Princeton, N.J.: Princeton University Press, 2011), 219–226.

18. Hugues-Félicité Robert de Lamennais, "Aux ouvriers," *Le Peuple constituant*, 24 April 1848.

19. On this point see Pierre Rosanvallon, *Society of Equals*, trans. Arthur Goldhammer (Cambridge, Mass.: Harvard University Press, 2013), 226–228.

20. My own writings on this topic include *La question syndicale: Histoire at avenir d'une forme sociale* (Paris: Calmann-Lévy, 1988), and *Le peuple introuvable: Histoire de la représentation démocratique en France* (Paris: Gallimard, 1998), neither one yet available in English.

21. The most illuminating writings on this decisive change are due to Peter Mair; see his "Representative versus Responsible Government," MPIfG Working Paper 09 / 8 (Cologne: Max Plank Institute for the Study of Societies, September 2009), and his posthumously published *Ruling the Void: The Hollowing of Western Democracy* (London: Verso, 2013). These late works seem to me to deepen Mair's pioneering theory of the "cartel party," formulated some fifteen years earlier with Richard Katz in "Changing Models of Party Organization and Party Democracy: The Emergence of the Cartel Party," *Party Politics* 1, no. 1 (1995): 5–31. For an empirical evaluation of this theory, see Yohann Aucante and Alexandre Dézé, eds., *Les systèmes de partis dans les démocraties occidentales: Le modèle du parti-cartel en question* (Paris: Presses de Sciences Po, 2008).

22. One is reminded of the old organic conception of representation, as the French revolutionaries and Edmund Burke conceived it. But drafting laws is no longer a matter of carrying out the nation's will; now it is a matter of carrying out the will of the executive.

23. This separation from society is aggravated in France by the fact that the members of the political class are, by and large, graduates of the same *grandes écoles*.

24. By "regular" I mean the rank and file, persons of firm partisan conviction, as opposed to those who participate more or less casually, whether directly or indirectly, in political life.

25. See Pierre Rosanvallon, *Le Parlement des invisibles* (Paris: Seuil, 2014).

26. This project comprises a book-publishing program and a website, both devoted to telling the real-life stories of ordinary people; for more information, see www.raconterlavie.fr.

27. Note that this almost ritualistic habit likewise presupposes that election is the privileged, if not in fact the unique, form of democratic expression.

28. Parties are therefore the guardians of certain parliamentary prerogatives, and help moreover to ensure that the rights of opposition are recognized—which, it will be agreed, furthers an undeniable democratic interest.

29. On this point see the very enlightening book by Isabelle Thireau and Hua Linshan, *Les ruses de la démocratie: Protester en Chine* (Paris: Seuil, 2010).

30. I say nothing of the problem of massive voting fraud, frequent in such cases.

31. See Pierre Rosanvallon, *Le sacre du citoyen: Histoire du suffrage universel en France* (Paris: Gallimard, 1992).

32. Originally the Seeley Lectures at Cambridge, first published in French and later in English as *Counter-Democracy: Politics in an Age of Distrust*, trans. Arthur Goldhammer (Cambridge: Cambridge University Press, 2008).

33. Rosanvallon, *Le peuple introuvable*.

34. Pierre Rosanvallon, *La démocratie inachevée: Histoire de la souveraineté du peuple en France* (Paris: Gallimard, 2000).

35. Rosanvallon, *Democratic Legitimacy*, originally published as *La légitimité démocratique: Impartialité, réflexivité, proximité* (Paris: Seuil, 2008).

36. Rosanvallon, *Le Parlement des invisibles*.

37. Rosanvallon, *Le sacre du citoyen*.

38. Rosanvallon, *Society of Equals*.

1. Consecration of the Law and Demotion of the Executive

1. See Michel Porret, ed., *Beccaria et la culture juridique des Lumières* (Geneva: Droz, 1997).

2. See Jacques Vanderlinden, "Code et codification dans la pensée de Jeremy Bentham," *Revue d'histoire du droit* 32 (1964): 45–78; Denis Baranger, "Bentham et la codification," *Droits* 27 (1998): 17–37; and François Ost, "Codification et temporalité dans la pensée de J. Bentham," in *Actualité de la pensée juridique de Jeremy Bentham*, ed. Philippe Gérard, François Ost, and Michel van de Kerchove (Brussels: Publications des Facultés universitaires Saint-Louis, 1987), 163–230.

3. The idea of a *pannomion* for the French nation is found in Bentham's manuscripts at University College London; see ms. 100, cited by Élie Halévy, *La formation du radicalisme philosophique*, 3 vols. (Paris: F. Alcan, 1901–1904), 1:367. See also *Pannomial Fragments*, in *The Works of Jeremy Bentham*, ed. John Bowring, 11 vols. (Edinburgh: William Tait, 1843), 3:211–230, as well as *Nomography; or The Art of Inditing Laws*, in the same volume, 3:231–283.

4. See also Rousseau's diatribe against "the enormous multitude of laws" in an undated fragment on politics posthumously published by G. Streckeisen-Moulton (Paris, 1861), and reproduced under the heading "Des Loix" as section 4.8 of *Fragments Politiques* in Jean-Jacques Rousseau, *Œuvres complètes,* ed. Bernard Gagnebin and Marcel Raymond, 5 vols. (Paris: Gallimard, 1959–1995), 3:493–494.

5. "We call a *royaume,*" observed Urbain Domergue, "a country already sovereignly ruled by a king; a country in which law alone commands, I will call a *loyaume.*" Quoted by Ferdinand Brunot, *Histoire de la langue française des origines à 1900,* 10 vols. (Paris: Armand Colin, 1905–1937), 9:641.

6. See the chapter "La suprématie de la loi" in Jean Belin, *La logique d'une idée-force: L'idée d'utilité sociale et la Révolution française (1789–1792)* (Paris: Hermann, 1939). See also Jean Ray, "La Révolution française et la pensée juridique: L'idée du règne de la loi," *Revue philosophique de la France et de l'étranger* 128 (1939): 9–12; and Catherine Larrère, "Le gouvernement de la loi est-il un thème républicain?," *Revue de synthèse* 118, no. 4 (1997): 237–258.

7. Montesquieu, *L'Esprit des lois* [1748], in *Œuvres complètes,* ed. Roger Caillois, 2 vols. (Paris: Gallimard, 1949–1951), 2:239.

8. These expressions are recalled by Marie-France Renoux-Zagamé, *Du droit de Dieu au droit de l'homme* (Paris: Presses Universitaires de France, 2003), 24.

9. Jean Carbonnier, "La passion des lois au siècle des Lumières," in *Essais sur les lois,* 2nd ed. (Paris: Defrénois, 1995), 240. "Thus it will be evident," he continues, "that there exists a passion to legislate, a passion for the law, which is in no way to be confused with the ordinary thirst for power, or even with the more singular pleasure that one may feel on making one's will. It is a phenomenon of juridical psychology—an indivisibly individual and collective psychology."

10. The Court was established by the law of 27 November 1790. On this point see the survey by Jean-Louis Halpérin, *Le tribunal de cassation et les pouvoirs sous la Révolution (1790–1799)* (Paris: Librairie générale de droit et de jurisprudence, 1987).

11. Bertrand Barère, speech of 8 May 1790, *Archives parlementaires de 1787 à 1860,* ser. 1 (1787–1799), 2nd ed., 82 vols. (Paris: Dupont, 1879–1913), 15:432.

12. Antoine Barnave, speech of 8 May 1790, *Archives parlementaires,* 15:432.

13. The mechanism actually put in place combined legislative interpretation and judicial determination. In those cases—supposed to be exceedingly rare—where the precise meaning of a passage in the statute was unclear, the legislator himself was called upon to settle the matter. "It is in the legislature that the Court of Cassation must be placed," Robespierre said, in order to emphasize that *cassation*—in the strict sense of the term, an act of annulment or repeal—was to be considered a measure of general interest, foreign to individual persons and therefore to the judicial order itself. Speech of 25 May 1790, *Archives parlementaires,* 15:671.

14. Intervention of 18 November 1790, *Archives parlementaires,* 20:516.

15. In this regard the Court scrupulously obeyed a decree of 27 November 1790, the third article of which stipulated that recourse to revisory jurisdiction ought to be had only in case of a *"deliberate* breach" of the text of a statute; see the examples given in the chapter "La notion de cassation," in Belin, *La logique d'une idée-force,* 94–96. This conception was carried over by the Constitutions of Year III and Year VIII, and later reaffirmed both in the law of 16 September 1807 and in the act of 22 April 1815 added to the imperial constitutions.

16. Rousseau, *Du contrat social* [1762], 3.1, in *Œuvres complètes,* 3:395–396.

17. See Robert Derathé, "Les rapports de l'exécutif et du législatif chez J.-J. Rousseau," *Annales de philosophie politique* 5 (1965): 153–169.

18. See Emmanuel-Joseph Sieyès, *Vues sur les moyens d'exécution dont les représentants de la France pourront disposer en 1789* ([n.p., n.p.], 1789).

19. Élysée Loustallot, *Introduction à la Révolution* (30 January 1790), 6.

20. See the opening chapter ("Le discrédit de la fonction ministérielle") of Édith Bernardin, *Jean-Marie Roland et le ministère de l'Intérieur (1792–1793)* (Paris: Société des études Robespierristes, 1964), 23–30.

21. For a more nuanced view than mine, see Guillaume Glénard, *L'Exécutif et la Constitution de 1791* (Paris: Presses Universitaires de France, 2010).

22. Bertrand Barère, speech of 27 August 1791, *Archives parlementaires,* 29:742. The same sentiment is expressed in a work by Abbé Mably, *Du gouvernement et des lois de la Pologne,* published posthumously in 1789.

23. One finds all these phrases in the fourth notebook of Sieyès's *Délinéaments politiques,* reproduced in Christine Fauré, ed., *Des manuscrits de Sieyès, 1773–1799* (Paris: Honoré Champion, 1999), 396–401.

24. See his "Lettre d'un jeune mécanicien aux auteurs du *Républicain*" (16 July 1791), in *Œuvres de Condorcet,* ed. A. Condorcet O'Connor and M. F. Arago, 12 vols. (Paris: Firmin Didot, 1847–1849), 12:239–241.

25. Condorcet, *De la nature des pouvoirs politiques dans une nation libre* (November 1792), in *Œuvres,* 10:607.

26. For a preliminary overview see Joseph Barthélemy, *Le rôle du pouvoir exécutif dans les républiques modernes* (Paris: Giard et Brière, 1907); also Michel Verpeaux, *La naissance du pouvoir réglementaire, 1789–1799* (Paris: Presses Universitaires de France, 1991).

27. The proposal was made by Pierre-Marie Roederer, intervening in parliamentary debate on 10 April 1791; see *Archives parlementaires,* 24:691.

28. The formulation is due to Bertrand Barère, in the debate of 4 December 1793 concerning codification; see *Archives parlementaires,* 80:637.

29. Maximilien Robespierre, intervention of 4 December 1793, *Archives parlementaires,* 80:637.

30. Article 1 of the decree of 4 December 1793.

31. See the account by Merlin de Douai in the article "Loi," in *Répertoire universel et raisonné de jurisprudence,* ed. J.-N. Guyot, P. J. J. G. Guyot, and

P.-A. Merlin, 4th ed., 17 vols. (Paris: Garnery, 1812–1825), 7:524. Note that, with the formation of the National Constituent Assembly in July 1789, all decrees cloaked in royal sanction bore the title "law," to emphasize that the king no longer had any will of his own.

32. See the report by Lazare Carnot on the abolition of the Executive Council, 1 April 1794, in *Archives parlementaires*, 81:694–698.

33. The phrase occurs in the report by Français de Nantes on Year VII; quoted by Bernard Gainot, *1799, un nouveau jacobinism? La démocratie représentative, une alternative à brumaire* (Paris: Éditions du Comité des travaux historiques et scientifiques, 2001), 452.

2. The Cult of Impersonality and Its Metamorphoses

1. The Greeks' pride in being governed by laws (as opposed to their enemies, the Persians, who were subject to the rule of a single man) is well attested. On this point, see Jacqueline de Romilly, *La loi dans la pensée grecque* (Paris: Les Belles Lettres, 2001); and David Cohen, "The Rule of Law and Democratic Ideology in Classical Athens," in *Die athenische Demokratie im 4. Jahrhundert vor Christi: Vollendung oder Verfall einer Verfassungsform?*, ed. Walter Eder (Stuttgart: Steiner, 1995), 227–247.

2. Whenever a problem arose, the ministers alone were held responsible. "Ah, if the king knew," it used to be said in absolving the monarch of blame.

3. Jacques Nicolas Billaud-Varenne, *L'Acéphocratie, ou le gouvernement fédératif* (Paris, 1791), 3. Note that two years later, in 1793, the Jacobins' adversaries were to interpret this term negatively. Thus, for example, General Dumouriez raged against the "democratic, or rather monstrous and acephalic, Republic"; quoted by Jean-Pierre Duprat, "Le 'monstre acéphale' dans la Constitution de 1793," in *La Constitution du 24 juin 1793: L'utopie dans le droit public français?*, ed. Jean Bart, Jean-Jacques Clère, Claude Courvoisier, and Michel Verpeaux (Dijon: Éditions Universitaires de Dijon, 1997), 241.

4. See Maurice Agulhon, *Marianne au combat: L'imagerie et la symbolique républicaine de 1789 à 1880* (Paris: Flammarion, 1979), 22–34.

5. The suggestion was made by Pierre Louis Manuel on 21 September 1792; see *Archives parlementaires*, 52:69.

6. Georges Couthon, intervention of 21 September 1792, *Archives parlementaires*, 52:69; the emphasis is mine. The idea of a triumvirate was subsequently rejected as well.

7. See the account of this proposal, made by Paul Barras in Year VII, and of its reception in Patrice Gueniffey, *Le dix-huit brumaire: L'épilogue de la Révolution française* (Paris: Gallimard, 2008), 257–258.

8. The Council was downgraded in March 1793 with the creation of the Committee of Public Safety, and formally abolished a year later.

9. See his "Exposition des principes et des motifs du plan de constitution" (15–16 February 1793), in *Œuvres de Condorcet*, ed. A. Condorcet O'Connor and M. F. Arago, 12 vols. (Paris: Firmin Didot, 1847–1849), 12:366–372.

10. Bertrand Barère, speech of 16 June 1793, *Archives parlementaires*, 66:574.

11. From the presentation by Antoine Claire Thibaudeau, in *Réimpression de l'ancien* Moniteur, 32 vols. (Paris: Bureau central, 1840–1845), 24:38.

12. The phrase was employed by François-Antoine Boissy d'Anglas, presenting the draft constitution to the Convention on 23 June 1795 (5 Messidor III), in *Réimpression de l'ancien* Moniteur, 25:92.

13. On Saint-Just's analysis in his speech of 24 April 1793, see Michel Troper, "Saint-Just et le problème du pouvoir exécutif dans le discours du 24 avril 1793," *Annales historiques de la Révolution française* 191 (1968): 5–13.

14. See Bronislaw Baczko, *Comment sortir de la Terreur: Thermidor et la Révolution* (Paris: Gallimard, 1989).

15. See Condorcet, "Sur l'institution d'un conseil électif" (23 July 1791), in *Œuvres,* 12:243–266. The only other important figure to support this position was Jacques-Pierre Brissot; see his article "Sur le projet de destituer le roi et de donner à son successeur un conseil électif et amovible," *Le Patriote français,* 1 July 1791.

16. Condorcet, "Exposition des principes."

17. In his famous speech of 2 Thermidor, Year III (20 July 1795).

18. Quoted in Patrice Gueniffey, *Bonaparte: 1769–1802*, trans. Steven Rendall (Cambridge, Mass.: Belknap Press of Harvard University Press, 2015), 604.

19. Madame de Staël, *Considérations sur les principaux événements de la Révolution française* [1818], in *Œuvres posthumes* (Paris: Firmin Didot, 1838), 204. Staël wrote these lines in the early 1810s.

20. See Gueniffey, *Bonaparte,* 532.

21. Daniel Stern, *Histoire de la Révolution de 1848,* 3 vols. (Paris: G. Sandré, 1850–1853), 3:342.

22. The phrase occurs in Quinet's preface to the first edition of his poem *Napoléon* [1835]. Beyond the borders of France, one also recalls Hegel's famous celebration of Napoleon as a man of action who revealed to humanity its creative possibilities, a figure who expressed the "soul of the world."

23. See Rosanvallon, *La démocratie inachevée: Histoire de la souveraineté du peuple en France* (Paris: Gallimard, 2000), 194.

24. Edgar Quinet, *Napoléon,* in *Œuvres complètes,* 10 vols. (Paris: Pagnerre, 1857–1858), 8:296. Quinet was later to repudiate his youthful Bonapartist enthusiasms.

25. Francis Bacon, *The New Atlantis* [1627], ed. G. C. Moore Smith (Cambridge: Cambridge University Press, 1919), 35.

26. See Sudhir Hazareesingh, *The Legend of Napoleon* (London: Granta, 2004); Bernard Ménager, *Les Napoléon du peuple* (Paris: Aubier, 1988); and Natalie Petiteau, *Napoléon, de la mythologie à l'histoire* (Paris: Seuil, 1999).

27. There is much in the novels of Balzac that supports this view. Even in the late nineteenth century, Barrès (preceded in this regard by Nietzsche) was still memorializing Napoleon as a "professor of energy."

28. Staël, *Considérations*, 237.

29. Jules Michelet, January 1866 preface to a new edition of *Histoire romaine* [1839], in *Œuvres complètes*, ed. Paul Viallaneix, 21 vols. (Paris: Flammarion, 1971–1987), 2:335.

30. Anacharsis Cloots, *Appel au genre humain* [1793]; quoted by Jules Michelet, *Histoire de la Révolution française* [1847–1853], 2 vols. (Paris: Gallimard, 1952), 2:1321.

31. The Republicans protested by passing a motion of no confidence (the famous "Manifeste des 363").

32. See the first chapter ("De l'origine des temps obscurs") of Daniel Halévy, *La fin des notables* (Paris: Grasset, 1930).

33. On this point see my argument in Chapter 12.

34. On this interpretation of the history of the executive branch in Britain see Denis Baranger, *Parlementarisme des origines: Essai sur les conditions de formation d'un exécutif responsable en Angleterre (des années 1740 au début de l'âge victorien)* (Paris: Presses Universitaires de France, 1999).

35. See Lord Balfour's remarks in this connection in his introduction to Walter Bagehot, *The English Constitution*, 2nd ed. (London: Oxford University Press, 1927).

36. Walter Bagehot, *The English Constitution*, with an introduction by R. H. S. Crossman (London: Fontana / Collins, 1963), 66.

37. Ibid.

38. Ibid., 68.

3. The Age of Rehabilitation

1. See Sighele's most famous work, *La folla delinquente* (Turin: Fratelli Bocca, 1891). [The first English edition has only now just appeared, in *The Criminal Crowd and Other Writings*, ed. Nicoletta Pireddu, trans. Andrew Robbins and Nicoletta Pireddu (Toronto: University of Toronto Press, 2017).—Trans.]

2. See, in particular, Gabriel Tarde, "Foules et sectes au point de vue criminel," *Revue des deux mondes* (15 November 1893): 349–387.

3. See Gustave Le Bon, *La psychologie des foules* (Paris: F. Alcan, 1895). It is hard for us today to appreciate the scale of its extraordinary success: reprinted more than fifty times and translated into some twenty languages, it was one of the greatest academic best-sellers of the nineteenth century. In Serge Moscovici's view, it remains still today "the most influential work in all of social psychology"; see Moscovici, *L'Âge des foules: Un traité historique de psychologie des masses* (Paris: Fayard, 1981), 81.

4. "The psychological crowd," Le Bon says, "is a provisional being. . . . In the aggregate which constitutes a crowd there is in no [way] a summing-up of or an average struck between its elements. What really takes place is a combination followed by the creation of new characteristics, just as in chemistry certain elements, when brought into contact—bases and acids, for example—combine to form a new body possessing properties quite different from those of the bodies that have served to form it. It is easy to prove how much the individual forming part of a crowd differs from the isolated individual." Gustave Le Bon, *The Crowd: A Study of the Popular Mind* (New York: Viking Press, 1960), 27.

5. Ibid., 32.

6. Tarde initially formulated the distinction in *L'opinion et la foule* (Paris: F. Alcan, 1901).

7. Le Bon, *The Crowd*, 19.

8. Ibid., 121.

9. Ibid., 118.

10. See Benoît Marpeau, *Gustave Le Bon: Parcours d'un intellectuel, 1841–1931* (Paris: CNRS Éditions, 2000); and Catherine Rouvier, *Les idées politiques de Gustave Le Bon* (Paris: Presses Universitaires de France, 1986).

11. Neither Lenin nor any of the others would have failed to notice Le Bon's insistence that "men gathered in a crowd lose all force of will, and turn instinctively to the person who possesses the quality they lack" (*The Crowd*, 119).

12. "The great questions to be resolved within parliaments," Le Bon wrote in a later work, "can be resolved only with a majority strongly grouped around a statesman capable of leading, and not with chance majorities that are seen to come into existence and disappear the same week." See Gustave Le Bon, *Le déséquilibre du monde* (Paris: Flammarion, 1924), 199.

13. See, in particular, Le Bon's article "L'évolution de l'Europe vers des formes diverses de dictature," *Annales politiques et littéraires*, no. 2123 (2 March 1924), as well as Le Bon, "Psychologie des récents mouvements révolutionnaires," *Annales politiques et littéraires*, no. 2102 (7 October 1923), published after the coup d'état by Miguel Primo de Rivera in Spain and the coming to power of Benito Mussolini in Italy.

14. This is the title of the second chapter of Moscovici's *L'Âge des foules*.

15. Le Bon, *The Crowd*, 176–177.

16. Indeed, it has often been argued that the triumph of parliamentarianism in the nineteenth century was connected with the fact that overall it had been a century of peace (with the exception of the brief Franco-Prussian conflict and the Crimean war before that).

17. Alexis de Tocqueville, *Democracy in America* [1835–1840], 2 vols., trans. Gerald Bevan (London: Penguin, 2003), 2.3.22, 755–756.

18. From the text of a lecture reproduced in Charles de Gaulle, *Lettres, notes et carnets*, 13 vols. (Paris: Plon, 1980–1997), 1:460.

19. Ibid., 1:473.
20. These letters first appeared in the *Revue de Paris* and were later collected in a single volume. In what follows I cite to the collection reprinted in vol. 3, pt. 1, of *L'Œuvre de Léon Blum,* 7 vols. (Paris: Albin Michel, 1955–1972), covering the years 1928–1934.
21. Ibid., 517.
22. Ibid., 509.
23. Ibid., 518.
24. Ibid., 522.
25. Ibid., 509.
26. Ibid., 511. "So long as a vote of Parliament will not have made them come down from their mountain top," Blum said by way of further emphasis, "our presidents of the Council are indeed kings" (ibid., 518).
27. Ibid., 515.
28. Ibid., 518.
29. On Blum's positions, and their evolution in response to what he called the problem of efficiency in a democracy, see Vincent Le Grand, *Léon Blum (1872–1950): Gouverner la République* (Paris: Librairie générale de droit et de jurisprudence, 2008).
30. Célestin Bouglé, "Ce que la guerre exige de la démocratie française," in Célestin Bouglé, Émile Doumergue, Henri Bois, and Henry Wickham Steed, *Les démocraties modernes* (Paris: Flammarion, 1921), 45.
31. Quoted by Nicolas Rousselier in his *mémoire d'habilitation* submitted to the Paris Institute of Political Studies in 2006, "Du gouvernement de guerre au gouvernement de la défaite: Les transformations du pouvoir exécutif en France (1913–1940)," 42.
32. On this point see Fabienne Bock, *Un parlementarisme de guerre, 1914–1919* (Paris: Belin, 2002); and also the classic work of Pierre Renouvin, *Les formes du gouvernement de guerre* (Paris: Presses Universitaires de France, 1925).
33. See Clemenceau's unsparing recollections in the chapter devoted to this topic in *Grandeurs et misères d'une victoire* (Paris: Plon, 1930), in which he describes Briand as the "conductor of [the orchestra of] French defeatism."
34. "Son de cloche," *L'Homme enchaîné,* 25 February 1917.
35. "On demande un gouvernement," *L'Homme enchaîné,* 15 November 1917.
36. "La vraie crise," *L'Homme enchaîné,* 4 September 1917.
37. "Un gouvernement français," *L'Homme enchaîné,* 9 September 1917.
38. "In administration," he wrote, "most qualifications can be acquired. . . . One learns to lead men as one learns to lead animals, things: a leader of men is not unlike a shepherd"; quoted by Yves Cohen, "Foucault déplace les sciences sociales: La gouvernementalité et l'histoire du XXᵉ siècle," in *Les sciences camérales: Activités pratiques et histoire des dispositifs publics,* ed. Pascale Laborier, Frédéric Audren, Paolo Napoli, and Jakob Vogel (Paris: Presses Universitaires de France, 2011), 71.

39. See, for example, Joseph Wilbois and Paul Vanuxem, *Essai sur la conduite des affaires et la direction des hommes* (Paris: Payot, 1919); and Robert Courau, *Psychologie du haut commandement des entreprises* (Paris: Berger-Levrault, 1930).

40. On the rise to power of leaders in all these countries, see the comprehensive survey by Yves Cohen, *Le siècle des chefs: Une histoire transnationale du commandement et de l'autorité (1890–1940)* (Paris: Éditions Amsterdam, 2013).

41. The slogan was due originally to the anarchist poet Joseph Déjacque (1821–1864), who used it as the title for an essay written in April 1859 and published posthumously as a pamphlet in Paris in 1912. It has been reprinted several times since, most recently in a collection of Déjacque's writings, *À bas les chefs! Écrits libertaires (1847–1863)*, ed. Thomas Bouchet (Paris: La Fabrique, 2016).

42. See the recent French edition of Berdyaev's 1918 work on the philosophy of inequality, *De l'inégalité*, trans. Anne and Constantin Andronikof (Lausanne: L'Âge d'homme, 2008), 51.

43. Thus Henry Bordeaux placed the following epigraph at the head of his book *Joffre, ou l'art de commander* (Paris: Grasset, 1933): "To the unknown soldier who in the name of his comrades, dead and alive, and in the very name of the country, cries out for leaders."

44. Bertrand de Jouvenal, "Sur l'évolution des formes de gouvernement," *Bulletin SEDEIS* 785, Futuribles suppl. (20 April 1961), 15.

45. See Peter A. Hall, ed., *The Political Power of Economic Ideas: Keynesianism across Nations* (Princeton, N.J.: Princeton University Press, 1989).

46. Pierre Mendès-France and Gabriel Ardant, *La science économique et l'action* (Paris: UNESCO-Julliard, 1954), 10.

47. See Georges Hispalis, "Pourquoi tant de loi(s)?," *Pouvoirs*, no. 114 (2005): 101–115.

48. Georges Burdeau, "Essai sur l'évolution de la notion de loi en droit français," *Archives de philosophie de droit*, no. 1–2 (1939): 44; also Burdeau, "Le déclin de la loi," *Archives de philosophie de droit*, new ser., no. 8 (1963): 35–41.

4. Two Temptations

1. Woodrow Wilson, "The Study of Administration," *Political Science Quarterly* 2, no. 2 (1887): 197–222. The French reader must keep in mind that in America the term *administration* refers both to the execution of public policy and to government in its policy-making capacity ("the administration").

2. See Samuel C. Patterson, "Remembering Frank J. Goodnow," *PS: Political Science and Politics* 34, no. 4 (2001): 875–881.

3. See the new edition of Frank J. Goodnow, *Politics and Administration: A Study in Government* [1900] (New Brunswick, N.J.: Transaction, 2003), with an introduction by John A. Rohr.

4. For both Wilson and Goodnow this was the great strength of the continental European model. France and Prussia are often held up as examples in their writings.

5. On this movement see in particular Samuel Haber, *Efficiency and Uplift: Scientific Management in the Progressive Era, 1890–1920* (Chicago: University of Chicago Press, 1964); Robert H. Wiebe, *The Search for Order, 1877–1920* (New York: Hill and Wang, 1967); Samuel P. Hays, *Conservation and the Gospel of Efficiency: The Progressive Conservation Movement, 1890–1920* (New York: Atheneum, 1969); and Judith A. Merkle, *Management and Ideology: The Legacy of the International Scientific Management Movement* (Berkeley: University of California Press, 1980).

6. Charles Ferguson, *The Great News* (New York: M. Kennerley, 1915), 59. Some years earlier Ferguson had written that democracy implies "the destruction of politicians," in *The Religion of Democracy: A Manual of Devotion* (London: F. Tennyson Neely, 1899), 100.

7. M. P. Follett, *The New State: Group Organization, the Solution of Popular Government* [1918], 3rd. ed. (New York: Longmans, Green and Co., 1934), 180.

8. Patrick Fridenson, "Un tournant taylorien de la société française (1904–1918)," *Annales ESC* 42, no. 5 (1987): 1031–1060.

9. Alfred Schatz, *L'entreprise gouvernementale et son administration* (Paris: Grasset, 1922), 90. Henri Fayol wrote a preface to Schatz's book.

10. Henri Fayol, "L'industrialisation de l'État," in *L'incapacité industrielle de l'État: Les PTT* (Paris: Dunot, 1921), 89. Fayol's lecture "La doctrine administrative dans l'État" was delivered at the Second International Congress of Administrative Sciences, held in Brussels in 1923, but not published until more than forty years later, in *Revue internationale des sciences administratives* 32, no. 2 (1966): 114–133. On Fayol's reception, see Alain Chatriot, "Fayol, les fayoliens et l'impossible réforme de l'administration durant l'entre-deux-guerres," *Entreprises et histoire* 34, no. 3 (2003): 84–97.

11. Intellectually, at least; administrative-executive power, as an ideal type, did little to transform the actual functioning and role of administration.

12. Benoist's remark, made during the 1 February 1916 session of the Chamber of Deputies, is quoted by Joseph Barthélemy, *Le problème de la compétence dans la démocratie* (Paris: F. Alcan, 1918), 221.

13. Émile Faguet, *Le culte de l'incompétence* (Paris: Grasset, 1910), 29–30.

14. On these experiments see three contemporary works: John J. Hamilton, *Government by Commission; or, the Dethronement of the City Boss [1910]*, 3rd ed. (New York: Funk and Wagnalls, 1911); Clinton R. Woodruff, ed., *City Government by Commission* (New York: Appleton, 1911); and the very complete collection of studies published in 1911, in Philadelphia, by the American Academy of Political and Social Science, *Commission Government in American Cities*. For a more recent survey, see Bradley Robert Rice, *Progressive Cities: The Commission Government Movement in America, 1901–1920* (Austin: University of Texas Press, 1977).

15. For an early evaluation of this system see Harold A. Stone, Don K. Price, and Kathryn H. Stone, *City Manager Government in the United States: A Review after Twenty-Five Years* (Chicago: Public Administration Service, 1940). The best recent study is Martin J. Schiesl, *The Politics of Efficiency: Municipal Administration and Reform in America, 1800–1920* (Berkeley: University of California Press, 1977). It should be noted that government service was becoming professionalized at all levels, federal, state, and municipal, during this period.

16. The term seems first to have come into use in 1919. See Raoul de Roussy de Sales, "Un mouvement nouveau aux États-Unis: La technocratie," *Revue de Paris*, no. 6 (March 1933): 431–454.

17. Henri Chardon, *L'organisation de la République pour la paix* (Paris: Presses Universitaires de France, 1926), xxvii. For reactions to his analysis, see Vida Azimi, "Administration et Parlement: La démocratie organisée de Henri Chardon," *Revue d'histoire du droit français et étranger* 76, no. 4 (1998): 557–558.

18. Henri Chardon, *Le pouvoir administratif: La réorganisation des services publics, la réforme administrative, le statut des fonctionnaires, et l'interdiction de la grève dans les services publics, la suppression du Ministère de l'intérieur* (Paris: Perrin, 1911), 29. "Public service," he added by way of further justification, "is permanent and necessary, whereas nothing is more fickle, and often more futile, than political judgment" (ibid., 111).

19. Ibid., 55.

20. Ibid., 191. In so doing, Chardon concluded, "each civil servant is, within the limits of his office, superior to any [administrative] authority."

21. In its initial form, the resort to dictatorship was limited to the three centuries of republican Rome, from 501 to the end of the Second Punic War in 202 BCE.

22. Dictatorship in Rome displayed five characteristic features: it could be put into effect only if circumstances required it, which is to say if the common law was incapable of meeting the demands of a given situation; a clear distinction was made between those who were authorized to call for the formation of a dictatorship and those who were responsible for appointing the holder of this office; whereas many institutions in republican Rome were collegial, the office of dictator was individual; the term of office of the dictator, appointed to perform a specific task, came to an end with the task's completion; finally, the dictator could take no measure of a general and long-lasting nature, and he was prohibited from enacting legislative or constitutional provisions by decree. My discussion here relies on Claude Nicolet, "La dictature à Rome," in *Dictatures et légitimité*, ed. Maurice Duverger (Paris: Presses Universitaires de France, 1982), 69–84; Theodor Mommsen, *Le droit public romain*, 7 vols., trans. Paul Frédéric Girard (Paris: E. Thorin, 1889–1896), 3:161–197; François Hinard, ed., *Dictatures: Actes de la Table Ronde réunie à Paris les 27 et 28 février 1984* (Paris: De Boccard, 1988); and Wilfried

Nippel, "Emergency Powers in the Roman Republic," in *La théorie politico-constitutionnelle du gouvernement d'exception,* ed. Pasquale Pasquino and Bernard Manin, published as a special issue of *Cahiers du CREA,* no. 19 (2000): 5–23.

23. Seventy-six dictatorships were declared during the three centuries of republican Rome (of which only six were instituted in response to proven cases of internal sedition), each one of them having been established and then discontinued in the prescribed manner.

24. The purpose of the institution was later subverted by Sulla and Caesar, who used it as a means of seizing power for themselves.

25. Among the great figures of modern political philosophy, only Locke directly addressed the question, this in the course formulating his doctrine of prerogative; see chaps. 14–15, second treatise, *Two Treatises of Government* [1689].

26. It was on the basis of this article that Charles X was to promulgate the famous ordinances restricting civil liberties that provoked the fall of the regime in July 1830.

27. In this regard see the impressive analysis by François Saint-Bonnet, *L'état d'exception* (Paris: Presses Universitaires de France, 2001).

28. On this point see Chapter 5.

29. Carl Schmitt, *Political Theology: Four Chapters on the Concept of Sovereignty* [1922], trans. George Schwab (Cambridge, Mass.: MIT Press, 1985), 5.

30. See Carl Schmitt, *The Concept of the Political* [1932], trans. George Schwab (Chicago: University of Chicago Press, 1996).

31. Schmitt, *Political Theology,* 12.

32. On this point see Olivier Beaud, *La puissance de l'État* (Paris: Presses Universitaires de France, 1994), 135–136.

33. This recalls both Lenin's idea of a dictatorship of the proletariat and the Jacobins' view in 1794 of the Terror as a means of national regeneration.

34. Carl Schmitt, *Dictatorship: From the Origin of the Modern Concept of Sovereignty to Proletarian Class Struggle* [1921], trans. Michael Hoelzl and Graham Ward (Cambridge: Polity, 2014), 119. Emphasis in the original.

35. From Schmitt's preface to the first edition, in ibid., xliii.

36. Emmanuel Joseph Sieyès, *Qu'est-ce que le Tiers-État?* [1789] (Paris: Presses Universitaires de France, 1982), 71.

37. Emmanuel Joseph Sieyès, *Quelques idées de constitution appliquables à la ville de Paris* (Versailles: Baudouin, 1789), 30. "Constituent power," Sieyès elaborated, "can do everything in this regard. . . . Thus the nation that exercises its greatest, its most important powers, must in this office be free from all constraint and from all form, other than that which it is pleased to adopt." Sieyès, *Préliminaire de la Constitution françoise: Reconnoissance et exposition raisonée des droits de l'homme & du citoyen* (Versailles: Pierres, 1789).

38. Carl Schmitt, *Constitutional Theory* [1928], trans. Jeffrey Seitzer (Durham, N.C.: Duke University Press, 2008), 129.

39. Ibid., 131.

40. Carl Schmitt, *The* Nomos *of the Earth in the International Law of the* Jus Publicum Europaeum [1950], trans. G. L. Ulmen (New York: Telos Press, 2003), 69. This discussion occurs in a chapter titled "On the Meaning of the Word *Nomos,*" 67–79.

41. Schmitt, *Constitutional Theory,* 156.

42. In these countries the resort to dictatorship was typically justified by the need to combat alleged threats of subversion to the nation's institutions.

43. The doctrine of sovereign democracy considers that popular election is in effect a kind of "acclamation," to use Schmitt's term, and that it therefore confers full powers. On this reformulation of Caesarist doctrine, see Chapter 7.

44. See, for example, the argument made by Giorgio Agamben in *State of Exception* [2003], trans. Kevin Attell (Chicago: University of Chicago Press, 2005).

45. It should be remembered that Greece, Spain, and Portugal, on emerging in the 1970s from long dark years of dictatorship, all made a point of adopting constitutional measures that strictly limited the future use of emergency powers.

5. The Pioneering Experiments: 1848 and Weimar

1. The minutes of the meeting, chaired by the Vicomte de Cormenin, are reproduced in Alexis de Tocqueville, *Écrits et discours politiques,* ed. André Jardin, 3 vols. (Paris: Gallimard: 1962–1990), 3:55–158.

2. French writers on politics from the 1820s to the 1840s constantly reminded their readers that the American republic had in addition, by instituting what was called government on the cheap, reduced the burden on taxpayers. See René Rémond, *Les États-Unis devant l'opinion française, 1815–1852* (Paris: Armand Colin, 1962); and Aurelian Crăiuţu and Jeffrey C. Isaac, eds., *America through European Eyes: British and French Reflections on the New World from the Eighteenth Century to the Present* (University Park: Pennsylvania State University Press, 2009).

3. Victor Considerant defended the same position on the ground that "the education of the people is not complete"; quoted in Paul Bastid, *Doctrines et institutions politiques de la Seconde République,* 2 vols. (Paris: Hachette, 1945), 1:272.

4. For a summary of these debates on executive power, see ibid., 2:105–116.

5. Quoted in ibid., 2:105–106.

6. Quoted in ibid., 2:106.

7. Pierre Leroux, *Projet d'une constitution démocratique et sociale* (Paris: G. Sandré, 1848), 1.

8. From an article entitled "The People" that appeared in a newspaper of the same name, *Le Peuple,* no. 3 [n.d. (October 1848?)], reproduced in

Pierre-Joseph Proudhon, *Mélanges: Articles de journaux (1848–1852)*, 3 vols. (Paris: Lacroix, 1868–1871), 1:161.

9. "Believe me," Proudhon urged the committee members, "the people do not trouble themselves over the distinction between *legislative* and *executive*. The executive, for them, is all that matters. [Selecting] a notary, no doubt that would be different; a fiancé, different as well. Provided that a president acts quickly and well, he will have, in the judgment of the people, wit enough. His virility will assure his worth. Your *legislature* is a eunuch, something less than nothing!" Proudhon, *Mélanges*, 1:161–162; emphasis in the original.

10. Ibid. [Proudhon humorously refers here to the pompous physician in Molière's *Le malade imaginaire.*—Trans.]

11. Quoted in Bastid, *Doctrines et institutions politiques*, 2:109.

12. Speech of 5 October 1848, in Tocqueville, *Écrits et discours politiques*, 3:212.

13. Ibid., 3:214.

14. "One will still find it hard to believe," Tocqueville noted in his memoirs in connection with the work of the constitutional committee, "that a subject so immense, so difficult, so new furnishes it with no material for a general debate or even for a very detailed discussion." These lines, written under the Second Empire, reflect the mature view of his later years that "appointing a president through the people was not a self-evident truth, and that the provision for electing him directly was as dangerous as it was novel." See Alexis de Tocqueville, *Souvenirs* [1893], ed. Luc Monnier (Paris: Gallimard, 1964), 187; also Arnaud Coutant, *Tocqueville et la constitution démocratique: Souveraineté du peuple et libertés* (Paris: Mare & Martin, 2008).

15. Letter from Beaumont to Tocqueville of 10 October 1848, in *Correspondance d'Alexis de Tocqueville et Gustave de Beaumont*, ed. André Jardin, 3 vols. (Paris: Gallimard, 1967), 2:57. The emphasis is mine.

16. Speech of 6 October 1848, quoted in Bastid, *Doctrines et institutions politiques*, 2:111.

17. Ibid., 2:111–112.

18. On the history of this constitution and of the Weimar regime, among works on the subject in French, see Christian Baechler, *L'Allemagne de Weimar, 1919–1933* (Paris: Fayard, 2007).

19. The expression is due to the veteran party official Hermann Molkenbuhr, quoted in Heinrich August Winkler, *Germany: The Long Road West*, 2 vols., trans. Alexander J. Sager (Oxford: Oxford University Press, 2006–2007), 1:362.

20. On the attitude of German Social Democrats toward referendum, see Karl Kautsky, *Parlementarisme et socialisme: Étude critique sur la législation directe par le peuple* [1893], trans. Édouard Berth (Paris: G. Jacques, 1900).

21. On this key point see Wolfgang Mommsen's analysis in *Max Weber and German Politics, 1890–1920* [1959], trans. Michael S. Steinberg (Chicago: University of Chicago Press, 1984), particularly the chapter on the making of the Weimar Constitution, 332–389. Not the least of Weber's concerns was

that any plan for constituting parliament on a unitary basis (one vote / one seat) would be poorly received by the Entente powers when the time came to negotiate peace terms.

22. Max Weber, *Economy and Society: An Outline of Interpretive Sociology* [1922], ed. Guenther Roth and Claus Wittich, trans. Ephraim Fischoff et al., 3 vols. (New York: Bedminster Press, 1968), 1:266.

23. Max Weber, *Économie et société* [1922], ed. and trans. Jacques Chavy and Éric Dampierre, 3 vols. (Paris: Plon, 1971), 1:275. [Here I have followed the more literal French version in preference to the misleading translation in the English edition cited in the previous note.—Trans.]

24. See Max Weber, *Parliament and Government in Germany under a New Political Order: Towards a Political Critique of Officialdom and the Party System* [1918], trans. Ronald Speirs, in *Weber: Political Writings*, ed. Peter Lassman and Ronald Speirs (Cambridge: Cambridge University Press, 1994), 130–271.

25. Ibid., 220–221; emphasis in the original.

26. "Such notions as the 'will of the people,' the true will of the people, ceased to exist for me years ago, they are *fictions*," he wrote in a letter dated 4 August 1908 to Michels. Quoted in Mommsen, *Max Weber and German Politics*, 395; emphasis in the original.

27. " 'The principle of small numbers' always rules in political action, i.e., the superior capacity for political maneuverability of *small* leadership groups," Weber insisted. This "Caesarist transformation" in mass democracies he considered to be unavoidable. Quoted in ibid., 186; emphasis in original.

28. "In a democracy," Weber observed, "the people choose a leader whom they trust. The one who has been chosen then says, 'Now be quiet and obey me. The people and the parties are no longer permitted to interfere in the leader's affairs.' After a certain time the people are called upon to judge the leader's performance. If he has made mistakes—to the gallows with him!" May 1919 meeting with Erich Ludendorff, quoted by Laurence Morel in "La Vᵉ République, le référendum, et la démocratie plébiscitaire de Max Weber," *Jus Politicum*, no. 4 (2010): 50.

29. Joseph Schumpeter, *Capitalism, Socialism, and Democracy* (New York: Harper and Bros., 1942), 273.

30. See Weber's remarks on the modernity of a figure such as Gladstone in England, in "The Profession and Vocation of Politics" [1919], in Lassman and Speirs, *Weber: Political Writings*, esp. 340–345; and more generally, on Caesarism, see *Parliament and Government in Germany under a New Political Order*, also in *Weber: Political Writings*, 220–222, 227–230.

31. Mommsen, *Max Weber and German Politics*, 409.

32. Ibid., 382. This question lay at the heart of the disagreement between Theodor Mommsen and Max Weber's liberal admirers, such as Raymond Aron and Karl Löwenstein, who were appalled at the thought of likening Weber to Schmitt ("the Mephistopheles of the pre-Hitler period," in Löwenstein's phrase [382, n. 156]).

33. Weber, *Parliament and Government*, 222.

34. "The whole structure of the German parliament today," he wrote, "is tailored to a merely *negative type of politics:* criticism, complaint, consultation, the amendment and dispatch of bills presented by the government. All parliamentary conventions correspond to this" (ibid., 177; emphasis in the original). The phrase "negative politics" frequently recurs in this essay.

35. Ibid., 187.

36. Parties now exhibited an essentially mechanical character (not for nothing were their organs called "machines"), having lost virtually all contact with the actual experience of the human beings whose votes they solicited.

37. In 1887 it was discovered that Jules Grévy's son-in-law, a deputy named Daniel Wilson, had used his office at the Élysée Palace to profit massively from bribes in the awarding of thousands of decorations. Grévy was forced to step down as president of the Republic the same year.

38. Named for Julius Barmat, a Dutch Jewish wholesale merchant of Russo-Ukrainian origin and a member of the Social Democratic Party in Holland, who was accused of embezzling funds from the Prussian State Bank.

39. See Nicolas Rousselier, *Le Parlement de l'éloquence: La souveraineté de la délibération au lendemain de la Grande Guerre* (Paris: Presses de Sciences Po, 1997). The same point is stressed in Nicolas Patin, *La catastrophe allemande, 1914–1945* (Paris: Fayard, 2014).

40. See Baechler, *L'Allemagne de Weimar*, 296.

41. Adolf Hitler, *Mon Combat* [1925] (Paris: Nouvelles Éditions Latines, 1934), 85, 97, 98.

42. Joseph Goebbels, *Journal, 1923–1933*, ed. Pierre Ayçoberry, trans. Denis-Armand Canal, Hélène Thiérard, and Dominique Viollet (Paris: Tallandier, 2006), 272.

43. Mommsen, *Max Weber and German Politics*, 380.

44. See Olivier Beaud, *Les derniers jours de Weimar: Carl Schmitt face à l'avènement du nazisme* (Paris: Descartes, 1997), 28–36.

45. Ibid., 32. [The votes of confidence that were frequently used by cabinets in the early years of Weimar came to be replaced by weaker "votes of tolerance" in the hope of preserving majority support in the Reichstag for the government's bills.—Trans.]

46. Quoted by Nikolai Wehrs, "Demokratie durch Diktatur? Friedrich Meinecke als Vernunftrepublikaner in der Weimarer Republik," in *Friedrich Meinecke in seiner Zeit: Studien zu Leben und Werk*, ed. Gisela Bock and Daniel Schönpflug (Stuttgart: F. Steiner, 2006), 116.

6. From Gaullist Exception to Standard Model

1. On this point see Henri Michel, *Les courants de pensée de la Résistance* (Paris: Presses Universitaires de France, 1962).

2. Léon Blum, "Un programme constitutionnel," *Le Populaire,* 22 November 1927; reprinted in *L'Œuvre de Léon Blum,* 8 vols. (Paris: Albin Michel, 1954–1972), vol. 3, pt. 2 [1928–1934], 14.

3. Léon Blum, "À l'échelle humaine" [1941]; reprinted in *L'Œuvre de Léon Blum,* vol. 5 [1940–1945], 430.

4. Léon Blum, "La lettre de démission," *Le Populaire,* 22 January 1946.

5. See National Constituent Assembly (elected 21 October 1945), *Séances de la commission de la Constitution: Comptes rendus analytiques* (April 1946): 83–84.

6. The MRP had proposed granting the prime minister this right. See the discussion on this point in National Constituent Assembly (elected 2 June 1946), *Séances de la commission de la Constitution: Comptes rendus analytiques* (October 1946): 68–75.

7. The final tally was nine million votes in favor and eight million against. Considering that there were six million abstentions and a million unmarked ballots, however, only 36 percent of the voters had voted in favor of the new constitution. The Gaullists, for their part, took a dim view of a document that had not put in place a chief of state "who would really be one of us," as the General put it.

8. The case of Portugal should be recalled as well. Six years after the military putsch of 1926, António Salazar became prime minister. The following year, 1933, an authoritarian regime was instituted in which the president of the Republic was to be elected by universal suffrage (though because illiterates, then numerous, were barred from voting, and only women with a secondary or higher education were considered to be qualified, the procedure fell far short of living up to its name). The election was, in any case, a mere formality, the presidency being occupied by minor figures of no political consequence and real power being exercised by Salazar.

9. Thus Alexander Hamilton defended the procedure in the following terms: "It was equally desirable, that the immediate election should be made by men most capable of analyzing the qualities adapted to the station, and acting under circumstances favorable to deliberation, and to a judicious combination of all the reasons and inducements which were proper to govern their choice. A small number of persons, selected by their fellow-citizens from the general mass, will be most likely to possess the information and discernment requisite to such complicated investigations." Federalist paper no. 68 (14 March 1788), in Alexander Hamilton, James Madison, and John Jay, *The Federalist* (Cambridge, Mass.: Belknap Press of Harvard University Press, 2009), 447.

10. The sole exception was North Carolina. Two states admitted to the union later (Florida in 1868 and Colorado in 1876) likewise adopted the practice of legislative appointment.

11. It sometimes happens, however, as in the case of George W. Bush in 2000 and Donald Trump in 2016, that the president elected by means of this system does not win a majority of the popular vote. Two other "minority"

presidents had been chosen previously, Rutherford B. Hayes in 1876 and Benjamin Harrison in 1888.

12. On this point, recall the faintly contemptuous remarks made by European political figures at the time.

13. René Capitant, preface to Léo Hamon, *De Gaulle dans la République* (Paris: Plon, 1958); reprinted in Capitant, *Écrits constitutionnelles* (Paris: Éditions du CNRS, 1982), 366.

14. Charles de Gaulle, *Mémoires de guerre,* 3 vols. (Paris: Plon, 1954–1959), 3:240. He had also spoken in his second Bayeux speech (16 June 1946) of a "gathering of delegations." It was for this reason that the simultaneous holding of ministerial and parliamentary offices was to be disallowed by Article 23 of the 1958 Constitution.

15. On this point see Odile Rudelle, "De Gaulle et l'élection directe du président de la République," *Revue française de science politique* 34, no. 4 (1984): 695, 700.

16. See Jean-Éric Callon, ed., *Les projets constitutionnels de la Résistance* (Paris: La Documentation française, 1998).

17. The Constitution of 1958 provided that the President be named by an electoral college composed of members of Parliament, department councillors, mayors of all the communes of France and, from the most populous of these, town councillors (or a total of about 80,000 popularly elected officials).

18. See his speech of 4 October 1962, reprinted in Charles de Gaulle, *Mémoires d'espoir,* 2 vols. (Paris: Plon, 1970–1971), 2:18, as well as conversations reported by Alain Peyrefitte and Roger Frey. Léo Hamon, for his part, was persuaded that these were no more than retrospective rationalizations; see his essay "La thèse gaullienne," in *L'élection du chef de l'État en France d'Hugues Capet à nos jours: Entretiens d'Auxerre 1987,* ed. Léo Hamon and Guy Lobrichon (Paris: Beauchesne, 1988), 185–195.

19. "At the time," de Gaulle later recalled, "in order not to oppose the almost unanimous longing for national unity, I thought it wise to take into consideration the passionate prejudices that, since Louis-Napoleon, the idea of a plebiscite aroused in many sectors of opinion. Once experience of the new Constitution had shown that the highest office created by it enjoys authority without resort to dictatorship, it would be time to propose to the people a final and lasting reform." *Mémoires d'espoir,* 2:19–20.

20. Ibid., 20.

21. On this point see Olivier Duhamel, *Le pouvoir politique en France* (Paris: Presses Universitaires de France, 1991).

22. See his remarks of 11 April 1961, quoted in Rudelle, "De Gaulle et l'élection directe," 702–703.

23. See the chapter devoted to this question ("Le refus total de la gauche communiste") in Olivier Duhamel, *La Gauche et la V* République* (Paris: Presses Universitaires de France, 1980), esp. 84–105.

24. Quoted in Serge Berstein, *Histoire du gaullisme* (Paris: Perrin, 2001), 105–106.

25. From an article in *Le Populaire,* 21 June 1946, reprinted in *L'Œuvre de Léon Blum,* vol. 6, pt. 2 [1945–1947], 218.

26. Pierre Mendès-France, *La République moderne: Propositions* (Paris: Gallimard, 1962); reprinted in *Œuvres complètes,* 6 vols. (Paris: Gallimard, 1984–1990), 4:739–888. Mendès-France refused to present himself as a candidate in a presidential election under the Fifth Republic.

27. Ibid., 4:775.

28. Ibid., 4:772.

29. "No doubt its beginnings seem favorable," de Gaulle conceded. "Amidst the enthusiasm of some and the resignation of others, in the strictness of the order it imposes, and owing to brilliant stage-setting and one-sided propaganda, there is a dynamism about it at first that stands in contrast to the anarchy that came before. But it is the destiny of dictatorship to exaggerate its undertakings." Charles de Gaulle, *Discours et messages,* 5 vols. (Paris: Plon, 1970), 3:10.

30. Mitterrand likened the constitution to a "rewriting of the [pact of] 2 December," apparently mistaking the date of de Gaulle's 1944 meeting in Moscow with Stalin for the signing of the Franco-Soviet Treaty of Alliance and Mutual Aid eight days later, on 10 December.—Trans.

31. These and other such charges occur throughout Mitterrand's book, *Le Coup d'État permanent* (Paris: Plon, 1964), reissued under the 10/18 imprint the following year.

32. See Raymond Aron, "La République gaulliste continue," *Preuves,* no. 143 (January 1963): 3–11.

33. See Raymond Aron, "Démission des français ou rénovation de la France?," *Preuves,* no. 96 (February 1959): 3–13. Both this article and Aron's "La République gaulliste continue" are reprinted in the collection edited by Christian Bachelier, *Une histoire du vingtième siècle* (Paris: Plon, 1996). On these positions see Frédéric Lazorthes, "Le libéral et la Constitution de la Ve République: Aron et le complex français du pouvoir exécutif," *Droits,* no. 44 (2007): 59–69.

34. The Council of State, overstepping the usual bounds of its advisory role concerning the legal aspects of administration, handed down a negative opinion on the proposed reform of the procedure for electing the President of the Republic. In this connection it is important to note that the left's traditional defense of parliamentary sovereignty was now extended to include a principled opposition to claims of executive prerogative in matters of constitutional review.

35. De Gaulle, moreover, had himself made it clear that he remained loyal to the anti-Bonapartist spirit of the early Third Republic. However great his commitment to "public-safety republican[ism]" may have been, he had no sympathy for Caesarism. On this point see Claire Andrieu, "Charles de Gaulle, héritier de la Révolution française," in *De Gaulle en son siècle: Actes des*

Journées internationales tenues à l'Unesco, Paris, 19–24 novembre 1990, 7 vols. (Paris: La Documentation française / Plon, 1991–1993), 2:43–68.

36. Mitterrand, *Le Coup d'État permanent,* 240.

37. Laurence Morel, "La Ve République, le référendum, et la démocratie plébiscitaire de Max Weber," *Jus Politicum,* no. 4 (2010): 34.

38. This conversion, it must be emphasized, did not in every case assume the form of a presidentialization of the executive.

39. See Maurice Duverger, *La monarchie républicaine* (Paris: Robert Laffont, 1974).

40. See the discussion in ibid., 63–72.

41. Brian Farrell, *Chairman or Chief? The Role of Taoiseach in Irish Government* (Dublin: Gill and Macmillan, 1971), x.

42. See, for example, Léo Hamon and Albert Mabileau, eds., *La personnalisation du pouvoir: Entretiens de Dijon* (Paris: Presses Universitaires de France, 1964).

43. For an overview see Thomas Poguntke and Paul Webb, eds., *The Presidentialization of Politics: A Comparative Study of Modern Democracies* (Oxford: Oxford University Press / European Consortium for Political Research, 2005).

44. Olivier Beaud, "À la recherche de la légitimité de la Ve République," *Droits,* no. 44 (2007): 88. On the evolution of French-style presidentialism, see Olivier Duhamel, "Vers une présidentialisation des institutions?," in *Le vote de rupture: Les élections présidentielle et législatives d'avril–juin 2007,* ed. Pascal Perrineau (Paris: Presses de Sciences Po, 2008), 271–282.

7. Unavoidable and Unsatisfactory

1. Particularly in relation to the development of television, which marked a decisive step in the process of personalization, above all in the context of presidential elections.

2. Jacques Necker, *Du pouvoir exécutif dans les grands États,* 2 vols. ([n.p.], 1792), 1:355.

3. These phrases occur in an article by Fréron that appeared in *Gazette nationale, ou le Moniteur universel,* 24 Floréal Year III.

4. See Yves Sintomer's critical edition of Max Weber, *La Domination* (Paris: La Découverte, 2013), which reprints the chapters of *Economy and Society* concerned with ruling together with a selection of Weber's unpublished writings on the subject.

5. Guglielmo Ferrero, *Pouvoir: Les génies invisible de la cité* (Paris: Plon, 1945), 18. [The book was originally published in French three years earlier in New York, on account of the Occupation.—Trans.]. Ferrero, for his part, distinguished four principles of legitimacy: elective, hereditary, aristocratic, and democratic.

6. Ibid., 269.

7. Max Weber, "The President of the Reich" (1919), in *Weber: Political Writings*, 308.

8. Two variables jointly determine the degree of representative correction, in other words, the type of electoral system and the representativeness of political parties.

9. On this duality see Rosanvallon, *Le peuple introuvable: Histoire de la représentation démocratique en France* (Paris: Gallimard, 1998), 43–56.

10. There have been various proposals for making increased use of lotteries or otherwise democratizing civic duties that require certain kinds of expertise, for example by means of citizen juries.

11. Political theory distinguishes between two main forms of representation: representation as delegation, which refers to the exercise of a mandate (acting for, or *Stellvertretung*), and representation as figuration, which is associated with the idea of incarnation (standing for, or *Repräsentation*); see my discussion in *Democratic Legitimacy: Impartiality, Reflexivity, Proximity*, trans. Arthur Goldhammer (Princeton, N.J.: Princeton University Press, 2011), 87–88. In this connection one thinks of the spirited debate in France about the "normalcy" of François Hollande, who had claimed this quality for himself when he was a candidate in the 2012 presidential election.

12. See Bernard Manin, "The Repeated Character of Elections," in *The Principles of Representative Government* (Cambridge: Cambridge University Press, 1997), 175–183.

13. See the theory formulated in Morris P. Fiorina, *Retrospective Voting in American National Elections* (New Haven, Conn.: Yale University Press, 1981).

14. There is a considerable literature on the subject in American political science. For a recent survey see Jeffrey M. Stonecash, *Reassessing the Incumbency Effect* (New York: Cambridge University Press, 2008).

15. These remarks were made in de Gaulle's press conference of 31 January 1964, reprinted in Charles de Gaulle, *Discours et messages*, 5 vols. (Paris: Plon, 1970), 4:164, 168. See also his press conference of 16 May 1967 (reprinted in vol. 5), in which he spoke disparagingly of legislative elections as "local competitions," whereas he had been elected by the entire nation.

16. See my discussion in *Democratic Legitimacy*, 1–2, 13–14.

17. "Without having the right to vote," wrote Bernard-Adolphe Granier de Cassagnac, a supporter of the regime, "[the press] seeks to control elections; without having the right to play a role in deliberative bodies, it seeks to influence deliberations; without having the right to sit in the councils of the sovereign, it seeks to bring about or to prevent acts of government; without having received from a department, or from an arrondissement, or from a commune, or from a hamlet any delegation whatever, it seeks to govern the nation; in a word, it seeks to substitute its action for the action of all the legally established powers without, in fact, being invested with any actual right." Both this quotation and the one from Napoleon III appear in the chapter devoted to Caesarism and liberal democracy in my book *La*

démocratie inachevée: Histoire de la souveraineté du peuple en France (Paris: Gallimard, 2000), 214–215.

18. I develop this idea at greater length in Pierre Rosanvallon, *Le sacre du citoyen: Histoire du suffrage universel en France* (Paris: Gallimard, 1992), 324–338.

19. The institution of a primary system, which allows citizens to take part in choosing candidates, can only serve to strengthen a sense of civic reappropriation, of giving politics back to its rightful owners.

8. Limiting Illiberalism

1. Hence the importance of adopting a distinct set of rules governing constitutional revision, for which the simple majority rule applied in the case of elections is apt to be insufficient.

2. Marx's famous pamphlet, many times reprinted and widely translated, first appeared in London in June 1871. Lenin's decree of 9 November 1917 on the formation of the Workers' and Peasants' Government gave the Congress of Soviets and its Central Committee the power to remove the people's commissars; see Vladimir Lenin, *Œuvres complètes,* 5th ed., 55 vols. (Paris: Éditions sociales, 1958–1965), 26:260–271.

3. I discuss this point in greater detail in Part IV.

4. The grounds specified by the Constitution for bringing a charge of impeachment ("treason, bribery, or other high crimes and misdemeanors") were taken from ancient English law.

5. The failure to act on campaign promises is not to be confused with what is sometimes called political nomadism, where a successful candidate changes party affiliation after being elected.

6. On this point see my discussion in Pierre Rosanvallon, *La démocratie inachevée: Histoire de la souveraineté du peuple en France* (Paris: Gallimard, 2000), 255–266.

7. See Thomas E. Cronin, *Direct Democracy: The Politics of Initiative, Referendum, and Recall* (Cambridge, Mass.: Harvard University Press, 1989), 125–156, 243–246. In Georgia, for example, recall is limited to evidence of misappropriation of public funds; in Rhode Island, to evidence of infringement of the code of ethics for elected representatives. As for the conditions under which the procedure may be set in motion, in California a petition must gather signatures equal in number to 12 percent of the votes cast in the last election (the lowest threshold), a percentage that rises to 40 percent in Kansas (the most common, and also the average, requirement being 25 percent).

8. Pierre Avril, *Rapport de la Commission de réflexion sur le statut pénal du Président de la République* (Paris: La Documentation française, 2002), 5. The quotations that follow are taken from the same report.

9. By the terms of the 1958 Constitution, the president of the Republic "shall incur no liability by reason of acts carried out in his official capacity"

(Article 67), but he may be removed from office in case of "a breach of his duties patently incompatible with his continuing in office" (Article 68), dismissal then being proclaimed by parliament sitting as High Court. Apart from crimes of murder and high treason, the Avril Commission gave further examples of conduct justifying removal, including "manifestly improper use of constitutional prerogatives leading to obstruction of institutions, as repeated refusals to promulgate laws, to convene the Council of Ministers, to sign the decrees of the Council of Ministers, to ratify treaties, indeed the decision to put into effect Article 16 [concerning the exercise of emergency powers] when the conditions for doing so are not fulfilled." See the commentary by Olivier Beaud and Philippe Lauvaux, "Sur le prétendu 'impeachment à la française': Réflexions sur le projet de loi constitutionnelle instaurant une responsabilité politique du président de la République," *Recueil Dalloz,* no. 39 (2003): 2646.

10. See Philippe Lauvaux, *Parlementarisme rationalisé et stabilité du pouvoir exécutif: Quelques aspects de la réforme de l'État confrontés aux expériences étrangères* (Brussels: Bruylant, 1988); and Pierre Avril, "Le parlementarisme rationalisé," *Revue de droit parlementaire,* special issue, 1988.

11. Resistance organizations in France had proposed several new parliamentary schemes at the end of the war. After 1945 the Gaullists and the MRP were the chief advocates of rationalizing parliamentary procedure, whereas the Socialists and the Communists championed classical parliamentarianism.

12. The scope of application of this procedure, often criticized, was limited in 2008 to two types of legislation sponsored by the government (bills concerning public finance and the funding of social security); for other types its use was restricted to one bill per session.

13. The American system of separation of powers is a notable outlier in this regard.

14. I leave to one side the specifically French question of the dual character of the executive. Its functioning continues to depend on circumstances, because a consecutive voting regime—the presidential election is held in advance of legislative elections, with both the president and deputies now holding office for the same term (five years)—is insufficient to determine who actually governs. This is why, in the case of so-called cohabitation between president and prime minister, one speaks of a "mixed constitution" under the Fifth Republic.

15. In this regard the differences between countries are ones of degree, not of kind.

16. Regarding the constitutional law of 23 July 2008, on the modernization of the institutions of the Fifth Republic, see Jean-Pierre Camby, Patrick Fraisseix, and Jean Gicquel, eds., *La Révision de 2008: Une nouvelle Constitution?* (Paris: Librairie générale de droit et de jurisprudence, 2011).

17. From the report of the commission headed by former prime minister Édouard Balladur, *Une Ve République plus démocratique* (Paris: La Documentation française, 2007), 4, 6.

18. Thus the president is now said in France to "define" the nation's policy (whereas the prime minister only "pursues" it). At the same time, however, the power of the president has been reduced by the limitation of his office to two terms of five years each.

19. See the works of Bastien François, most recently *La 6ᵉ République: Pourquoi, comment* (Paris: Éditions Les petits matins, 2015). Advocates of this plan include Arnaud Montebourg among the Socialists and Jean-Luc Mélenchon in the Left Party.

20. Here, and in what follows, I refer to the constitutional design proposed by Arnaud Montebourg and Bastien François, *La Constitution de la 6ᵉ République: Réconcilier les Français avec de démocratie* (Paris: Odile Jacob, 2005).

21. Most populist or antiestablishment parties call for such independent bodies to be abolished. In so doing they make it clear that in their view democracy is nothing more than a way of authorizing government action with the approval of a majority (hence, too, their reverence for the referendum).

22. In the United States they are known as "independent regulatory agencies," in the United Kingdom as "nondepartmental public bodies," in France as "independent administrative authorities." See the chapter on the history and problems of such authorities in my *Democratic Legitimacy: Impartiality, Reflexivity, Proximity,* trans. Arthur Goldhammer (Princeton, N.J.: Princeton University Press, 2011), 75–86.

23. Here I adopt Dominique Rousseau's fine phrase in his *Droit du contentieux constitutionnel,* 9th ed. (Paris: Montchrestien, 2010).

24. See James M. Buchanan, *Constitutional Economics* (Oxford: Blackwell, 1991), which develops this notion chiefly in relation to fiscal and budgetary policy, and my commentary ("The Mirage of the Absolute Constitution") in chapter 8 of *Democratic Legitimacy,* 150–153.

25. See Finn E. Kydland and James C. Prescott, "Rules Rather than Discretion: The Inconsistency of Optimal Plans," *Journal of Political Economy* 85, no. 3 (1977): 473–492. Kydland and Prescott won the 2004 Nobel Prize in Economics for their work on this question.

26. The phrase is due to Alain Supiot in *La gouvernance par les nombres: Cours au Collège de France (2012–2014)* (Paris: Fayard, 2015).

27. On this point see the influential article by R. Kent Weaver, "Setting and Firing Policy Triggers," *Journal of Public Policy* 9, no. 3 (1989): 307–336.

9. The Governed and Their Governors

1. The verb *eseguire* (to execute, carry out) frequently recurs in Machiavelli's writings.

2. From the dedication to Justus Lipsius, *Politicorum libri sex* [1589], quoted in Michel Senellart, *Les arts de gouverner: Du regimen médiéval au concept de gouvernement* (Paris: Seuil, 1995), 232. Lipsius's work appeared in the same year as Giovanni Botero's *Della ragion di Stato.*

3. Daniel de Priezac, *Des secrets de la domination, ou de la raison de l'État*, in part 1 of *Discours de politiques* (Paris: 1652–1654); the passage quoted here appears on p. 202 of the complete edition published in 1666.

4. Naudé's *Considérations politiques sur les coups d'État* first came out in Rome. In what follows I cite to the text of the second edition, published in Paris in 1667, as it appears in the modern critical edition by Frédérique Marin and Marie-Odile Perulli, published in 1989 and reissued by Gallimard in 2004.

5. Quoted in Étienne Thuau, *Raison d'État et pensée politique à l'époque de Richelieu* (Paris: Armand Colin, 1966), 323.

6. Naudé, *Considérations politiques*, 83.

7. Ibid., 104.

8. Ibid., 87.

9. Cardinal Mazarin, *Bréviaire des politiciens*, trans. François Rosso (Paris: Arléa, 1997), 123.

10. On this point see Gabriel Naudé, *Addition à l'histoire de Louis XI* [1630], ed. Yves-Charles Zarka and Robert Damien (Paris: Fayard, 1999), 24–29.

11. Ibid., 24–25.

12. Naudé, *Considérations politiques*, 67.

13. Ibid., 155. "This rabble," he went on to say, "is like unto a sea subject to all sorts of winds and storms; to a chameleon that can admit all sorts of colors except white; and to the sink and sewer into which all the filth and refuse of a house flow. It is for the most part of an inconstant and variable nature, approving and disapproving some thing at the same time, running always from one contrary to another, believing without due reflection, quick to rise up in revolt, forever grumbling and complaining; in brief, all that it thinks is but vanity, all that it says is false and absurd, what it disapproves is good, what it approves bad, what it praises infamous, and all that it does and undertakes is but pure folly."

14. See René Pintard's magnum opus *Le libertinage érudit dans la première moitié du XVIIᵉ siècle* (Paris: Boivin, 1943), still the standard reference on this point; a reprint was issued in 2000 by Éditions Slatkine in Geneva.

15. Quoted in Antoine Adam, ed., *Les libertins au XVIIᵉ siècle* (Paris: Buchet / Chastel, 1964), 124.

16. Also known in inferior manuscripts as *De petitione consulatus* [On Running for the Consulship]; Quintus Tullius Cicero's authorship is disputed. In French, see *Petit manuel de campagne électorale*, trans. Jean-Yves Boriand (Paris: Arléa, 1992); in English, the Loeb translation by M. I. Henderson (revised by E. H. Warmington and D. R. Shackleton Bailey), *Handbook of Electioneering*, in vol. 28 of the works of Cicero (Cambridge, Mass.: Harvard University Press, 2002), 393–445. —Trans.

17. See Cicero, *Handbook of Electioneering*, esp. 439–443. [The English versions given here are mine.—Trans.]

18. See Maurice Joly, *Dialogue aux enfers entre Machiavel et Montesquieu, ou la politique de Machiavel au XIXᵉ siècle* (Brussels: A. Mertens et fils, 1864); reissued

in 1968, with a preface by Jean-François Revel, by Calmann-Lévy in Paris, from which the following extracts are taken. Joly's satire is also famous for having been plagiarized and distorted by the authors of the pamphlet *Protocols of the Elders of Zion* (accusations of Machiavellianism on the part of Napoleon III being converted into denunciation of a Jewish plot).

19. Joly, *Dialogue aux enfers,* 112.

20. Ibid., 114–116.

21. Ibid., 120. And furthermore: "In order to fathom the extent of my system, it is necessary to see how the language of my press manages to converge with the official acts of my policy: suppose that I wish to contrive a solution to this or that external or internal complication; this solution, recommended by my newspapers, which for several months have been guiding public opinion, each in its own way, is brought forth one fine morning as an official event. You well know with what discretion and what ingenious circumspection authoritative documents must be drawn up at important moments: the problem to be solved in such cases is how to give some measure of satisfaction to each party. Well, then, every one of my newspapers, each according to its own lights, will seek to persuade its party that the solution that has been adopted is the one most favorable to it. What is not written down in an official document will be made to emerge through interpretation; what is only suggested, the semi-official newspapers will express more openly and the democratic and revolutionary papers will shout from the rooftops; and while they are arguing with one another, giving the most varied interpretations of my acts, my government will always be able to respond to one and all: you mistake my intentions, you have misconstrued what I have said; I never meant to say this or that. The main thing is never to be found in contradiction with oneself."

22. Hannah Arendt, *Crises of the Republic: Lying in Politics; Civil Disobedience; On Violence; Thoughts on Politics and Revolution* (New York: Harcourt Brace Jovanovich, 1972), 13.

23. "It is not good," Rousseau observes, "that he who makes the laws should enforce them as well, *nor that the body of the people should turn its attention away from general purposes and concentrate it on particular objects." Du contrat social,* 3.4, in Jean-Jacques Rousseau, *Œuvres complètes,* ed. Bernard Gagnebin and Marcel Raymond, 5 vols. (Paris: Gallimard, 1959–1995), 3:404 (the emphasis is mine).

24. I will discuss the problems raised by collegial forms of executive power particularly with regard to responsibility, in Chapter 11.

25. In this connection see my first book, *L'âge de l'autogestion* (Paris: Seuil, 1976).

26. I borrow this notion from Cornelius Castoriadis. See the commentary by Bruno Bernardi, "En marge de Castoriadis, sur le concept d'auto-institution de la société," in *Cornelius Castoriadis et Claude Lefort: L'expérience démocratique,* ed. Nicolas Poirier (Lormont, France: Le Bord de l'eau, 2015), 147–156.

27. See Melvin Edelstein's overview, *The French Revolution and the Birth of Electoral Democracy* (London: Routledge, 2014). Note that the constitutions of the "sister republics" formed by Bonaparte in Italy, in 1797–1798, were also adopted as a result of "plebiscites" held among the nations concerned. The American Constitution of 1787 had earlier been ratified by specially elected conventions in the thirteen states of the Union.

28. The reunion of Avignon and the Comtat Venaissin with France, in 1791, gave rise to the first modern juridical and political debate on the rights of nations to assert their own authority, free from outside interference. See Jean-Jacques Clère, "Le rattachement d'Avignon et du Comtat à la France: Approche juridique (1789–1791)," *Annales historiques de la Révolution française* 290, no. 1 (1992): 571–587. In the 1860s, Nice and Savoy were reattached to France with the sanction of a referendum held among the peoples most directly concerned. At about the same time, during the period of the *Risorgimento* in Italy, the same procedure was used, in each of the various political entities then in existence, to decide the terms of the country's unification.

29. From an article published in *Le Peuple*, no. 4 (8–15 November 1848), reprinted in Pierre-Joseph Proudhon, *Mélanges*, 3 vols. (Paris: Librairie internationale, 1868), 1:190.

30. Ibid. "Master and servant," he added, "have nothing in common."

31. Pierre-Joseph Proudhon, "Qu'est-ce que le gouvernement? Qu'est-ce que Dieu?," *La Voix du peuple*, 5 November 1849, reprinted in ibid., 2:261.

32. From the first of a series of polemical articles published under the title "À propos de Louis Blanc: De l'utilité présente et de la possibilité future de l'État," in *La Voix du peuple*, 26–27 December 1849, reprinted in ibid., 3:53; emphasis in the original. Note that Proudhon analyzed religion in the same terms.

33. Pierre-Joseph Proudhon, *Carnets*, ed. Pierre Haubtmann, 4 vols. (Paris: M. Rivière, 1960–1971), 3:216.

34. Pierre-Joseph Proudhon, *Idée générale de la Révolution au XIXᵉ siècle* [1851] (Paris: M. Rivière, 1923), 199. See, too, the entire fourth study, on the principle of authority.

35. Note, too, that Proudhon was, like them, very critical of Rousseau. "The vogue of Rousseau," he went so far as to say, "has cost France more gold, more blood, more shame than the detested reign of the three famous courtesans (la Châteauroux, la Pompadour, la Dubarry)." Ibid., 195.

36. Ibid., 187; emphasis in the original.

37. Available in English as Pierre Clastres, *Society against the State: Essays in Political Anthropology*, trans. Robert Hurley, 2nd ed. (New York: Zone Books, 1987), and Clastres, *Archeology of Violence*, trans. Jeanine Herman, 2nd ed. (Los Angeles: Semiotext(e); Cambridge, Mass.: MIT Press, 2010), respectively.—Trans.

38. See Pierre Clastres, *Recherches d'anthropologie politique* (Paris: Seuil, 1980). "To hold power is to exercise it; to exercise it is to dominate those over whom it

is exercised," Clastres remarks. "This is precisely what primitive societies do (did) not want, this is why their leaders are powerless, why power is not detached from the body of society as a whole" (108).

39. See, for example, Jean-William Lapierre, "Sociétés sauvages, sociétés contre l'État," *Esprit,* May 1976, 996–997.

40. Clastres, *Recherches d'anthropologie politique,* 106–107.

41. Ibid., 192. "The leader does not have a monopoly on legitimate violence," Lapierre comments, "because he has a monopoly on the use of legitimate speech, because no one can speak up against him without committing a sacrilege unanimously condemned by public opinion" ("Sociétés sauvages," 996–997).

42. Pierre Clastres, *La Société contre l'État* (Paris: Minuit, 1974), 159. "Engraved on the body," he continues in a discussion of the role of torture, "the law expresses primitive society's refusal to run the risk of division, the risk of a power separate from itself, *a power that escapes its control*" (160; emphasis in the original).

43. Raymond Aron summarized the matter thus, referring to "a theory that today is called Machiavellian, and that one finds expressed in many books, Pareto's *Treatise of General Sociology,* Mosca's book on *The Ruling Class,* as well as the book by J. Burnham entitled *The Machiavellians.* The central idea of these authors, in my words—words they would nonetheless accept—is that *every political regime is oligarchic.* All societies, they say, at least all complex societies, are governed by a small number of men; the regimes vary according to the character of the minority that exercises authority." See Aron, *Démocratie et totalitarisme* [1965] (Paris: Gallimard, 2005), 133.

44. Robert Michels, *Les partis politiques: Essai sur les tendances oligarchiques des démocraties* [1911] (Paris: Flammarion, 1971), 33; Vilfredo Pareto, *Trattato di sociologia generale,* 2 vols. (Florence: G. Barbèra, 1916), §2053.

45. Recall that Weber distinguishes rule by reason of authority from rule by reason of a configuration of interests (economic monopoly, for example). [The German word *Herrschaft* is variously translated in this context as "rule," "authority," "domination," "dominion"; Weber's essay "Die drei reinen Typen der legitimen Herrschaft" (1922), alluded to here, is usually referred to in English as "The Three Types of Legitimate Rule."—Trans.]

46. In this case domination operates through the mental incorporation of a certain view of the world and of social arrangements to which Bourdieu gives the name *habitus.*

47. See, in particular, the important work done by Tom R. Tyler, summarized in his book *Why People Obey the Law,* 2nd ed. (Princeton, N.J.: Princeton University Press, 2006).

48. See Susan J. Pharr, "Officials' Misconduct and Public Distrust," in *Disaffected Democracies,* ed. Susan J. Pharr and Robert D. Putnam (Princeton, N.J.: Princeton University Press, 2000), 173–201.

49. See John R. Hibbing and Elizabeth Theiss-Morse, *Stealth Democracy: Americans' Beliefs about How Government Should Work* (New York: Cambridge University Press, 2002), esp.107–128.

10. Legibility

1. There is a considerable literature on this subject. See the recent work by Jacob Soll, *The Reckoning: Financial Accountability and the Rise and Fall of Nations* (New York: Basic Books, 2014).

2. The manuscript record of this survey has come down to us as the Domesday Book. See V. H. Galbraith, *Domesday Book: Its Place in Administrative History* (Oxford: Clarendon Press, 1974); and David Roffe, *Decoding Domesday* (Woodbridge, Suffolk, UK: Boydell Press, 2007).

3. See Pierre Fröhlich, "Remarques sur la reddition de comptes des stratèges athéniens," *Dike* 3 (2000): 81–111, and Fröhlich, *Les cités grecques et le contrôle des magistrats (IVᵉ–Iᵉʳ siècle avant J.-C.)* (Geneva: Droz, 2004).

4. See Paul Seaward, "The Cavalier Parliament, the 1667 Accounts Commission and the Idea of Accountability," in *Parliament at Work: Parliamentary Committees, Political Power, and Public Access in Early Modern England,* ed. Chris R. Kyle and Jason Peacey (Woodbridge, Sussex, UK: Boydell Press, 2002), 149–168.

5. See Paul Seaward, "Parliament and the Idea of Political Accountability in Early Modern Britain," in *Realities of Representation: State Building in Early Modern Europe and European America,* ed. Maija Jansson (New York: Palgrave Macmillan, 2007), 45–62.

6. On this point, see the groundbreaking article by Peter Mathias and Patrick O'Brien, "Taxation in Britain and France, 1715–1810: A Comparison of the Social and Economic Incidence of Taxes Collected for the Central Governments," *Journal of European Economic History* 5, no. 3 (1976): 601–650.

7. See Jacques Necker, *Compte rendu au Roi* [1781], in *Œuvres complètes,* 15 vols. (Paris: Treuttel et Würtz, 1820), 2:1–7.

8. Ibid., 1–2.

9. Ibid., 2–3.

10. From the introduction to Jacques Necker, *De l'administration des finances de la France* [1784], in *Œuvres complètes,* 4:10. Necker strongly supported a system of provincial administration for this same reason, that it could help to restore public trust through greater transparency.

11. Ibid., 16.

12. Necker, *Compte rendu au Roi,* 2:3.

13. Under the Empire, it should be noted, emphasis was placed on the *internal* oversight of state finances. Napoleon I, though he spoke of the need for "active supervision" of the use of public funds, entrusted responsibility to a state audit office, the Cour des comptes (created in 1807), parliament having ceased to exercise its authority in this domain.

14. Jacques-Pierre Brissot, *Plan de conduite pour les députés du peuple aux États-généraux de 1789* ([n.p.], April 1789), 13.

15. Pierre-Victor Malouet, intervention of 28 May 1789, *Archives parlementaires,* 8:55. In the first months of the meeting of the Estates-General that year, the public often mixed with representatives.

16. Constantin-François Volney, intervention of 28 May 1789, ibid.

17. Maximilien Robespierre, *Œuvres,* 10 vols. (Paris: Société des études robespierristes, 1912–1967), 9:503. See also his speech of 10 February 1792 (*Œuvres,* 8:174), in which he pleaded for the construction of a "majestic edifice" on the ruins of the Bastille, so that "the people may comfortably come and freely hear and see their mandatories."

18. Ibid., 9:503.

19. Ibid., 9:502–503.

20. The public had access to Westminster Hall, but not to members' meeting rooms. See Chris R. Kyle and Jason Peacey, " 'Under cover of so much coming and going': Public Access to Parliament and the Political Process in Early Modern England," in Kyle and Peacey, *Parliament at Work,* 1–23.

21. Note that Jeremy Bentham, a foremost advocate of publicity in many other respects, had strongly justified this exclusion in an essay translated from a work written in French by Étienne Dumont, *Tactique des assemblées politiques délibérantes* [1816], based on Bentham's manuscripts, and later incorporated with Bentham's earlier unpublished "Essay on Political Tactics" [1791] in Bowring's edition of the collected works. "The seductions of eloquence and ridicule are most dangerous instruments in a political assembly," he wrote. "Admit females—you add new force to these seductions." *An Essay on Political Tactics, or Inquiries concerning the Discipline and Mode of Proceeding Proper to Be Observed in Political Assemblies,* in *Works of Jeremy Bentham,* ed. John Bowring, 11 vols. (Edinburgh: William Tait, 1838–1843), 2:237.

22. See Terry Fewtrell, "A New Parliamentary House: A New Parliamentary Order," *Australian Journal of Public Administration* 44, no. 4 (1985): 323–332.

23. In Australia, government ministers remain members of the House of Representatives and the Senate.

24. From the prospectus for the *Gazette nationale, ou le Moniteur universel,* 24 November 1789.

25. On the prehistory of parliamentary publicity in Great Britain, see Courtenay Ilbert, *Parliament: Its History, Constitution and Practice,* 3rd. rev. ed. (London: Oxford University Press, 1948); and Thomas Erskin May, *Treatise on the Law, Privileges, Proceedings and Usage of Parliament* [1844], 23rd ed. (London: LexisNexis UK, 2004).

26. Article 9 of the Bill of Rights of 1689 recognized the right of "proceedings in Parliament" to be neither "impeached or questioned" in any place or court of justice outside of Parliament itself. For a commentary on this article, and the uncertainties over its precise meaning that were a source of debate until quite recently, see May, *Treatise on the Law,* 108–115.

27. This point is considered in some detail in J. R. Pole, *The Gift of Government: Political Responsibility from the English Restoration to American Independence* (Athens: University of Georgia Press, 1983), 93–113.

28. On this idea of representation see John P. Reid, *The Concept of Representation in the Age of the American Revolution* (Chicago: University of Chicago Press, 1989); and J. R. Pole, *Political Representation in England and the Origins of the American Republic* (London: Macmillan, 1966).

29. See Bentham, *Essay on Political Tactics,* in *Works of Jeremy Bentham,* 2:299–373.

30. The well-known English title of Foucault's 1975 book deliberately departs from the original French; see the translator's note in Foucault, *Discipline and Punish: The Birth of the Prison,* trans. Alan Sheridan (New York: Vintage, 1977), ix.—Trans.

31. In this regard, too, see Foucault's contribution to a 1977 debate about Bentham's Panopticon, later published as "L'œil du pouvoir" in Michel Foucault, *Dits et écrits,* ed. Daniel Defert and François Ewald, 4 vols. (Paris: Gallimard, 1994), 3:190–207.

32. Bentham, *Essay on Political Tactics,* in *Works of Jeremy Bentham,* 2:310.

33. Ibid., 2:310–311; emphasis in the original.

34. Ibid., 2:311–312.

35. In the French literature on this subject see Romain Huret, *De l'Amérique ordinaire à l'État secret: Le cas Nixon* (Paris: Presses de Sciences Po, 2009); and Alexandre Rios-Bordes, "Les précurseurs sombres: L'émergence de 'l'État secret' aux États-Unis (1911–1941)," doctoral thesis, École des hautes études en sciences sociales, Paris, 2014.

36. See John Street, "Celebrity Politicians: Popular Culture and Political Representation," *British Journal of Politics and International Relations* 6, no. 4 (2004): 435–452; John B. Thompson, "La nouvelle visibilité," *Réseaux,* nos. 129–130 (2005): 59–87; Jamil Dakhila, *Politique People* (Rosny-sous-Bois: Bréal, 2008); and Antoine Lilti, *Figures politiques: L'invention de la célébrité (1750–1850)* (Paris: Fayard, 2014).

37. On the history of this reversal see Fabrice d'Almeida, *La politique au naturel: Comportement des hommes politiques et représentations publiques en France et Italie du XIXᵉ au XXIᵉ siècle* (Rome: École française de Rome, 2007).

38. Quoted in Joël Cornette, "Versailles, architecture parlante de l'État absolu," *Cahiers de Malagar,* no. 16 (September 2007): 27–50.

39. These were opposed by Pascal to the "cords of necessity."

40. Cornette, "Versailles," rightly speaks in this connection of the "dual nature" of the king's absolutism.

41. These expressions occur in an enlightening book by Antoine Vauchez, *Démocratiser l'Europe* (Paris: Seuil, 2014).

42. Thus the symbolic importance of the national referendums held in 2005 on a proposed European constitution, and the feeling that democratic values had been betrayed with the adoption two years later of a mere agreement, the Treaty of Lisbon, which then took effect in 2009.

43. It should be kept in mind that the European budget has hardly changed since the signing of the Treaty of Rome in 1957, still being limited today to roughly 1 percent of the gross domestic product of the member states.

44. Here I follow the suggestions made by Vauchez in *Démocratiser l'Europe*, 10.

45. Benjamin Constant, *De la responsibilité des ministres* (Paris: H. Nicolle, 1815), 53.

46. These three institutions, it will be recalled, are authority, trust, and legitimacy.

47. The literature on the subject is considerable. For Europe, see for example the many works of Pierre-André Targuieff, as well as Emmanuelle Danblon and Loïc Nicolas, eds., *Les rhétoiques de la conspiration* (Paris: CNRS Éditions, 2010); for the United States, Peter Knight, ed., *Conspiracy Theories in American History: An Encyclopedia* (Santa Barbara: ABC-CLIO, 2003); and, for the Arab world, Matthew Gray, *Conspiracy Theories in the Arab World: Sources and Politics* (New York: Routledge, 2010), and Jean-Pierre Filiu, *Apocalypse in Islam*, trans. M. B. DeBevoise (Berkeley: University of California Press, 2011).

48. For a contemporary French example of this view (and one of the most customer-reviewed books on amazon.fr), see Alain Soral, *Comprendre l'Empire: Demain la gouvernance globale ou la révolte des nations?* (Paris: Blanche, 2011).

49. "Conspiratorialism," Emmanuel Taïeb has rightly remarked in "Logiques politiques du conspirationnisme," *Sociologie et sociétés* 42, no. 2 (2010): 275, "claims to identify the real power behind the empty space of democratic government."

50. Alexis de Tocqueville, *Democracy in America* [1835–1840], 2 vols., trans. Gerald Bevan (London: Penguin, 2003), 1.1.8, 193.

51. See Arlette Farge, "Rumeur," in *Dictionnaire européen des Lumières*, ed. Michel Delon (Paris: Presses Universitaires de France, 1997), 958–960; also her earlier book, *Dire et mal dire: L'opinion publique au XVIIIᵉ siècle* (Paris: Seuil, 1992).

52. I borrow these expressions from François Ploux, *De bouche à oreille: Naissance et propagation des rumeurs dans la France du XIXᵉ siècle* (Paris: Aubier, 2003).

53. See Marc Bloch, "Réflexions d'un historien sur les fausses nouvelles de la guerre," *Revue de Synthèse* 33 (1921): 13–35; reprinted in 1999 under the same title by Éditions Allia in Paris.

54. On this point see two classic essays: Richard Hofstadter, "The Paranoid Style in American Politics," in *The Paranoid Style in American Politics and Other Essays* (New York: Alfred A. Knopf, 1965), 3–40; and Gordon S. Wood, "Conspiracy and the Paranoid Style: Causality and Deceit in the Eighteenth Century," *William and Mary Quarterly* 39, no. 3 (1982): 401–441.

55. See his famous *Thoughts on the Cause of the Present Discontents* [1770], in *The Writings and Speeches of Edmund Burke*, ed. Paul Langford, 9 vols. (Oxford: Clarendon Press: 1981–), 2:241–323.

56. On this point see Pierre Rosanvallon, ed., *Science et démocratie: Actes du colloque de rentrée du Collège de France 2013* (Paris: Odile Jacob, 2014); and Gérald Bronner, *La démocratie des crédules* (Paris: Presses Universitaires de France, 2013).

57. On American public interest groups of the period, see the overview in Michael W. McCann, *Taking Reform Seriously: Perspectives on Public Interest Liberalism* (Ithaca, N.Y.: Cornell University Press, 1986). I am grateful to Pauline Peretz for her guidance on this question, and regret that for reasons of space it is impossible to make full use here of all that I found in the course of my research.

58. See Sandrine Baume, "La transparence dans la conduite des affairs publiques: Origines et sens d'une exigence," *Raison-publique.fr* (11 July 2011): 10.

59. On the history of CADA see Corinne Bouchoux and Jean-Jacques Hyest, "Refonder le droit à l'information publique à l'heure du numérique: Un enjeu citoyen, une opportunité stratégique," Senate Report no. 589, tome 1 (2013–2014), 5 June 2014.

60. In the United States, citizen associations and consumer groups in many fields have campaigned on behalf of such a right (in particular the Right-to-Know Network, which provides free access to databases and resources on the environment). Small wonder, then, that in France the founder of the Mediapart.fr website, Edwy Plenel, titled a recent book summarizing his conception of journalism *Le droit de savoir* (Paris: Don Quichotte, 2013).

61. See James C. Goodale, *Fighting for the Press: The Inside Story of the Pentagon Papers and Other Battles* (New York: CUNY Journalism Press, 2013).

62. Hannah Arendt, "On Lying in Politics: Reflections on the Pentagon Papers" [1971], reprinted in *Crises of the Republic*, 9.

63. On this point see the reservations and warnings expressed in Archon Fung, Mary Graham, and David Weil, *Full Disclosure: The Perils and Promise of Transparency* (New York: Cambridge University Press, 2007).

64. In the event that independent media outlets cannot obtain financial support from private nonprofit organizations, the practical value of their contribution to public debate should be recognized as justifying specific grants of public assistance (by contrast with the present system of press subsidies in France, which today place all reputable "general interest" publications on an equal footing). On this point see Julia Cagé, *Saving the Media: Capitalism, Crowdfunding, and Democracy* [2015], trans. Arthur Goldhammer (Cambridge, Mass.: Belknap Press of Harvard University Press, 2016).

65. Here it is important to make a clear distinction between critical thinking, an indispensable element of the scientific outlook, and the relativist view that the incompleteness of knowledge is independent of the question whether advances in knowledge are possible.

66. The question of the limitations imposed by respect for private life and for the confidentiality of various kinds of personal information falls outside the scope of the present work. For the same reason I do not discuss the circum-

stances under which aspects of the private life of public figures may or may not be considered to have a public character.

67. The contrast with the American system is well analyzed by Kimberly J. Morgan and Monica Prasad, "The Origins of Tax Systems: A French-American Comparison," *American Journal of Sociology* 114, no. 5 (2009): 1350–1394.

68. It is instructive to consider what has come of the proposals made by Thomas Piketty. In this connection one may profitably read Nicolas Delalande's suggestive article "L'économie politique des réformes fiscales: Une analyse historique," *Revue de l'OFCE,* no. 122 (2012): 35–59.

69. See John Rawls, *A Theory of Justice* (Cambridge, Mass.: Belknap Press of Harvard University Press, 1971), esp. 1.3.24, 136–142.

11. Responsibility

1. From the introduction to Olivier Beaud and Jean-Michel Blanquer, eds., *La responsabilité des gouvernants* (Paris: Descartes, 1999), 12.

2. Denis Baranger, *Parlementarisme des origines: Essai sur les conditions de formation d'un exécutif responsable en Angleterre, des années 1740 au début de l'âge victorien* (Paris: Presses Universitaires de France, 1999), 25.

3. The French text speaks of *mal-gouvernement,* which in its earliest application is to be understood as being limited to corruption and treason. These high crimes were later supplemented by a larger class of high misdemeanors, the chief one of which Blackstone called "mal-administration" (a term that today tends to be restricted to mere bureaucratic incompetence). The word "misgovernment," used by Burke but less often now than in his time, conveys the more general sense, intended by the author in what follows, of bad government, whether of a country or a state.—Trans.

4. Burke, *Thoughts on the Cause of the Present Discontents,* in *Writings and Speeches of Edmund Burke,* ed. Paul Langford, 9 vols. (Oxford: Clarendon Press: 1981–), 2:294. The phrase is italicized in Burke's original text.

5. Lord Latimer was found guilty of, among other things, extorting huge sums, seizing spoils of war for his own personal profit, and committing military crimes. The list of charges spoke of "frauds and misdeeds toward the King and the people." See T. F. T. Plucknett, "The Origin of Impeachment," *Transactions of the Royal Historical Society* 24 (1942): 47–71.

6. See bk. 4, chap. 9 ("Of Misprisions and Contempts, Affecting the King and Government"), in William Blackstone, *Commentaries on the Laws of England* [1765–1769], 8th ed., 4 vols. (Oxford: Clarendon Press, 1778), 4:119–126.

7. The phrase occurs in Coke's speech to the House of Lords on behalf of the impeachment of Sir Lionel Cranfield in 1624, reproduced in J. P. Kenyon, ed., *The Stuart Constitution, 1603–1699: Documents and Commentary* (Cambridge: Cambridge University Press, 1966), 100–102.

8. On this history see Baranger's very carefully researched study *Parlementarisme des origines,* esp. 352–356.

9. The criticism directed against the king's private advisors—that they acted in secret, and therefore in effect as unaccountable ministers—had the effect in its turn of stabilizing, and even reinforcing, the power of the king's actual ministers, who were held responsible for their actions.

10. On the complicated history of these developments, see once again Baranger, *Parlementarisme des origines,* 191–380. Baranger argues that the implementation of the principle of political responsibility should actually be understood as the *vehicle* of this increase in executive power.

11. In 1839, in the midst of the gravest ministerial crisis that the July Monarchy had yet known, the regime's apologists were to publish a great many articles in support of the position that the royal prerogative had in no way been compromised or diminished. See my treatment of this subject in Pierre Rosanvallon, *La monarchie impossible: Les Chartes de 1814 et de 1830* (Paris: Fayard, 1994), 149–181.

12. On this distinction see Alain Laquièze, *Les origines du régime parlementaire en France, 1814–1848* (Paris: Presses Universitaires de France, 2002).

13. Eugène François Auguste d'Arnauld, baron de Vitrolles, *Du ministère dans le gouvernement représentatif* (Paris: Dentu, 1815), 10.

14. Pierre-Paul Royer-Collard, speech of 12 February 1816, reprinted in *La vie politique de M. Royer-Collard; ses discours et ses écrits,* ed. Prosper de Barante, 2 vols. (Paris: Didier, 1861–1863), 1:217. Tellingly, Royer-Collard described England as "a republic disguised as a monarchy."

15. See Benjamin Constant, *De la responsibilité des ministres* (Paris: H. Nicolle, 1815); and Lucien Jaume, "Le concept de responsabilité des ministres chez Benjamin Constant," *Revue française de droit constitutionnel* 42 (2000): 227–243.

16. Philippe Ségur, *La responsabilité politique* (Paris: Presses Universitaires de France, 1998), 17.

17. This model is analyzed in Diana Woodhouse, *Ministers and Parliament: Accountability in Theory and Practice* (Oxford: Clarendon Press, 1994).

18. John Stuart Mill, *Considerations on Representative Government* [1861], in *On Liberty, Utilitarianism, and Other Essays,* ed. Mark Philp and Frederick Rosen (Oxford: Oxford University Press, 2015), 235–236. This quotation and the ones that follow occur in chap. 5 ("Of the Proper Functions of Representative Bodies").

19. Ibid., 235, 246.

20. Ibid., 246.

21. The only exception to this in Europe is Italy prior to the reforms of the early 2000s; on this point see Christian Bidégaray, "Le principe de responsabilité fondement de la démocratie: Petite promenade dans les allées du 'jardin des délices démocratiques,'" *Pouvoirs,* no. 92 (January 2000): 5–16.

22. See Paul Ricoeur, "Le concept de responsabilité: Essai d'analyse sémantique," *Esprit* (November 1994): 28–48.

23. On the problem of imputability in a complex modern society see Dennis F. Thompson, "Moral Responsibility of Public Officials: The Problem of Many Hands," *American Political Science Review* 74, no. 4 (1980): 905–916; and Mark Bovens, *The Quest for Responsibility: Accountability and Citizenship in Complex Organizations* (Cambridge: Cambridge University Press, 1998).

24. Ulrich Beck, *Risk Society: Towards a New Modernity* [1986], trans. Mark Ritter (London: Sage, 1992), 183; emphasis in the original. This is why, historically, the notion of risk has been associated with a socialization of responsibility—an "accident" being a matter of chance, a fortuitous and nonimputable event.

25. On this crucial development see Olivier Beaud, "La responsabilité politique face à la concurrence d'autres formes de responsabilité des gouvernants," *Pouvoir*, no. 92 (January 2000): 17–30; also Antoine Garapon and Denis Salas, *La République pénalisée* (Paris: Hachette, 1996), and the section "Taking Accountability to the Courts" in chap. 3 of Robert D. Behn, *Rethinking Democratic Accountability* (Washington, D.C.: Brookings Institution Press, 2001), 56–58.

26. See Olivier Beaud, *Le sang contaminé: Essai critique sur la criminalisation de la responsabilité des gouvernants* (Paris: Presses Universitaires de France, 1999).

27. Jean-Michel Blanquer and Olivier Beaud, "Le principe irresponsabilité: La crise de la responsabilité politique sous la Vᵉ République," *Le Débat*, no. 108 (January–February 2000), 39, 41. The authors see the act of resignation furthermore as "a *simulacrum* of modern societies, the mimicked sacrifice of one man permitting the reconciliation of the community, government in the narrow sense, society in the broad sense."

28. For an overview of the relevant topics see Mark Bovens, Robert E. Goodin, and Thomas Schillemans, eds., *The Oxford Handbook of Public Accountability* (New York: Oxford University Press, 2014).

29. Mark Bovens, "Analysing and Assessing Accountability: A Conceptual Framework," *European Law Journal* 13, no. 4 (2007): 447.

30. On this way of looking at the opposition's role see my further remarks in *Counter-Democracy: Politics in an Age of Distrust*, trans. Arthur Goldhammer (Cambridge: Cambridge University Press, 2008), esp. 156–160; also, from a more juridical perspective, the analysis of Carlos-Miguel Pimentel, particularly in his article "L'opposition, ou le procès symbolique du pouvoir," *Pouvoirs*, no. 108 (January 2014): 45–62.

31. I have elaborated on this point in two earlier books: *Le peuple introuvable: Histoire de la représentation démocratique en France* (Paris: Gallimard, 1998); and Rosanvallon, *La démocratie inachevée: Histoire de la souveraineté du peuple en France* (Paris: Gallimard, 2000).

32. See my remarks in this connection in two other books: *Le moment Guizot* (Paris: Gallimard, 1985); and *Le sacre du citoyen: Histoire du suffrage universel en France* (Paris: Gallimard, 1992).

33. Bovens speaks of situations in which there are too many eyes; see "Analysing and Assessing Accountability," 455–457.

34. In France, Article 24 of the Constitution of the Fifth Republic explicitly refers to this state of affairs in assigning Parliament three functions: passing statutes, monitoring the actions of the government, and assessing public policies.

35. The tasks of monitoring and evaluation account for a significant share of the activity of social science research institutes today. In France, a notable example is the work being done under the auspices of the Institute for Public Policy at the Paris School of Economics.

36. See Weber's famous 1919 lecture "Politics as a Vocation," reprinted in *The Vocation Lectures,* ed. David Owen and Tracy B. Strong, trans. Rodney Livingstone (Indianapolis: Hackett, 2004), 32–94. Weber considered this "responsibility to the future" to be of overriding importance, and nowhere more so than in Germany following World War I, where sharp divisions persisted over the causes of its defeat and the extent of German responsibility for bringing about the war.

37. The phrase occurs in Beaud and Blanquer, eds., *La responsabilité des gouvernants,* 9.

38. Facile—but hardly mistaken!

39. "Anyone who witnessed the outbreak of the War in its full intensity will agree that it was essentially a flight from peace." See section 16 of Musil's 1922 essay "Helpless Europe," translated by Philip H. Beard in the collection *Precision and Soul: Essays and Addresses,* ed. Burton Pike and David S. Luft (Chicago: University of Chicago Press, 1990), 128–129.

40. Ibid., 128.

41. This phrase is found in an unpublished draft chapter ("Schmeisser und Meingast") of the projected fourth part of Robert Musil, *Der Mann ohne Eigenschaften* [1930–1943], corresponding to §82 in the 1952 German edition published in Hamburg by Rowohlt, p. 1371. —Trans.

42. Ibid.

43. Musil, "Ruminations of a Slow-Witted Mind" [1933], in Pike and Luft, *Precision and Soul,* 221.

12. Responsiveness

1. Jacques Necker, *Du pouvoir exécutif dans les grands États,* 2 vols. ([n.p.], 1792), 1:15.

2. Ibid., 1:22–23. Necker made a detailed study of the circumstances under which the committees of the National Assembly were established, which he believed had prevented it from grasping the peculiar nature of executive power. He saw this misunderstanding as the source of the uncontrollable escalation of revolutionary fervor, rightly considering it to be a corollary

of the utopian fantasy of a people that directly makes its own laws (see ibid., 45).

3. The passage occurs in Guizot's review of Charles-Antoine Scheffer's book *Essai sur la politique de la nation anglaise et du gouvernement britannique* (Paris, 1817), in *Archives philosophiques, politiques et littéraires* 1, no. 3 (September 1817): 274.

4. François Guizot, *Des moyens de gouvernement et d'opposition dans l'état actuel de la France* (Paris: Ladvocat, 1821), 122.

5. François Guizot, *Du gouvernement de la France depuis la Restauration et du ministère actuel* (Paris: Ladvocat, 1820), 155.

6. Guizot, *Des moyens de gouvernement et d'opposition,* 128–130. See, too, the whole of chap. 7 ("On the means of government in general").

7. In the eleventh of his series of lectures on European civilization, Guizot called for a way of "governing by managing minds, not by ruining lives." See his *Histoire générale de la civilisation en Europe depuis la chute de l'Empire romain jusqu'à la Révolution française* [1828], 17th ed. [Paris: Didier, 1878], 307.

8. Balzac reports that Louis XVIII sometimes used this term (*gouvernementabilité*) himself; see Honoré de Balzac, *Le Bal de Seaux* [1830] (Paris: Garnier, 1963), 128.

9. Guizot, review of Scheffer's *Essai,* 278.

10. François Guizot, "Session de 1817: Débats des chambres," *Archives philosophiques, politiques et littéraires* 2, no. 6 (December 1817): 184.

11. Guizot, *Des moyens de gouvernement et d'opposition,* 121.

12. François Guizot, "Des garanties légales de la liberté de la presse," *Archives philosophiques, politiques et littéraires* 5, no. 18 (December 1818): 278.

13. The lectures delivered between 1820 and 1822 were published serially and collected some thirty years later; the quotation given here is found in François Guizot, *Histoire des origines du gouvernement représentatif en Europe,* 2 vols. (Paris: Didier, 1851), 1:124.

14. Ibid., 2:242.

15. On this point see Pierre Karila-Cohen, *L'État des esprits: L'invention de l'enquête politique en France, 1814–1848* (Rennes: Presses Universitaires de Rennes, 2008).

16. See Anne Kupiec, "La Gironde et le Bureau de l'esprit public: Livre et révolution," *Annales historiques de la Révolution française* 302, no. 1 (1995): 571–586.

17. Jürgen Habermas, *The Structural Transformation of the Public Sphere: An Inquiry into a Category of Bourgeois Society* [1962], trans. Thomas Burger (Cambridge, Mass.: MIT Press, 1989), 101. I have tried to develop this intuition more fully in *Le moment Guizot* (Paris: Gallimard, 1985), esp. 64–72. On Necker's approach to the question of governability in its relation to opinion, see Léonard Burnand, *Necker et l'opinion publique* (Paris: Honoré Champion, 2004).

18. See article 34 of the decree of 22 December 1789.

19. Adhémar Esmein, *Éléments de droit constitutionnel français et comparé* [1899], 8th ed., 2 vols. (Paris: Sirey, 1927), 1:590.

20. On the form this provision assumed in practice, see André Castaldo, *Les méthodes de travail de la Constituante: Les techniques délibératives de l'Assemblée nationale, 1789–1791* (Paris: Presses Universitaires de France, 1989), 360–364.

21. Louis-Marie de Cormenin, *Questions de droit administratif* [1822], 4th ed., 3 vols. (Paris: A. Guyot et Scribe, 1837), 3:384. Pellegrino Rossi, a leading legal authority of the time, went so far as to describe it as a "right of women and proletarians." See Rossi, *Œuvres complètes: Cours de droit constitutionnel* [1866–1867], 2nd ed., 4 vols. (Paris: Guillaumin, 1877), 3:159–175.

22. From an unsigned article ("Sur le droit de pétition") in the *Gazette nationale, ou le Moniteur universel,* 6 April 1791. A whole movement had arisen urging the prohibition of collective petitions and a restriction of the right to enter individual pleas. See, too, the 26 April 1791 report by Isaac Le Chapelier, suggesting that the right of petition be abolished altogether, in *Archives parlementaires,* 25:678–682.

23. From a 2 March 1820 speech by Pierre Claude François Daunou, principal author of the Constitution of Year III, reprinted in his *Essai sur les garanties individuelles que réclame l'état actuel de la société* [1819], 3rd ed. (Paris: Bobée, 1822).

24. Alexandre Ledru-Rollin, "Travailleurs, faites des pétitions," *La Réforme,* 2 November 1844; subsequently issued as a pamphlet under the title *Manifeste aux travailleurs: Travailleurs, faites des pétitions* and reprinted in Ledru-Rollin, *Discours politiques et écrits divers,* 2 vols. (Paris: G. Baillière, 1879), 1:117–124.

25. From Girardin's 1851 article "Du droit de pétition," reprinted in Émile de Girardin, *Questions de mon temps, 1836–1856,* 12 vols. (Paris: Serrière, 1858), 10:132.

26. Ibid., 10:131.

27. Jean-Jacques Clère, "Le droit de pétition aux Chambres de 1789 à nos jours," in *1791, la première constitution française,* ed. Jean Bart and Françoise Naudin-Patriat (Paris: Economica, 1993), 299.

28. The Constitution of 1793 called it "the most sacred of duties"; see the chapter on illegitimate demonstration in Danielle Tartakowsky, *Le pouvoir est dans la rue: Crises politiques et manifestations en France* (Paris: Aubier, 1998), 18–22.

29. From an untitled editorial by Camille Pelletan in *L'Éclair,* 22 October 1898.

30. From an article in *Radical,* 30 July 1888, quoted in Tartakowsky, *Le pouvoir est dans la rue,* 236. See too Michelle Perrot, *Les ouvriers en grève: France, 1871–1890,* 2 vols. (Paris: Mouton, 1974): 2:552–568.

31. From a parliamentary intervention by Waldeck-Rousseau of 11 February 1884 (*Annales de la Chambre des députés: Débats parlementaires,* 12 vols. [1885–1940], vol. 1, ordinary session of 1884, tome 1, p. 427) in connection with the discussion of a proposed law clarifying the terms of the prohibi-

tion of gatherings on public thoroughfares enacted by a prior statute of 1881.

32. From the session of 21 January 1907, recorded in *Annales de la Chambre des députés*, vol. 6, ordinary session of 1907, tome 1, p. 140.

33. The phrase is due to Jules Guesde. See his article "Le droit à la rue," *Le Cri du peuple*, 15 February 1885; later reprinted in a collection of his essays, *État, politique et morale de classe* (Paris: Giard et Brière, 1901), 140–143.

34. On the difference between the "essentialist" type of representation offered by unions and electoral representation, see my discussion in *La question syndicale: Histoire at avenir d'une forme sociale* (Paris: Calmann-Lévy, 1988), 208–213. The expression of opinion via unions subsequently declined with the emergence of other opportunities for social interaction connected with changing patterns of housing, consumption, and leisure.

35. For the French case, see Danielle Tartakowsky, *Les droites et la rue: Histoire d'une ambivalence, de 1880 à nos jours* (Paris: La Découverte, 2014).

36. See my chapter on negative politics in *Counter-Democracy: Politics in an Age of Distrust*, trans. Arthur Goldhammer (Cambridge: Cambridge University Press, 2008), 173–190.

37. Quoted in Hadley Cantril / Office of Public Opinion Research, *Gauging Public Opinion* (Princeton, N.J.: Princeton University Press, 1944), viii.

38. Quoted in Dominique Reynié, *Le triomphe de l'opinion publique: L'espace public français du XVIe au XXe siècle* (Paris: Odile Jacob, 1998), 345.

39. In the 11 April 1945 issue of *Combat*, quoted in Loïc Blondiaux, "Le règne de l'opinion: Chronique d'une prise de pouvoir," *Le Débat*, no. 88 (January–February 1996): 17–30. See also Blondiaux, *La fabrique de l'opinion: Une histoire sociale des sondages* (Paris: Seuil, 1998).

40. On the use of "misgovernment" in the sense of bad government, see Chapter 11; on "malrepresentation," intended here especially to mean underrepresentation, see the author's explanation in the Introduction. —Trans.

41. See the literature on citizens' juries and consensus conferences, in particular.

42. From the seventh lecture in Émile Durkheim, *Leçons de sociologie: Physique des mœurs et du droit* [1898–1900], ed., Georges Davy (Paris: Presses Universitaires de France, 1950), 94.

43. Ibid., 95.

44. Ibid., 102.

45. Recall Durkheim's two definitions of democracy: (1) "The political system by means of which society achieves the purest consciousness of itself. A people is all the more democratic as deliberation, reflection, and critical thinking play a more considerable role in the course of public affairs" (ibid. [eighth lecture], 107–108); and (2) "A regime in which the state, while remaining distinct from the mass of the nation, is in close communication with it" (ibid. [ninth lecture], 118).

13. The Good Ruler in Historical Perspective

1. On the interpretation of these paintings see Patrick Boucheron, *Conjurer la peur: Sienne 1338: Essai sur la force politique des images* (Paris: Seuil, 2013); and Quentin Skinner, "Imbroglio Lorenzetti: The Artist as Political Philosopher," *Proceedings of the British Academy* 72 (1986): 1–56.

2. See the chapter on the "profession of king" in Jacques Krynen, *L'empire du roi: Idées et croyances politiques en France, XIIIᵉ–XVᵉ siècle* (Paris: Gallimard, 1993), 2.1, 167–239.

3. See Marie Dejoux, *Les enquêtes de Saint Louis: Gouverner et sauver son âme* (Paris: Presses Universitaires de France, 2014).

4. See John of Salisbury, *Policraticus: Of the Frivolities of Courtiers and the Footprints of Philosophers,* ed. and trans. Cary J. Nederman (Cambridge: Cambridge University Press, 1990), 27–63.

5. Jacques Krynen, *Idéal du prince et pouvoir royal en France à la fin du Moyen Âge, 1380–1440: Études de la littérature politique du temps* (Paris: Picard, 1981), 108.

6. Giles of Rome, *De regimine principium,* 2.2.8; quoted in Jean-Marie Carbasse and Guillaume Leyte, eds., *L'État royal, XIIᵉ–XVIIIᵉ siècle: Une anthologie* (Paris: Presses Universitaires de France, 2004), 102.

7. See Marcel Demongeot, *Le meilleur régime politique selon saint Thomas* (Paris: André Blot, 1928), as well as Aquinas's *Sententia libri Politicorum* [ca. 1270], a commentary on Aristotle's *Politics;* also Jacques Dalarun, *Gouverner, c'est servir: Essai de démocratie médiévale* (Paris: Alma, 2012).

8. This phrase occurs as the title of bk. 1, chap. 11, of Pizan's treatise; see Christine de Pizan, *Le livre du corps de policie,* ed. Angus J. Kennedy (Paris: Honoré Champion, 1998), 17.

9. The title of bk. 1, chap. 9; see ibid., 13.

10. Here Foucault's argument concerning this pastoral model is of interest. To my way of thinking he likens it too readily to modern liberal governmentality, on the basis of a distinction between the management of peoples and the management of territories, even if both models do, of course, stand at some remove from *raison d'état* theories. See the lectures of 8 February, 15 February, and 22 February 1978 in Michel Foucault, *Sécurité, territoire, population: Cours au Collège de France, 1977–1978* (Paris: Seuil / Gallimard, 2004), 119–193; also Foucault, *"Omnes et singulatim:* Vers une critique de la raison politique" [1981], in Michel Foucault, *Dits et écrits,* ed. Daniel Defert and François Ewald, 4 vols. (Paris: Gallimard, 1994), 4:134–161.

11. For a survey see Jean Meyer, *L'éducation des princes en Europe du XVᵉ au XIXᵉ siècle* (Paris: Perrin, 2004); and Bruno Neveu, "Futurs rois très chrétiens," in Ran Halévi, ed., *Le savoir du prince: Du Moyen Âge aux Lumières* (Paris: Fayard, 2002), 197–233.

12. Quoted in Antoine Boulay de la Meurthe, *Théorie constitutionnelle de Sieyès: Constitution de l'an VII* (Paris: P. Renouard, 1836), 14.

13. Abbé de Sieyès, "La Nation," undated draft manuscript (prior to 1789) in the collection of Sieyès's personal papers at the Archives Nationales, Paris, 284 AP3, 2(3).

14. Paul-Philippe Gudin de la Brenellerie, *Supplément au Contrat social* (Paris: Maradan et Perlet, 1791), 18.

15. This conception was consistent with the fact that representation was not thought of as a matter of standing for society, of holding up a mirror to it, but only as an *office*. Representatives existed only in the plural, in order to express the nation's will; none of them was *the* representative of his constituency.

16. Privilege results from the recognition and institutionalization of an inequality. Eminence, by contrast, results from a volatile sort of differentiation, one that is capable at any instant of being challenged. "Election," Patrice Gueniffey notes in this connection, "continually cancels the difference that it creates between citizens. . . . The elite instituted by suffrage is an essentially unstable elite, continually recomposed in response to modifications of a [public] trust; modifications that themselves result from the displacement of qualifications in a society that has become fluid, open, with the advent of equality of rights. For the public consideration owed to personal merits, 'by its nature freely given, is withdrawn the moment it ceases to be merited,' as Sieyès put it." Gueniffey, *Le nombre et la raison: La Révolution française et les élections* (Paris: Éditions de l'EHESS, 1993), 128.

17. Thomas Paine, *Rights of Man: Being an Answer to Mr. Burke's Attack on the French Revolution* [1791–1792], 2.3, in *Rights of Man, Common Sense, and Other Political Writings*, ed. Mark Philp (Oxford: Oxford University Press, 1995), 227–228.

18. See the illuminating discussion of this fundamental point in chap. 8 of Gueniffey, *Le nombre et la raison*, esp. 359–377.

19. Quatremère de Quincy propounded this thesis with great eloquence: "Every measure that tends to concentrate public discussion on individuals awakens passions, irritates them and excites partisan feeling anew, whereas [this feeling] ought to be forgotten altogether. True *candidacy*, to the contrary, [the candidacy] of public opinion, that which alone suits our government and our customs, prefers to generalize what the other particularizes. . . . The true list of candidates ought to be, not a gathering together of individual portraits of such-and-such figures, but a blending of the traits suited to forming the model or type that each candidate should resemble." M. Quatremère de Quincy, *La Véritable Liste des candidates, précédée d'observations sur la nature de l'institution des candidats, et son application au gouvernement représentatif,* 2nd ed. (Paris: Fauvelle et Sagnier, Year V [1797]), 17–18; emphasis in the original).

20. This idea has survived in our very word for "intrigue." [The modern French word, *brigue*, is cognate with the verb *briguer*, meaning to solicit or to canvass for votes, which additionally carries the related sense of currying favor. The corresponding Latin term for electoral corruption in the most general

sense, including bribery and graft, was *ambitus* (formed from the same root as the word from which both French and English were to derive "ambition").—Trans.]

21. "The Emperor is not a man, he is a people," as one prominent eulogist of the Second Empire was to say; see Arthur de la Guéronnière, *Portraits politiques contemporains: Napoléon III* (Paris: Amyot, 1853), 93.

22. Napoléon-Louis Bonaparte, *Des idées napoléoniennes* (Paris: Paulin, 1839), 27–28.

23. There is, in fact, a necessary connection between the leader's claim to embody society and the presumptive existence of a single, uniform—and therefore readily representable—people.

24. Vladimir Lenin, *Œuvres complètes*, 5th ed., 55 vols. (Paris: Éditions sociales, 1958–1965), 44:456.

25. Aleksandr I. Solzhenitsyn, *L'Archipel du Goulag, 1918–1956: Essai d'investigation littéraire*, 3 vols. (Parts 1–7), trans. Geneviève Johannet et al. (Paris: Seuil, 1974–1976), 1:73; italicized in the original. [Thomas Whitney's English version translates the Russian term simply as "Autocrat." Neither rendering fully captures the richness of Solzhenitzyn's neologism—Единодержавец, literally, "mono-sovereign" or "one-world-ruler" (the root держава also signifies an orb, in the sense of a royal device or insignia, a sphere surmounted by a cross symbolizing kingly power and justice, in effect identifying Stalin with the world he rules)—though the French does manage to convey the implied sense of megalomania. —Trans.]

26. Claude Lefort, *Un homme en trop: Réflexions sur "L'Archipel du Goulag"* (Paris: Seuil, 1976), 68–69; emphasis in the original.

27. Quoted in Guy Hermet, "Les populismes latino-américains," *Cités*, no. 49 (2012): 37–48.

28. Juan Domingo Perón, speech of 1 May 1974, in *El modelo argentino para el proyecto nacional* (Gualeguaychú, Argentina: Editorial Tolemia, 2011), 11.

29. See her extraordinary autobiography, *La razón de mi vida* (Buenos Aires: Ediciones Peuser, 1951); published in English as *My Mission in Life*, trans. Ethel Cherry (New York: Vantage Press, 1952).

30. Quoted in Roger Caillois, *Les jeux et les hommes: Le masque et le vertige* [1958], rev. and aug. ed. (Paris: Gallimard, 1967), 239.

31. This passage, from the widely circulated French version of a speech of 12 July 2012, was repeated word for word in speeches delivered the following 9 September and 24 September.

32. It should be noted that the Mexican guerilla leader Subcomandante Marcos justified wearing a balaclava in very similar terms. Asked why he hid behind a mask, he replied, "If you wish to know who Marcos is, pick up a mirror, the face you will see is that of Marcos. For Marcos is you, woman; he is you, man; he is you, indigenous person, peasant, soldier, student. . . . *We are all Marcos, a whole insurgent people.*" Quoted in Ignacio Ramonet, *Marcos, le dig-*

nité rebelle: Conversations avec le sous-commandant Marcos, trans. Laurence Villaumel (Paris: Galilée, 2001); the emphasis is mine.

33. Hugo Chávez, *Seis discursos del Presidente constitucional de Venezuela Hugo Chávez Frías* (Caracas: Ediciones de la Presidencia de la República, 2000), 47.

34. See Patrice Duran, "Max Weber et la fabrique des hommes politiques," in *Max Weber et le politique,* ed. Hinnerk Bruhns and Patrice Duran (Paris: Librairie générale de droit et de jurisprudence, 2009); and Catherine Colliot-Thélène's preface to her new translation of Max Weber, *Le savant et le politique* (Paris: La Découverte, 2003).

35. See Weber, "Politics as a Vocation," in *The Vocation Lectures,* 32–94.

36. Max Weber, *Parliament and Government in Germany under a New Political Order: Towards a Political Critique of Officialdom and the Party System* [1918], trans. Ronald Speirs, in *Weber: Political Writings,* ed. Peter Lassman and Ronald Speirs (Cambridge: Cambridge University Press, 1994), 169. [The French edition translates both more succinctly and more vividly, speaking of a choice between "a breeding ground of leaders or a swamp of careerists." —Trans.]

37. Weber, "Politics as a Vocation," 76–77.

38. From the interview with Nora in François Fourquet, ed., *Les comptes de la puissance: Histoire de la comptabilité nationale et du Plan* (Fontenay-sous-Bois: Recherches, 1980); quoted in Pierre Rosanvallon, *Democratic Legitimacy: Impartiality, Reflexivity, Proximity,* trans. Arthur Goldhammer (Princeton, N.J.: Princeton University Press, 2011), 52.

39. All these expressions occur in a series of interviews with another prominent civil servant, François Bloch-Lainé; see *Profession, fonctionnaire: Entretiens avec Françoise Carrière* (Paris: Seuil, 1976).

40. From the interview with Simon Nora, "Servir l'État," in *Le Dèbat,* no. 40 (May–September 1986): 102.

41. It is hardly an exaggeration to say that these technocrats considered their agencies the equal of those bodies of superior knowledge [*corps de lumière*] that Henri François d'Aguesseau imagined to have been constituted by the magistracy of his time, seventeenth-century France.

42. Georg Simmel, *Sociology: Inquiries into the Construction of Social Forms* [1908], ed. and trans. Anthony J. Blasi, Anton K. Jacobs, and Matthew Kanjirathinkal, 2 vols. (Boston: Brill, 2009), 1:315.

43. "Trust, as the hypothesis for future behavior, which is certain enough to ground practical action," Simmel observes, "is, as hypothesis, a middle position between knowledge and ignorance of others. Someone who knows all need not *trust,* someone who knows nothing cannot reasonably trust at all" (ibid.; emphasis in the original).

44. Here *trust between persons,* one of the indispensable invisible institutions of democracy, must be distinguished from its corresponding counterdemocratic impulse, *mistrust of institutions.*

45. On this point, see Bernard Manin, *The Principles of Representative Government* (Cambridge: Cambridge University Press, 1997), 202–203, 220–221, 233.

14. Truthfulness

1. The former French prime minister, Manuel Valls, in a speech of 8 April 2014.
2. Polybius, *The Histories* 2.38.6. [Here and below the renderings from the Greek are my own.—Trans.]
3. The fact that *parrēsia* referred to speech of every kind meant that it could also be used negatively to characterize someone who speaks falsely or talks nonsense.
4. See Michel Foucault, *Le gouvernement de soi et des autres: Cours au Collège de France, 1982–1983* (Paris: Gallimard / Seuil, 2008), particularly the lectures of 2 February, 9 February, and 2 March 1983; and Foucault, *Le courage de la vérité: Le gouvernement de soi et des autres II: Cours au Collège de France, 1984* (Paris: Gallimard / Seuil, 2009), lecture of 1 February 1984. See also Foucault, "La *parrêsia*," *Anabases*, no. 16 (2012): 157–188, another lecture that gives a fair idea of his thinking on the subject.
5. "It seems to me," Foucault says, "that by examining the notion of *parrêsia* one can see that the analysis of modes of truthsaying, the study of techniques of governmentality, and the detection of forms of practice of the self are all bound up together"; *Le courage de la vérité* (lecture of 1 February 1984), 10.
6. For Greece, see Roland Barthes, "L'ancienne rhétorique: Aide-mémoire," *Communications* 16, no. 1 (1970): 172–223; and Françoise Desbordes, *La rhétorique antique: L'art de persuader* (Paris: Hachette, 1966). For Rome, see George A. Kennedy, *The Art of Rhetoric in the Roman World* (Princeton, N.J.: Princeton University Press, 1972). For the modern period in Europe, see Marc Fumaroli, ed., *Histoire de la rhétorique dans l'Europe moderne, 1450–1950* (Paris: Presses Universitaires de France, 1999), and Fumaroli's own classic work *L'Âge de l'éloquence: Rhétorique et "res literaria" de la Renaissance au seuil de l'époque classique* [1980], 2nd ed. (Paris: Albin Michel, 1994).
7. Thus the accusations brought by Plato and his followers against the Sophists.
8. See the very carefully researched study by Noémie Villacèque, *Spectateurs de paroles! Délibération démocratique et théâtre à l'Athènes à l'époque classique* (Rennes: Presses Universitaires de Rennes, 2013).
9. Foucault, *Le courage de la vérité* (lecture of 1 February 1984), 15.
10. See, for example, Demosthenes, *On the Peace* 5.
11. In this connection Demosthenes explicitly invokes the concept of *parrēsia*, reproaching his fellow Athenians with the words: "One cannot always speak freely among you" (*Third Olynthiac*, 32).

12. Demosthenes, *Third Philippic* 4.

13. From the draft version of an unpublished seventh issue of the journal edited by Camille Desmoulins, *Le Vieux Cordelier* [1793–1794], ed. Pierre Pachet (Paris: Belin, 1987), 107.

14. Ibid., 123.

15. Joseph-Emmanuel Sieyès, intervention of 14 May 1789, *Archives parlementaires,* 8:109.

16. Jean-Baptiste Target, intervention of 14 May 1789, *Archives parlementaires,* 8:118.

17. Jacques-Guillaume Thouret, intervention of 14 May 1789, *Archives parlementaires,* 8:114.

18. Quoted in Jacques Guilhaumou, *Sieyès et l'ordre de la langue: L'invention de la politique moderne* (Paris: Kimé, 2002), 31.

19. Heinrich Heine, *De la France* (Paris: Renduel, 1833), 19–20.

20. Augustin Cochin, *Les sociétés de pensée et la démocratie moderne: Études d'histoire révolutionnaire* [1921] (Paris: Copernic, 1978), 19.

21. Hannah Arendt, *The Origins of Totalitarianism* [1951] (New York: Harcourt, Brace and World, 1967), 3.11, 352–353. On the rejection of the "factuality of the real world" in favor of a "fictitious world," see also 3.11, 387, and 3.13, 473–474.

22. See Victor Klemperer, *The Language of the Third Reich:* LTI, Lingua Tertii Imperii: *A Philologist's Notebook* [1947], trans. Martin Brady (London: Athlone Press, 2000). Here I follow Aubry and Turpin's introduction to a volume of essays comparing the approaches of Arendt, Klemperer, and Jean-Pierre Faye to this question: *Victor Klemperer: Repenser le langage totalitaire,* ed. Laurence Aubry and Béatrice Turpin (Paris: CNRS Éditions, 2012).

23. See A. Ciliga, *Au pays du mensonge déconcertant* (Paris: Plon, 1950). [The book first appeared in 1938 with Plon as *Au pays du grand mensonge,* and then in English two years later as *The Russian Enigma,* trans. Fernand G. Renier and Anne Cliff (London: Routledge and Sons, 1940). A new and augmented edition, of which this material constitutes the first part, was later published as *Dix ans au pays du mensonge déconcertant* (Paris: Champs libre, 1977). —Trans.]

24. See Jonathan Swift, "The Art of Political Lying," *The Examiner,* no. 14 (9 November 1710), reprinted in *The Prose Works of Jonathan Swift,* ed. Herbert Davis, 14 vols. (Oxford: Basil Blackwell, 1939–1968), 3:8–13. Political lying, he says [in a an anonymous pamphlet sometimes attributed to Swift but more commonly to his friend John Arbuthnot —Trans.], is "the art of convincing the people of salutary falsehoods for some end." See *Proposals for Printing a very Curious Discourse, in Two Volumes in Quarto, intitled Pseudologia Politikē; or, A Treatise of the Art of Political Lying, with an Abstract of the First Volume of the Said Treatise* (London: Printed for John Morphew, 1712). The peculiar property of this art, Swift maintained, is that it is "lawful and

permitted." The question of whether or not lying for the good of the people is morally justifiable was a subject of great debate during the eighteenth century, most notably perhaps in the competition sponsored by the Prussian Academy at the urging of Frederick II in 1778.

25. The words quoted from Blanqui are found in *La Patrie en danger* (Paris: A. Chevalier, 1871), 265, and the London toast of 25 February 1851, "Avis au peuple," reprinted in *Écrits sur la Révolution*, ed. Arno Münster (Paris: Galilée, 1977), 329.

26. A mutual attraction undeniably existed between the two. In France, Joseph de Maistre was read in Blanquist circles; in Germany, Carl Schmitt later gave proof of this same affinity.

27. M. Donoso Cortès, *Essai sur le catholicisme, le libéralisme et le socialisme* [1851] (Paris: Bibliothèque nouvelle, 1851), 223.

28. On this and many other points see Dominique Colas's incisive analysis in *Le Léninisme: Philosophie et sociologie politiques du Léninisme* (Paris: Presses Universitaires de France, 1982).

29. See Immanuel Kant, *Anthropology from a Pragmatic Point of View*, ed. and trans. Robert Louden (Cambridge: Cambridge University Press, 2006); on the interpretation of this thought experiment see François Calori, "*Laut Denken:* De la transparence chez Kant," *Raison-publique.fr*, 11 July 2011.

30. In the introduction to Jon Elster, ed., *Deliberative Democracy* (Cambridge: Cambridge University Press, 1998), 12.

31. Quoted in Élisabeth Guibert-Sledziewski, "Le peuple représenté," *Les Cahiers de Fontenay*, nos. 24–25 (December 1981): 19.

32. Quoted in Ferdinand Brunot, *Histoire de la langue française des origines à 1900*, 13 vols. (Paris: Armand Colin, 1905–1938), 9:653–654.

33. From p. 10 of the prospectus of this journal, co-founded by Condorcet with Abbé Sieyès and Jules-Michel Duhamel, director of the National Institute for Deaf Mutes in Paris.

34. Ibid., 10–11.

35. Sieyès spoke of "fixing the language by means of a preliminary convention that would consist in a system determined by combinations, operations between words adequate to new ideas, at the end of an analytic transaction"; quoted in Guilhaumou, *Sieyès et l'ordre de la langue*, 132. The phrasing is somewhat muddled, but the basic idea is clear enough.

36. On this point see Brigitte Schlieben-Lange, *Idéologie, révolution et uniformité de la langue* (Liège: Mardaga, 1996); and Rose Goetz, *Destutt de Tracy: Philosophie du langage et science de l'homme* (Geneva: Droz, 1993).

37. See Georges Clemenceau, *Démosthène* (Paris: Plon, 1926).

38. Ibid., 50–51.

39. Ibid., 81–86.

40. See R. Kent Weaver, "The Politics of Blame Avoidance," *Journal of Public Policy* 6, no. 4 (1986): 371–398.

41. George Orwell, "Politics and the English Language" [1946], reprinted in *The Collected Essays, Journalism, and Letters of George Orwell,* ed. Sonia Orwell and Ian Angus, 4 vols. (New York: Harcourt Brace Jovanovich, 1968), 4:127–140.

42. Ibid., 136.

43. See Annie Ernaux, *Les Années* (Paris: Gallimard, 2008).

44. On this point see the suggestive work by Jeffrey E. Green, *The Eyes of the People: Democracy in an Age of Spectatorship* (New York: Oxford University Press, 2010), esp. 201–211.

45. The sculpture is still in Rome today, set against a wall of the basilica Santa Maria in Cosmedin.

46. See Jean Starobinski, "Éloquence antique, éloquence future: Aspects d'un lieu commun d'ancien régime," in *The French Revolution and the Creation of Modern Political Culture,* vol. 1, *The Political Culture of the Old Regime,* ed. Keith Michael Baker (Oxford: Pergamon Press, 1987), 311–329.

47. Condorcet, *Troisième mémoire sur l'instruction publique* [1791], in *Œuvres de Condorcet,* ed. A. Condorcet O'Connor and M. F. Arago, 12 vols. (Paris: Firmin Didot, 1847–1849), 7:270–271.

48. Jean Charles Léonard Simonde de Sismondi, *Études sur les constitutions des peuples libres* (Brussels: Dumont, 1836), 253.

49. The points at issue were summarized under the Third Republic by Eugène Pierre, *Traité de droit politique, électoral et parlementaire* [1893], 2nd rev. and aug. ed. (Paris: Librairies-Imprimeries Réunies, 1902), 1033–1035. No modifications of this system have been made in the meantime. It should be noted that its main features had been proscribed by the Constitution of Year VIII.

50. See the section entitled "Of the exclusion of written discourses" in Bentham, *Essay on Political Tactics,* 9.4, in *Works of Jeremy Bentham,* ed. John Bowring, 11 vols. (Edinburgh: William Tait, 1838–1843), 2:361–362.

51. This passage occurs in the chapter devoted to representative assemblies in Constant's *Principes de politique applicables à tous les gouvernements représentatifs* [1815], reprinted in tome 9 of the *Œuvres complètes de Benjamin Constant,* 2 vols., ed. Olivier Devaux and Kurt Kloocke (Tübingen: M. Niemeyer, 2001), 2:746. Note that Constant managed to insert a provision into the "Acte additionnel aux constitutions de l'Empire" of 22 April 1815 (title I, article 26) prohibiting the reading of speeches in either of the Chambers.

52. Timon [Louis-Marie de Cormenin], *Livre des orateurs* [1836], reprinted in *Œuvres,* 3 vols. (Paris: Pagnerre, 1869–1870), 1:37.

53. See Dominique Schnapper, "La Commission de la nationalité, une instance singulière," *Revue européenne des migrations internationales* 4, nos. 1–2 (1988): 9–29.

54. Among French newspapers, for example, see the "Les décodeurs" column in *Le Monde* and the "Info-intox" column in *Libération;* among online journals, see the investigative work done by *Mediapart.*

15. Integrity

1. Administrative memorandum no. 5.078 / SG circulated by the Hôtel de Matignon to the members of Raffarin's government on 30 June 2005.
2. The claim that Commynes was the first writer to use this term is advanced in Joël Blanchard, *Commynes l'Européen: L'invention du politique* (Geneva: Droz, 1996), 320–325.
3. Jean-Jacques Rousseau, *Les Confessions* [1763], bk. 4, in *Œuvres complètes*, ed. Bernard Gagnebin and Marcel Raymond, 5 vols. (Paris: Gallimard, 1959–1995), 1:175.
4. See Pierre Burgelin, *La philosophie de l'existence de J.-J. Rousseau* (Paris: Presses Universitaires de France, 1952), 293–295.
5. Rousseau, *Confessions*, bk. 9, in *Œuvres complètes*, 1:446.
6. Jean-Jacques Rousseau, *Discours sur l'origine et les fondements de l'inégalité parmi les hommes* [1755], in *Œuvres complètes*, 3:112.
7. Jean-Jacques Rousseau, *Considérations sur le gouvernement de Pologne* [1782], in *Œuvres complètes*, 3:970.
8. Ibid., 3:1019.
9. Recall what Rousseau wrote in the first book of *Émile, ou De l'éducation* [1762]: "Forced to combat nature or social institutions, one must choose between making a man or a citizen; for one cannot make both at the same time"; in *Œuvres complètes*, 4:248.
10. Rousseau gives special emphasis to the personal pronoun here: "je serais *moi* sans contradiction" (ibid., 4:604–605).
11. Jean Starobinski, *Jean-Jacques Rousseau: Transparency and Obstruction* [1971], trans. Arthur Goldhammer (Chicago: University of Chicago Press, 1988), 255.
12. Bruno Bernardi has rightly emphasized the importance of these "chemical images" in Rousseau's conceptualization of the general will; see his study *La fabrique des concepts: Recherches sur l'invention conceptuelle chez Rousseau* (Paris: Champion, 2006).
13. Jean-Jacques Rousseau, *Institutions chimiques* [1747], ed. Bruno Bernardi and Bernadette Bensaude-Vincent (Paris: Fayard, 1999), 24–25.
14. The parallel is explicitly drawn in the *Considérations sur le gouvernement de Pologne*: "All large nations groan that are crushed under the weight of their own numbers, or that are in anarchy, or under the petty tyrants that their kings are obliged out of respect for a necessary hierarchy to set over them. As God alone can rule the world, so men of more than human faculties would be needed to govern a large nation" (in *Œuvres complètes*, 3:970–971).
15. See Arthur Weinberg and Lila Weinberg, eds., *The Muckrakers: The Era in Journalism That Moved America to Reform, the Most Significant Magazine Articles of 1902–1912* (New York: Simon and Schuster, 1961).
16. See Stanley K. Schultz, "The Morality of Politics: The Muckrakers' Vision of Democracy," *Journal of American History* 52, no. 3 (1965): 527–547.

17. Quoted in ibid., 529–530.

18. Louis D. Brandeis, "What Publicity Can Do," *Harper's Weekly,* 20 December 1913; reprinted in *Other People's Money and How the Bankers Use It* (New York: Stokes, 1914), 92. The essays collected in this book are principally devoted to transparency in business affairs.

19. The stele is today at the Louvre. See Dominique Charpin, "L'historien de la Mésopotamie et ses sources: Autour du Code de Hammu-rabi," *Journal asiatique* 301, no. 2 (2013): 339–366.

20. Jean Bodin, *Les Six Livres de la République* [1576], 6 vols. (Paris: Fayard, 1986), 6:17–18.

21. Quoted in Frédéric Monier, "Enquêter sur la corruption: Jaurès et la commission Rochette," *Cahiers Jaurès,* no. 209 (2009): 72.

22. Jean Bouvier, *Les deux scandales de Panama* (Paris: Julliard, 1964), 8.

23. For the reactions of the left, see Christophe Portalez, "*La Revue socialiste* face à la corruption politique: Du scandale de Panama à l'affaire Rochette," and, for the right, Olivier Dard, "Le moment Barrès: Nationalisme et critique de la corruption," both in *Cahiers Jaurès,* no. 209 (2009): 15–32, 93–111. These articles, along with Monier, "Enquêter sur la corruption," appear in a very interesting special issue of *Cahiers Jaurès* devoted to corruption in the late nineteenth and early twentieth centuries in Europe.

24. See Albert Meijer, "Transparency," in *The Oxford Handbook of Public Accountability,* ed. Mark Bovens, Robert E. Goodin, and Thomas Schillemans (New York: Oxford University Press, 2014), 507–524.

25. See the sharply critical reaction of Lawrence Lessig, "Against Transparency," *The New Republic,* 9 October 2009; available via https://newrepublic.com/article/70097/against-transparency.

26. I am pleased to adopt the definition of transparency given by Meijer, as "the availability of information about an actor allowing other actors to monitor the workings or performance of this actor"; see Meijer, "Transparency," 511.

27. Here one thinks especially of the controversies aroused by the surveillance activities of the National Security Agency in the United States, among other less sophisticated and more generalized forms of surveillance.

28. On the historical roots of the way in which the private and the public are combined in the lives of celebrities, see Antoine Lilti, *Figures politiques: L'invention de la célébrité (1750–1850)* (Paris: Fayard, 2014), esp. chap. 6 ("Pouvoirs de la célébrité"), 221–294.

29. See, for example, its ruling in the case of *Jones and Others v. United Kingdom,* App nos. 34356 / 06 and 40528 / 06 (14 January 2014).

30. This dissymmetry marks a difference between instrumental transparency and transparency as a state of society in Rousseau, the latter serving to equalize and generalize the prying glances of others.

31. Jérôme Cahuzac, budget minister under François Hollande, was forced to resign in March 2013 amid revelations of tax fraud and money laundering.

He was convicted in December 2016 and sentenced to three years in prison. —Trans.

32. Recommending the creation of a body of this type were two reports published in the years immediately prior, one by Jean-Marc Sauvé, Didier Migaud, and Jean-Claude Magendie, *Pour une nouvelle déontologie de la vie publique* (Paris: La Documentation française, 2011), summarizing the findings of a study group formed to examine conflicts of interest in public life; the other by Lionel Jospin, *Pour un renouveau démocratique* (Paris: La Documentation française, 2012), on the work of the commission Jospin chaired on democratic renewal and ethics in public life.

33. On this point see the *Receuil des textes juridiques,* published by the High Authority for Transparency in Public Life via www.HATVP.fr in 2014, for further detail concerning its powers and procedures.

34. See the decisions of the Constitutional Council regarding transparency (no. 2013-675 / 676 DC) handed down on 9 October 2013.

35. A former public prosecutor at the Court of Cassation, Nadal is noted for his independence and also for speaking his mind.

36. See Jean-Louis Nadal, *Renouer la confiance publique: Rapport au Président de la République sur l'exemplarité des responsables publics* (Paris: La Documentation française, 2014).

37. Bentham, *Essay on Political Tactics,* in *Works of Jeremy Bentham,* 2.1, 2:310.

38. See Matthew Neufield, "Parliament and Some Roots of Whistleblowing during the Nine Years War," *Historical Journal* 57, no. 2 (2014): 397-420.

39. Originally the title given by the former Socialist minister (now leader of the Left Party) Jean-Luc Mélenchon to his book *Qu'ils s'en aillent tous* (Paris: Flammarion, 2010).

40. Filters (or "screens," as Pettit also calls them) are preventive forms of control that apply to everyone. Sanctions he considers to be less effective because, being aimed only at deviants, they do not help improve the behavior of all citizens; see Pettit, *Republicanism: A Theory of Freedom and Government* (Oxford: Clarendon Press, 1997), 212-230.

41. On this point see Jacques Chiffoleau, "Le crime de majesté, la politique et l'extraordinaire," in *Les procès politiques (XIVᵉ–XVIIᵉ siècle),* ed. Yves-Marie Bercé (Rome: École française de Rome, 2007), 577-662.

42. See C. P. Jones, "Stigma: Tattooing and Branding in Graeco-Roman Antiquity," *Journal of Roman Studies* 77 (1987): 139-155.

43. See Pierre-François Muyart de Vouglans, *Mémoire sur les peines infamantes* [1780], published as an appendix to Michel Porret's recent article, "Atténuer le mal de l'infamie: Le réformisme conservateur de Pierre-François Muyart de Vouglans," *Crime, histoire & sociétés / Crime, History & Societies* 4, no. 2 (2000): 95-120.

44. See, for example, John Braithwaite, "Shame and Modernity," *British Journal of Criminology* 33, no. 1 (1993): 1-18; also Dan M. Kahan, "The Progressive Appropriation of Disgust," in *The Passions of Law,* ed. Susan A. Bandes (New

York: NYU Press, 1999), 63–79. For a careful examination of the question, see Martha C. Nussbaum, *Hiding from Humanity: Disgust, Shame, and the Law* (Princeton, N.J.: Princeton University Press, 2004); and James Q. Whitman, "What Is Wrong with Inflicting Shame Sanctions?," *Yale Law Journal* 107 (1998): 1055–1092.

45. See the doctoral thesis by Clément Bur, "La citoyenneté dégradé: Recherches sur l'infamie à Rome de 312 avant J.-C. à 96 après J.-C." (Université Paris 1, 2013).

46. See the examples cited in Merlin de Douai, "Dégradation," in *Répertoire universel et raisonné de jurisprudence,* ed. J.-N. Guyot, P. J. J. G. Guyot, and P.-A. Merlin, 4th ed., 17 vols. (Paris: Garnery, 1812–1825), 3:391–392.

47. This phrase occurs in the decree of the National Assembly of 29–30 December 1789 concerning elections.

48. This concept is not to be confused with the notion of a *crime de lèse-nation,* vaguer still from the legal point of view, which was used essentially for political ends; see the chapter on the imputation of this crime in Charles Walton, *Liberté d'expression en révolution: Les mœurs, l'honneur et la calomnie* [2011] (Rennes: Presses Universitaires de Rennes, 2014): 223–245.

49. This penalty and two other types of *peine infamante* (the pillory and banishment) are enumerated, without elaboration, in article 8; their details were specified in the revision of 1832, where they correspond to the category of civil death.

50. Recorded by Merlin de Douai in "Dégradation civique," in Guyot et al., *Répertoire universel et raisonné de jurisprudence,* 3:392.

51. On this episode see the standard work by Anne Simonin, *Le déshonneur dans la République: Une histoire de l'indignité, 1791–1958* (Paris: Grasset, 2008).

52. See Pierre Couvrat, "Les catégories des peines afflictives ou infamantes et des peines accessoires au regard du Conseil d'État," *Revue de science criminelle et de droit pénal comparé* 65, no. 1 (2004): 153–157.

53. Nadal's argument, at least implicitly, is that leaving it to the courts to administer this punishment would be preferable to counting on voters not to reelect a corrupt official.

54. See Nadal, *Renouer avec la confiance publique,* 143. A recent OpinionWay poll indicates that 85 percent of the French people would look favorably on such a possibility (see *Libération,* 25 November 2014). Nadal's chief regret is that ineligibility penalties remain for the moment optional and complementary to other sanctions, and are relatively seldom applied by judges.

55. Debate in France was sidetracked in early 2015 by the government's resolve to apply to terrorists a penalty of national unworthiness, with the result that the question is no longer considered primarily to be a matter of political integrity. See the report submitted to the National Assembly by the Commission for Constitutional Laws, Legislation, and the General Administration of the Republic, chaired by Jean-Jacques Urvoas, on 25 March 2015.

Conclusion

1. I have explored the forms assumed by this disenchantment in France in *Le sacre du citoyen: Histoire du suffrage universel en France* (Paris: Gallimard, 1992); see esp. 3.1 ("Le pouvoir du dernier mot"), 299–338.

2. See Pierre Rosanvallon, *Democratic Legitimacy: Impartiality, Reflexivity, Proximity*, trans. Arthur Goldhammer (Princeton, N.J.: Princeton University Press, 2011), esp. 203–218.

3. See Pierre Rosanvallon, *Counter-Democracy: Politics in an Age of Distrust*, trans. Arthur Goldhammer (Cambridge: Cambridge University Press, 2008), esp. 61–66, 253–257, 291–299.

4. I explain the reasons for my reluctance to proceed in this direction in the postface to Florent Guénard and Sarah Al-Matary, eds., *La démocratie à l'œuvre: Autour de Pierre Rosanvallon* (Paris: Seuil, 2015).

5. In France these tasks are partly combined in the mission of the High Authority for Transparency in Public Life and, to a lesser degree, that of the Commission for Access to Administrative Documents.

6. In France, the constitutional nonrecognition of a fourth branch of government has led the Constitutional Council to restrict the prerogatives of the High Authority for Transparency in Public Life. On the intellectual history of plans for such a fourth branch, see my discussion of new directions for popular sovereignty in Rosanvallon, "From the Past to the Future of Democracy" [2000], in the volume of my selected essays edited and translated by Samuel Moyn, *Democracy Past and Future* (New York: Columbia University Press, 2006), esp. 199–204; also my books *Counter-Democracy*, 76–103, and *Democratic Legitimacy*, 154–167.

7. It is in accordance with such just such a principle of functional representativeness that unions in France have a seat on the boards of directors of a whole range of public agencies. On this point see Rosanvallon, *La question syndicale: Histoire at avenir d'une forme sociale* (Paris: Calmann-Lévy, 1988), 35–44.

8. In the French case this would lead also to a reconsideration of the role of the Economic, Social, and Environmental Council, which in its present form constitutes a rough-and-ready compromise between the commission model as I have described it here and the parliamentary assembly model.

9. Recall that this is what representation was once expected to do, before it came to be associated with the idea of mere electoral ratification. On this point see John P. Reid, *The Concept of Representation in the Age of the American Revolution* (Chicago: University of Chicago Press, 1989), esp. 31–42, 140–146.

10. It should be kept in mind that the prohibition against running for office during the French Revolution, which no one today would think for a mo-

ment of reinstating, had exactly this effect—of preventing candidates from promising too much.

11. One might imagine choosing at random the members of a certain type of representative assembly, but not the president of the Republic and his ministers, or their counterparts in systems similar to that of France.

12. "Things were better in the old days," as many people say today.

INDEX

Abandonment, sense of, 196. *See also* Powerlessness
Absolutism, 10
Abuse of words, 227
Accountability, 16, 146, 147, 173, 183–186; linked with responsibility, 178–179; responsibility-evaluation, 183–186; responsibility-presentation, 183
Accounts Commission, 147, 149, 255
Acéphocratie, 33
Achaeans, 225
Aeschines, 233–234
Age of crowds. *See* Crowds
Algeria, 97, 99
Ambiguities, of language, 227, 236
American Revolution, 115, 163
Anarchism, 138–139
Antiparliamentarianism, 60, 63, 87–89
Aquinas, Thomas, 212
Arendt, Hannah, 133, 169, 229
Aristocracy, elective, 109; place of in democracies, 55
Aron, Raymond, 99
Assange, Julian, 169
Assemblies, election of, 3–5
Auditing of accounts. *See* Accountability
Australia, 152

Authenticity, 234
Authoritarianism, 114–124
Authority, constitutional, 69; political, 7, 42, 52, 84

Babeuf, Gracchus, 36
Bacon, Francis, 38
Bagehot, Walter, 43
Balladur Commission, 119
Balzac, Jean-Louis Guez de, 130, 195
Barère, Bertrand, 35
Barthélemy, Jean-Jacques (known as Abbé), 213
Beaumont, Gustave de, 76, 80
Beccaria, Cesare, 23–24
Becher, Johann Joachim, 248
Beck, Ulrich, 181
Becket, Thomas, 211
Benoist, Charles, 63
Bentham, Jeremy, 24, 155, 161, 239, 255
Berdyaev, Nikolai, 55
Bismarck, Otto, 81
Blackstone, William, 174
Blanqui, Auguste, 229, 230
Bloch, Marc, 163
Blum, Léon, 51–52, 53, 92, 98, 102
Bodin, Jean, 128, 129, 249

Bonaparte, Napoléon, 10, 34, 36, 37–38, 39, 188, 209, 215, 259
Bonapartism, fears of, 79
Bossuet, Jacques-Bénigne, 212
Bourbon Restoration, 149, 176–177
Bourdieu, Pierre, 143
Bourgeois, Léon, 40
Brandeis, Louis, 249
Branding. See Stigmatization, penalties of
Brissot, Jacques-Pierre, 33, 150
Brüning, Heinrich, 89
Buchanan, James, 122, 123
Budget chapters. See Government, parliamentary oversight of
Burke, Edmund, 163, 173

Caesarism, 10, 41, 75, 86–87, 95, 96, 112–113, 118, 215–216. See also Man-as-people
Campaigns, 132. See also Election
Capitant, René, 93, 96, 97
Carbonnier, Jean, 27
Castro, Fidel, 218
Central African Republic, 100
Chardon, Henri, 64–65
Charismatic leader. See Dictatorship, charismatic; Leaders
Charles X, 177
Charron, Pierre, 131
Charter of democratic action, 263
Chávez, Hugo, 218
Chief of state, 96, 117. See also Executive; President
Churchill, Winston, 234
Cicero, Marcus Tullius, 132–133, 210
Cicero, Quintus Tullius, 132–133
Ciliga, Ante, 229
Citizenship, 17, 167
Civic vigilance organizations, 263, 265
Civil rights, 168, 259
Civil servants, 220–221
Class, 8, 13, 39
Clastres, Pierre, 139–142
Clemenceau, Georges, 53, 199, 233–234
Cloots, Anacharsis, 39
Cochin, Augustin, 228
Coke, Edward, 174
Colombia, 217–218
Combes, Émile, 40
Command, rhetoric of, 52–53
Commission de la comptabilité, 149

Commission for Access to Administrative Documents (CADA), 166
Commission government, 64
Commission on Nationality, 240
Commitment. See Responsibility, to future
Committee of Public Safety, 35
Common Cause. See Good government organizations
Common-law systems, 42
Communism, 48
Communist: governments, 216; parties, 13, 88, 97
Commynes, Philippe de, 127, 244
Competence, ideal of, 62
Condorcet, Nicolas de, 33, 36, 232, 238
Conspiracy theories, 162–164
Constant, Benjamin, 4, 161–162, 177, 239
Constituent power, 69
Constituents, relationship to representatives, 9. See also Governing-governed relation
Constitution, France: of 1791, 30; of 1793, 34, 228; of Year III, 30, 35, 36; of Year VIII, 37; of Third Republic, 40; of Fourth Republic, 93, 118; of Fifth Republic, 95, 97, 99, 103, 118–120
Constitution, United States: 67, 94
Constitutional authority, theory of in Schmitt, 69
Constitutionalism, economic, 122–123
Contracts, rule of according to Proudhon, 139
Cordeliers Club (Society of the Friends of the Rights of Man and the Citizen), 237
Cormenin, Louis-Marie de Lahaye, 197, 239
Corruption, 63–64, 87, 212, 243, 250, 256
Council of the European Union, 160
Council of the Republic, 93
Council on democratic performance, 263–264
Court of Cassation, 27–28
Crosby, Ernest, 249
Crowds, 46–49. See also Masses

Debate, parliamentary, 238–240
Deception, importance of in governing, 130
Decision, technique of, 111
Decisionism, 65–70, 230

Declaration of the Rights of Man and the
    Citizen, 25, 149, 213
De Gaulle, Charles, 50, 75, 92, 96, 97, 99,
    100, 103, 110, 111, 112, 215, 234.
    See also Gaullism
Degradation, penalties of, 258–260;
    indignité nationale, crime punished by,
    259–260; reputation, as element of,
    258; trust and worthiness, role of in,
    258–259
Demarchy, 122
Democracy: abstracting executive from,
    59; of appropriation, 11, 167; aristocracy
    in, 55; of authorization, 9–10, 16–17,
    107, 168; competitive, 266–267;
    domination effects in, 143–144;
    elements in, 262; executive power in,
    144–145; of expression and interaction,
    190; as form of government, 18; as form
    of society, 18, 205; governing organs of,
    6; institutions for, 263–265; of interac-
    tion, 190, 196, 204–205; intrinsic
    indeterminacy of, 236; liberal, 70;
    lotteries in, 8; mass, 45; meaning of,
    268; as mode of government, 205;
    networked, 10; objective, 61–62;
    parliamentary-representative model of,
    6; participatory, 8; permanent, 10, 16,
    223; plebiscitary, 83–86, 100; prospects
    for reforming, 261–262; of the public,
    149; readiness for, 90; as regime, 17;
    relation with authority, 52; representa-
    tive, 151; representative dimension of,
    14; trust of, 11; Weber on, 85
Democratic universalism, 17
Demonstration, right to, 199–200, 201
Demosthenes, 226–227, 233–234
Depersonalization. *See* Impersonality
Deschamps, Léger Marie (known as Dom
    Deschamps), 248
Desmoulin, Camille, 227
Despotism, 25, 169
Destutt, Antoine Louis Claude, comte de
    Tracy, 232
Dictatorship, 68, 87, 89. *See also* Nazism
Dictatorship, charismatic, 86; classical,
    66; sovereign, 68–70
Directory, 35, 36
Disraeli, Benjamin, 43
Distinction, principle of, 108–109
Domination, in Bourdieu and Weber,
    143

Donoso Cortés, Juan, marqués de
    Valdegamas, 230
Dufaure, Jules, 40, 76
Dupin, Louis-Claude, seigneur de
    Franceuil (known as Dupin de
    Franceuil), 247–248
Dupuy, Charles, 40
Duquesnoy, Adrien, 231
Durkheim, Émile, 204–205
Duverger, Maurice, 101–102

Ebert, Friedrich, 82, 89
Education, 169–170
Egalitarianism, as an ideal, 37
Egocrat. *See* Stalin, Joseph
Electability, vs. governing, 108, 132,
    235
Election, 195, 266; of chief executive, 3;
    democratization of, 7; governed-
    governing relation and, 9–10; identified
    with universal suffrage, 3; old vs. new
    senses of, 213–215; presidential, 14;
    structural tensions in, 107–110; as
    vehicle of civic expression, 190. *See also*
    Legitimacy
Electoral college, 94–95
Electoral controls, 114–117
Electoral mandates. *See* Imperative
    mandate; Mandates
Ellsberg, Daniel, 169
Elster, Jon, 231
Emergency powers, 65, 71
Emergency rule, 67
Empowerment, 204
England: development of parliamentary
    institutions in, 147; ministers in, 175;
    responsibility in, 178. *See also* Great
    Britain
Equality, 18, 225
Ernaux, Annie, 237
European Commission, 160
European Council, 160
European Court of Human Rights, 252
European Parliament, 160
European Union, 161
Euroscepticism, 159
Exception, rejection of executive power
    as, 41–44
Execution, art of, 128. *See also* Governing
Executive, 9; abstracting from democracy,
    59; as adjunct of legislature, 35;
    concentration of power in, 87; election

Executive (*continued*)
  of, 3, 9; increased strength of, 91;
  power of, 4, 57; rehabilitation of, 50;
  Weber's view of, 86
Executive branch: government used to
  refer to, 5–6; Necker on, 192
Executive power. *See* Power
Expertise / experts, 64, 65, 70, 109
Expression, political, 196–201. *See also*
  Demonstration
Exteriority, impossibility of doing away
  with, 138–142
Eyes of democracy, in Bentham, 155–157

Faguet, Émile, 63
Farge, Arlette, 163
Farrell, Brian, 102
Fascism, 48, 91
Fayol, Henri, 62
Fénelon, François, 212
Ferrero, Guglielmo, 106
Ferry, Jules, 40
Finances, administration of, 148–150.
  See also Accountability; Transparency
Finland, 94
Flaubert, Gustave, 261
Follet, Mary Parker, 62
Forums, special, 203
Foucault, Michel, 155, 225, 226
France, 60, 62, 118, 128, 178; accessibility
  of representatives in, 150–151; ancien
  régime in, 158; after Second World War,
  92; budget chapters, 149–150; colonial
  system, 97–98; colonies, 100–101;
  electoral committees, 12; Gaullist
  regime, 95–100, 102, 119; High
  Authority for Transparency in Public
  Life, 253–255; ministers in, 176;
  parliament, 118, 150; presidential
  election of 1848, 75–81; presidentialism
  in, 5; removal of chief of state in, 117;
  responsibility in, 176–178; taxation in,
  170. *See also* Constitution, France
Freedom of Information Act (FOIA), 166
French Revolution, 8, 33, 115, 163, 227,
  237; conception of law in, 25–27;
  Declaration of the Rights of Man and
  the Citizen, 25, 149, 213; Executive
  Council during, 34–35; National
  Convention during, 33
French Section of the Workers' International, 92

French Union, 97
Fréron, Louis, 104–105
Future, responsibility to, 186–189

Gaitán, Jorge Eliécer, 217–218
Galbraith, John Kenneth, 13
Gallup, George, 201
Gambetta, Léon, 40
Gaullism, 95–100, 102, 119
General Confederation of Labor (CGT),
  201
Generality, principle of, 26, 27, 32, 61,
  136
George, David Lloyd, 53
German National People's Party (DNVP),
  88
German Social Democratic Party, 219
Germany, 4, 219; antiparliamentarianism
  in, 87–89; cult of personality under
  Nazi regime, 87; federal organization
  of, 83; reconstruction of Reichstag in,
  152–153; transition to dictatorship in,
  89; Weimar experiment, 59, 67, 75,
  81–90, 94, 116
Giles of Rome (Aegidius Romanus),
  211
Girardin, Émile de, 198
Gladstone, William Ewart, 43
Goebbels, Joseph, 88–89
Good government organizations, 16,
  165
Goodnow, Frank J., 60–61
Governance, 123–124, 180
Governing: art of, 127–134; vs. electability, 108–109, 132, 235; language of,
  235; law as means of, 57. *See also*
  Executive; Governing-governed
  relation; Leaders; Princes
Governing-governed relation, 9, 15,
  129–145, 222; distrustful nature of,
  202; domination relations in, 132–134,
  143–144; elements of, 145; structural
  asymmetry in, 134–136, 137, 138
Government: art of, 130; bad, 1; bureaucratization of, 84; coalition, 15;
  commission, 64; democracy as form of,
  18; incompetence in, 63; intervention
  by, 62; open, 10, 157, 167; parliamentary oversight of, 147–150; popular
  distrust of, 244; principles of, 10–11;
  representative, 149; separated from
  sovereignty, 135; theories of, 127–145,

191–195; used to refer to executive branch, 5–6

Governmentability, 193

Great Britain, 42–44, 151–152. *See also* England

Great War, 49, 67

Greece, 4

Grévy, Jules, 40, 78, 79

Grievances, redress of, 196–198

Guayaki Indians, 139–142

Guizot, François, 191–192

Habermas, Jürgen, 195

Halévy, Daniel, 41

Hamilton, Alexander, 115

Hayek, Friedrich, 122, 123

Hébert, Jacques-René, 36

Heine, Heinrich, 228

Henry II, 211

High Authority for Transparency in Public Life, 253–255

Hindenburg, Paul von, 90

Hitler, Adolf, 67, 88

Hitlerism, 188

Hobbes, Thomas, 38

Hollande, François, 209

Honor. See *peine d'infamie*

Housing, ministerial, 243–244

Human rights, 168

Identity, politics of, 219

Ideology, 229, 248–251

Illegibility, 159, 162. *See also* Legibility

Illiberalism, 110–112, 114–124

Impartiality, legitimacy of, 18

Impeachment, 115, 173–175

Imperative mandate, 115–116

Impersonality, 7, 32, 105, 161; associated with parliamentarianism, 39; faith in virtues of, 38–41; functional, 123; new forms of, 121–124; revoking principle of, 37–38

Imputation, crisis of, 180–181

Indignité nationale. See Degradation, penalties of

Individualism of singularity, 13

Individualization, 102

Information: ability to analyze, 168–170; conspiracy theories and, 164; public disclosure of, 164; right to, 164–170

Initiative (electoral procedure), 116

Integrity, 11, 145, 223, 253–255. *See also* Transparency

Intelligibility, 169

Intentions, language of, 240–241

Internet, 164, 184–185

Ireland, 94

Italy, 4, 91, 128

Jaucourt, Louis de, 24

Jaurès, Jean, 250

John of Salisbury, 211

Joly, Maurice, 133

Journalism, 133–134, 227, 237, 240, 248–249

Jouvenal, Bertrand de, 55

Judicial error, 24

Judiciary, 27, 121

Justice, 24, 181; principle of, 26

Justification, principle of, 111–112

Kant, Immanuel, 229, 231, 234

Keynesianism, 56, 57

King, 32. *See also* Monarchy

Klemperer, Victor, 229

Kydland, Finn, 122–123

Labor movement, 164, 200

La Mothe Le Vayer, François de, 132

Lamartine, Alphonse de, 80, 229

Lamennais, Hugues-Félicité Robert de, 12

Language: absolute, 231; ambiguities of, 227, 236; debate, 238–240; electoral, 235; plain speaking, 230–242; political, 234–235; powerlessness and, 240–241. *See also* Speech

Language of intentions, 240–241

Law: change in nature of, 57–58; codification of, 26–27; conception of, 25–27; as expression of general will, 7; impersonality of, 32; as means of governing, 57; reverence for, 39; role of, 140

Law, rule of, 6–7, 23, 24–31, 256

Leaders, 83–84, 145. *See also* Princes

Le Bon, Gustave, 46, 47–49

Le Chapelier law (June 1791), 200

Ledru-Rollin, Alexandre, 198

Lefort, Claude, 216

Legibility, 10, 145, 146–171, 204, 251

Legislation: parliaments' role in, 13–14; as a science, 24

Legislature: executive as adjunct of, 35; inferiority of, 48; power in, 7; subordination of, 6; supremacy of, 39

Legitimacy: classical theories of, 106; constitutional-parliamentary, 85; revolutionary, 85; source of, 84. *See also* Election

Legitimation: vs. selection, 107–108; through voting, 111; by universal suffrage, 107

Lenin, Vladimir Ilyich, 48, 54, 115, 216, 230

Leroux, Pierre, 77–78

"Lettres sur la réforme gouvernementale" (Blum), 51

Lincoln, Abraham, 201

Lipsius, Justus, 129

Lorenzetti, Imbroglio, 210

Louis IX, 210

Louis-Philippe, 176, 243

Louis XIV, 158, 217

Machiavelli, 66, 69, 127, 133

MacMahon, Marie Esme Patrice Maurice, comte de, 39–40

Madagascar, 100

Majority rule, 111

Malrepresentation, 13–14

Management, rational, 62

Man-as-people, 38, 41, 215–218

Mandates, 115–116, 204

Marcus Aurelius, 210

Marianne (symbol of the French republic), 33

Marrast, Armand, 76

Marx, Karl, 56, 115

Masses, 46, 85, 131–132. *See also* Suffrage, universal

Mazarin, Jules Raymond, Cardinal, 130, 191

Meinecke, Friedrich, 88, 90

Mendès-France, Pierre, 57, 98

Michelet, Jules, 25, 39, 203

Michels, Robert, 12, 142

Mill, John Stuart, 179

Ministers, 30, 176; in England, 175–176; in France, 176; responsibility of, 177, 178–179

Mirabeau, Honoré-Gabriel Riqueti, comte de, 227

Mirrors of princes (*specula principum*), 210–211, 221

Misgovernment, 173, 202

Mitterrand, François, 99

Monarch, elected, 120; republican 101–102

Monarchies, constitutional, 4

Monarchy, 43; executive power and, 32–33; presidency as, 77–78

Monologues, political, 238–240

Montesquieu, Charles-Louis de Secondat, baron de la Brède et de, 25

Morelly, Étienne-Gabriel, 248

Muckrakers, 248–249

Musil, Robert, 188

Mussolini, Benito, 217

Nadal, Jean-Louis, 254, 260

Nader, Ralph, 165

Napoleon III, 112, 133, 215

National Commission for Public Debate, 204

National Constituent Assembly, 26

National Security Agency, 169

Naudé, Gabriel, 129, 191

Nazis, 88–89, 90, 188

Nazism, 59, 67, 75, 91

Necker, Jacques, 104, 148–149, 191

News, false, 163

Nicole, Pierre, 212

Nine Years' War, 255

No confidence, vote of, 118

Nora, Simon, 220–221

Norms, 69–70, 191

Notables, 39, 41, 43

Obama, Barack, 71; administration of, 166

Objective democracy, 61–62

Occupy Wall Street, 15

Office for Correspondence Relating to the Formation and Propagation of Public Feeling, 195

Officials, prosecution of, 181

Oligarchy, democratic, 142

One-party states, 216

Opacity, 158, 161–164, 166, 169, 170–171, 251

Open government, 157, 167

Opinion, 182, 184, 186, 191, 195; manipulation of, 133–134, 190

Opinion polls, 201–202

Opposition party, role of, 183–184

Order, principle of, 26

Orwell, George, 229, 237
Ostrogorski, Moisei 12
Overinformation, 169

Paine, Thomas, 214
Panama scandal, 250
Panopticon, 155
Pareto, Vilfredo, 142
Paris Commune, 115
Parliament, 147; debates in, 153–155;
    functions of, 13–14; galleries in,
    151–152; popular oversight of, 150–155;
    purpose of, 191–192
Parliamentarianism, 7, 40; Blum on,
    92–93; in France, 118, 150; in Great
    Britain, 42–44; impersonality
    associated with, 39; rationalized, 117;
    return to, 92–94
Parliamentary: architecture, modern,
    151–153; institutions, development of,
    147; proceedings, publication of,
    153–155
Parliamentary-representative model of
    democracy, 2, 6–9
Parrēsia, 225, 226, 227, 233, 234
Participatory democracy, 8
Particularity, principle of, 26, 136
Parties, political, 84, 86; abandonment of
    representative dimension, 14; as
    machines, 86; class-based, 8; conven-
    tions of, 95; criticisms of, 12–13;
    decline of, 13–14; and democracy of
    authorization, 168; functions of, 11–15;
    in Germany, 88, 89; malrepresentation
    by, 12–13; opacity and, 166; opposition
    party, 183–184; professionalization of,
    190; reaction against, 60
Pascal, Blaise, 158
Past, responsibility to, 183–186
Peine d'infamie, 258–260
Pensions Advisory Council, 240
Pentagon Papers, 168
People, the, 7, 203; use of word, 227–228,
    231–232
People-as-legislator, 7
People's Lobby, 165
Permanent democracy. See Democracy,
    permanent
Perón, Eva, 218
Perón, Juan, 218
Personalization, 6, 7, 17, 91, 102–103, 219
Personhood, right of, 168

Petition, right of, 196–198
Pettit, Philip, 256
Philip IV (Philippe le Bel), 211
Pizan, Christine de, 212
Plain speaking. See Truthfulness
Plebiscitary democracy, 83–86, 100
Plebiscite, 85, 98
Plutarch, 210, 213
Podemos, 15
Poincaré, Raymond, 53
Polarization, 6, 17, 196
Policy, evolution of term, 56–57
Political correctness, 241
Political expression, 196–200
Politicians, 48–49, 50, 70, 84, 209, 219,
    220, 234–236, 240, 246, 249, 252, 256,
    266
Politics, 67; desocialization of, 190;
    detached from real life, 190; lack of
    interest in, 221; shift in center of, 1–2;
    as sphere of decision, 24; as a vocation,
    219–222
Polls, 201–202
Polybius, 225
Popular Republican Movement (MRP), 93
Popular sovereignty, transparency as, 253
Populist movements, 196, 217
Portugal, 4
Postal and telecommunications service
    (PTT), 62
Power, 1, 42, 43; active, 86; administra-
    tive, 60–65; in age of popular sover-
    eignty, 191; auditing of accounts,
    146–147; authorization of, 106;
    autonomy of, 42; balance between, 65;
    of chief executive, 4; collegial, 34–36;
    constituent, 69; in democracy,
    144–145; directly elected by citizens,
    36; discrediting of, 28–29; exercise of,
    30;; generative source of, 7; Guizot on,
    192; holding on to, 132–134; indi-
    vidual, 34; increase in, 3; legislative,
    86; in legislature, 7; literature on
    exercise of, 127; mistrust of, 2;
    monarchy and, 32–33; personalization
    of, 219; political, 64; rejection of as
    exception, 41–44; responsibility and,
    172–173; separation of, 29–30, 31, 111,
    115; social appropriation of, 204;
    solitary exercise of, 32–34; sovereign
    dictatorship as, 68–70; as sovereign
    exercise of will, 68; supervision of, 174;

Power (continued)
supremacy of, 6; tendency to personalization, 6; tendency to polarization, 5
Powerlessness, 240–241, 245; prudence
of, 113
Prescott, Edward, 122–123
President, 75; conception of as individual,
33–34; direct election of, 75–81,
96–100; in Fourth Republic, 93; need
for, 51–52; selection of in United States,
94–95; under Weimar Constitution,
81–83
Presidential-governing model, 2, 103
Presidentialism, 95; conception of, 2;
growing influence of executive branch
and, 5–6; growth of, 2–5; illiberalism
of, 110–112, 114–124; in relation to
social desires, 105; shift to, 14; spread
of, 100–101
Presidentialization-personalization, 103
Press, the, 133–134
Pretense, importance of in governing, 130
Preuss, Hugo, 83
Priezac, Daniel de, 129
Primary system, 7, 64, 95
Prime minister, in British system, 42, 43
Princes, 127, 129, 131, 210–212. See also
Governing; Leaders
Privacy, 251, 252
Privileged bodies, British houses of
parliament as, 154
Progress, Napoleonic notion of, 38
Promising, role of in democracy, 108,
267
Prosecution, of officials, 181
Proudhon, Pierre-Joseph, 78; conception
of property and socialism, 138–139
Proximity, legitimacy of, 18
Prussia, 83
Public administration, 60, 61, 84. See also
Government
Public Citizen movement, 165
Public commissions, 263, 264–265
Public shaming. See Stigmatization,
penalties of
Public interest research groups (PIRGs),
170
Public office: removal from, 114–117;
resignation of, 175,178, 182
Publicity, 155–156, 157, 161, 194–195,
245, 248, 249, 252
Pyat, Félix, 76–77

Quatremère de Quincy, Antoine-
Chrysostome, 214
Quinet, Edgar, 38

Raison d'État theorists, 129–131, 154
Rally of the French People (RPF), 99
Rawls, John, 171
Reasoned nonconfrontation, rhetoric of,
238
Recall (electoral procedure), 115–116
Reelection, 109–110
Referendum, introduction of, 8
Reflexivity, legitimacy of, 18, 136, 137
Regime: democracy as, 17; use of
term, 2
Regulation, as essential activity of
government, 56–57
Regulatory bodies, 121–122
Reichstag, 81, 82–83, 85, 87, 88, 116,
152–153
Reparliamentarization, 119–120
Representation: crisis of, 2; as delegation,
202; as figuration, 109, 202–203, 222;
as mirror, 218; nature of, 7–9; need for
revitalization of, 15–16
Representative democracy, 151
Representatives: vs. governors, 9;
constitutional function of, 154;
oversight of, 150; personal commitment of, 234; relationship to constituents, 9. See also Governing-governed
relation; Leaders; Parliament
Reputation. See Degradation, penalties of
Responsibility, 10, 106, 118, 145, 204;
breakdown of idea of, 180; defined,
172; electoral, 179–180; in England,
178; to future, 186–189; modern
concept of, 175–176; objects of,
172–173; parties' retreat from, 13–14;
to past, 183–186; political, 173, 178; to
popular opinion, 182; principle of,
181–183; as a test of ability, 173
Responsibility-evaluation, 183–186
Responsibility-justification, 183–185
Responsibility-presentation, 183
Responsiveness, 10, 145, 190–205
Rhetoric, 225–226
Ribot, Alexandre, 41
Right to know, 164, 167
Risk society, 181
Robespierre, Maximilien, 28, 30, 35, 36,
151, 248

Roland, Jean-Marie, vicomte de la
Platière, 195
Rousseau, Jean-Jacques, 28, 66, 134, 135,
246–248
Royer-Collard, Pierre-Paul, 177
Rule of law, 6–7, 23, 24–31, 256
Rule of public opinion, 195
Ruler. *See* Election; Governing-governed
relation; Leaders; Representatives
Ruler, good, 209–223
Rumors, spread of, 163

Saint-Just, Louis Antoine Léon de, 35,
213, 248
Sanctions regimes, 255–260
Schmitt, Carl, 59, 60, 67–68, 69–70,
86, 89
Schumpeter, Joseph, 85
Second World War, 70, 259
Secrecy, right to, 154, 161
Seduction, rhetoric as art of, 226
Selection, vs. legitimation, 107–108
Self-determination, right of nations to,
137
Self-government, vs. self-management,
136–137
Senegal, 100
Separation of powers, 29–30, 31, 111, 115
Shadow cabinet, 179
Siena, Town of Hall of, 210
Sieyès, Emmanuel-Joseph (known as
Abbé), 28, 36, 69, 213, 227, 228, 232
Sighele, Scipio, 46
Similarity, principle of, 108–109
Simon, Jules, 40
Sincerity, Kantian notion of, 231, 234
Sismondi, Jean Charles Leonard Simonde
de, 238
Sixth Republic, calls for in France, 120
Slogan, authority of in Leninist Russia,
230
Snowden, Edward, 169
Social Democrats, in Weimar Germany,
82, 83
Social groups, representation of, 8–9,
12–13
Society: democracy as form of, 18;
self-institution of, 137
Solzhenitsyn, Aleksandr, 216
Sovereign immunity, 33
Sovereignty, 17, 128, 135
Spain, 4, 15

Speech: vs. action, 230; false, 228–229;
freedom of, 225; public, 224; *parrēsia*,
225, 226, 227, 233, 234; rhetoric,
225–226
Speeches, 238–240
Staël, Germaine de, 37, 39
Stalin, Joseph, 216–217
Starobinski, Jean, 247
Status domination, Weber's theory of,
143
Steffens, Lincoln, 249
Stigmatization, penalties of, 257–258;
branding and, 257; public shaming
and, 257–258
Subordination, political, 138
Suffrage, universal, 45, 84–85, 96–100,
198; association with election of
representative assemblies, 3–5; crowds
and, 47; direct election and, 75–81;
election identified with, 3; election of
executive by, 94; election of president
by, 96–100; election of president of
Reich and, 81–83, 85; legitimation by,
107; spread of, 100–101; vs. petition,
197–198; women's, 82
Sunlight Foundation, 250
Super-legitimacy, 111–112
Suspicion. *See* Publicity
Swift, Thomas, 229

Tarde, Gabriel, 46, 47
Target, Jean-Baptiste, 227
Taylor, Frederick, 54, 62
Technocracy, 70; as ideal, 60–65
Thiers, Adolphe, 39
Thinking out loud [*Laut-Denken*], Kantian
ideal of, 229
Third Republic, 39–41, 70, 81, 92, 177
Thouret, Jacques-Guillaume, 228
Tocqueville, Alexis de, 50, 76, 79, 80, 162
Totalitarianism, 10; discourse of, 241
Transparency, 10, 105–106, 145, 157,
244–253; in business, 164–165; and
common good, 249; demands for,
164–165; empowering, 252; financial,
148, 149; as form of social existence,
247; as ideology, 248–251; instrumental, 251, 252; intrusive, 252;
personal behavior and, 245–246;
popular sovereignty as, 253; sanctions
and, 256; utopian view of, 246–248; vs.
opacity, 164. *See also* Legibility

Transparency International, 254
Trust, 222–223, 225. *See also* Degradation, penalties of
Trustee, 222–223
Truth, 226, 228
Truthfulness, 11, 145, 223, 224–242; commitment to, 229; reflexive dimension of, 236
Tsípras, Alexis, 241

Ultra-presidentialism, 118–119
United States of America, 60; de Gaulle's criticism of, 96; electoral college in, 94–95; impeachment in, 115; recall in, 116
Unworthiness. *See* Degradation, penalties of

Vaillant, Édouard, 199–200
Venezuela, 116–117
Visibility, vs. legibility, 158
Vitrification, Rousseau's understanding and use, 248
Vitrolles, Eugène François Auguste d'Arnauld, baron de, 177

Von Papen, Franz, 90
Voting: legitimation through, 111; vs. petition, 197–198; retrospective, 109–110. *See also* Suffrage

Waldeck-Rousseau, Pierre, 199
Wars of Religion, 128
Watchwords. *See* Slogan
Weber, Max, 69, 83–86, 100, 106, 107, 143, 186, 209, 219–220, 221
Weimar Republic, 59, 67, 75, 81–90, 94, 116
Welfare state, 171
Whistle-blowers, 254, 255
WikiLeaks, 169
Wilkes, John, 154
Will: Bonaparte's redefinition of, 38; crisis of, 187; democratic, 38; executive power as exercise of, 68; general, 7, 18, 26, 111; Musil on, 188; projective, 187–188, 189; reflexive, 189
Wilson, Woodrow, 60
World War I, 67
World War II, 70, 259
Worthiness. *See* Degradation, penalties of